HOLINESS, ETHICS AND RITUAL IN LEVITICUS

Hebrew Bible Monographs, 29

Series Editors
David J.A. Clines, J. Cheryl Exum, Keith W. Whitelam

HOLINESS, ETHICS AND RITUAL IN LEVITICUS

Leigh M. Trevaskis

SHEFFIELD PHOENIX PRESS

2011

Copyright © 2011 Sheffield Phoenix Press

Published by Sheffield Phoenix Press
Department of Biblical Studies, University of Sheffield
Sheffield S3 7QB

www.sheffieldphoenix.com

A CIP catalogue record for this book
is available from the British Library

Typeset by CA Typesetting Ltd
Printed on acid-free paper by Lightning Source UK Ltd, Milton Keynes

ISBN-13 978-1-906055-98-1
ISSN 1747-9614

CONTENTS

Acknowledgments   vii
Abbreviations   viii

Chapter 1
INTRODUCTION   1

Chapter 2
METHODOLOGY   11

Chapter 3
LEVITICUS 11.43-45: AN INVITATION TO EXPLORE P'S
'DIETARY PRESCRIPTIONS' AS MOTIVATIONAL FOR HOLINESS   47

Chapter 4
MORTAL 'FLESH' (בשר) AS SYMBOLIC SOURCE
OF 'UNCLEANNESS' (טמא) IN LEVITICUS 12–15   108

Chapter 5
'A MALE WITHOUT DEFECT' (תמים זכר: תמים) AS AN
ASPECT OF קדש IN THE 'BURNT OFFERING' OF LEVITICUS 1   172

Chapter 6
THE USE OF תמים TO DENOTE AN ASPECT OF
'HOLINESS' (קדש) WHEN APPLIED TO ANIMALS IN H   208

Chapter 7
CONCLUSION   230

APPENDIX 1   238
APPENDIX 2   251

Bibliography   262
Index of References   274
Index of Authors   283
Index of Subjects   286

ACKNOWLEDGMENTS

The impetus for writing this book, a modified version of my doctoral thesis, arose from an interest in the idea of holiness found in Leviticus 1–16. In particular I wanted to assess the widely held assumption that an ethical dimension to holiness did not exist before a prophetic critique of the priestly cultic tradition. The research itself was undertaken under the supervision of Dr Gordon Wenham through Trinity College and the University of Bristol in the United Kingdom. I am grateful for Dr Wenham's generous supervision and wise advice, on more than theological matters, and for the care that he and his wife Lynne extended to my family. It saddens me that a 24-hour flight now prevents me from spontaneously dropping-in at their place. My studies and family were generously supported by Australian friends, most notably SMBC, Croydon.

Dr Walter Houston of Mansfield College, Oxford, provided more input than is expected from one's second supervisor. His identification of several areas where my argument could be strengthened, clarified or abandoned has made this a better work. I would also like to thank Dr N. Kiuchi (Tokyo), Dr Shani Berrin (Jerusalem) and Dr Paul Williamson (Sydney) for their early contributions to the shape of this book. I am grateful for Professor David Clines's acceptance of this book for publication and for the editorial work provided by Sheffield Phoenix Press.

Finally, few wives would agree to move across the globe with two children and a third on the way. My wife Elisa was selfless in her facilitation and support of my studies in the United Kingdom. She is an extraordinary wife, my best mate and tireless mother to our four children Cicely, Clancy, Sidney and Lillian. I dedicate this book to her.

ABBREVIATIONS

AB	Anchor Bible
ABD	David Noel Freedman (ed.), *The Anchor Bible Dictionary* (New York: Doubleday, 1992).
AnBib	Analecta biblica
AOAT	Alter Orient und Altes Testament
BA	*Biblical Archaeologist*
BBB	Bonner biblische Beiträge
BJS	Brown Judaic Studies
BKAT	Biblischer Kommentar: Altes Testament
BN	*Biblische Notizen*
BR	*Biblical Research*
BZAW	Beihefte zur *Zeitschrift für die Alttestamentliche Wissenschaft*
CAT	Commentaire de l'Ancien Testament
CBQ	*Catholic Biblical Quarterly*
DJD	*Discoveries in the Judaean Desert*
EJT	*European Journal of Theology*
ESV	English Standard Version
FRLANT	Forschungen zur Religion und Literatur des Alten und Neuen Testaments
HALOT	L. Koehler and W. Baumgartner, *The Hebrew and Aramaic Lexicon of the Old Testament* (trans. M.E.J. Richardson; Leiden: E.J. Brill, 1994–2000).
HKAT	Handkommentar zum Alten Testament
Int	*Interpretation*
HR	*History of Religions*
JAOS	*Journal of the American Oriental Society*
JBL	*Journal of Biblical Literature*
JEA	*Journal of Egyptian Archaeology*
JJS	*Journal of Jewish Studies*
JNES	*Journal of Near Eastern Studies*
JPS	Jewish Publication Society
JQR	*Jewish Quarterly Review*
JSNTSup	*Journal for the Study of the New Testament* Supplement Series
JSOT	*Journal for the Study of the Old Testament*
JSOTSup	*Journal for the Study of the Old Testament* Supplement Series
JTS	*Journal of Theological Studies*
LHB	Library of Hebrew Bible
NAS	New American Standard Bible
NCB	New Century Bible
NCBC	New Century Bible Commentary
NEB	New English Bible
NIV	New International Version

NJB	The New Jerusalem Bible
NRS	New Revised Standard Bible
NITDOTTE	Willem A. VanGemeren (ed.), *New International Dictionary of Old Testament Theology and Exegesis* (5 vols.; Grand Rapids: Zondervan, 1997).
OBO	Orbis biblicus et orientalis
OTL	Old Testament Library
PEQ	*Palestine Exploration Quarterly*
SBL	Society of Biblical Literature
SJLA	Studies in Judaism in Late Antiquity
SJT	*Scottish Journal of Theology*
STDJ	Studies on the Texts of the Desert of Judah
SUNT	Studien zur Umwelt des Neuen Testaments
TDOT	G.J. Botterweck and H. Ringgren (eds.), *Theological Dictionary of the Old Testament*
THAT	Ernst Jenni and Claus Westermann (eds.), *Theologisches Handwörterbuch zum Alten Testament* (Munich: Chr. Kaiser, 1970–76)
VT	*Vetus Testamentum*
VTSup	*Vetus Testamentum* Supplement Series
WBC	Word Biblical Commentary
WMANT	Wissenschaftliche Monographien zum Alten und Neuen Testament
ZAW	*Zeitschrift für die alttestamentliche Wissenschaft*
ZLThK	*Zeitschrift für die gesamte lutherische Theologie und Kirche*

Chapter 1

INTRODUCTION

The present study examines whether the concept of 'holiness' (קדשׁ) in the Priestly material of Leviticus (i.e. Leviticus 1–16, traditionally 'P') includes an ethical dimension similar to that which is characteristic of holiness in the Holiness Code (Leviticus 17–26; traditionally 'H').[1] Such a goal is provocative because scholars traditionally make a distinction between the ideas of holiness found in P and H along the following lines.

First, apart from a command for the priests to sanctify God,[2] holiness in P is *static*, a status assigned to items or priests which are restricted to the confines of the sanctuary. With the exception of Lev. 11.43-45, which scholars assign to H on theological, stylistic and terminological grounds, holiness terminology is not applied to the laity or places outside the sanctuary.[3] Moreover, P's holiness is described as a *cultic* concept because it is produced by rituals rather than ethical behaviour. For example, the priests, their garments, the altar, and the sanctuary's furniture and utensils are made holy when they are anointed with consecrating oil and blood (Lev. 8.10-11, 15, 30).

---

1. Leviticus 27 is commonly viewed as an appendix composed later than the rest of the 'book'. B.D. Eerdmans, *Das Buch Leviticus* (Giessen: Alfred Töpelmann, 1912), pp. 136-37; Jacob Milgrom, 'H$_R$ in Leviticus and Elsewhere in the Torah', in *The Book of Leviticus. Composition and Reception* (ed. Rolf Rendtorff and Robert A. Kugler; VTSup, 93; Leiden: E.J. Brill, 2003), pp. 26-27.

2. In Lev. 10.3b God commands that בקרבי אקדשׁ ('among those who are near me I will be sanctified'). For a discussion concerning the translation of the niphal אקדשׁ see Jacob Milgrom, *Leviticus 1–16: A New Translation with Introduction and Commentary* (AB, 3; New York: Doubleday, 1991), pp. 601-603. Milgrom translates it as a reflexive: 'I will sanctify myself' and suggests that on this occasion Yahweh sanctifies himself before the Israelites through the burning of Nadab and Abihu.

3. A more comprehensive treatment of why scholars assign Lev. 11.43-45 to H is delayed until Chapter 3 which argues that this H text may explicate the implicit purpose of P's dietary legislation (Leviticus 11). To summarize what is said there, scholars argue that a different concept of holiness, a hortatory literary style and a synonymous use of certain terms (e.g. תמא and שׁקץ), which are not synonyms in P, reflect that Lev. 11.43-45 is the work of H not P. See Milgrom, *Leviticus 1–16*, pp. 39, 694-96; Eerdmans, *Das Buch Leviticus*, p. 65.

Second, in contrast to P, holiness in H is *dynamic* and inseparable from *ethical* concerns because Israel is commanded to obey cultic *and* ethical laws to become holy (Lev. 19.2, 20.7, 26). Whereas holiness is achieved by rituals in P, the behaviour of the laity can sanctify the priests (Lev. 21.8), the name of God (Lev. 22.32-33) and achieve their own sanctification (Lev. 19.2). Moreover, God identifies himself as the one 'who sanctifies *you* [plural; i.e. the laity]' (מקדשכם, Lev. 20.8; 21.8; 22.32). Broadly speaking, whereas holiness resides in those things which enjoy close proximity to the holy divine presence in P, God's holiness is displayed by people who express his rule in their behaviour (cf. Lev. 19.2), in addition to its cultic representation (i.e. Leviticus 21–23, 25), in H.[4]

Presented in this way, the argument that one must make a distinction between two kinds of holiness in Leviticus seems reasonable. Scholars were unable to account for how the 'cultic' concept of holiness, in Leviticus 1–16, relates to the 'ethical' concept in Leviticus 17–26. For example, when contemplating the relationship between Leviticus 1–16 and 17–26, Carl F. Keil (1875) attempted to avoid this difficulty by shifting the focus away from holiness as the central theme of Leviticus. He suggested that Leviticus 1–16 is concerned with the restoration of fellowship between the Israelites and Yahweh and that Leviticus 17–26 proceeds to strengthen the Israelites's fellowship with Yahweh through the sanctification of life.[5] From such a perspective the connection between the two units resides not in their concern for holiness but in a general program for spiritual (i.e. Leviticus 16) and physical (i.e. Leviticus 25) *liberation*.[6] Similarly, S. Kellogg (1899) argued that entrance into fellowship with Yahweh is the central concern of Leviticus 1–16 whereas Leviticus 17–26 focuses on how this fellowship should be reflected in Israel's lifestyle.[7] Keil and Kellogg arguably resorted to a Christian theology of salvation too quickly when considering how the two halves

---

4. S.R. Driver, *An Introduction to the Literature of the Old Testament* (Edinburgh: T. & T. Clarke, 1897), p. 48; Walter Houston, *Purity and Monotheism: Clean and Unclean Animals in Biblical Law* (JSOTSup, 140; Sheffield: Sheffield Academic Press, 1993), pp. 222, 225; Israel Knohl, *The Sanctuary of Silence: The Priestly Torah and the Holiness School* (Minneapolis: Fortress Press, 1995), p. 69; Baruch J. Schwartz, 'Israel's Holiness: The Torah Traditions', in *Purity and Holiness* (ed. M.J.H.M. Poorthuis and Baruch J. Schwartz; Leiden: E.J. Brill, 2000), p. 53; Jacob Milgrom, *Leviticus 17–22: A New Translation with Introduction and Commentary* (AB, 3; New York: Doubleday, 2000), pp. 1397-1400.

5. C.F. Keil, *Commentary on the Old Testament. II. The Pentateuch* (1866–91; repr. Peabody, MA: Hendrickson, 1996), p. 262.

6. Keil, *The Pentateuch*, pp. 263-64.

7. S.H. Kellogg, *The Book of Leviticus* (The Expositor's Bible; New York: Funk & Wagnalls, 1900), p. 28.

are related. For example, Kellogg concludes that Leviticus 1–16 deal with 'new birth' and Leviticus 17–26 relate to the living of a 'holy life'.[8]

Another approach to these seemingly different kinds of holiness in P and H was to explain their existence in historical terms. Differences in vocabulary, idiom, style, and theology between Leviticus 1–16 and Leviticus 17–26 were interpreted as evidence for two independent literary sources.[9] Karl Graf first argued that Leviticus 17–26 was an independent corpus of literature on the basis of its linguistic and stylistic features,[10] and in 1893 August Klostermann coined its now widely accepted name as 'das Heiligkeitsgesetz' ('The Holiness Law') on the basis of the recurring, even if occasionally modified, formula: 'You shall be holy, for I Yahweh your God am holy' (קדשים תהיו כי קדוש אני יהוה אלהיכם).[11] At roughly the same time Chapters 1–16 were assigned to the Priestly source ('Priesterschrift'), which scholars accepted as postexilic, and they assumed that Leviticus 27 was attached at a later time.[12] Scholars established specific historical contexts that would account for the different views of holiness in P and H according to Julius Wellhausen's model for dating the sources of the Pentateuch.[13]

An important presupposition of the new 'Documentary Hypothesis',[14] developed and popularized by Wellhausen, was that Israel's religious life and practice developed from an originally spontaneous 'popular' form of worship

8. Kellogg, *The Book of Leviticus*, p. 28.

9. Julius Wellhausen, *Prolegomena to the History of Israel* (trans. J. Sutherland Black and A. Menzies; Atlanta: Scholars Press, 1994 [1883]), pp. 377-87; Martin Noth, *Leviticus* (trans. J.E. Anderson; Old Testament Library; Philadelphia: Westminster Press, 1965), pp. 14, 128. More recently there has been a tendency to view H as a redaction rather than a literary source. See especially Knohl, *The Sanctuary of Silence*; Milgrom, *Leviticus 1–16*, pp. 13-35.

10. Karl Heinrich Graf, *Die geschichtlichen Bücher des Alten Testaments. Zwei historische-kritische Untersuchungen* (Leipzig: T.O. Weigel, 1866).

11. Lev. 19.2; 20.7, 26; see also Lev. 21.8; 22.32-33. August Klostermann, *Der Pentateuch* (Leipzig: Deichert, 1893), pp. 368-418. Otto Eissfeldt indicates that the relevant pages of this work were already published as August Klostermann, 'Beiträge zur Entstehungsgeschichte des Pentateuchs', *ZLThK* 38 (1877), pp. 401-45. This article was not available to the present writer.

12. Milgrom argues that Leviticus 27 was written in the eighth century BCE and attached to Leviticus during the exile (Jacob Milgrom, *Leviticus 23–27: A New Translation with Introduction and Commentary* [AB, 3; New York: Doubleday, 2001], p. 2409).

13. For a concise history of the development of historical criticism in the area of Pentateuchal studies see Otto Eissfeldt, *The Old Testament. An Introduction* (trans. Peter R. Ackroyd; Oxford: Blackwell, 1965), pp. 158-70.

14. As opposed to the 'old' Documentary Hypothesis proposed by Jean Astruc, *Conjectures sur la Genése: Introduction et notes de Pierre Gibert* (1773; Classiques de l'histoire des religions. Paris: Noêsis, 1999).

into a formalized, ritualistic legalism, made necessary by the unification of the nation under the monarchy.[15] P's emphasis on sacrificial ritual within the sanctuary, and silence regarding the pre-exilic social organization of Israel, reflected a maturation of Josiah's Deuteronomic reforms within the postexilic community.[16] Moreover, the lack of imperatives within P was a sign that these customs had long been adopted by postexilic Israel.[17] With the removal of the earlier popular forms of Israelite worship by the postexilic period, Wellhausen proposed that the priestly school projected the newly established postexilic traditions onto Israel's ancient history, claiming that it originated from Sinai.[18]

In contrast to postexilic P, H's predominantly 'popular' content and similarities to Deuteronomic legal formulations led Wellhausen to the conclusion that it was written some time between Deuteronomy and P, although it was thought to be an expansion of a much earlier Sinai source.[19] In addition to the many stylistic and linguistic elements that are unique to this material, Wellhausen observed that H's concept of holiness differed from that found in P.[20] Whereas H's concept of holiness embraced the people and the land, reflecting a pre-exilic agricultural setting, holiness in P had been abstracted from such matters.

> If the [concept of holiness] was formerly a belief supporting the natural ordinances of human society, it was now set forth in visible form as a divine state, in an artificial sphere peculiar to itself *and transcending the ordinary life of the people*. The idea had formerly informed and possessed the natural body, but now, in order that it might be thoroughly realized, it was to have a spiritual body of its own. There arose a material, external antitheses of a sacred and profane; men's minds came to be full of this, and it was their great endeavour to draw the line as sharply as possible and to repress the natural sphere more and more.[21]

For most of the last century scholars have accepted Wellhausen's assumption that P's cultic view of holiness reflected the institutionalization of Israel's religion in postexilic Israel.

---

15. Wellhausen, *Prolegomena*, p. 36.
16. Wellhausen, *Prolegomena*, p. 41.
17. Wellhausen, *Prolegomena*, p. 35.
18. Wellhausen, *Prolegomena*, p. 38.
19. It shares some similarities with standard biblical legal codes commonly accepted as quite early (e.g. Exod. 20.22–23.33; Deut. 11.31–28.68). As with these, H begins with laws and sacrifices (Leviticus 17) and ends with blessings and curses (Leviticus 26). See Wellhausen, *Prolegomena*, p. 86.
20. Wellhausen, *Prolegomena*, p. 378.
21. Wellhausen, *Prolegomena*, p. 422. Emphasis mine.

A recent challenge to Wellhausen's view of the compositional history of Leviticus has come from Israel Knohl and Jacob Milgrom.[22] Identifying what they perceive as major weaknesses with his explanation,[23] these scholars propose an alternative theory for the relative dating of P and H, suggesting that P is pre-exilic and was redacted by H.[24] They share the traditional view that different concepts of holiness are found in P and H but identify different historical contexts from which these arose. Nevertheless, though Knohl and Milgrom generally agree on the historical situation that gave rise to H's concept of holiness they account for the composition of P and its theology in significantly different ways.

On the one hand, Knohl suggests that P's cultic view of holiness reflects an historical situation in which a priestly class became elitist in connection with the establishment of the 'King's Temple'.[25] 'It is these circles that

22. Milgrom, *Leviticus 1–16*; Knohl, *The Sanctuary of Silence*.

23. Several weaknesses identified in his idea are as follows. First, similar ritual customs to those in P existed within the second millennium BCE (W. von Soden, 'Religiöse Unsicherheit, Säkularisierungstendenzen und Aberglaube zur Zeit der Sargoniden', in *Studie biblica et orientalia* (AnBib, 12; Rome: Pontifical Biblical Institute Press, 1959), pp. 356ff.; Moshe Weinfeld, 'Social and Cultic Institutions in the Priestly Source against their Near Eastern Background', in *Proceedings of the Eighth World Congress of Jewish Studies, Bible Studies, and Hebrew Language* (1981; Jerusalem: World Union of Jewish Studies, 1983), pp. 95-129. Second, the existence of H material outside of the 'Holiness Code' lacks a convincing explanation if it is post-dated by P (see on this issue Christophe Nihan, *From Priestly Torah to Pentateuch: A Study in the Composition of the Book of Leviticus* [PhD dissertation; University of Lausanne, 2005], pp. 503-504). Third, Wellhausen's postexilic dating of P has become increasingly suspect in view of certain archaeological and literary observations. Archaeological findings have emerged that undermine Wellhausen's 'evolutionary' model for the development of Israelite religion. Kaufmann and Weinfeld have argued that ancient societies tended to secularize, rather than formalize, with time. Even if Wellhausen's assumption in this regard were correct, there are literary observations that undermine his position. For example, his theory does not satisfactorily explain why a postexilic P document exhibits no literary dependence on the earlier Deuteronomic material. Y. Kaufmann, *The History of Israelite Religion*, I (Tel Aviv: Dvir, 1937–56), pp. 1-220 (Hebrew); Weinfeld, 'Social and Cultic Institutions in the Priestly Source against their Ancient Near Eastern Background', pp. 95-129; Moshe Weinfeld, *Deuteronomy and the Deuteronomic School* (Winona Lake, IN: Eisenbrauns, 1992), pp. 180-89.

24. Milgrom argues that the final redaction of H occurred no later than the Babylonian exile whereas Knohl suggests that this might have happened as late as the beginning of the Persian period. The difference is not overly significant for my argument considering that both scholars agree that H reflects the work of a priestly school at the time of Hezekiah's reforms (i.e. *c.* 743-701 BCE). See Milgrom, *Leviticus 1–16*, p. 28; Knohl, *The Sanctuary of Silence*, pp. 209, 226.

25. Elitist, and unconnected with the social welfare of the kingdom, because 'after Solomon ascended the throne, we no longer hear of any involvement of the priests in

generate the ideal of superior faith, completely detached from social, national, or material needs.'[26] This presupposition has two implications for Knohl. First, it explains why holiness is unrelated to ethics in P. Second, he argues that it accounts for why P is largely uninterested in ethics.[27]

On the other hand, Milgrom dates P earlier than Knohl, contending that it reflects the cultic customs of the sanctuary at Shiloh and Solomon's temple.[28] And though he agrees with Knohl that P's concept of holiness is unrelated to ethical concerns he remains adamant, contra Knohl, that P exhibits specific ethical concerns. For example, he argues that P adapts the ANE concept of ritual 'uncleanness' to encourage an ethical respect for life.[29] This ethical concern does not contradict Milgrom's contention that P has a narrow cultic concept of holiness because he assumes that the root קדש ('holiness') acquired an ethical aspect only at a later time in Israel's history. In this regard it is noteworthy that though Knohl attempts to provide an historical explanation for why P's concept of holiness was originally unrelated to ethics, Milgrom does not.

By contrast Knohl and Milgrom agree that H's highly ethical view of holiness reflects a priestly response to the classical prophetic critique of the cult. In this regard, Knohl makes the following statement.

> Classical prophecy grew out of a deep social and religious crisis. The prophets of the period [e.g. Amos, Micah, Jeremiah] decry the sharp social cleavages and condemn the rich for their abandonment of social justice and their valueless devotion to the cult. The extreme solution of classical prophecy to these phenomena is the rejection of ritual service and the insistence on moral purity as God's highest command.[30]

In terms of H's theology, Knohl and Milgrom argue that H expands P's cultic notion of holiness in such a way that requires all of Israel to 'be holy'. Thus, Milgrom contends that

affairs of the kingdom, with the exception of Jehoiada the priest (2 Kgs 11.4-20). This singular exception was probably provoked by the religious threat posed by Athaliah's actions (see 2 Kgs 11.18). See Knohl, *The Sanctuary of Silence*, p. 221.

26. Knohl, *The Sanctuary of Silence*, p. 222.

27. That is, while P may assume a universal ethic Knohl argues that it does not exhibit an interest in developing a specific ethic for Israel (*The Sanctuary of Silence*, p. 147). We shall see in Chapter 3 that Milgrom opposes Knohl's assumption that P has no interest in ethics.

28. Milgrom, *Leviticus 1–16*, p. 34.

29. See Milgrom, *Leviticus 1–16*, pp. 42-51. This aspect of Milgrom's argument is discussed at some length in Chapter 3.

30. Knohl, *The Sanctuary of Silence*, p. 215.

H serves as a polemic against P, which rigidly reserves the notion of קדוש solely for the priests, Nazirites and the *sancta*. To be sure, H—also a priestly school—does not deny the genetically transmitted holiness of the priesthood. But even this holiness, limited to the exclusive prerogative of the inherited priesthood to officiate at the altar, can only be sustained by the priests' adherence to a rigorous ritual code (see Lev. 21). Israel, on the other hand, achieves holiness by its obedience to all the revealed commandments, ritual and moral alike.[31]

It should now be apparent that, regardless of how one construes the compositional history of Leviticus (i.e. Wellhausen *versus* Knohl/Milgrom) modern scholarship accounts for the different use of holiness terminology, within P and H, in diachronic terms.

By contrast, the present study examines if there is more coherence between the concepts of holiness in P and H than scholars assume. Specifically it shall investigate whether an ethical dimension to P's concept of holiness exists that has previously gone unnoticed. There are two reasons for why such an investigation seems reasonable.

First, diachronic studies have not identified an historical context which would account for a concept of holiness that is unrelated to ethics.[32] As already mentioned, Wellhausen's assumption that it was the product of the institutionalization of Israel's religion has been found unconvincing by recent

---

31. Jacob Milgrom, 'The Changing Concepts of Holiness in the Pentateuchal Codes with Emphasis on Leviticus 19', in *Reading Leviticus: A Conversation with Mary Douglas* (ed. John F.A. Sawyer; Sheffield: Sheffield Academic Press, 1996), pp. 65-75 (68-69).

32. It is true that many scholars assume that 'holiness' (קדש) was essentially a relational rather than ethical concept. That is, things and people that were holy had to be separated from that which was not (e.g. Otto, Eichrodt, von Rad, Kornfeld, Ringgren, Houston, Joosten). For these scholars 'holiness' does not naturally connote the idea of ethics. Thus, when one begins with this presupposition it may seem unnecessary to have to justify, on historical terms, why holiness was limited to an abstract concept of separation at an earlier period in Israel's history. But this assumption does not negate the point being made above, which is that in the absence of a convincing historical hypothesis for why holiness should be an abstract concept in P we are entitled to explore if this is the meaning of holiness in this material. See Rudolf Otto, *The Idea of the Holy* (London: Oxford University Press, 1923); Walther Eichrodt, *Theology of the Old Testament*, II (London: SCM Press, 1967), pp. 270-82; Gerhard von Rad, *Old Testament Theology. II. The Theology of Israel's Historical Traditions* (1957; trans. D.M.G. Stalker; Edinburgh: Oliver & Boyd, 1973), pp. 203-12; W. Kornfeld and H. Ringgren, 'קדש', in *Theological Dictionary of the Old Testament*, XII (ed. G.J. Botterweck and H. Ringgren; Grand Rapids: Eerdmans, 1975), pp. 521-45 (521-23); Houston, *Purity and Monotheism*, pp. 54-55; Jan Joosten, *People and Land in the Holiness Code: An Exegetical Study of the Ideational Framework of the Law in Leviticus 17–26* (Leiden: E.J. Brill, 1996), p. 123.

scholars. Conversely, Knohl's proposal that it reflects an elitist priesthood that was uninterested in the ethics of society has received sufficient criticism from Milgrom to make one doubt its validity.[33] And, surprisingly, though Milgrom argues that holiness in P is not an ethical concept, he does not explain how an amoral concept of holiness relates to what he proposes is the historical context for this stratum. Thus, in the absence of any historical evidence for why we should expect that P's view of holiness did not have an ethical dimension, we seem entitled to examine if this is really the case.[34]

Second, and in relation to the point that has just been made, studies of P's concept of holiness are limited to the propositional content of Leviticus 1–16. With the exception of Lev. 11.43-45, which almost all scholars assign to H,

33. This criticism is reviewed in Chapter 3.

34. There may be another problem with the view that H extended and applied P's cultic concept of holiness to the entire nation. In response to Knohl's assertion that H's theology reflects 'the rejection of ritual service and the insistence on moral purity as God's highest command', one may ask why a distinction continues to be made between the holiness of priests and laity in Leviticus 17–26. The following statement by Saul Olyan draws attention to this distinction. 'Is there a difference between priestly sanctification and that of the people [in H]? A number of Holiness texts suggest that there is indeed. Lev. 21.6, 7, 8 recognize the special status of priests and connect it to their sanctification. A priest shall not marry a prostitute or divorced woman "for holy is he to his god," says Lev. 21.7. "You shall sanctify him," says Lev. 21.8, "for the food of your god he brings near; holy shall he be for you, for holy am I, Yhwh, who sanctifies you." Other texts explicitly restrict access to the holy foods to priests and their dependents (Lev. 22.10-13). If all Israel is holy, as Lev. 22.32 and other texts seem to suggest, why must access to the holy foods be restricted, as Lev. 22.10-13 makes plain? And why is the special status of the priesthood, with its attendant rights and obligations, connected to their holiness by Lev. 21.6, 7, 8? If all the people are holy, what makes the holiness of the priesthood significant? The holiness of the priest must be of a different order than that of the people. The people's separation and holiness in Holiness texts does not privilege them in any concrete way vis-à-vis the priesthood; it seems mainly to be rhetorical. In contrast, some Holiness materials emphasize the privileges of priests vis-à-vis the people: they bring near Yhwh's offerings (Lev. 21.6, 8); they eat holy foods (Lev. 22.10-13). Thus, priestly holiness has concrete ramifications in texts of the Holiness School. It is very likely conferred through rites such as anointing, setting it apart from the holiness of the people, as some scholars have argued. But however it is conferred, concrete differences in privilege distinguish priestly sanctification from that of the people. And when all is said and done, *the people, though sanctified, have no greater privileges in the cultic sphere than do the people according to the Priestly Writing*' [Saul M. Olyan, *Rites and Rank. Hierarchy in Biblical Representations of Cult* (Princeton, NJ: Princeton University Press, 2000], pp. 121-22 [emphasis mine]; cf. Knohl, *The Sanctuary of Silence*, p. 215). Does Olyan's conclusion, in the final sentence, support Knohl's idea concerning H's agenda to diminish the importance of ritual and uphold moral purity? Though this idea remains possible, perhaps it is more likely that the distinction between the holiness of priests and people reflects what is already implicit within P.

such an approach yields only a 'cultic' view of holiness. But what if an ethical dimension to P's view of holiness remains *implicit* within the rituals of Leviticus 1–16? Milgrom makes a similar argument for why music and prayer may have accompanied the rituals prescribed in P. In response to Knohl's contention that this was not the case, because no prescriptions for such practices are given, Milgrom comments that the

> main fault that recurs in Knohl's reasoning is that it is frequently based on the argument from silence. Thus the ostensible absence of music and prayer from P's prescriptions need not mean that it had no use for them or that it tolerated them in other sanctuaries but not in the Temple.[35]

Perhaps we are also within our rights to ask whether the argument, that P's concept of holiness is devoid of ethical concerns, has been too hastily built on an argument from silence. In other words, what if the symbolic meaning of P's ritual texts reflects a relationship between holiness and ethics?[36] The present study examines this possibility. However, before one can attempt a symbolic interpretation of these texts a relatively objective method for this purpose will need to be established in Chapter 2.

Let me be clear about what this study does not attempt. I am not arguing against the existence of H as either a literary source or a later priestly redaction of P. Since a specific time in Israel's history that would account for P's amoral view of holiness has not been identified by scholars, I do not see why the proposal that P has an ethical view of holiness would threaten diachronic theories. Anyway, hypotheses concerning H are not only based on the assumption that the view of holiness found in Leviticus 17–26 is different from that found in Leviticus 1–16. The distinction scholars make between P and H also derives from well-documented differences in vocabulary, idiom and

35. Milgrom, *Leviticus 1–16*, p. 19.

36. For evidence that one may assume that there is a symbolic dimension to ritual texts within Leviticus see Leigh M. Trevaskis, 'The Purpose of Leviticus 24 within its Literary Context', *VT* 59 (2009), pp. 295-312; see also Jonathan Klawans's argument for the symbolic nature of some aspects of priestly ritual on the basis that the prophets occasionally performed symbolic actions ('Methodology and Ideology in the Study of Priestly Ritual', in *Perspectives on Purity and Purification in the Bible* [ed. Baruch J. Schwartz and David P. Wright; London: T. & T. Clark, 2008], p. 8). From a historical point of view the symbolic interpretation of priestly rituals is not a new development. Klawans has documented the use of symbolic approaches to ritual during the second temple period (Klawans, *Purity, Sacrifice, and the Temple: Symbolism and Supersessionism in the Study of Ancient Judaism* [Oxford: Oxford University Press, 2006], pp. 111-44). However the symbolic interpretation of priestly rituals gained in popularity following the publication of Mary Douglas, *Purity and Danger* (London: Routledge & Kegan Paul, 1966).

style.[37] A far more comprehensive study than the present one would be required to challenge what has been the long-standing consensus concerning the compositional history of Leviticus. Nevertheless, these differences between P and H do not rule out the possibility that the H provenance assigned to certain texts outside Leviticus 17–26 may be challenged as part of the present study. If an ethical dimension to P's view of holiness is demonstrated this would have implications for those texts that are identified as H more or less on the basis that they display an interest in ethical holiness.

Save for the Introduction (Chapter 1) and Conclusion (Chapter 7), the argument of the present work is conducted over five Chapters. Chapter 2 seeks to establish a coherent methodological framework for analyzing the symbolic meaning of ritual words and texts. Such a method is required to identify whether a possible ethical dimension to P's idea of holiness is implicit within the symbolic dimension of its ritual texts. Chapter 3 asks whether H's command to 'be holy' in Lev. 11.43-45 explicates the symbolic meaning of P's preceding 'dietary regulations'. In support of this hypothesis it argues that the symbolic dimension of these regulations was intended to persuade the Israelites to refrain from rebelling against Yahweh. Chapter 4 examines if the proposed symbolic dimension of Leviticus 11 extends into P's remaining purity regulations (Leviticus 12–15). On the one hand this Chapter is intended to support the argument concerning the symbolic mean-ing of Leviticus 11 and ethical holiness. On the other hand, it sets out to confirm that P desired to persuade the Israelites to refrain from rebellion against Yahweh. Chapter 5 investigates if the prescription for the 'burnt offering' (Leviticus 1) anticipates the proposed ethical aspect of P's view of holiness in Leviticus 11 (cf. Chapter 3). This prescription is selected because the concept of holiness is arguably implicit (i.e. the 'burnt offering' is 'most holy'). Chapter 5 argues that, within this context, the term תמים ('without defect') is intended to evoke the meaning it has when applied to humans, namely human 'integrity'. Chapter 6 seeks to confirm that a relationship exists between the terms 'holy' and תמים, in ritual texts, in an exegetical study of Leviticus 21–22. This passage belongs to H but scholars maintain that it uses the relevant terms in the same way as P.

---

37. Consult Milgrom, *Leviticus 1–16*, pp. 35-42; Knohl, *The Sanctuary of Silence*, pp. 106-10. See also Klaus Gründwaldt's review of the history of research on Leviticus 17–26 (*Das Heiligkeitsgesetz. Leviticus 17–26* [Berlin: W. de Gruyter, 1999], pp. 5-22). Stylistic and linguistic differences between P and H are also documented by J. Begrich, 'Die priesterliche Torah', in *Werden und Wesen des alten Testament* (BZAW, 66; Berlin: Alfred Töpelmann, 1936), pp. 63-88 (82); Christian Feucht, *Untersuchungen zum Heiligkeitsgesetz* (Berlin: Evangelische Verlagsanstalt, 1964), pp. 11-12; A. Cholewinski, *Heiligkeitsgesetz und Deuteronomium* (AnBib, 66; Rome: Biblical Institute Press, 1976), p. 137.

Chapter 2

METHODOLOGY

Determining the Meaning of Words, Concepts and Ritual Texts

To test the hypothesis, that P's view of holiness has an ethical dimension similar to what is found in H, requires exegesis of the relevant Levitical terminology and ritual texts. Moreover, the proposal made in Chapter 1, that such a dimension may exist on a symbolic plane of meaning, requires, first, a defence of the assumption that these texts have symbolic meaning and, second, the establishment of a coherent framework for interpreting their symbolism. Thus, an account of how I shall determine the meaning of words, concepts and ritual prescriptions, and a basis for my assumption that P's ritual texts have a symbolic dimension is provided in the four sections of this Chapter.

The first section recommends that one must attend to a word's linguistic context to interpret its primary meaning. The second explains how cognitive linguistic theory provides a relatively objective means for identifying a term's symbolic meaning. The third section makes a case for assuming that the purpose of ritual texts extends beyond practical concerns which includes a symbolic function. The fourth attempts to avoid confusion concerning terms used to describe words and concepts (i.e. ethical, cultic, symbolic, metaphorical) by defining how they are used in this book.

The Meaning of Words: Distinguishing between Sense, Term, and Concept

Within a literary context a word may be conceptualized as comprising a *term* (or *symbol*), a *referent* (i.e. the *concept* to which the term refers), and a *sense* (i.e. what the term says about the concept to which it refers).[1] When approached in this way, the sense of a term is *independent* from the concept to which the term refers. That is, *a term's sense is the idea this term evokes*

---

1. See C.K. Ogden and I.A. Richards, *The Meaning of Meaning* (New York: Harcourt, Brace & Co, 1945), p. 11.

about a concept when used within a particular context. A corollary of this observation is that the description of a concept may comprise a multiplicity of senses evoked by more than one term. This understanding has practical importance for the present study since it alerts us that the sense(s) of the term קדש may not exhaust the full meaning of the concept of holiness. One must avoid confusing the sense of a term (e.g. קדש) with the concept to which it refers (e.g. holiness). James Barr illustrates this point when describing the two valid approaches a person may use in describing the sense of the Greek term ἐκκλησία in the NT.[2] On the one hand, the sense of ἐκκλησία can be described by equating it with the many senses it can have in the NT.

> [W]e might say (a) 'the Church is the Body of Christ' (b) 'the Church is the first installment of the Kingdom of God' (c) 'the Church is the Bride of Christ', and other such statements. The 'meaning of ἐκκλησία in the NT' could then be legitimately stated to be the totality of these relations.[3]

On the other hand, one may describe the sense in which a term is used *within a particular context*. This approach to the interpretation of an individual occurrence of a term is essential because it cannot be assumed that each occurance of a term automatically evokes its multiplicity of senses. However, according to Barr, it is possible to neglect this task and transfer the general meaning a term has across the literature to its use within a particular context.

> The error that arises, when the 'meaning' of a word (understood as the total series of relations in which it is used in the literature) is read into a particular case as its sense and implication there, may be called 'illegitimate totality transfer'.[4]

When such a thing happens, the interpreter erroneously assumes that a singular occurrence of a particular term (e.g. ἐκκλησία) evokes all the senses this term may have, in relation to a specific concept, across a particular corpus of literature. In terms of the present study, Barr's work cautions against assuming that the term קדש carries all the connotations theologians normally associate with *the concept of holiness* whenever it occurs. As Barr points out, such an

> attempt to relate the individual word directly to the theological thought leads to the distortion of the semantic contribution made by words in contexts.[5]

His observation is relevant to the present study which asks whether P's view of holiness shares the characteristics this concept has in H. It may be tempting to force a preconceived concept of holiness onto the relevant terminology

---

2. James Barr, *The Semantics of Biblical Language* (Oxford: Oxford University Press, 1961), p. 218.
3. Barr, *Semantics of Biblical Language*, p. 218.
4. Barr, *Semantics of Biblical Language*, p. 218.
5. Barr, *Semantics of Biblical Language*, p. 128.

wherever it is used. However, the inverse of this error is possibly just as dangerous: in seeking to achieve our goal, one must avoid equating, or confusing, the sense of קדשׁ as it appears in a particular context with the concept to which it refers. That is, having determined the meaning of this term as it occurs in a specific text, one must not fall into the temptation of arguing that the term retains this meaning wherever it occurs in Leviticus. Such a move would confuse the term's sense with the concept to which it refers. For example, if it is possible to demonstrate that קדשׁ is used with an ethical sense in P, one must remember that this sense remains just one aspect of P's concept of holiness. There are other cases in which the term has what appears to be a sense of 'ritual separation' (e.g. Lev. 6.18-20).[6] To demonstrate that P's concept of holiness has an ethical dimension *one does not need to demonstrate that it always uses the term קדשׁ with the same sense, but that it is aware of an ethical sense.*

Barr maintains that one identifies the sense of a term within a given context by paying attention to how the term is *used.*

> It is the sentence (and of course the still larger literary complex such as the complete speech or poem) which is the linguistic bearer of the usual theological statement, and not the word (the lexical unit) or the morphological and syntactical connection.[7]

Similarly, Moisés Silva comments that

> lexical meaning—which cannot be reduced to the concept of denotation—consists largely in the sets of (structural) relations obtaining between the senses of different symbols.[8]

There are two sets of structural relations that govern the sense of a particular term, namely its *paradigmatic* and *syntagmatic* relations. This distinction, and its importance for determining the meaning of words, is described by Silva in *Biblical Words and Their Meaning* (1983). The following, which relies heavily on Silva's work, explains how an analysis of these two structural relations is necessary in the identification of a term's sense within a given context.

Paradigmatic Relations
A term's paradigmatic relations consist of those other terms which 'can occupy the same slot in a particular context (or syntagm)'.[9] Thus, in an example provided by Silva, within the clause 'the man is working slowly' the

---

6. Moreover, it remains possible that P uses other terms to refer to its concept of holiness.

7. Barr, *Semantics of Biblical Language*, p. 263.

8. Moisés Silva, *Biblical Words and their Meaning: An Introduction to Lexical Semantics* (Grand Rapids: Academie Books, 1983), p. 119.

9. Silva, *Biblical Words and their Meaning*, p. 119.

term *man* 'is in paradigmatic relation with *woman, boy,* etc.; *working* with *running, walking,* etc'.[10] The identification of a term's paradigmatic relations draws attention to what may have governed the choice of this term over other possibilities.. So long as the terms are not synonymous, the answer will relate to the sense of the term within that context. Barr contends that this process is essential for an accurate interpretation of a term's contextual meaning.

> [I]t can be argued that the real meaning of a word has to be expressed paradigmatically, that is, in terms of the difference that it makes to choose this word rather than some other word, in a related field, that might have been in the same place: for instance, what does it mean when the text says bārā' rather than *'āśāh* or *geber* rather than *'iš* or *'ādām?*[11]

N. Kiuchi employs an awareness of paradigmatic relations in his semantic analysis of the term כִּפֶּר.[12] Listing terms that are sometimes juxtaposed with כִּפֶּר he identifies two fields of paradigmatic relations. The first includes terms used to denote ritual cleansing (i.e. חָטֵא and טָהֵר) and the second is limited to the phrase נָשָׂא עָוֹן ('to bear guilt'). Beginning with an analysis of the use of כִּפֶּר in the first field he finds that, while the concept of ritual cleansing is a component of what it means to make כִּפֶּר, the term refers more generally to 'the act which enables progression from uncleanness to cleanness, from cleanness to holiness and from uncleanness to holiness'.[13] Thus, rather than synonyms of כִּפֶּר these terms are *hyponyms*, meaning that their overlap in sense is incomplete. Within ritual cleansing contexts this observation implies that an author's decision to use כִּפֶּר, rather than one of its paradigmatic relations, is intended to focus on the *action*, rather than the outcome, of ritual cleansing.

By contrast, in the second field of paradigmatic relations (i.e. נָשָׂא עָוֹן) Kiuchi argues that כִּפֶּר is used to refer to the act of 'bearing guilt'. Nevertheless, since כִּפֶּר has another, seemingly unrelated, field of paradigmatic relations (i.e. ritual cleansing), he infers that it cannot be a synonym of the phrase נָשָׂא עָוֹן. Instead,

> the fact that the concept of *kipper* includes the notion of 'purification' expressed by טָהֵר, קֹדֶשׁ and חָטֵא, while the latter is clearly distinct from the notion of 'bearing guilt', suggests that *kipper* is also [a] *supernym* of the concept of נָשָׂא עָוֹן.[14]

10. Silva, *Biblical Words and their Meaning*, p. 119.

11. James Barr, 'Hebrew Lexicography', in *Linguistics and Biblical Hebrew* (ed. Walter R. Bodine; Winona Lake,IN: Eisenbrauns, 1992), pp. 137-51 (144).

12. N. Kiuchi, *The Purification Offering in the Priestly Literature: Its Meaning and Function* (Sheffield: JSOT Press, 1987), Chapter 4.

13. Kiuchi, *The Purification Offering*, pp. 97-98.

14. Kiuchi, *The Purification Offering*, p. 99. Kiuchi adopts this semantic category of *supernym* from Benjamin Kedar. According to Kedar, a word is a supernym of another word when it contains and exceeds the 'elements' signified by the latter, and it is a hypo-

In this regard, when כִּפֶּר, rather than נשׂא עוֹן, is used in relation to the removal of guilt it probably intends the reader to understand that something in addition to this occurs, namely cleansing from defilement.[15]

By paying attention to the paradigmatic relations of the term כִּפֶּר Kiuchi establishes its range of *potential* lexical meaning. However, if he were to posit that a combination of these senses is the meaning of כִּפֶּר in whatever context it is used, which he does not, then it would be an example of what Barr refers to as 'illegitimate totality transfer': the concept and term would be confused. To determine what aspect of a concept is being referred to by a particular term, one must consult the latter's syntagmatic relations.

Syntagmatic Relations

Within Silva's illustrative clause, 'the man is working slowly', *man* is in syntagmatic relation with the terms *the, is, working, slowly*. He emphasizes the importance of this kind of structural relationship as follows.

> [I]t should be noted that the syntagmatic combinations play the determinative role in language. While the paradigmatic relations alert us to the potential for lexical expression in a particular language, this potential becomes 'actualized' only when words are in fact combined with one another by a specific speaker or writer to form sentences.[16]

An example of how attention to syntagmatic relations is vital for the identification of a word's meaning is provided in Kiuchi's determination of what sense the term חִטֵּא is used within Exod. 29.36. Though many commentators regard it as meaning 'to purify' within this context, Kiuchi arrives at the conclusion that it means 'to offer a חַטָּאת [sin/purification offering]' by taking into account the term's syntagmatic relations.

> Elsewhere חִטֵּא never takes עַל. In fact, חִטֵּא usually takes a direct object, and if not, as in Ezek. 43.22, 23 the object is self-evident. In this regard חִטֵּא עַל in our passage appears unique. Now the term חִטֵּא itself can mean either 'de-sin, purify' or 'bring a *ḥaṭṭāʾt* offering, perform the rite of the *ḥaṭṭāʾt*.' However, the lack of a direct object and the presence of עַל הַמִּזְבֵּחַ suggest that the idea of 'purify/de-sin the altar' is not the right one. Rather another meaning of חִטֵּא, 'offer a *ḥaṭṭāʾt*', better suits the context.[17]

nym to another word when it shares only some of the 'elements' signified by the latter. See examples provided in Benjamin Kedar, *Biblische Semantik* (Stuttgart: W. Kohlhammer, 1981), pp. 76-77.

15. Cf. Lev. 4.20, 26, 31, 35; 5.6, 10; etc., and Kiuchi, *The Purification Offering*, p. 109.

16. Silva, *Biblical Words and their Meaning*, p. 120.

17. Kiuchi, *The Purification Offering*, pp. 95-96.

This example illustrates Silva's point that 'the syntagmatic combinations play the determinative role in language'.[18] Though the potential semantic value of the term חַטָּא is suggested by its paradigmatic relations, its sense in Exod. 29.36 is settled by its syntagmatic relations.

The Meaning of Words: The Use of Cognitive Linguistics

The symbolic meaning of ritual terms has importance for the present study which is interested in whether P's 'cultic' texts reflect a concept of holiness, on a symbolic plane, that is made explicit in texts thought to belong to H. But how can one demonstrate that a term has a meaning that extends beyond the literal to the symbolic? Though Barr's contention that an interpreter must consult a term's paradigmatic and syntagmatic relations when determining its meaning is accepted, this approach seems limited in its ability to identify more than a term's primary meaning. Extra-linguistic factors that may have significance for how a term should be interpreted are not taken into account. In other words, though the interpretative approach advocated by Barr identifies the primary meaning of a term within a particular context, it does not entertain the possibility that a reader's experience may result in this term evoking other secondary meanings.

For example, imagine a short story within which the word 'empty' occurs numerous times to qualify terms such as 'life', 'love', 'relationship', and 'feeling'. In the final scene of this story 'empty' occurs once more when the depressed protagonist arrives at his family house to find it 'empty'. Attention to the paradigmatic and syntagmatic relations of this final use of the term 'empty' would lead to the conclusion that it has a practical rather than emotional meaning. Yet this conclusion overlooks the possibility that the term is intended to evoke the emotional feelings it conveys when it is used previously in the story. In other words, the reader, though admitting that the term 'empty' is *primarily* used to describe the absence of furniture and people in the house, may suspect that this 'spatial emptiness' corresponds in some way to the protagonist's 'emotional emptiness'. The latter would be a *secondary* meaning that is not identified by restricting one's attention to the paradigmatic and syntagmatic relations of 'empty' within this context.

Cognitive linguistics is a method of interpretation that may be used in conjunction with the method recommended by Barr to register a reader's cognitive processing of words.[19] However, before an explanation is given for

---

18. Silva, *Biblical Words and their Meaning*, p. 120.

19. George Lakoff and Mark Johnson, *Metaphors We Live By* (Chicago: University of Chicago Press, 1980); George Lakoff, *Women, Fire, and Dangerous Things: What Categories Reveal about the Mind* (Chicago: University of Chicago Press, 1987); Ronald W. Langacker, *Concept, Image, and Symbol: The Cognitive Basis of Grammar*

how one goes about using a cognitive linguistic approach more needs to be said about why it is relevant to the present study.

The advantage of employing a cognitive linguistic approach in the interpretation of words, in the present study, is that it provides a relatively objective basis for the identification of symbolic meaning. The weakness of symbolic interpretations of Leviticus in the late 19th century was that, where the symbolism was not explicit (e.g. Lev. 17.11), they tended to be arbitrary.[20] By contrast cognitive linguistic interpretations are more objective because they seek to describe why a reader would access secondary, possibly symbolic, meanings of words. They register the various meanings a term has elsewhere and assess the probability that one or more of these meanings is evoked, in addition to the primary meaning, within a particular context. To return to my example concerning the use of the term 'empty' within a short story, a cognitive linguistic approach assesses the likelihood that a reader would access a meaning that extends beyond a house devoid of people and furniture. It may be that there are enough literary cues within the final scene to prompt a reader, from his experience of reading the entire text, to recall the protagonist's earlier 'empty' feelings and associate these with the mention of an 'empty' house.

Since the cognitive science underlying cognitive linguistic theory is well-documented it does not need to be reproduced here.[21] Instead we may proceed by describing the cognitive linguistic method used in the present study. To begin with, a definition of several concepts which are essential for understanding this method is necessary.[22]

The Semantic Frame
A cognitive linguistic approach to interpretation presupposes that each term, which is referred to as a *profile*, has a *semantic frame*. This frame may be

---

(2nd edn; Cognitive Linguistics Research, 1; Berlin: W. de Gruyter, 2002); George Lakoff, *Philosophy in the Flesh* (New York: Basic Books, 1999); J. Allwood, 'Meaning Potential and Context: Some Consequences for the Analysis of Variation in Meaning', in *Cognitive Approaches to Lexical Semantics* (ed. H. Cuyckens, R. Dirven and J.R. Taylor; Berlin: W. de Gruyter, 2003), pp. 29-65 (39-41); William Croft and D. Alan Cruse, *Cognitive Linguistics* (Cambridge: Cambridge University Press, 2004).

20. For example see the works of J.H. Kurtz, *Sacrificial Worship of the Old Testament* (repr. 1863 edn; Grand Rapids: Baker, 1980) and K.C.W.F. Bähr, *Symbolik des mosaischen Cultus* (2 vols.; Heidelberg: Mohr, 1837–39).

21. See the literature cited above.

22. In the following I am heavily indebted to the description of this method provided by T.R. Wardlaw, *Conceptualizing Words for 'God' within the Pentateuch: A Cognitive-Semantic Investigation in Literary Context* (LHB, 495; New York: T. & T. Clark, 2008), pp. 23-53.

conceptualized as a matrix which comprises a number of *semantic domains*.[23]
For example, the term (i.e. profile) 'dog' has a semantic frame which includes the domains of 'pet', 'canine', 'friend', etc. When interpreting the
term 'dog' a person may access any one of these domains and assume that
this corresponds to its intended meaning within a given context. But as we
shall see, more than one domain may be accessed depending on a reader's
previous experience or exposure to this term.

A term's semantic frame is the sum of an interpreter's experience of this
term and cognitive linguists refer to this bank of experience as the reader's
encyclopaedic knowledge. An awareness of a term's semantic frame enables
the interpreter to 'describe the relation of a profile to various domains within
a larger conceptual matrix'.[24] In this way, instead of confining an interpretation to a term's primary meaning, one may evaluate the likelihood that
other domains within its semantic frame are accessed. This facility may
enable us to identify the symbolic meaning of terms within the ritual texts of
Leviticus.

Centrality
Of vital importance in avoiding Barr's charge of 'illegitimate totality transfer', is the concept of 'centrality' developed by Ronald Langacker.[25] In order
to prevent an arbitrary assignment of meaning (i.e. semantic domains) to a
term from one's encyclopaedic knowledge (i.e. the term's 'semantic frame'),
Langacker emphasizes that there will be a gradation in the saliency of these
domains in relation to the meaning of a term within any given context.

> The multitude of specifications that figure in our encyclopedic conception of
> an entity clearly form a gradation in terms of their centrality. Some are so
> central that they can hardly be omitted from even the sketchiest characteri-
> zation, whereas others are so peripheral that they hold little significance even
> for the most exhaustive description.[26]

Thus, the task of the cognitive linguist is to estimate the saliency various
domains have for the use of a term within a particular context. Between the
two extremes of a 'primary domain' (i.e. most central) and an insignificant
domain (most peripheral) a range of 'secondary domains' may exist which
have significance for how a text should be interpreted. With regard to the
present study, it seems feasible to think of the symbolic dimension of ritual
texts as residing within the field of 'secondary domains'.

23. Langaacker, *Foundations*, p. 147.
24. Wardlaw, *Conceptualizing Words*, p. 30.
25. Langacker, *Foundations*, p. 159.
26. Langacker, *Foundations*, p. 159.

The Prescriptive Context
Where does the context of a particular term's semantic frame terminate (i.e. what is its 'prescriptive context'?)? Langacker suggests that it is restricted by 'the physical, social, and cultural context, both the immediate context and presumed shared knowledge'.[27] Within an ancient text, for which the living audience is no longer accessible, this would mean that the context prescribing a term's encyclopaedic knowledge is limited to the larger text it presupposes. The implications of this observation for my interpretation of Leviticus are summed up by Wardlaw in his study of words for 'God' in the Pentateuch:

> In relation to defining the meaning of words for 'God' within the Pentateuch, the nature of canonical scripture seems to be prescriptive. As such, it may not be the case that comparative evidence defines the meaning of the words, but rather that the meaning of these words is embedded and developed within the language-system of the text itself, and that this was prescriptive both within the religious community of ancient Israel, as well as within the present Christian Church. Therefore the present investigation seeks to describe the prescriptive meaning of words for 'God' since this accords better with the nature of the biblical text when read in a confessional context. Thus the text is its own contextualized linguistic system situated within a community of speakers and readers.[28]

In the present study, it seems reasonable to limit the context, in which we define the semantic frame of Levitical terminology, to the Pentateuch.

Interpretation as Dynamic Construal
Cognitive linguists view interpretation as a person's *dynamic* construal of meaning.[29] It is dynamic because meaning is construed from a particular linguistic expression

> alongside non-linguistic knowledge, information available from context, knowledge and conjectures regarding the state of mind of hearers and so on.[30]

For this reason an interpreter is required to go beyond the term's paradigmatic and syntagmatic relations in identifying its meaning. As far as a term within Leviticus is concerned, assuming that its semantic frame is coterminus with the use of this term within the Pentateuch, the interpreter will need to take into consideration any factors which are likely to encourage a reader to access domains beyond that which is primary. This method of reading presupposes that interpretation is a process and Croft and Cruse characterize this process as follows.

27. Langacker, 'Context, Cognition, and Semantics', p. 194.
28. Wardlaw, *Conceptualizing Words*, p. 37.
29. Croft and Cruse, *Cognitive Linguistics*, p. 98.
30. Croft and Cruse, *Cognitive Linguistics*, p. 98.

When we encounter a piece of language in the course of normal communication, there is an instant of comprehension, a kind of crystallization of the perception of meaning—we know what somebody has said (or written etc.). This is similar to our recognition of a familiar face, or when we realize that what we are seeing is a dog and so on. In the case of the face, we do not merely recognize whose face it is, but at the same instant we see perhaps that the person is tired, or worried, and the hair is windblown and so on. On further reflection, we might infer what the person has been doing, or what the cause of worry is. The processing can continue indefinitely, but there is nonetheless a prior moment of recognition.

Something similar happens when we encounter a piece of language. We recognize in an instant what has been said, but we can go on working out consequences and further inferences indefinitely. It is what constitutes the focus of our attention at the moment of understanding that is referred to here as the interpretation of an expression. Phenomenologically, it is a fairly clearcut event. It will be useful to distinguish pre-crystallization processes, processes preceding and leading up to crystallization, and post-crystallization processes. In many approaches to meaning, there is a determinate starting point for the process of constructing an interpretation, but an indeterminate end point.[31]

We may illustrate this way of conceptualizing the process of interpretation by returning to our short story that concludes with the protagonist finding his house 'empty'. Within this final scene various cues may remind us of the emptiness characterizing this man in the preceding pages. For example, as he turns onto his street the narrator has him recall how his wife used to comment on the state of a neighbour's garden; reflect on the fact that she is no longer with him; even consider driving his car into a brick wall. When reading this text the interpreter is in the 'pre-crystallization process'. Perhaps the reader is building expectations that the protagonist is about to experience a worsening of his 'empty' life experience. The 'moment of crystallization' arrives when the interpreter reads that the man found his family house 'empty'. Immediately the reader accesses the domain of 'spatial emptiness' because this is what the term normally means within the syntagm 'house was empty'. However, after the 'moment of crystallization' some of the contextual cues (i.e. the thoughts he was having as he drove towards his house) may encourage an interpreter to begin accessing other domains from this term's semantic frame. Though the primary domain of meaning relates to the fact that there is nothing in his house, it might occur to the reader that the house's emptiness is figurative of the man's own emptiness. This is the 'post-crystallization process' and the domain accessed is secondary.

A cognitive linguistic approach does not reinvent what Barr describes as 'illegitimate totality transfer'. Instead, as Wardlaw points out, this approach

31. Croft and Cruse, *Cognitive Linguistics*, pp. 99-100.

is a refinement of Barr's description of illegitimate totality transfer in his critique of the Biblical Theology movement. On the one hand, the present approach limits the information which the mind realistically processes in the instant of initial interpretation. On the other hand, the subsequent process of interpretation allows for the cognition of further encyclopedic knowledge that may be associated with a given word.[32]

The benefit of supplementing the method of interpretation proposed by Barr with cognitive linguistic insights, for the present study, is that it may increase the objectivity by which symbolic meaning is assigned to various terms.[33]

The Meaning of Biblical Ritual Texts

So far we have discussed how one should attend to the linguistic and extra-linguistic factors that govern the meaning of words. However, before we proceed to examine the texts of Leviticus it is necessary to establish the nature of ritual texts. Chapter 1 argued that by classifying ritual texts as 'cultic', scholars may have overlooked their symbolic meaning. This insight has significance for the study of holiness in Leviticus 1–16 because it allows for the possibility that ethical holiness is present on the symbolic dimension of this material.[34] Nevertheless, in order to test this hypothesis at least two methodological issues require attention. First, we must demonstrate that the purpose of ritual texts extends beyond practical concerns. Most scholars assume that the purpose of these texts is confined to practical rather than theological matters.[35] But may one also assume that these texts have a

32. Wardlaw, *Conceptualizing Words*, pp. 40-41.

33. In this way I hope to avoid the following charge James Watts claims can be levelled against symbolic interpretations of P. 'If texts, such as P, do not provide symbolic explanations of the rituals they describe, interpreters find themselves open to the charge of imposing symbolic systems not intrinsic or necessary to the rituals' [James W. Watts, *Ritual and Rhetoric in Leviticus: From Sacrifice to Scripture* (Cambridge: Cambridge University Press, 2007], p. 33).

34. The kind of ethical concern I seek to demonstrate as operative within Leviticus 1–16 is different from the ethical purpose Milgrom assigns to this material. Milgrom rejects the notion that P calls upon its readers to be ethically holy by directing their attention to God's ethical law. Instead, he views P's ethical interest as relating to a desire to conserve life, and in this way imitate God. In this regard, the Israelites behave ethically as a *consequence* of observing, for example, the food laws (Leviticus 11) by confining their diet to a relatively small part of the animal kingdom (*Leviticus 1–16*, pp. 731-36). By contrast, the view proposed here, concerning the ethical concern of Leviticus 1–16, is that the symbolic meaning of the ritual texts is intended to persuade the audience to observe the ethical and cultic commands received at Sinai.

35. For example, Martin Noth assumes that 'the rituals in Lev. 3 are only interested in what the "layman" needed to know about sacrificial procedure in the narrower sense'

symbolic meaning which is of theological importance? Second, we shall need to clarify what the object of interpretation should be, namely the text or the enacted ritual it prescribes, and how one should interpret it. Scholars sometimes assume that the theological meaning of a rite is found in how it is *used* or *interpreted* within narrative texts (e.g. Baruch Levine), or in how one envisages the *enacted* rite may have functioned within its original context (e.g. Frank Gorman). I intend to argue that an interfusion between the theology and literary art of ritual texts requires that the latter should be the focus for interpretation.

The Purpose of Biblical Ritual Texts

Traditionally scholars assign a practical purpose to the ritual texts of Leviticus. For example, Leviticus 1–7 is commonly referred to as a 'Handbook for Priests',[36] on the assumption that it served as a reference for people desiring to make its prescribed offerings.[37] In line with this approach to ritual texts, Rolf Rendtorff sought to establish the existence of a 'ritual' genre in Leviticus 1–5.[38] On the one hand, he claims that all of the prescriptions in these

(Noth, *Leviticus*, p. 31). See also A. Noordtzij, *Leviticus* (trans. T. Togtman; Bible Student's Commentary; Grand Rapids: Zondervan, 1982), pp. 23-24; John E. Hartley, *Leviticus* (Dallas: Word Books, 1992), p. 3. More recently, William Gilders has argued that questions concerning the symbolic meaning of ritual texts are not answered by 'most ritual texts'. 'Biblical texts offer very little in the way of interpretation or explanation of ritual acts. Their obvious concern is with the details of practice, with telling the reader how ritual actions were enacted or in prescribing how to carry them out. Questions that focus on the symbolic meanings or instrumental effects of ritual acts are external to the purposes of most of the texts. They were not written to answer such questions. Rather, they invite questions about formal practice' (William K. Gilders, *Blood Ritual in the Hebrew Bible: Meaning and Power* [Baltimore: The John Hopkins University Press, 2004], p. 6). But, as we shall see below, there seems to be too much information missing if the purpose of the relevant texts was to answer 'questions about formal practice'. Moreover, Gilders assumes a practical purpose for the ritual texts without demonstrating this to be the case.

36. Eissfeldt suggests that the genre of Leviticus 1–5 is to direct priests on how to make offerings (*The Old Testament: An Introduction*, pp. 30-31); see likewise A. Rainey, 'The Order of Sacrifices in Old Testament Ritual Texts', *Biblica* 51 (1970), pp. 485-98 (487); followed by D.W. Baker, 'Leviticus 1–7 and the Punic Tariffs: A Form Critical Comparison', *ZAW* (1987), pp. 188-97 (196). Rendtorff opposes the view of these scholars. Pointing out that the prescriptions are addressed to the lay offerer in Lev. 1.2, he prefers the view that the style of Leviticus 1–5 instructs the lay-person rather than the priests (*Leviticus* [BKAT, 3/1; Neukirchen–Vluyn: Neukirchener Verlag, 1985], p. 21.

37. Baker, 'Leviticus 1–7', pp. 196-97. See also Rolf P. Knierim, *Text and Concept in Leviticus 1:1-9* (Tübingen: J.C.B. Mohr, 1992).

38. Rolf Rendtorff, *Die Gesetze in der Priesterschrift* (FRLANT, 62; Göttingen: Vandenhoeck & Ruprecht, 1963). Though, in his later commentary on Leviticus,

chapters prescribe six actions for the priests to perform.[39] On the other, he suggests that the similarity in style of these prescriptions reflects that they come from a recognized genre of ritual. In this regard, he points out that the legislator confines himself to using an indirect verbal form (3ms) and a *waw-qatal-X* construction.[40] On the presupposition that these texts served a practical purpose, many scholars restrict their exegesis to an explanation of the practical significance of the ritual elements. When questions of ritual theology arise they typically refer to observations of how the prescribed rites are *used* in the narrative texts or, by tracing their etymology, in ANE texts. Only on rare occasions, when explicit theological explanations are supplied, do scholars draw theology from the ritual text.[41] And the existence of theological statements within the ritual texts is assumed to serve the latter's practical goal rather than expound the theological purpose for readers.[42]

Baruch Levine's analysis of the 'peace offering' (שלמים) reflects the traditional assumption that ritual texts have a primarily practical function.[43]

Rendtorff refers to a ritual 'style' rather than 'genre', he still regards such texts as serving both practical and theological functions. He introduces his commentary by stating that chaps. 1–7 have 'eine ganz spezifische Absicht: Anweisungen zu geben über die Art und Beschaffenheit des Opfermaterials, über die Durchführung der jeweiligen Opferhandlung sowie über weitere mit dem Opfervollzug zusammenhängende praktische, kultrechtliche und kulttheologische Fragen' (Rendtorff, *Leviticus*, pp. 1, 19-20). Nevertheless, one cannot help thinking that the extent to which he views them as theological is limited to occasions when he views terms as being loaded with 'cultic theology'. For example, see his discussion of the root רצון as it occurs in Lev. 1.3 (*Leviticus*, pp. 30-32).

39. Rendtorff, *Leviticus*, pp. 32-60.

40. The introductory clause is an exception. Rendtorff, *Die Gesetze in der Priesterschrift*, p. 12. Knierim has exposed difficulties associated with the assumption that these texts constitute a genre of 'ritual instruction'. Nevertheless, his recommendation that they should be viewed as 'ritual procedure' that is intended for standardizing ritual conduct at a future time does not shift their purpose beyond practical concerns (Knierim, *Text and Concept*, pp. 91-94). Against Rendtorff, Nihan utilizes V. Fritz's contention that the repetition of the construction *waw-qatal-X* is not sufficient evidence for the existence of a unique ritual genre (V. Fritz, *Tempel und Zelt: Studien zum Tempelbau in Israel und zu dem Zeltheiligtum der Priesterschrift* [WMANT, 47; Neukirchen–Vluyn: Neukirchen Verlag, 1977], p. 116; Nihan, *From Priestly Torah to Pentateuch*, pp. 18-19).

41. For example, most commentators attempt to infer the theological significance of the statement וסמך ידו על ראש העלה ונרצה לו לכפר עליו ('and he shall lean his hand upon its head so that it will be accepted for him to make atonement for him', Lev. 1.4).

42. Knierim suggests that '[t]he act of information appears to be an important procedural element' (Knierim, *Text and Concept*, pp. 43-45).

43. Baruch Levine, *In the Presence of the Lord* (Leiden: E.J. Brill, 1974); cf. Baruch Levine, 'The Descriptive Tabernacle Texts of the Pentateuch', *JAOS* 85 (1965), pp. 307-18. This assumption does not prevent Levine from suggesting that there is a theological

In defining this offering's theological significance he pays no attention to its prescriptive texts (Leviticus 3; 7.11-35). Instead, he constructs the offering's theology from how this sacrifice is used within biblical narratives and in the ANE literature, an approach which necessitates the framing of his conclusion in historical terms.

> Underlying the entire history of the *šelāmîm*, with its developments in Israel, is the notion of sacrifice as an efficacious gift of greeting, offered 'in the presence of the Lord.'[44]

Levine does not explain why he omits the offering's prescriptive texts from his analysis, though it presumably reflects his assumption that these have a practical rather than theological purpose. This assumption is also evident from his contention that the meaning the peace offering has in the biblical narratives occasioned its incorporation into the (later) priestly tradition. He speculates that P

> sought to avail itself of a sacrifice identified with great cultic moments in Israelite history—the initiation of the monarchy under Saul, sanctioned by a cultic convocational the bringing of the ark to Jerusalem, marking the rise of that city to cultic pre-eminence, and the dedication of Solomon's temple… The *šelamîm* epitomized significant beginnings, and we know that the cultic establishment frequently attempted to routinize the momentous, thus rendering it part and parcel of the ongoing religious experience of the individual Israelite and of the people, collective.[45]

For Levine it appears that the purpose of the ritual text does not extend to theological concerns. Instead, these texts *evoke* the theology their prescribed rites have in the narrative texts, and in keeping with this assumption, he

meaning inherent within Israel's ritual worship. For example, in his later commentary he makes the following statement: 'For all students of biblical religion and history, Leviticus poses a genuine challenge: Are we able to penetrate forms and actions to arrive at the dimension of their underlying meanings? Are we limited to statements about how religious devotion was expressed, or can we say something as well about why it was expressed in prescribed ways? One of the major purposes of the present Commentary will be the attempt to fathom the significance of biblical religion, in essence and manifestation' (Baruch Levine, *Leviticus* [Philadelphia: The Jewish Publication Society of America, 1989], p. xl). Nevertheless, as we shall see, Levine goes about this task by looking outside the ritual texts for answers concerning their theological meaning.

44. Levine, *In the Presence of the Lord*, p. 52.

45. Thus, Levine assumes, rather than interprets, that the meaning of the ritual text in Leviticus 3 conforms to what he judges is the historical meaning of this offering—a gift of greeting (Levine, *In the Presence of the Lord*, p. 52). By contrast, Baker considers that this 'genre of practical, prescriptive ritual texts, as the basic groundwork for the cult, would appear logically to be needed as early as, or perhaps earlier than, a theological explanation or interpretation of the cult or its origins' (Baker, 'Leviticus 1–7', p. 197).

confines his commentary on Leviticus 3 to an explanation of its practical significance.[46]

Levine is not alone in presupposing that the ritual texts are of limited theological importance. The same presupposition compels John Hartley to insert a theological excursus on each offering, similarly gained through an analysis of narrative texts, before his exegetical comments on each prescription.[47] This approach reflects his view that within the ritual texts

> there is no extensive treatment of the theological significance of the various sacrifices or of sacrifice in general. Emphasis is on the kinds and forms of sacrificial materials and the rituals for each kind of sacrifice.[48]

Thus, like Levine, Hartley restricts his exegesis to an explanation of *how* things happened in their enactment, referring to the narrative texts when commenting on issues of theology.[49]

Assessment. Describing a ritual's theology as it occurs across the OT and ANE is similar to describing all the ways in which a term such as ἐκκλησία is used in the NT. Not only is this kind of study necessary for the construction of a systematic theology of biblical rituals, but the identification of the potential aspects of meaning a rite may have across the OT provides a useful guide to the interpretation of individual ritual elements.[50] Nevertheless, several problems underlie the assumption that the theological meaning(s) a ritual has across the OT must constitute the meaning of its prescriptive text.

The first problem is that it makes the same error Barr refers to as 'illegitimate totality transfer' in the field of lexical semantics: it wrongly assumes that a ritual text automatically evokes the complete set of meanings its prescribed rite has across the OT without investigating how the text is *used* within a particular context.[51] This assumption overlooks the possibility that

46. Levine, *Leviticus*, pp. 15-17.

47. Hartley, *Leviticus*. A similar approach is taken in Noordtzij, *Leviticus*; J.P. Budd, *Leviticus* (NCB; Grand Rapids: Eerdmans, 1996); E.S. Gerstenberger, *Leviticus* (OTL; Louisville, KY: Westminster/John Knox Press, 1996).

48. Hartley, *Leviticus*, p. 3.

49. See also William Barron Stevenson, 'Hebrew *'Olah* and *Zebach* Sacrifices', in *Festschrift für A. Bertholet* (ed. W. Baumgartner; Tübingen: Mohr, 1950), pp. 488-97 (489-92).

50. For example, Wenham comments that 'though other passages of Scripture and neighbouring cultures may suggest meanings for elements of rites, ultimately this interpretation must be compatible with the overall purpose and function of the rite as recovered by the systematic analysis of that rite and similar ones' (Gordon J. Wenham, *Numbers* [Leicester: IVP, 1981], p. 37).

51. Kevin Vanhoozer has pointed out that scholars who have heeded Barr's corrective on the lexical level are 'in danger of repeating the linguistic sins of [their] forefathers, only this time on the literary rather than the lexical level' (Kevin J. Vanhoozer, 'The

a ritual prescription's composition is intended to emphasize a certain aspect of its implicit theological meaning. This possibility does not appear at all unlikely when one takes into account the literary context of Leviticus.. Though a surface reading of Exodus 25–40 may suggest that it simply reports Yahweh's instructions for, and Israel's construction of, the tabernacle, scholars agree that the composition of this material invites an interpretation of this tent-structure through the lens of Israel's creation theology.[52] Despite such agreement, scholars have not recognized that a similar theological concern may have governed the composition of the ritual texts in Leviticus. Yet if the latter is the case it would require the exegete to interpret the theological meaning of the prescription at hand, rather than assume that its theology must be evoked from elsewhere in the OT.[53]

Second, Hartley's observation that there is no 'extensive treatment' of theology in ritual texts does not imply that they are uninterested in theology. One should not expect that theological treatment be propositional in form when this is not the case in some other genres. For example, though an 'extensive treatment' of the theology of God's providence does not exist in the Joseph narratives (Genesis 37–50), scholars do not suggest that an excursus on divine providence in the OT is necessary before a discussion can take place about the theology of these narratives.[54] Should we not allow for the

Semantics of Biblical Literature: Truth and Scripture's Diverse Literary Forms', in *Hermeneutics, Authority, and Canon* [ed. D.A. Carson and John D. Woodbridge; Carlisle: Paternoster Press, 1986], p. 54).

52. See Chapter 3 and Nahum Sarna, *Exploring Exodus*, pp. 190-220. Terence Fretheim, hypothesizing that the 'sociohistorical setting for the basic form of the tabernacle texts is the exile' makes the stimulating suggestion that in addition to providing plans for a sanctuary beyond exile, the 'extensive detail' of these chapters 'creates a tabernacle in the minds of those who have none. A sanctuary begins to take shape within, where it can be considered in all of its grandeur and beauty, living once again in the memory'. Fretheim considers that when the Israelites became aware of the allusions made to Genesis 1 they possibly reflected on the tabernacle's 'grandeur and beauty' in terms of the creation. If it is possible for these texts to serve this purpose, it does not seem unlikely that Leviticus 1–16 could have provided a similar reflective experience for the reader (Terence E. Fretheim, *Exodus* [Louisville, KY: John Knox Press, 1991], p. 264). Nihan suggests that '[t]he building of Yhwh's sanctuary in Exod 25ff. follows another conflict against the primeval waters, this time in the context of the crossing of the Sea in Exod 14 where the division (בדל *hi.*) of the sea unmistakably echoes the separation of the waters from below and waters from above and the delineation of a distinct area of dry land in Gen 1:6-10' (Nihan, *From Priestly Torah to Pentateuch*, p. 79).

53. For the similarities in the genres of Exodus 25–40 and Leviticus 1–16 see K. Koch, *Die Priesterschrift von Exodus 25 bis Leviticus 16: Eine überlieferungsgeschichtliche und literarkritische Untersuchung* (FRLANT, 53; Göttingen: Vandenhoeck & Ruprecht, 1959), pp. 102-103.

54. 'The Joseph narrative is a finely crafted piece of literature with a subtle theologi-

possibility that the ritual texts convey their theological significance in something other than propositional form? Gordon Wenham likens biblical ritual to 'a drama on a stage watched by human and divine spectators'.[55] If he is correct, why should we expect an explicit interpretation of this drama anymore than we would if we attended a Shakespearean play?

Relevant to this point is the absence of an 'extensive treatment' of how the various rites are enacted in ritual texts.[56] This observation is noteworthy because if these texts are intended to have a practical purpose, as most scholars assume, then a lack of explanation cannot indicate a lack of interest. Nevertheless, the absence of an extensive treatment of practical information favours the possibility that these texts are constructed for theological, rather than practical, purposes. It seems more likely that one can interpret implicit theological ideas than implicit practical directives. This suggestion becomes more persuasive when the importance of implicit theological meaning in Exodus 25–40 is recalled.

Third, following what has just been said, the traditional assumption that the purpose of ritual texts is limited to the *instruction* of practical matters is far from certain. Knierim demonstrates that an instructional purpose is unlikely.[57] On the one hand, the prescribed sequence of actions does not

---

cal theme. The lack of explicit theological language throughout the story has led some to categorize it as wisdom literature. However, the theme becomes explicit at the end of the account when Jacob dies...This theme of God's providence protecting the bearers of the promise accounts for the selection of episodes from the life of Joseph' (Iain Provan, V. Philips Long, and Tremper Longman III, *A Biblical History of Israel* [Louisville, KY: Westminster/John Knox Press, 2003], p. 123).

55. Wenham, *Numbers*, p. 29.

56. Jonathan Z. Smith, commenting on the incomplete nature of biblical ritual texts concludes that 'we don't have ritual texts in the Bible. We have very poor ethnographic descriptions. You cannot perform a single biblical ritual on the basis of what is given to you in the text. If you can't perform it, then by definition it is not a ritual. The biblical texts are scattered, theoretical reconstructions of what may have happened' (cited in Klawans, *Purity, Sacrifice, and the Temple*, p. 52). Cf., Gerstenberger, *Leviticus*, pp. 23–24; Wesley J. Bergen, *Reading Ritual. Leviticus in Postmodern Culture* (JSOTSup, 417; London/New York: T. & T. Clark, 2005), p. 4. It is not only the sacrificial prescriptions (Leviticus 1–7) which seem incomplete in terms of practical procedure. The same is true for the purity regulations of Leviticus 11–15. For example, these regulations do not indicate whether washing one's body is required after eating unclean food (Lev. 11.24-28); what measurements are taken to establish if a skin complaint has spread (Leviticus 13); what to do with the mixture of blood and water after the completion of the rite involving two-birds in Leviticus 14; whether one is permitted to wash off the blood applied to one's body (Leviticus 14); if the person who removes the stones of the צרעת-afflicted house is unclean (Lev. 14.45), and what is to be done with an unclean bed in Leviticus 15.

57. Knierim, *Text and Concept*, p. 100.

reflect how these were enacted in practice.[58] On the other hand, too much practical information appears missing if these texts exist solely for the purpose of practical instruction.[59] For example, not only do these texts fail to identify the subject of some actions, but the actions themselves are represented by verbs which do not explain how an act, such as slaughtering, is to be carried out in practice.[60]

> The way in which the verbs function in the text, individually and in relation to one another, deserves special attention. Individually, they are used in a twofold sense. They characterize an action without describing how it is to be performed; and they refer to the totality of an action that consists of more than one act by expressing only one of those acts.[61]

Though most scholars interpret the paucity of practical information in the ritual texts as reflecting a loss of presupposed knowledge, Knierim, citing the inclusion of many seemingly obvious instructions, contends that this cannot be the only explanation.[62] For example, the 'without defect' (תמים) requirement for sacrificial animals must have been presupposed by the offerer before arriving at the sanctuary with such an animal. One could also cite the recurring instruction concerning 'hand-leaning'. Surely offerers would need to make or observe only a limited number of animal offerings before they presuppose that the 'hand-leaning' rite is an essential component of these offerings? These observations raise questions concerning what governed the selection of material for inclusion in the ritual prescriptions and how it was arranged.[63] We may tentatively suggest that an *author* included and arranged various ritual elements in order to make, among other things, a theological point.

---

58. Knierim, *Text and Concept*, pp. 25-26.

59. See footnote 57.

60. 'The individual acts of the procedure are scarcely "exactly described." What controls the language of the individual prescriptions? Descriptive language would have to say, among other things, how, and not only that the acts are done' (Knierim, *Text and Concept*, p. 48).

61. Knierim, *Text and Concept*, pp. 87-88.

62. In this regard, Knierim asks several relevant questions. 'As for the offerer, who is assumed to know all the unsaid things, why is he not assumed to know also the most elementary of all? Does he really have to be instructed about the most basic actions, the most self-explanatory ones, if there is no need for instructing him about at least some important details of which he may not be aware? Is the text lay instruction?' (Knierim, *Text and Concept*, pp. 24-25).

63. Knierim makes a similar point when he asks does 'a comparison between the inexplicit and the explicit, rather than the declaration of the text's "disinterest" in the inexplicit, point to a possibly different intention or function of the text?' (Knierim, *Text and Concept*, pp. 24-25).

From what has just been argued the assumption that ritual texts convey information that is practical, rather than theological, may be misleading. As Knierim points out,

> [i]t seems that our assumptions of the instructional purpose or intention of the texts about the sacrifices are inherited more from a general perception of Torah as instruction than from observations of their specific nature.[64]

Sufficient evidence exists to suggest that these texts are intended to do something more than instruct offerers on how to make sacrifices. In this regard, Milgrom is on the right track when he claims that

> [t]heology is what Leviticus is all about. It pervades every chapter and almost every verse. It is not expressed in pronouncements but embedded in rituals. Indeed, every act, whether movement, manipulation, or gesticulation, is pregnant with meaning: 'at their deepest level rituals reveal values which are sociological facts.'[65]

But unfortunately Milgrom's own commentary does not reflect this view. In his six page discussion concerning the 'Name, Antiquity, and Function' of the עלה he refers to just one verse, albeit on three occasions, of its prescription (Lev. 1.4).[66] In the equivalent section for the מנחה (eight pages), Milgrom makes 14 references to this offering's prescription, but not one of these is used to make an argument concerning this offering's theology.[67] And in relation to the function of the שלמים, an offering whose rationale he believes 'can be satisfactorily explained',[68] not a single reference is made to its prescription in nine pages of discussion.[69] This scant, and sometimes non-existent, attention to the prescriptive texts when describing their rationales characterizes Milgrom's treatment of the remaining prescriptive sacrificial and purity texts in Leviticus 1–16. As such it remains unclear what he means

---

64. It is yet to be seen if Knierim's criticism is applicable to how scholars read the purity laws of Leviticus 11–15 (Knierim, *Text and Concept*, p. 101).

65. Milgrom, *Leviticus 1–16*, p. 42; he is quoting Victor Turner's summary of Monica Wilson's view of ritual (Victor W. Turner, *The Forest of Symbols* [Ithaca, NY: Cornell University Press, 1967], p. 44).

66. What is more, on one of these occasions he suggests that this verse, which interprets the עלה as an expiatory offering, 'may reflect an early stage in the history of this offering' (Milgrom, *Leviticus 1–16*, pp. 172-77). Does this suggestion mean that the only verse he refers to reflects an earlier theology than the theology that Leviticus 1 'is all about?

67. Milgrom, *Leviticus 1–16*, pp. 195-202.

68. Milgrom, *Leviticus 1–16*, p. 49.

69. Milgrom, *Leviticus 1–16*, pp. 217-25. We might add that in the prescription for the חטאת (Leviticus 4) Milgrom similarly makes few references (i.e. nine) to this text in a five-page discussion of this offering's function. More striking is that he does not even refer to this prescription in his four-page treatise on this offering's theology. See Milgrom, *Leviticus 1–16*, pp. 254-61.

when he says that theology 'pervades every chapter and almost every verse' of Leviticus 1–3, unless, in keeping with Levine and Hartley, he is referring to the theology evoked from the use of these rituals elsewhere in the OT. Consequently, though Milgrom champions a symbolic approach to the cultic material of Leviticus,[70] it seems that his conclusions are derived from somewhere other than his close reading of the text.[71]

The Object of Interpretation: Ritual Text or Enacted Ritual?

Even if one may infer a rite's theology from its prescription, the object of interpretation still requires clarification: should we interpret the prescriptive text or the enacted ritual presupposed by the text? Frank Gorman argues for the latter, contending that, even though it is no longer possible to observe the enacted rituals, the interpreter must ask what such rituals, *when enacted*, would have meant to those who observed them in their original socio-historical context.[72] He defends this claim as follows.

> Ritual is an enactment; something is done. Indeed, it is only as rituals are enacted that they are realized. At the same time, however, rituals say some-thing about the participants in the ritual and world in which they live. Symbols are the vehicles for communication in ritual. It is *only* by analyzing these symbols in their socio-cultural setting and in light of the world view they presuppose, that the communicative aspects of rituals may be understood.[73]

For Gorman, the text does not induct one into a rite's theology but into the worldview of those who originally partook in its enactment. Nevertheless, while it is not disputed that an appreciation of P's worldview would assist in the interpretation of its rituals, the assumptions underlying Gorman's argument for why the object of study should be the enacted ritual rather than the ritual text *per se*, are questionable.

First, Gorman's claim that 'ritual *is* an enactment' is too narrow because it overlooks that sometimes a 'ritual *is* a text'.[74] Returning to Wenham's

---

70. '[T]he ritual complexes of Lev 1–16 make sense only as aspects of a symbolic system' (Milgrom, *Leviticus 1–16*, p. 45).

71. A similar criticism of Milgrom's approach to sacrificial rituals in Leviticus is made by Klawans, *Purity, Sacrifice, and the Temple*, pp. 29-32.

72. Frank H. Gorman, Jr, *The Ideology of Ritual: Space, Time and Status in the Priestly Literature* (JSOT Press; Sheffield: Sheffield Academic Press, 1990), p. 13.

73. Gorman, *The Ideology of Ritual*, pp. 24-25 (emphasis mine). See similarly Frank H. Gorman, 'Ritualizing, Rite and Pentateuchal Theology', in *Prophets and Paradigms: Essays in Honor of Gene M. Tucker* (ed. Stephen Breck Reid; Sheffield: Sheffield Academic Press, 1996), pp. 173-86 (177).

74. In answering the question of what constitutes the essence of religious ritual in the Bible, Wenham says, 'It is a means of communication between God and man, a drama on a stage watched by human and divine spectators. Old Testament rituals express religious truths visually as opposed to verbally' (Wenham, *Numbers*, p. 29). This state-

suggestion that ritual is drama we could liken the ritual text to the book-form of Chekhov's plays: one may interpret these plays by attending them as either performance *or* text. On a practical level the latter remains the only possibility in relation to biblical 'plays' because they exist only in textual form. Surely this entitles us to ask what a person does when reading them. Are they doing theology, or ethics, etc? Before an attempt to answer this question is made it is necessary to demonstrate that the ritual texts of Leviticus were intended to be read as literature for the purpose of theological understanding.[75]

Second, the assumption that the purpose of ritual texts is to instruct the enactment of rituals within a particular socio-cultural setting is not supported by the textual evidence. In this regard Gorman's proposal is open to the same criticisms leveled at Levine and Hartley above, so that we need not repeat them here.[76]

Third, it is unlikely that the kind of socio-historical context Gorman attempts to recreate is presupposed as important for an individual ritual text's interpretation. In the absence of an 'actual social field' Gorman seeks to infer one from the priestly texts.

> It must be granted that the ideal situation for the interpretation of rituals and their symbols is an actual social field... In examining biblical texts as here suggested, the social field of action is obviously not available for direct study. If, however, there is indeed a close relationship existing between ritual and its socio-cultural context, then it should be possible to gain clues to the shape of the socio-cultural context through the rituals. In this case, close attention

ment is certainly correct of enacted ritual, but is it an accurate portrayal of the essence of ritual in textual form? What if it is the language used to prescribe the ritual that draws the reader to make certain conclusions about the drama that is read?

75. This suggestion is similar to Rendtorff's speculation that the recitation of these prescriptions was intended to replace their enactment. However, Rendtorff's view that this quality of these texts reflects their composition during the time of Babylonian exile is not persuasive (Rendtorff, *Die Gesetze in der Priesterschrift*, pp. 22-23). Bergen argues that 'texts about rituals likely arise from and certainly highlight the absence of a ritual. Why would you need a text about a ritual if you had the ritual? There is nothing in Leviticus 1 that could not be learned from simple observation, except for the three comments about Yahweh's attitude. The text is a sign of the absence of ritual' (Bergen, *Reading Ritual*, p. 7). But, while the present study is sympathetic to the emphasis Bergen places on the fact that the rituals of Leviticus are texts, rather than texts about rituals, one may ask why a ritual as text presupposes the 'absence of ritual'. Did not Chekov's plays exist in written form at the time of their enactment? Do written prescriptions for how one should address the present English monarch not exist?

76. Though we may add Knierim's contention that the prescription 'may differ from the description of any observed performances. It must, therefore, be interpreted in its own right as a linguistically based expression and conceptuality of ritual reality' (Knierim, *Text and Concept*, p. 18). The burden for proof lies with Gorman to demonstrate that the prescriptive texts of Leviticus are a description of 'what happened'.

to the language used to depict the ritual situation must be a focal point of attention. Language is the means for opening up the possibilities of what the social field of the Priestly ritual might have been. At the same time, however, it can also act as a constraint on what the social field was not.[77]

But, in an unrelated context, Knierim points out that such a reconstruction requires 'a virtually complete body of literature rather than individual texts or confined groups of texts'.[78] He proceeds to argue that the resultant reconstructed worldview might have little significance for an individual text's interpretation because it may

> neither self-evidently, nor necessarily, represent the concepts or assumptions…that belong to the immediate reason for and meaning of an individual text, or of a coherent group of texts, or of a larger literary work.[79]

And he contends that only those '*conceptualities that are operative in the immediacy of a text are directly important for exegetical work*'.[80] Thus, while Gorman correctly argues that the conceptual world of the ritual is essential for its interpretation, it is more precisely the worldview presupposed by an individual text that is required. This insight would seem to shift the object of interpretation away from a resynthesis of the enacted ritual toward the individual ritual prescription.[81]

Finally, the most unsatisfying part of Gorman's argument is that he appears to justify his method for interpreting ritual texts on the basis that they constitute a different genre. In his introduction he argues that

---

77. Gorman, *The Ideology of Ritual*, p. 25.

78. Knierim, *Text and Concept*, p. 2. Indeed, the high degree of uncertainty surrounding the dating of texts must be imputed to the socio-historical context one attempts to reconstruct from them. The following statement made by Bryan Bibb is relevant in this regard: 'Even if one could firmly situate the Pentateuchal ritual texts within a particular historical setting, it still would be impossible to observe these rituals in practice. Aside from the historical uncertainties, the texts themselves do not provide enough information to allow the interpreter fully to imagine a real performance' (Bryan D. Bibb, *This is the Thing That the Lord Commanded You to Do: Ritual Words and Narrative Worlds in the Book of Leviticus* [PhD dissertation: Princeton Theological Seminary, 2005], p. 58). Elsewhere in an assessment of Gorman's methodology Bibb observes that, while Gorman claims that he intends to interpret the reconstructed enacted ritual, he does not do this but uses the text to create an imaginary ritual world without addressing how this relates to the real world. Nevertheless, even if this is the case, the above quoted comments made by Knierim are still relevant to Gorman's approach (Bibb, *This is the Thing*, p. 62).

79. Knierim, *Text and Concept*, p. 2.

80. Knierim, *Text and Concept*, p. 2 (emphasis mine).

81. This statement does not imply that a larger coherent group of texts has no significance for interpreting a specific text. For example, one needs to infer the significance of the tent to which the offerings are brought in Leviticus 1–5 from the text of Exodus 25–40.

[i]f literary genres are distinct, calling for the interpreter to understand their distinctiveness, it follows that distinct genres would call for distinct methods of analysis. So, it might well be asked, are methods of interpretation used in the study of narrative texts equally useful in the study of ritual texts? More important is the methodological issue of whether the analysis of ritual *texts* should focus on texts or the ritual depicted in the texts.[82]

It is apparently because he begins with the premise that actions are at the heart of ritual and that '[r]itual produces its effects only in and through the performance and enactment of particular actions', that Gorman concludes that this genre requires the interpreter to focus on the enacted ritual.[83] Thus, he outlines his methodology as follows.

The present analysis is concerned with the interpretation of texts which spell out in some detail the performance of specific rituals. *The texts will be used to deduce what the rituals might have looked like if actually enacted, and it is the meaning and significance of that enactment that will be the focus of study.*[84]

But though different genres require different methods of interpretation, it does not follow that the object of interpretation should change, in this case from text to enacted ritual.[85] Gorman's appeal to the fact that the ritual text prescribes enactment is inadequate since the same argument could be made for why the actual history underlying a historical narrative should be the object of interpretation. Yet, as is widely acknowledged by scholars, the

---

82. Gorman, *The Ideology of Ritual*, p. 7.
83. Gorman, *The Ideology of Ritual*, p. 36.
84. Gorman, *The Ideology of Ritual*, p. 31 (emphasis mine).
85. The same criticism of Gorman is made by Gilders, who explains his alternative approach as follows: 'Although we have access to a textually represented ritual only through the text, in the reading of the text we may seek to construct an image of the living enactment of a ritual complex. This ritual enactment takes place in what may be termed "the world of the text," which is that image of a world constructed by the reader, in which the action of the narrative takes place. This world comes into being in the interaction of reader with text and is part of that "meaning" which can exist only through the process of reading. For this reason, we must distinguish carefully between the "world of the text" and a living, historical context in which ritual activity takes place. The latter context is not immediately accessible to the reader of the Bible. Only after we have developed a clear picture of the world of the text can we attempt to reconstruct an image of the real world in which ritual actions might have been carried out' (Gilders, *Blood Ritual in the Hebrew Bible*, pp. 9-11). Though I largely agree with Gilders's proposal for reading ritual texts, the difference in our respective approaches is that whereas Gilders assumes that the meaning of ritual texts is to be found in 'formal practice', I allow for the possibility that the author has used literary art to convey a theological purpose. Moreover, I argue that there is a symbolic dimension to these texts which Gilders seems to assume is of little significance for the meaning of ritual texts.

latter is unacceptable because historical narratives reflect their author's interpretation of history. They may even be composed in a way that detracts from 'what happened' in order to emphasize a theological concern.[86] But what if a similar process has occurred in the composition of the Bible's ritual texts? As we have already seen, this process of composition is not unlikely considering the use of literary art to draw attention to the symbolic meaning of the tabernacle in Exodus 25–40. Just as the literary nature of historical narratives invites the reader to interpret the text, rather than a reconstruction of 'what happened', so too does the literary nature of ritual texts invite an interpretation of the text rather than the enacted rites they prescribe.

It is helpful to introduce Robert Alter's treatment of Hebrew narrative at this point. Alter is critical of those scholars who approach the Hebrew Bible *as* literature, as though it could also be studied *as* theology, or *as* ethics etc, and contends that it should be interpreted on the presupposition that it *is* literature.

> Rather than viewing the literary character of the Bible as one of several 'purposes' or 'tendencies'… I would prefer to insist on a complete interfusion of literary art with theological, moral, or historiosophical vision, the fullest perception of the latter dependent on the fullest grasp of the former.[87]

This understanding of the Hebrew Bible may provide a helpful starting point for our interpretation of ritual texts. On the one hand, contra Levine and Hartley, it opens up the possibility that there is interfusion between the theology of the prescribed rites in Leviticus and their prescriptive texts. Such an interfusion would obviate the need to interpret their theology from elsewhere. On the other hand, contra Gorman, if the rites of Leviticus *are* texts then the text, rather than an enactment they presuppose, forms the proper object of interpretation.[88] Thus, the following statement Alter makes concerning the interpretation of 'narrative art' is possibly just as relevant to the interpretation of 'ritual art'.

> [T]o understand a narrative art so bare of embellishment and explicit commentary, one must be constantly aware of two features: the repeated use of narrative analogy, through which one part of the text provides oblique commentary on another; and the richly expressive function of syntax, which often bears the kind of weight of meaning that, say, imagery does in a novel

---

86. For this reason, '*biblical accounts must be appreciated first as narratives before they can be used as historical sources*' (Provan, Long, and Longman, *A Biblical History of Israel*, p. 93). See also Pierre Grelot, *The Language of Symbolism. Biblical Theology, Semantics, and Exegesis* [trans. Christopher R. Smith; Peabody, MA: Hendrickson Publishers, 2006], pp. 104-108).

87. Robert Alter, *The Art of Biblical Narrative* (London: George Allen & Unwin, 1981), pp. 18-20.

88. See similarly Gilders, *Blood Ritual in the Hebrew Bible*, p. 9.

by Virginia Woolf or analysis in a novel by George Eliot. Attention to such features leads not to a more 'imaginative' reading of biblical narrative but to a more precise one; and since all these features are linked to discernible details in the Hebrew text, the literary approach is actually a good deal *less* conjectural than the historical scholarship that asks of a verse whether it contains possible Akkadian loanwords, whether it reflects Sumerian kinship practices, whether it may have been corrupted by scribal error.[89]

Alter's contention that a literary approach should lead to a 'less conjectural' interpretation is important for the present study which seeks to explore the symbolic dimension of ritual texts. Moreover, if my presupposition that theology is implicit within the ritual texts is correct, then attention to 'the discernible details of the text' will yield falsifiable results. This hermeneutic is an improvement on the approach taken by some previous symbolic interpretations of ritual texts which are rightly criticized as being somewhat arbitrary in their assignment of symbolic meaning.[90]

Kiuchi has attempted to undertake the kind of literary approach advocated here in his commentary on Leviticus.[92] He justifies this method of interpretation on the basis that

---

89. Alter, *The Art of Biblical Narrative*, p. 21. It is noteworthy that while Alter has written on the art of biblical narrative, and the art of biblical poetry, he has not written on the 'art of biblical ritual'.

90. E.g. Bähr, *Symbolik des mosaischen Cultus*; K. Keil, *Die Opfer des A. Bundes nach ihrer symbolischen und typischen Bedeutung* (Luth. Zeitschrift, 1856); Franz Delitzsch, *Commentar zum Hebräerbrief* (Leipzig: Dörffling & Franke, 1857); Kurtz, *Sacrificial Worship of the Old Testament*.

91. Nobuyoshi Kiuchi, *Leviticus* (Apollos; Leicester: IVP, 2007). A scholar who advocates a similar approach to ritual texts is Hannah Liss. Liss makes the stimulating suggestion that P has removed cultic rituals from the historical sphere and created a timeless 'cult in the text' (*Kultus im Text*). In this way, the meaning of the cult is no longer found within the sphere of history but in the 'interpretative sphere' ('Auslegungs-Raum') so that one may interpret P's ritual prescriptions as a 'theological-play' ('theologischen Bühnenstück'). Hanna Liss, 'Kanon und Fiktion: Zur literarischen Funktion biblischer Rechtstexte', *Biblische Notizen* 121 (2004), pp. 7-34 (32-33). The present study does not adopt a thoroughly postmodern hermeneutic which assumes that the meaning of ritual texts is independent of the ideology of their authors, contra the position taken by Anne Fitzpatrick-McKinley, *The Transformation of Torah from Scribal Advice to Law* (JSOTSup, 287; Sheffield: Sheffield Academic Press, 1999), p. 80. The use of the German term 'fiktive' to describe the ritual texts is affirmed in so far as these are written in 'fictive mode'. This view is expressed well, albeit in relation to narrative texts, in Garret Green's summary of Manfred Oeming's use of the term 'fiktion'. That is, it is a 'kind of narrative presentation that relates what is historically inaccurate [*historisch Unzutreffendes*] but that is still related to history in that it intends to disclose a truth in the past that does not become apparent in mere description' (Garrett Green, '"The Bible as…": Fictional Narrative and Scriptural Truth', in *Scriptural Authority and Narrative Interpretation* [ed. Garrett Green; Philadelphia: Fortress Press, 1987], pp. 79-96 [84]).

> [a]lthough the laws…are commonly viewed as no more than an instruction
> manual describing how rituals should be conducted, their formulation and
> presentation indicates they have a different agenda. They are aimed to convey
> a certain message through their formulation, and not least through the sym-
> bolic meaning of the rituals found therein… For example, the stipulation in
> 7.30 that 'His hands shall bring the Lord's food offerings' seems unneces-
> sary if this is just a prescription. Thus we are invited to explore the under-
> lying rationales for the various formulations.[92]

Kiuchi proceeds to identify the use of repetition and non-repetition as one
way in which prescriptive texts convey their theology. Though he acknowledges that some variations are 'dictated purely by stylistic concerns',[93] he
identifies three other ways in which the principle of repetition/non-repetition
is used to accomplish the author's theological purpose. He provides examples
of each of these from the prescription of the חטאת in Leviticus 4.

First, sometimes a case's introductory formula is varied to reflect 'the
degree of sinfulness that characterizes the person standing before God'.[94] For
example, in Leviticus 4 all but one case refers to its subject as 'realizing
guilt' (אשם).[95] The exception is found in the prescription for the high priest's
offering (Lev. 4.3) which presupposes a case in which the high priest sins 'so
that the people realize guilt' (לאשמת העם). Kiuchi is possibly correct in
arguing that, on the presupposition that the high priest does not feel guilty, a
sense of urgency is achieved concerning this case. However, it seems even
more likely that the people's realization of guilt when the priest sins implies

---

92. Kiuchi, *Leviticus*, pp. 25-26. The methodological approach advocated by Kiuchi
has implications for the main conclusion Knierim draws concerning the purpose of the
prescriptive sacrificial texts, namely that they are composed in such a way as to establish
a *sacrificial procedure*. 'The primary purpose of the prescription of procedure means
only that it aims at securing the standardized and, in that sense, legitimate performance
itself, to whatever extent and at whatever place and time it is taught' (Knierim, *Text and
Concept*, p. 105). However, this conclusion relies on his assumption that the principle
governing what is not mentioned is whether or not it was essential to the successful
completion of the entire procedure: 'Whatever subsidiary actions are presupposed (and
presupposed to be important), the absence of their explication is caused by the focus on
what is decisive, in the individual actions, for the ritual goal of the whole procedure'
(Knierim, *Text and Concept*, p. 89). But if Kiuchi is correct then some of this information was omitted to make a theological assertion which detracts from Knierim's
suggestion that the purpose of these texts is confined to the establishment of ritual
procedure.

93. Kiuchi, *Leviticus*, p. 26. For example, some ritual details are not repeated in sub-
cases of a general case for stylistic reasons.

94. Kiuchi, *Leviticus*, p. 26.

95. For Kiuchi's translation of אשם as 'to realize guilt' as opposed to Milgrom's
rendering of this term as 'to feel guilt' see Kiuchi, *The Purification Offering*, pp. 31-34.

something about the theological relationship between priest and people.[96] It raises the theological question of why the people should realize guilt when it is the high priest who sins.

Second, the author may make an explicit reference to something to draw attention to an implicit assumption. Kiuchi interprets the fact that the phrase 'for a soothing aroma' (לריח ניחח) occurs only in connection with the burning of fat in the lay person's prescription (Lev. 4.31) as indicating that the preceding cases are of a more serious nature. Since the burnt fat presumably results in the same 'soothing aroma' in the preceding cases, 'the omission of this phrase in relation to the other cases achieves a literary function. It stresses the serious, rather than joyful, character of those rituals.'[97]

Third, the striking omission of significant terms in the body of the prescription may imply a theological intention. For example, Kiuchi thinks that the non-mention of כפר in the case for the high priest implies that it was not possible for him to make כפר for himself.[98]

Kiuchi's insights concerning the use of repetition/non-repetition are adopted in the present interpretation of ritual texts. In addition to repetition, other forms of literary art may exist within these texts that draw attention to matters of theology. For example, given that several scholars identify terminology or concepts that are common to various P-texts in Genesis,[99] it is conceivable that something akin to Alter's 'narrative analogy' is operative in the ritual texts. An example is apparent in the occurrence of the term 'belly' (גחון) in Leviticus 11, which occurs elsewhere only in relation to the cursed serpent in Gen. 3.14. It seems possible that we are intended to observe some kind of interplay between these texts so that this term introduces a theological interpretation of the unclean animals in Leviticus 11.[100]

---

96. To be fair, previous scholars have drawn attention to the theological significance of the non-mention of the priest realizing his guilt. However, these scholars are not consistent in applying this method of interpretation to the ritual text as a whole. See Noth, *Leviticus*, p. 38; Noordtzij, *Leviticus*, p. 57; Hartley, *Leviticus*, p. 59.

97. Kiuchi, *Leviticus*, p. 26.

98. Kiuchi, *The Purification Offering*, pp. 126-28. Rendtorff, commenting on the absence of any reference to כפר being made for the high priest concludes 'Niemand kann für den »gesalbten Priester« die Sühnehandlung vollziehen. Das kann er nur selbst tun, und er tut es am Versöhnungstag (Lev 16,6 u.ö.)' (Rendtorff, *Leviticus*, pp. 172-73, 322).

99. Douglas, *Purity and Danger*, p. 361; Howard Eilberg-Schwartz, 'Creation and Classification in Judaism: From Priestly to Rabbinic Conceptions', *HR* 26 (1987), pp. 357-81 (361); Edwin Firmage, 'The Biblical Dietary Laws and the Concept of Holiness', in *Studies in the Pentateuch* (ed. J.A. Emerton; Leiden: E.J. Brill, 1990), pp. 177-208 (196-97); Milgrom, *Leviticus 1–16*, p. 689; Nobuyoshi Kiuchi, *A Study of Ḥāṭā' and Ḥaṭṭā't in Leviticus 4–5* (Tübingen: J.C.B. Mohr [Paul Siebeck], 2003).

100. See discussion in Chapter 3.

Another form of literary art that may enhance my interpretation of ritual texts is the use of rhetorical progression. Yairah Amit has defined this literary device within narrative texts as follows.

> Progression…is a rhetorical technique, or contrivance, that organizes the data for the author in a multi-phased, hierarchical structure, wherein the elements are arranged in an ascending or descending order: from the general to the particular, or vice versa; from minor to major, or the reverse; from the expected to the unexpected; the impersonal to the personal, and so on. Often the final step in the progression is the climactic one, while each of the preceding steps plays its part in expanding or narrowing the sequence, and thereby shedding more light on the subject.[101]

Amit cites an example of rhetorical progression, from the expected to the unexpected, in the narrative concerning the report of the death of the high priest Eli's two sons, Hophni and Phinehas, in 1 Sam. 4.12-18.

> [The bearer of the news] begins by informing Eli about the defeat, which was not news, since he had already alerted the city, which 'broke out in a cry' (v. 13), so that Eli probably knew about it and expected it. Then the messenger states that there were many casualties. Casualties in defeat are to be expected, but the number in this case was so great that the news-bearer describes it as 'a great slaughter' (מגפה גדולה). The term מגפה, with its connotation of divine punishment, a spreading, deadly epidemic, indicated the unexpectedly large number of the fallen. Only then did the news-bearer mention the death of Eli's two sons, which was to him the least expected outcome, since priests were not foot soldiers, though of course their presence at the battlefield exposed them to danger. Finally, he mentions that the Ark of God was captured by the Philistines—the most unexpected event of all, especially in view of the hopes of deliverance that the Israelites placed in it (vv. 3, 5) and the Philistines' fear of it (vv. 6-9). How unexpected was the loss of the ark to Eli is shown in the sequel. Although Eli's heart 'trembled for the Ark of God', he did not imagine that it might fall into the hands of the Philistines, as his reaction shows: 'When he mentioned the Ark of God, [Eli] fell backward off the seat beside the gate, broke his neck and died…' (v. 18).[102]

There appears to be no reason why we should not allow for the presence of rhetorical progression within ritual texts. Chapters 3 and 4 shall investigate if this is the case in the purity texts (i.e. Leviticus 11–15). To anticipate, it appears as though these prescriptions progress from the general (i.e. matters of diet and skin complaints) to the particular (i.e. the symbolic meaning of these things).

A final word is required about the identification of presuppositions which have a bearing on the text's meaning. Such a discussion is necessary because

---

101. Yairah Amit, 'Progression as a Rhetorical Device in Biblical Literature', *JSOT* 78 (2003), pp. 3-32 (9).

102. Amit, 'Progression as a Rhetorical Device', p. 11.

the method of interpretation advocated above requires one to ask what extra-linguistic information is important for a text's interpretation. In doing so we are taking up the following challenge made by Knierim.

> The surface level of a text communicates to the reader explicit information, but it also points to aspects beneath itself which are, nevertheless, implicitly operative in it and which generate and control its form and content. Texts are linguistic semantic entities in which explicit statements and their presuppositions interact. Exegesis must, therefore, do more than paraphrase what a text says. It must also, however hypothetically, reconstruct a text's assumptions which lie underneath its surface.[103]

Knierim alerts exegetes to the potentially misleading nature of this task as follows.

> It is problematic when the exegete dismisses the interpretation of one inexplicit presupposition in a text while placing a high priority on another one. Such judgments demonstrate that presuppositions are not irrelevant for or inoperative in the text because they are inexplicit. They rest instead on the exegete's differentiation between those presuppositions that belong to the plan of the text and those that do not. That differentiation, however, rests on the exegetical reconstruction of a certain plan, a reconstruction that may be right or wrong.[104]

In line with this observation, it is essential that we justify, on a textual basis, why one inexplicit presupposition is prioritized over another in the process of interpretation. Kiuchi exemplifies this approach in his argument for why no mention is made of כפר being made for the high priest in Leviticus 4. Before he concludes that this omission has theological significance for the meaning of כפר in Leviticus, it is necessary for him to demonstrate why this omission has more significance than that of other terms.[105] A good textual basis exists for assuming that the non-mention of כפר in connection with the high priest is intended to provide an important presupposition concerning the meaning of כפר. Elsewhere in Leviticus 1–5 the non-repetition of a particular term that is clearly presupposed occurs after it is mentioned in the first case. However, since the case for the high priest introduces Leviticus 4, the silence concerning כפר seems deliberate. Thus we are invited to presuppose that כפר is not achieved for the high priest. Essentially, when reading the ritual texts we are required to ask 'Why is said what is said, and why not what is not said?'[106]

103. Knierim, *Text and Concept*, p. 1.
104. Knierim, *Text and Concept*, pp. 25.
105. For example, though v. 8 specifies where the fat that will be burned should be taken from, this is not mentioned in the cases that follow.
106. Knierim, *Text and Concept*, p. 24.

The Definition of Terms Relevant to the Present Study

Before the methodological insights gained in this Chapter are used to examine some ritual texts of Leviticus it remains necessary to define certain descriptive terminology. These terms, which will be frequently used, do not always mean the same thing to all scholars. Therefore some clarification is required concerning what I mean when using the terms *ethics, cultic, metaphorical,* and *symbolic.*

Ethics

The *Oxford English Dictionary* (1989) defines *ethics* as 'the science of morals; the department of study concerned with the principals of human duty'. In keeping with this definition the present study uses the adjective *ethical* to refer to the moral concerns comprised by H's view of holiness which, scholars contend, distinguish it from P's amoral concept of holiness. That is, whereas P does not explicitly identify moral or ethical behaviour as an aspect of holiness, H does (see Lev. 19.2-3a, 9-18).

The use of the term *ethics* within Levitical studies introduces a behavioural distinction not made explicit by either P or H. For example, when H commands the Israelites to 'be holy' it urges the observance of ethical *and* cultic laws (cf. Leviticus 19). Since scholars maintain that the difference in the views of holiness expressed by P and H is the absence of ethical concerns in the former, the use of this terminology remains unavoidable. In other words, we shall need to explore whether P's notion of holiness has in view behaviour which modern scholars regard as ethical.

Cultic

Scholars use the term *cultic* to refer to biblical laws, and their associated terminology, that govern Israel's system of worship in relation to the sanctuary. Moreover, when one introduces the modern cultic-ethical distinction into biblical studies cultic legislation is viewed as amoral.

The use of the term cultic within this book requires some qualification because my hypothesis that the Levitical cultic material has an ethical purpose does not allow for a clear-cut distinction between ethics and cult. Thus, when referring to cultic material, or cultic rituals, I have in mind physical activity, allowing for the possibility that the symbolic dimension of these things may have ethical significance.

Symbolic and Metaphorical Language[107]

An investigation of the symbolic meaning of the cultic texts of Leviticus requires a definition of what is meant by the term symbolic. A helpful

107. In the present study the terms 'metaphor' and 'metaphorical' are used in their

starting point for such a definition is the following statement made by Larry P. Jones.

> [A] symbol both points toward something other than itself and in some way presents and represents that to which it points.[108]

Since this definition could equally apply to metaphorical language, Jones attempts to identify three distinctive differences between symbolic and metaphorical language.[109] As shall become apparent, though I agree with the first of these I find the remaining two unconvincing. The third of these proposed differences seems irrelevant to the present study.[110]

'narrow' sense. That is, rather than referring broadly to all non-literal language such as irony, metonymy, synecdoche, hyperbole etc, 'metaphor' and its adjective will denote the use of language that is distinct from the literal use of language and the other non-literal forms just mentioned. For the 'narrow' and 'wide' sense of the term 'metaphor' see Josef Stern, *Metaphor in Context* (Cambridge: MIT Press, 2000), p. 23.

108. Larry Paul Jones, *The Symbol of Water in the Gospel of John* (JSNTSup, 145; Sheffield: Sheffield Academic Press, 1997), p. 14.

109. Some semantic overlap exists between the terms metaphor and symbol. In reality a symbol is 'a kind of developed metaphor'. Nevertheless, my attempt to distinguish between the two is intended to refine my understanding of how language can be used in a non-literal sense. See Grelot, *The Language of Symbolism*, 18; René Wellek and Austin Warren, *Theory of Literature* (London: Jonathan Cape, 1949), p. 186.

110. This third distinction Jones makes between symbols and metaphors relates to his contention that, unlike a metaphor, a symbol allows readers to experience what they cannot objectively know (p. 15). He suggests that this aspect of a symbol is two-sided. First, the referent of the symbol must defy 'clear and perceptual expression', because the referential meaning will be either transcendental or existential (p. 19). For example, we have no direct perception of where God is because he is other to our space-time continuum. Therefore, his location must be spoken of symbolically: 'above the dome over their heads there was something like a throne, in appearance like sapphire; and seated above the likeness of a throne was something that looked like a human form' (Ezek. 1.26; I owe this example to Grelot, *The Language of Symbolism*, p. 71). Second, the symbol must not 'merely point to the reality it represents, but also in some way renders that reality present' (p. 17). An obvious NT example is the 'Lord's Supper'. Not only does it represent the transcendental reality of God's sacrificial love for his people, but this reality is experienced in the eating and drinking of the symbolic meal. Similarly Ezekiel's symbolic imagery (Ezek. 1.26) could render God as present either in the reader's imagination or by the contemplation of its interpretation by an artist.

However, as shall be observed in relation to Jones's second point above, these two characteristics, which he identifies as characteristic of symbolic language, do not seem to distinguish it from metaphorical language. On the one hand, though the debate is ongoing, a persuasive case can be made that one cannot exhaustively state the meaning of a metaphor (see the discussion of this issue in Stern, *Metaphor in Context*, pp. 262-71). In line with this understanding Dan Stiver suggests that '[m]etaphor sometimes says what has not been said before and cannot be said in any other way. In other words, metaphor is often irreducible to literal language' (Dan R. Stiver, *The Philosophy of*

First, Jones argues that the inflexibility of a symbol's meaning distinguishes it from a metaphor. The meaning of a metaphor is an entirely flexible literary device. As colourfully put by Vanhoozer, it 'is the imagination making creative connections, thinking laterally, talking out loud'.[111] And, quoting Paul Ricoeur, Vanhoozer affirms that a metaphor works by 'confusing the established logical boundaries for the sake of detecting new similarities which previous categorization prevented from our noticing'.[112] By contrast to the relatively *ad hoc* employment of metaphors, a symbolic meaning of a word or action often recurs persistently throughout a given narrative.[113] As it recurs 'a symbol typically expands in meaning and that to which it points becomes more clearly defined'.[114] According to this definition, we should expect the same core symbolic meaning identified for a specific term, phrase, or ritual to apply each time it recurs in Leviticus. *In this regard, we will need to ask what the reader learns about the symbolic meaning of a term, phrase, or ritual as it recurs throughout an unfolding text.*

The second distinction Jones makes between a symbol and a metaphor is less certain. He suggests that, whereas the *tenor* (meaning) to which a symbol points is not explicit, both *vehicle* (the thing to which a term normally refers) and *tenor* are discernible in the use of metaphorical language.[115] That is,

---

Religious Language: Sign, Symbol and Story [Oxford: Blackwell Publishers, 1996], p. 115). On the other hand, can it be denied that a metaphor renders present the reality to which it points? It seems that within Robert Frost's statement 'Two roads diverged in a wood, and I—I took the one less traveled by, And that has made all the difference', the phrase 'two roads' provides a relatively tangible form of what are two ideological possibilities. Nevertheless, though one may not be able to distinguish between symbolic and metaphorical language in this way, it remains possible that these two kinds of language vary in the degree to which they convey the 'transcendental or existential' and render these realities present.

111. Kevin J. Vanhoozer, *Is There a Meaning in This Text?* (Grand Rapids: Zondervan, 1998), p. 129. This is not to say that there is no such thing as an established metaphor. See Stern, *Metaphor in Context*.

112. Ricoeur quoted by Vanhoozer, *Is There a Meaning in this Text?*, p. 129.

113. Even so, within a specific text, a symbol may first occur as a metaphor. For example, René Wellek and Austin Warren make the following comment. 'Is there any important sense in which "symbol" differs from "image" and "metaphor"? Primarily, we think, in the recurrence and persistence of the "symbol". An "image" may be invoked once as a metaphor, but if it persistently recurs, both as presentation and representation, it becomes a symbol, may even become part of a symbolic (or mythic) system' (Wellek and Warren, *Theory of Literature*, p. 189).

114. '[W]hereas an image or a metaphor usually appears once or only a few times in a narrative, a symbol recurs persistently' (Jones, *The Symbol of Water*, p. 14). Chapter 3 suggests that the definition and expansion in meaning of a symbol throughout a ritual text is a form of rhetorical progression.

115. The concepts of *vehicle* and *tenor* are described as follows by G.B. Caird. 'To refer

unlike a metaphor in which the tenor is explicit (i.e. God [tenor] is a rock [vehicle]), a symbol

> [p]resents the vehicle and leaves it to the reader to discern the tenor (meaning). The literary context in which the symbol appears and any cultural influences or background information shared by the reader and the narrator must suffice to enable the reader to discern the meaning.[116]

However, though the tenor of a metaphor *can be* explicit (e.g. '*God* is a rock') this is not always the case. Take, for example, in the statement already noted by Robert Frost:[117]

> Two roads diverged in a wood, and I—I took the one less traveled by, And that has made all the difference.

The tenor of the metaphorical 'roads' is not explicit so that it is just as true to say of this metaphor that the literary context in which it appears 'and any cultural influences or background information shared by the reader and the narrator must suffice to enable the reader to discern the meaning'.[118] In this way it does not seem that a distinction can be drawn between symbol and metaphor according to the explicitness of tenor. *However, this observation aside, Jones's suggestion that the discernment of symbolic meaning requires one to consult a context larger than the immediate literary context seems apt in relation to what has already been said about a cognitive linguistic approach to interpretation.* This aspect of symbolic interpretation is taken up in more detail below.

In view of the above considerations, it seems prudent to limit the distinction between symbolic and metaphorical language to Jones's first point, namely that the former retains an inflexible meaning as it recurs throughout a text. Apart from this distinction, the identification and interpretation of symbolic language would seem very similar to that which is used in relation to metaphorical language.

---

to the two constituent elements of a metaphor Ogden and Richards invented the useful terms *vehicle* and *tenor*: *vehicle* being the thing to which the word normally and naturally applies, the thing from which it is transferred, and *tenor* the thing to which it is transferred. In a living metaphor, although both speaker and hearer are aware that vehicle and tenor are distinct entities, they are not grasped as two but one. When we look at an object through a lens, we concentrate on the object and ignore the lens. Metaphor is a lens; it is as though the speaker were saying, "Look through this and see what I have seen, something you would never have noticed without the lens"' (G.B. Caird, *The Language and Imagery of the Bible* [Philadelphia: Westminster Press, 1980], p. 152 [emphasis mine]).

116. Jones, *The Symbol of Water*, p. 14.

117. Quotation is from Stern, *Metaphor in Context*, p. 4.

118. Jones, *The Symbol of Water*, p. 14.

My definition of symbolic language will have significance for how it is identified and interpreted within the ritual texts of Leviticus. Some previous studies presuppose that one identifies symbolic language by discerning occasions in which it is not possible to interpret a particular term or utterance literally. For example Douglas Miller argues that before identifying a symbol

> the audience must recognize the inadequacy of the literal use of the P [metaphor] term within its context, e.g., 'Truth (S [subject]) is a fire (P).'[119]

But, though Miller stands within a tradition of scholars who identify metaphors and symbols in this way (i.e. as 'defective' or 'deviant' when read literally')[120] Josef Stern argues that it is 'subject to fatal descriptive and explanatory problems'.[121] Though he accepts that many metaphors are 'literally' defective, he claims that there are 'countless counter examples' which have

> perfectly good literal as well as metaphorical interpretations, and some are even 'twice-true,' that is, true in the very same contexts *both* when they are interpreted metaphorically and when they are interpreted literally.[122]

---

119. This requirement for the identification of symbolic language is based on his assumption concerning how one interprets metaphorical language. Thus, in order to interpret a metaphor he contends that a 'determination must first be made whether an utterance actually involves a metaphor, that the literal statement does not work, e.g., "She (S) is solid gold (P)." For a metaphor to be recognized, a speech phenomenon must first be identified as 'defective'. This may be because a statement is clearly false (the person is not made of gold), or tritely true ("No man is an island"). The audience employs the strategy, "Where the utterance is defective if taken literally, look for an utterance meaning that differs from sentence meaning"' (Douglas B. Miller, *Symbol and Rhetoric in Ecclesiastes: The Place of Hebel in Qohelet's Work* [Atlanta: Society of Biblical Literature, 2002], pp. 42, 46).

120. See R. Matthews, 'Concerning a "Linguistic Theory" of Metaphor', *Foundations of Language* 7 (1971), pp. 413-25; H.P. Grice, 'Logic and Conversation', in *Syntax and Semantics. III. Speech Acts* (ed. P. Cole and J. Morgan; New York: Academic Press, 1975), pp. 41-58; S. Levin, *The Semantics of Metaphor* (Baltimore: The John Hopkins University Press, 1977); M. Beardsley 'Metaphorical Senses', *Nous* 12 (1978), pp. 3-16. It is true that Searle suggests that the first step in interpreting metaphor requires one to, where 'the utterance is defective if taken literally, look for an utterance meaning that differs from sentence meaning'. However, he does qualify this method as applicable to 'the simple sorts of cases we have been discussing', so that it is possible that he allows for metaphorical language that can be understood literally. See John R. Searle, 'Metaphor', in *Metaphor and Thought* (ed. Andrew Ortony; Cambridge: Cambridge University Press, 1979), pp. 92-123 (114).

121. Stern, *Metaphor in Context*, p. 4.

122. He includes, among a number of examples, Mao Tse-Tung's comment, 'A revolution is not a matter of inviting people to dinner' (p. 4). Stern suggests that the underlying difficulty with what he refers to as the 'deviance account' of metaphor is that it wrongly assumes that 'every utterance is first interpreted literally. Following a serial or linear model of processing, the speaker-hearer turns to a nonliteral interpretation only after the literal interpretation has been eliminated' (p. 5). But citing evidence to the con-

Stern's argument has importance for the present research. According to the 'deviance account' of metaphor it would almost be impossible to embark on a metaphorical or symbolic interpretation of cultic prescriptive texts. Take, for example, the following statement made in Lev. 13.14.

וביום הראות בו בשר חי יטמא: ('When raw flesh appears on him he shall be unclean').

The 'deviancy account' does not require one to propose a metaphorical or symbolic meaning for any of the terms within this verse because a literal interpretation seems appropriate. However, according to Stern, the audience is permitted to assess both literal and non-literal interpretations of this text before concluding which of these is the most accessible within the context.[123] And, as was noted for cognitive linguistic theory, he reasons that the

> context in which an expression is interpreted metaphorically must be broadened to include not only its immediate linguistic environment, but also its extralinguistic situation (including nonverbalized presuppositions and attitudes).[124]

The present study presupposes that a reader's 'extralinguistic situation' includes his experience of reading the Pentateuch and the attitude he has come to take in relation to the various terms used in a text such as Lev. 13.14. Chapter 4 shall argue that, using a cognitive linguistic approach, a reader may access the negative ethical connotations the term בשר ('flesh') has elsewhere in the Pentateuch when reading the prescriptive text of Leviticus 13. If this argument is correct, then keeping in mind Stern's view of metaphorical (and by implication symbolical) language, we may assume that an interpreter would evaluate the possibility that this term is used metaphorically or symbolically within this prescription.

---

trary, he proposes that 'both literal and nonliteral interpretations are processed and evaluated in parallel or simultaneously. Among such parallel alternatives, the preferred interpretation is the one that is most *accessible* (where accessibility is itself context relative) rather than the one that is most literal... Adherents of the grammatical deviance condition narrowly focus on the limiting case where the metaphorical interpretation is the *only possible* interpretation of the utterance. But their tunnel vision obscures the fact that we may select one over another interpretation because it is the *best* (or better) rather than the only candidate' (Stern, *Metaphor in Context*, pp. 4-6).

123. See previous footnote.

124. In this regard Stern follows George Lakoff, 'The Contemporary Theory of Metaphor', in *Metaphor and Thought* (ed. A. Ortony; 2nd edn; Cambridge: Cambridge University Press, 1993), pp. 202-51. Stern's approach to metaphor implies that 'strictly speaking, there are no literal or metaphorical *expressions* per se (except in terms of art); there are only literal and metaphorical *interpretations* of expressions'. See Stern, *Metaphor in Context*, pp. 22, 307; Josef Stern, 'Metaphor, Literal, Literalism', *Mind and Language* 21 (2006), pp. 243-79 (243).

Conclusion

This Chapter has attempted to improve the objectivity with which one can interpret the symbolic meaning of ritual texts. First it presents what should be the first step in interpretation, namely the identification of a term's primary meaning by attending to its paradigmatic and syntagmatic relations. Nevertheless, a limitation of this method is that it may overlook a term's symbolic meaning if the latter occupies a domain that is secondary to a term's primary meaning. Thus, a symbolic dimension within P's ritual texts may go unnoticed when attention is restricted to a term's immediate linguistic context. The second section of this Chapter seeks to address this limitation. It examines the feasability of using cognitive linguistics to identify secondary meanings, possibly symbolic, that may be evoked by extra-linguistic factors. Though a term has a primary domain of meaning, cognitive linguistics provides a relatively objective means for establishing whether secondary domains are likely to be accessed by a competent reader. The concept of a secondary domain(s) of meaning provides a useful philosophical basis for describing the symbolic meaning of terms within ritual texts. However, since many scholars regard ritual texts as having no more than a primary meaning, the third section contemplated the nature of these texts and whether one can assume that they have a symbolic dimension. It concludes that the purpose of ritual texts extends beyond practical concerns to matters of theology. Moreover, following the work of Robert Alter on Hebrew narrative, there is possibly an interfusion between the theology of the priestly ritual texts and their literary art. On this assumption one should consult the ritual texts themselves for their theological meaning rather than by (a) reconstructing how these rituals may have once been enacted or (b) investigating how the prescribed rituals are used within narrative texts.

The conclusions reached in this Chapter encourage an interpretation of ritual texts that (a) when interested in the theology of a ritual text, presupposes that the latter is the object of interpretation and (b) uses the insights of cognitive linguistics to examine the secondary, possibly symbolic, meaning of terms. These methodological insights are employed in Chapter 3 to see if H's concluding call for holiness in Leviticus 11 (e.g. vv. 43-45) explicates the symbolic meaning of P's dietary regulations.

Chapter 3

LEVITICUS 11.43-45:
AN INVITATION TO EXPLORE P'S 'DIETARY
PRESCRIPTIONS' AS MOTIVATIONAL FOR HOLINESS

This Chapter uses the interpretive methods presented in Chapter 2 to estab-lish that an ethical view of holiness is implicit within the ritual 'dietary prescriptions' of Leviticus 11. This P-text concludes with what scholars assume is H's dynamic view of holiness (i.e. Lev. 11:43-45), raising the possibility that H may have made explicit what is implicit, in a symbolic dimension, within P's dietary prescriptions. Nevertheless it seems that schol-ars have not investigated this possibility for two reasons.

First, the nature of holiness that characterizes P seems too far at odds with H's dynamic concept to allow for such a possibility. Milgrom exemplifies such a view when he comments that the view that Lev. 11.43-45 stems from H's redactional activity

> is strongly corroborated by the imperative to Israel to make itself holy (v. 44), which is the most distinctive characteristic of H (hence its name) but which *stands in flat contradiction* to the opposing doctrine of P, that holiness of persons is reserved exclusively for priests and Nazirites.[1]

Second, any suggestion that the avoidance of *cultic* uncleanness (טמא) is a means to a person becoming ethically holy (i.e. Lev. 11.44) is deemed at odds with the intended function of P's purity laws, namely to protect the sanctuary.[2]

Since it assumes that the dynamic concept of holiness in these verses *ought* to occur elsewhere in P if written by the same author, the first argu-

---

1. Milgrom, *Leviticus 1–16*, p. 694. Emphasis mine.
2. For a review of approaches to the function of Israel's purity laws, see Hartley, *Leviticus*, pp. 141-46. Milgrom is the leading proponent of the idea that 'uncleanness' accumulates in the sanctuary thereby threatening Yahweh's residence there. Thus, 'uncleanness' is envisaged as a metaphysical substance independent of the offerer and this interpretation has led to his suggestion that the 'purification offering' (חטאת) cleanses not the offerer but the sancta. Milgrom, *Leviticus 1–16*, 253-61. For a critique of this position see Kiuchi, *Purification Offering*; Jay Sklar, *Sin, Impurity, Sacrifice, Atonement: The Priestly Conceptions* (Sheffield: Sheffield Phoenix Press, 2005).

ment can be set aside for the moment.[3] Since the second argument poses an immediate challenge to an ethical reading of holiness in P, because it prevents the interpretation of its ritual prescriptions as ancillary to the achievement of personal holiness, we shall evaluate it first.

The validity of the second argument depends on whether cultic terminology sufficiently accounts for the purpose of P's impurity regulations in Leviticus 11–15. Modern scholarship employs the word 'cultic' with reference to rituals, and their associated terminology, that are associated with the preservation of the sanctuary. Although these rituals may preserve the offerer's well-being, their performance is often regarded as *amoral*, occupying a realm separate from that of ethics. From this assumption scholars infer that no overlap exists between the cultic view of holiness in Leviticus 1–16, achieved by ritual, and ethics.[4] However, though these scholars assume that P's concept of holiness excludes an ethical component, they do not necessarily assume that P is uninterested in ethics.[5]

The universal description of P as 'cultic' is assumed rather than derived from exegesis.[6] This observation is significant considering that it is this assumption which leads to the common translation of the term טמא as *'ceremonial/ritual* uncleanness',[7] a translation that no doubt encourages the

3. Subsequent chapters investigate the claim that the offerer is not required to be holy in P.

4. For example, with regard to the nature of 'uncleanness', Noordtzij suggests that '[t]hese notions are not primarily concerned with the realm of the physical or even that of the ethical, but they belong rather within the sphere of the cult and ritual. Uncleanness shut off the possibility of participating in the ceremonial service of the Lord' (Noordtzij, *Leviticus*, p. 116).

5. Knohl and Snaith are unique in their contention that P has no direct interest in ethical behaviour. Knohl says that P's cultic system is 'detached from morality', and Snaith suggests that the concepts of clean and unclean in P never 'had any ethical association whatever in early days, and it is hard to see what ethical content there ever was or is. The ethical content of [קדש] developed because of the teaching of the prophets and whatever non-ritualistic elements there were in the priestly teaching.' See N.H. Snaith, *Leviticus and Numbers* (London: Thomas Nelson, 1967), pp. 60-61; Knohl, *The Sanctuary of Silence*, passim. For a rebuttal of Knohl's idea, that P is uninterested in ethics, see Milgrom, *Leviticus 1–16*, pp. 21-26.

6. To my knowledge no study has been undertaken to establish that the material of Leviticus 11–15 is purely cultic in the modern sense of that word. It would seem that the current distinction scholars maintain between 'cultic' and 'ethical/moral' laws derives from the work of Thomas Aquinas, who was the first person to refer to those laws that pertain to the 'Divine worship' as *ceremonial*. He regarded these laws as 'moral' when that term refers to human action directed by law. Cf. Thomas Aquinas, *Summa theological*, II (Chicago: William Benton, 1952), pp. 247-48.

7. NIV; Richard E. Averbeck, 'טמא', in *NIDOTTE*, I (ed. W.A. VanGemeren; Grand Rapids: Zondervan , 1997), pp. 365-76; Ludwig Koehler and Walter Baumgartner, *The*

interpretation of Leviticus 11–15 as no more than cultic.[8] This assumption, that Leviticus 11 is cultic, makes the emphasis on personal holiness in Lev. 11.43-45 appear alien to its context, so that these verses are interpreted as a novel addition rather than an invitation to explore how the purity system of Leviticus may function in relation to the personal (ethical) holiness of the Israelites. I am not trying to argue that Lev. 11.43-45 was original to P. Chapter 1 acknowledged stylistic and linguistic features, in addition to its use of holiness terminology, which distinguish it from its literary context. What is questioned is the assumption that H introduces a concept of holiness that is not already implicit within Leviticus 11. By making this assumption previous studies have overlooked the possibility that the author of Lev. 11.43-45 included the explicit command for holiness to complement what he understood was the original intention of the preceding ritual prescriptions.

Since we are interested in whether there is an ethical component to P's concept of holiness, the present Chapter investigates the proposed incongruence between P's 'cultic' regulations and dynamic (personal) holiness in Leviticus 11. If it is found that these regulations are misrepresented by the term 'cultic', and that they encourage a person to act with ethical integrity, then H's dynamic concept of holiness in Lev. 11.43-45 may explicate what is already implicit within P's preceding 'dietary regulations'.[9] If such a conclusion is accepted it invites a renewed assessment of the dichotomy scholars draw between the concepts of holiness in P and H.

To assess the accuracy of the description of 'uncleanness' (טמא) as a purely cultic term, we need to investigate its occurrence in Leviticus 1–16, especially in relation to the concepts of מות, שקץ and קדש in the 'dietary regulations' of Leviticus 11. If the term 'cultic' inadequately accounts for what is meant by 'uncleanness', we shall attempt to offer a better understand-

---

Hebrew and Aramaic Lexicon of the Old Testament (Leiden: E.J. Brill, 1995), pp. 375-76; G. André, 'טמא', in *TDOT*, I , pp. 330-42 (331).

8. With regard to the significance of the regulations of Leviticus 11, Noth comments that, '[t]he real ground is to be sought in the cultic field, for we are dealing throughout with the ideas of "cultically clean" and "cultically unclean". The real "unclean" was all that did not accord with Israel's lawful cultus, all that—outside the cultic field in the narrower sense—was forbidden for the Israelites, bound as they were to their God by their worship, and might therefore not be eaten' (Noth, *Leviticus*, p. 92).

9. As will be observed below, several scholars argue that an ethical purpose underlies Leviticus 11 without concluding that this purpose is subsumed under P's view of holiness. This is because the nature of ethics that they contend is present within Leviticus 11 is different from that which characterizes H's view of holiness. Thus, the present study will need to demonstrate that the ethical concern of P's legislation is comparable to that found in H before I can argue that these sources (redactions?) have a similar ethical concept of holiness.

ing of this term that may in turn reveal something of its relationship to personal holiness in Leviticus 11.

An Evaluation of the Cultic Description of Leviticus 11

Modern scholarship's tendency to categorize offerings, rituals and their associated terminology, as either cultic or ethical, is most apparent in the work of Israel Knohl.[10] Knohl contends that P's innovative contribution is to separate the *cultic* religion of Israel from the *ethical*,[11] suggesting that this moment in the development of Israel's religion occurred after Yahweh's revelation of his name which represented Him as holy and inapproachable to *un*holy humankind (Exod. 3.15; 19).[12]

> The revelation of the name of Yahweh results in a Copernican revolution. Moses and, following him, Israel learn to recognize the essence of the divine nature, which is unrelated to creation, or to humanity and its needs. This dimension cannot be fully comprehended by humans and surpasses the limits of morality and reason, since morality and its laws are only meaningful in relation to human society and human understanding. The aspect of divine essence that surpasses reason and morality—the 'numinous' element—is represented in [P][13] by the name of Yahweh.[14]

The revelation of Yahweh's name generates P's development of a *cultic* system that expresses humanity's status in light of the *numinous* holy God who had become abstracted from his practical functions in the world.[15] In this regard, Knohl favourably quotes Kaufmann:

10. Knohl, *The Sanctuary of Silence*, passim.

11. Knohl does not dispute that P had an ethical standard. However, he assumes that P's interest in ethics is limited to a universal ethic for mankind (*The Sanctuary of Silence*, p 147).

12. Knohl argues that whereas in the Genesis period God is described in anthropomorphic terms (e.g. talking to mankind without intermediaries), after he reveals his name as Yahweh, 'his actions are described…in impersonal, indirect language, and anthropomorphic imagery is absent from the descriptions of God and his cult' (*The Sanctuary of Silence*, p. 137).

13. Knohl prefers to speak of a Priestly Torah (PT) than a Priestly School (P). For the sake of uniformity, only P will be used in the present work to refer to the Priestly School or to Knohl's Priestly Torah.

14. Knohl, *The Sanctuary of Silence*, p. 146. Rudolf Otto coined the term 'numinous' to refer to the abstract concept of 'holy' separated from 'all subordinate forms or stages of development it may show'. The numinous concept of holiness suits Knohl's contention that P knows of only a holy God who is removed from the moral realm. See Rudolf Otto, *The Idea of the Holy* (London: Oxford University Press, 1923), pp. 5-7.

15. Knohl, *The Sanctuary of Silence*, p. 149.

> The purpose of the cult in the ideal temple is to sanctify it…so that God may appear there to Israel and its prophet; …the actions performed in the temple itself…are all directed towards a single goal: the sanctification of the place, in which the name of God dwells and where the symbol of his word is to be found.[16]

Accordingly, the purpose of the offerings and rituals of Leviticus 1–16 is viewed as the maintenance of the sanctuary's *cultic* holiness rather than the sanctification of individuals. In line with this, Knohl concludes that the concept of holiness in P

> has a ritual character devoid of any moral content; thus, holiness is imparted to objects and to people in the same way (Exod. 30.26-30, Lev. 8.10-12)—through ceremonies of sanctification which combine rituals of purification, atonement, and anointing (Exod. 29.1-37; 30.26-30; Lev. 8.10-30)…[P's] cult expresses humanity's position vis-à-vis the sublime holy. Such an encounter necessarily engenders feelings of guilt and the need for atonement. This guilt is not associated with any particular sin; rather, it is a result of human awareness of insignificance and contamination in comparison with the sublimity of God's holiness.[17]

With regard to the concept of 'uncleanness', Knohl adopts Milgrom's view that it is a metaphysical substance, the import of which is its ability to pollute the sanctuary.[18] Yet Knohl's proposal that P strives to separate the cultic and ethical realms forces him to conclude, contra Milgrom, that cultic 'uncleanness' is completely detached from ethics: it is with reference to the threat it poses to the sanctuary that the offerer feels guilt, rather than any wrongdoing on his part. This aspect of Knohl's argument is criticized by Milgrom who, while similarly denying that the cultic regulations of Leviticus 1–16 are aimed at sanctifying persons, suggests that P's regulations protect Yahweh's sanctuary ('a symbol of life') from the *cultic* 'uncleanness' ('representing death') produced by Israel's violation of *ethical* commands.[19] Milgrom's response to Knohl helps to justify the present study, for if Knohl is correct

16. Cited in Knohl, *The Sanctuary of Silence*, p. 149.

17. Knohl, *The Sanctuary of Silence*, p. 151.

18. Knohl, *The Sanctuary of Silence*, p. 155; cf. Milgrom, *Leviticus 1–16*, pp. 45-46, 257.

19. Milgrom, *Leviticus 1–16*, pp. 50-51. For his criticism of Knohl's contention that P is uninterested in ethics, see pp. 17-26. Milgrom's proposal that an ethical concern underlies Leviticus 1–16 does not require him to associate this concern with P's view of holiness. On the one hand, he would dispute that the root קדשׁ naturally carries an ethical meaning and, on the other hand, he argues that P's ethical concern is different from that which characterizes H's view of holiness. As we shall see below, whereas Milgrom argues that the ethical concern of H relates to the keeping of cultic and ethical commandments, he proposes that in P it is a more general notion of 'respect for life'.

there would be no point in asking whether an ethical concern underlies the commands of Leviticus 11.

Milgrom's primary contention with Knohl is that he argues from silence: *the non-mention of ethics does not imply a disinterest in ethics*.[20] In addition to this contention, he offers four reasons for why it is reasonable to assume that the realms of ethics and cult are integrated in P, and more specifically the dietary regulations of Leviticus 11.

First he points out that Knohl's restriction of 'all of Yahweh's prohibitive commandments' (מכל מצות יהוה אשר לא תעשינה, Lev. 4.2, 13, 22) to mean cultic, but not ethical, regulations seems excessive given the relative scarcity of the former type of prohibitions in Leviticus 1–16.[21]

Second, conceding that a paucity of ethical commands characterizes Leviticus 1–16, Milgrom cites several Mesopotamian ritual documents that do not reflect the kind of distinction Knohl draws between the ethical and cultic realms.[22] In view of these documents, Milgrom suggests that it is unlikely such a distinction was made in ancient Israel.

Third, Milgrom argues that Aaron's confession of Israel's פשעים on the Day of Atonement (Lev. 16.16, 21) reflects an integration of cult and ethics in P. On the one hand, he urges that, since the language of 'inadvertence' (שגג) is not present in Leviticus 16, פשעים refers to Israel's 'brazen, presumptuous sins'.[23] On the other hand, contra Knohl's contention that sin refers only to the transgression of cultic regulations in P, Milgrom argues that the semantic range of these פשעים possible encompasses ethical sins because the term עונת, by which the פשעיהם and חטאתם are collectively described (i.e. 'all the iniquities' [את־על־עונת], Lev. 16.21),[24] is elsewhere used to refer to ethical sins (Lev. 5.1, 5.17-16; Num. 5.15-16, 30.16) in

---

20. Milgrom, *Leviticus 1–16*, p. 19.

21. Milgrom, *Leviticus 1–16*, p. 21.

22. For example, Milgrom cites Mesopotamian texts which have a clear interest in the 'ethical' activity of the worshippers. 'If NN, son of NN, has sinned…if he committed an assault, if he committed murder…if he had intercourse with a wife of his friend…if he talked to a sinner…if he interceded for a sinner, if he committed grievous sin, if he sinned against his father, if he sinned against his mother…' (E. Reiner, 'Lipšur Litanies', *JNES* 15 [1956], pp. 129-49 [137], cited in Milgrom, *Leviticus 1–16*, pp. 21-22).

23. Therefore, Milgrom assumes that these sins are premeditated and intentional (Milgrom, *Leviticus 1–16*, p. 25). See also Snaith, *Leviticus and Numbers*, p. 80; Hartley, *Leviticus*, p. 240. However Milgrom's equation of פשעים with 'brazen, presumptuous sins' does not take into account Knierim's study of this term in which he concludes that it does not include a reference to a person's attitude (i.e. a *deliberate* transgression). See Rolf Knierim, *Die Hauptbegriffe für Sünde im Alten Testament* (2nd edn; Gütersloh: Mohn, 1967), pp. 176-84. Nevertheless, Milgrom's argument that the term refers to both cultic and ethical transgressions still stands.

24. Literally, v. 21 says, 'confess over it all the iniquities of the Israelites—all their transgressions (and) their sins—and place them'.

addition to cultic sins (cf. Exod. 28.38, 43; Lev. 7.18). From this argument he concludes that P has cultic *and* ethical concerns.

Fourth, Milgrom demonstrates that P is aware that the 'Lord's command-ments' encompass more than legislation which scholars refer to as cultic. He cites the omission of the term מעל in Lev. 5.17 as evidence that the author understands the offence, mentioned in this verse, as embracing 'the entire gamut of sins subsumed under the rubric of 'the Lord's prohibitive commandments' (4.2)'.[25] He considers that מעל refers to the desecration of sancta (Lev. 5.14-16) or oaths (Lev. 5.17-19),[26] and since it is used in contexts that emphasize the violation of cultic violations (e.g. Lev. 5.15) its omission in Lev. 5.17 signifies that, in the mind of the legislator, something more than cultic regulations is transgressed.

Overall, Milgrom's opposition to Knohl's view that P has no direct inter-est in ethics seems persuasive. Thus, we may proceed for the moment, by examining the approaches Milgrom and Mary Douglas take in accounting for the ethical basis for the food laws of Leviticus 11.

It may seem surprising that, though Milgrom argues that an ethical con-cern underlies P's purity laws (Leviticus 11–15) he maintains that its concept of holiness excludes ethics.[27] Would not an ethical concern in P reflect an idea of holiness that is similar to that found in H? Milgrom would deny that this is the case because he contends that P's ethical concern (i.e. a 'respect for life'; see below) differs from that which characterizes the idea of holiness in H (i.e. the observance of cultic and ethical commandments). Thus, it seems that prior to any suggestion that there is an ethical aspect to P's view of holiness we will need to do more than identify an ethical dimension to Leviticus 11. One must demonstrate that the ethical purpose of Leviticus 11 is *comparable* to that associated with H's view of holiness.

In what follows the proposals that Milgrom and Douglas offer for the ethical purpose of Leviticus 11 will be assessed. If these are found to be unsatisfactory I shall undertake my own analysis of Leviticus 11 to see if it shares a similar ethical concern to that which characterizes H's concept of holiness. If it exhibits the same concern this would encourage the conclusion that H's command to 'be holy' in vv. 43-44 explicates what is implicit within P's dietary regulations.

25. Milgrom, *Leviticus 1–16*, p. 24.

26. Milgrom, *Leviticus 1–16*, p. 320. See also Rendtorff, *Leviticus*, p. 201.

27. Though Douglas does not deny that the ethical concerns of Leviticus 11 are unre-lated to holiness, I shall contend that her argument, in this regard, is inconsistent. Nevertheless, like Milgrom, her view of the ethical purpose of this chapter differs from that which characterizes H's view of holiness. Thus, it will need to be assessed before we can examine whether Leviticus 11 reflects an ethical concern that is similar to that found in H.

Theories for an Ethical Basis to P's Purity Legislation[34]

Both Milgrom and Douglas attempt to identify an ethical basis to P's purity regulations.[29] The latter adopts Milgrom's conceptualization of 'uncleanness' as a metaphysical force that threatens God's residence in the sanctuary. However, though both scholars agree that the dietary regulations of Leviticus 11 serve to inculcate an ethical respect for life, Douglas's proposal for what kind of ethics are on view in this Chapter is more elaborate than Milgrom's. She maintains that they also teach the Israelites specific societal values.

Jacob Milgrom

Presumably arising from his conviction that cult and ethics are integrated within P, Milgrom seeks to identify an ethical basis for the food-laws of Leviticus 11. As just observed, such a move may seem somewhat ironic because elsewhere he argues that the *ethical* concept of holiness in Lev. 11.43-45 [i.e. H] is 'assiduously avoided—and, by implication, denied—by P, which holds that only the priests (and temporary Nazarites) are holy'.[30] Nevertheless, as we shall see, the kind of ethical basis he proposes for Leviticus 11 is unrelated to the kind of ethics H subsumes under the idea of holy.[31] In other words, the ethical purpose he assigns to Leviticus 11 does not invite a comparison between the concepts of holiness found in P and H respectively.

28. A recent proposal for interpreting an ethical dimension to the laws of Leviticus 11 is offered by Houston (Walter Houston, 'Towards and Integrated Reading of the Dietary Laws of Leviticus', in *The Book of Leviticus. Composition and Reception* [ed. Rolf Rendtorff and Robert A. Kugler; VTSup, 93; Atlanta: SBL, 2003], pp. 142-61). More specifically, after evaluating the attempts of Milgrom and Douglas 'to view the ritual and morality of Leviticus as parts of a unified whole rather than as unrelated systems', Houston offers his own theory for this. His view of the ethical concern of Leviticus 11 is not mutually exclusive of the argument I shall make in this chapter. In order to conserve space I shall not deal with it here.

29. In this regard, Douglas's approach is the more innovative one. By contrast, Milgrom's view of the ethical purpose of these laws stands 'very much in the tradition of Philo and Maimonides with their conviction that the purpose of the dietary laws in general is to discipline the appetite and to prevent human beings becoming dehumanized by the violence involved in the killing of meat' (Houston, *Purity and Monotheism*, p. 76).

30. Milgrom, *Leviticus 1–16*, pp. 686-87.

31. That is, whereas Milgrom argues that the ethical purpose of P's purity regulations (Leviticus 11–15) is to inculcate a 'respect for life' among the Israelites, he contends that in H it is for Israel to observe God's 'moral and ritual commandments'. In this way 'Israel can become holy' (*Leviticus 1–16*, pp. 686-87).

In conceptualizing the ethical function of Israel's purity laws Milgrom draws on his understanding of the nature of impurity in ancient pagan religion, particularly that found in Mesopotamian ritual texts. This comparison arises from his assumption that P's cultic material serves as a polemic against demonology in pagan religion.[32] Milgrom observes that the deities portrayed in pagan religions are typically limited by a meta-divine realm, comprised of demonic entities that could be persuaded, by magic, to influence the deity's behaviour.[33] These demonic forces are capable of repelling the deity housed, fed and worshipped within the temple, by polluting the latter with metaphysical impurity. Hence, purity rites are a cultic means by which devotees protect their deity's presence from demonic impurity, thereby guaranteeing their god's reciprocation of their care.

In comparing P's cultic prescriptions with his observations on pagan religion, Milgrom concludes that the Levitical concept of impurity is similarly a metaphysical substance, quite independent of the worshipper, capable of repelling Yahweh from his sanctuary. But he notes that a difference exists between the two which stems from Israel's monotheism which excludes the demonic realm from their worldview. This eviscerates

> impurity of its magic power. Only in its nexus with the sancta does it spring to life. This malefic impurity does not inhere in nature; it is the creation of man. Only man, even by inadvertence, can generate the impurity that will evict God from his earthly abode.[34]

Humans are the only creatures that have 'demonic power' since they are endowed with free-will.

> The demons have been expunged from the world, but man has taken their place. This is one of the major contributions of the priestly theology: man is 'demonized.' True, man falls short of being a demon, but he is capable of the demonic. He alone is the cause of the world's ills. He alone can contaminate the sanctuary and force God out.[35]

Thus Israel's world is not suffused with demonic impurity, but the *cultic* impurity of humankind. Although the evisceration of the demonic from impurity is thought to serve as a polemic against its pagan counterparts, Milgrom suggests that its dynamic power, which is inherent in pagan impurity, is retained by P to serve a *theological purpose* within Israel:[36] *The ability of cultic טמא to 'force God out' of his sanctuary serves as an ethical*

---

32. Milgrom, *Leviticus 1–16*, p. 43. An evaluation of this presupposition is offered below.
33. Milgrom, *Leviticus 1–16*, pp. 42-43.
34. Milgrom, *Leviticus 1–16*, p. 261.
35. Milgrom, *Leviticus 1–16*, p. 260.
36. Milgrom, *Leviticus 1–16*, p. 43.

impetus for Israel to choose life and reject death.[37] In summary, this impetus derives from the fact that טמא represents the 'forces of death' released upon the sanctuary by humankind's violation of God's commandments that are intended to conserve life. Thus the priestly regulations concerning 'uncleanness' are given to protect the holy sanctuary from the 'uncleanness' incurred through the violation of what are essentially *ethical* commands. By implication, and contra Knohl, both the prescriptions for offerings (Leviticus 1–7) and the purity laws (Leviticus 11–15) have an ethical basis.[38] The logic by which Milgrom reaches this conclusion is reviewed and evaluated in what follows.

'Uncleanness' as Symbolic of the 'Forces of Death'

Milgrom provides a twofold defense of his claim that 'uncleanness' is symbolic for the 'forces of death'. The first derives from his view that death is the common denominator of what he identifies as P's three categories of impurity, namely corpse/carcass (Leviticus 11; 21.1-4);[39] scale disease (Leviticus 13–14) and genital discharge (Leviticus 12; 15).

Second, he argues that a consideration of the conceptual relations between the terms טהור, טמא, חל, and קדש in Lev. 10.10 implies that 'uncleanness' represents the 'forces of death'. A summary and evaluation of these two arguments follows.

1. *Death as the Common Denominator of the 'Three Categories of Impurity'*. Of the three categories of impurity Milgrom identifies within P, the first (i.e. corpse/carcass; Leviticus 11; 21.1-4) exhibits the clearest relationship between death and impurity: dead human bodies defile (Lev. 21.1-4) and animals pollute only when they are dead (Leviticus 11).[40] But since death is not mentioned in the categories of 'scale disease' (צרעת, Leviticus 13–14) and genital discharge (Leviticus 12; 15), Milgrom and others are left to deduce that death is the *symbolic* referent of these kinds of 'uncleanness':[41] צרעת (Leviticus 13–14) symbolizes the appearance of death and the loss of

---

37. Milgrom, *Leviticus 1–16*, p. 43 (emphasis mine).

38. Milgrom, *Leviticus 1–16*, pp. 48-51.

39. In addition to the contamination by corpse-carcass contact in Leviticus 11, Milgrom adds contact with human corpses (Lev. 21.1-4; Num. 5.2-4; 6.9-12; Ezek. 44.26-27). Since these examples are not from Leviticus 1–16 they are not further examined (Milgrom, *Leviticus 1–16*, pp. 986-89).

40. With the exception of 'clean' animals that are sacrificed or slaughtered for food.

41. Other scholars who concur with this position include Keil, *The Pentateuch*, p. 358; Gordon J. Wenham, 'Why Does Sexual Intercourse Defile (Lev. 15:18)?' *ZAW* 95 (1983), pp. 432-34; Hyam Maccoby, *Ritual and Morality: The Ritual Purity System and its Place in Judaism* (Cambridge: Cambridge University Press; 1999); Gordon J. Wenham, 'Purity', in *The Biblical World*, II (ed. John Barton; London: Routledge, 2002), pp. 378-94 (385-86).

vaginal blood and semen (Leviticus 12; 15) represents the loss of life.[42] While I would dispute Milgrom's argument for how 'uncleanness' relates to death in this material, I agree that the meanings of 'uncleanness' and 'death' are closely related.

2. 'Uncleanness' as Metaphysical Force in Leviticus 10.10. Having concluded that P's concept of 'uncleanness' represents 'death', Milgrom marshals additional support from the syntactical relationship between קדש and טמא in Lev. 10.10.[43] More specifically he uses this text to establish that these concepts are 'forces', an argument intended to buttress his claim that Israel's purity regulations are a polemic against those found in the ANE: *just as impurity in the latter is a force that threatens the deity, so impurity within Israel is a force that threatens to chase God out of the sanctuary.*

Lev. 10.10 refers to קדש and טמא and the closely related concepts חל and טהר. Of these, Milgrom suggests that only קדש and טמא cannot coexist and he concludes that these terms are 'exact' semantic opposites: if the referent of טמא is 'death' then its proposed antonym קדש must refer to 'life'. Moreover, since the two are antagonistic to one another, they are more properly referred to as meaning the *'forces of* death' and the *'forces of* life' respectively. Thus,

> *ṭumʾâ* and *qĕdûšâ*, biblical impurity and holiness, are semantic opposites. And as the quintessence and source of *qĕdûšâ* resides with God, it is imperative for Israel to control the occurrence of impurity lest it impinge upon the realm of the holy God.[44]

Assuming that 'uncleanness' represents the *'forces* of death', Milgrom contends that the ultimate aim of P's purity regulations is to preserve Yahweh's presence in the sanctuary from the metaphysical entity of טמא—the 'forces of death'.[45] With regard to the dietary regulations of Leviticus 11, by making the death of animals the source of metaphysical impurity, Milgrom suggests that P intends these laws to fulfil the ethical function of conserving animal

---

42. It is noteworthy that if death is an intrinsic conceptual component of 'uncleanness' it would seem at once to negate Knohl's premise that this cultic term is unrelated to the *life* of the Israelite. Milgrom does not explore this weakness in Knohl's proposal. However, there appears to be a clear intention, if death is a semantic element of 'uncleanness', to encourage the Israelites to shun death. It is yet to be seen what kind of 'death' they are to shun. Is it simply the incidence of physical death, as envisaged by Milgrom, or that representing exclusion from Yahweh's immediate presence (cf. Genesis 3)? See Milgrom, *Leviticus 1–16*, p. 1002.

43. Milgrom, *Leviticus 1–16*, p. 616.

44. Milgrom, *Leviticus 1–16*, pp. 1002-1003.

45. Milgrom, *Leviticus 1–16*, p. 696. Feldman proposes a similar relationship between קדש and טמא (E. Feldman, *Biblical and Post-Biblical Defilement and Mourning* [New York: Ktav, 1977], p. 65).

life: *each time the Israelites spare the lives of unclean animals uncleanness is not 'released against' the holy sanctuary, thereby 'chasing' God away.*[46]

The Avoidance of Uncleanness as Ethical Impetus to Conserve Life

Milgrom's most innovative contribution to the study of Israel's purity regulations is his idea that an ethical concern to conserve life explains the symbolic relationship between 'uncleanness' and the metaphysical 'forces of death'. Approached in this way the Levitical impurities are viewed as the 'precipitates of a filtering process initiated by the priests', and the filter is an ethical concern to limit the occurrence of death which could in turn threaten the sanctuary.[47] But how does Milgrom know that an ethical concern to conserve animal life is foundational to Leviticus 11?

In the absence of any direct indication of what ethical principle might underlie the food prohibitions of Leviticus 11, Milgrom infers what it might have been from what he considers is the ethical basis of the other elements of Israel's so-called 'dietary system'.[48] According to him, this system comprises the 'blood prohibition' (Lev. 17.10-14; Gen. 9.3-6), 'instructions for ritual slaughter',[49] the 'kid prohibition' (Exod. 23.19; 34.26; Deut. 14.21) and the 'prohibited animals' of Leviticus 11.[50] In short, he posits that an ethical concern to conserve life and limit the occasion of death is fundamental to each of these.[51]

First, he understands the 'blood prohibition' of Lev. 17.10-14 and Gen. 9.3-6 is understood to inculcate a 'respect for life' among humankind (Gen. 9.3-6) and, more specifically, Israel (Lev. 17.1-11). Departing from the tra-

---

46. Even before we examine this argument in more detail it is worth taking into consideration the following criticism it has received from Houston. 'There seems to be a failure of logic here. The unclean animals symbolize *the forces of death*, yet the purpose of forbidding access to them is to maintain reverence for life *by limiting the exploitation of life*. Either of the two italicized phrases may be capable of making sense of the law as a consistent principle, though, as I have shown, neither accounts for its details; but taken together they are hopelessly contradictory' (Houston, 'Towards an Integrated Reading of the Dietary Laws of Leviticus', p. 149).

47. Milgrom, *Leviticus 1–16*, pp. 46-47.

48. The suggestion that there was such a 'system' possibly reflects a modern tendency to systematize. There is no reference to such a system within the OT. Thus, Milgrom's appeal to the 'dietary system' is already speculative (*Leviticus 1–16*, pp. 704-42).

49. He derives this category from no single text but from the verb (i.e. שׁחט) used to describe how one is to kill a sacrificial animal. See discussion below.

50. The 'Kid Prohibition' will not be dealt with here since Milgrom infers its ethical basis from his observations of the other three aspects of Israel's so-called dietary system (*Leviticus 1–16*, pp. 737-42).

51. Milgrom suggests that within P 'we can detect the earliest gropings toward an ecological position' (*Leviticus 1–16*, p. 47).

ditional interpretation, Milgrom argues that the כֹּפֶר capacity of sacrificial blood in Lev. 17.11 refers exclusively to that of the 'peace offering' (שׁלמים). This argument is based on his assumption that the prohibition against eating blood (vv. 10, 12) limits its reference to the 'peace offering' because this is the only meat offering eaten by the Israelites.[52] Although acknowledging with the consensus that the 'peace offering' is a non-expiatory sacrifice in P,[53] he is adamant that H developed a new function for the sacrifice: the blood of the 'peace offering' could כֹּפֶר for the 'life' (נֶפֶשׁ) of the offerer to save the latter from the charge of murder.

Milgrom renders כֹּפֶר 'to ransom' in Lev. 17.11 because he interprets the sacrificial blood of the 'peace offering' as the means by which the offerer could escape the death penalty for murdering an animal. This conclusion derives from his opinion that the law of Lev. 17.3-4 means: 'he who commits profane slaughter is reckoned to be a murderer because he has shed blood'.[54] Thus,

> [t]hese two laws complement each other perfectly. The first states that an Israelite who slaughters the animal for its meat without offering it as a sacrifice is a murderer. The second provides the rationale that the purpose of this sacrifice—indeed, of dousing the animal's blood on the altar—is to atone for killing it.[55]

The offerer's life must be ransomed because he has murdered an animal for food (i.e. the שׁלמים).[56] Although this function of the 'peace offering' is restricted to H, Milgrom contends that the same ethical concern for the life of animals is adumbrated in Gen. 9.4 (P).

> H's innovation is not without some precedent. P ordains that the non-Israelite commits murder if he does not drain the slain animal of its blood (Gen. 9.4). H extends this notion to the Israelite and revises it: to ransom the Israelite from the charge of murder, for taking the life of the animal, he must drain the animal's blood on a sanctuary altar—that is, offer the animal as a *šelāmîm*.[57]

According to Milgrom, this innovation serves to sharpen the principle of the inviolability of life.[58]

---

52. This argument assumes that the reference to 'eating' (אכל) blood (Lev. 17.10) refers to blood in the flesh rather than that drained from an animal (Milgrom, *Leviticus 17–22*, p. 1470).

53. Although see Kiuchi's contention that the שׁלמים is indeed expiatory and pro-pitiatory (N. Kiuchi, 'Propitiation in the Sacrificial Ritual', in *Christ and the World*. XV [Inzai, Chiba: Tokyo Christian University, 2005], pp. 35-50).

54. Milgrom, *Leviticus 1–16*, p. 710.

55. Milgrom, *Leviticus 1–16*, p. 711.

56. Milgrom, *Leviticus 1–16*, pp. 704-13.

57. Milgrom, *Leviticus 17–22*, p. 1478.

58. Milgrom, *Leviticus 1–16*, p. 49.

> The Bible decrees that blood is life; human blood may not be spilled and animal blood may not be ingested. Israel is enjoined to observe an additional safeguard: Blood of sacrificial animals must be drained on the authorized altar… The human being must never lose sight of the fundamental tenet for a viable human society. Life is inviolable; it may not be treated lightly. Mankind has a right to nourishment, not to life. Hence, blood, the symbol of life, must be drained, returned to the universe, to God.[59]

Second, Milgrom maintains that a respect for animal life underlies the 'ritual for slaughter'. Though acknowledging that the OT does not prescribe a technique for ritual slaughter, he argues that Deut. 12.21 implies that there is a standardized technique.[60] Moreover, he equates this method with that represented elsewhere by the verb שחט which he translates as 'to slit the throat'.[61] P's use of this method reflects its desire that 'the death of the animal should be effected in such a way (by painless slaughter and the immediate drainage of blood) that the slaughterer's sense of reverence for life will never be blunted'.[62]

These two findings regarding the ethical basis of Israel's so-called 'dietary system' lead Milgrom to suspect that the ethical basis of the dietary regulations of Leviticus 11 is likewise a desire to inculcate a 'respect for life' by encouraging Israelites to avoid the incursion of טמאה—a symbol of 'death'.[63]

His logic can be summarized as follows. First, the sanctuary and its contents are קדש; they represent the 'forces of life'. Second, טמאה represents the 'forces of death', incurred when the ethical concern to conserve life is violated. Third, קדש and טמאה are necessarily antithetical: life cannot exist where there is death and vice versa. Fourth, (therefore) the food prohibitions and associated purity regulations aim to inculcate a respect for life by emphasizing the threat cultic טמאה poses to the sanctuary.

Evaluation of Milgrom's Integration of Cultic טמאה and Ethics

An Inconsistency in Milgrom's View of Holiness in P?
An apparent inconsistency exists in Milgrom's explanation of the ethical rationale underlying the formulation of Leviticus 11. He claims that '[a]

---

59. Milgrom, *Leviticus 1–16*, p. 713.

60. Milgrom, *Leviticus 1–16*, p. 715.

61. Koehler and Baumgartner do not translate this term so precisely. They make the more general observation that it refers to the ceremonial slaughter of animals (L. Koehler and W. Baumgartner, *The Hebrew and Aramaic Lexicon of the Old Testament*, IV [trans. M.E.J. Richardson; Leiden: E.J. Brill, 1994–2000], pp. 1458-59).

62. Milgrom, *Leviticus 1–16*, p. 718.

63. Milgrom, *Leviticus 1–16*, pp. 729-30.

rationale, it turns out, is not at all absent from Leviticus 11. It is found in one concept—holiness'.[64] Expanding on this, he suggests that

> because the demand for holiness occurs with greater frequency and emphasis in the food prohibitions than in any other commandment, we can only conclude that they are Torah's personal recommendation as the best way of achieving this higher ethical life.[65]

But the difficulty with this line of argument is that he cites the rationale of holiness from Lev. 11.43-45—a passage he considers as belonging to the redactional work of H.[66] As such, Milgrom cannot avoid the charge of inconsistency by maintaining, on the one hand, that P's concept of holiness is unrelated to ethics and, on the other hand, concluding that the food prohibitions '...are Torah's personal recommendation as the best way of achieving this higher ethical life'.[67] Milgrom must *either* conclude that P's concept of holiness coheres with H's ethical concept *or* jettison his theory that the food prohibitions were a means by which the Israelites became God-like in their reverence for life.[68] To do the former would forfeit what Milgrom regards as 'the most distinctive characteristic of H'.[69] To do the latter would require him to advocate a view of ethics that is not grounded in the image of God.[70]

Israel's Purity System as Polemic against Demonology in Pagan Religion?

Foundational to Milgrom's conceptualization of 'uncleanness' as a metaphysical force that is capable of 'forcing God out' of his sanctuary, is his hypothesis that P's purity regulations serve as a polemic against the pagan religions of the ancient world. Unfortunately, however, he provides no evi-

64. Milgrom, *Leviticus 1–16*, p. 729.
65. Milgrom, *Leviticus 1–16*, p. 731.
66. And a passage which he views as advocating a view of holiness that contradicts the concept of holiness espoused by P (Milgrom, *Leviticus 1–16*, p. 694).
67. This conclusion would be valid if Milgrom were claiming that H has made explicit P's original purpose of these laws. However, for him to make this claim would be to accept that P and H share the same view of holiness (Milgrom, *Leviticus 1–16*, p. 731). Paul Heinisch is of the opinion that though vv. 44-45 come from the hand of H, the purpose they attribute to the 'dietary regulations' was already the intention of the more ancient regulations. 'Der religiöse Zweck, den ein späterer Ergänzer angab, das Volk sollte zu einem heiligen Leben angeleitet warden V. 44, 45, lag gewiss auch in der Absicht des älteren Gesetzgebers' (Paul Heinisch, *Das Buch Leviticus* [Bonn: Hanstein, 1935], p. 55).
68. Milgrom, *Leviticus 1–16*, p. 735.
69. Indeed, in this regard, he argues that H's concept of holiness 'stands in flat contradiction to the opposing doctrine of P' (Milgrom, *Leviticus 1–16*, p. 694).
70. Milgrom admits that '[w]e have to remember that the Godhead of Israel is the seat of ethics' (Milgrom, *Leviticus 1–16*, p. 731).

dence to defend this claim. Though there are several texts of the Pentateuch that are readily accepted as serving as a polemic against ANE religious ideas, these exhibit many literary similarities to the literature of the ANE.[71] The burden for proof remains with Milgrom to demonstrate that this is the case with Leviticus 1–16.

There are two more difficulties with Milgrom's proposal in this regard. The first has to do with his proposal that Israel's purity laws are a polemic against an ANE view that impurity is a demonic force which threatens the divinity's residence in the sanctuary. Problematic for this proposal is that Leviticus 1–16 seems to emphasize the consequences of impurity for the offerer rather than God's residence in the sanctuary.[72] The effect of uncleanness on the sanctuary is not acknowledged in Leviticus 11, whereas the consequence of uncleanness for individuals is (cf. Lev. 11.24-28).

Second, Israel's monotheistic faith is not necessarily unable to accommodate the existence of other supernatural beings. Though there are laws that prohibit the offering of sacrifices to other deities (Lev. 18.21; 20.2) and even 'the goat demons' (לשעירם, Lev. 17.7), the legislator does not indicate that these do not exist.

In conclusion, it seems that Israel's purity system may not have had the same dynamic qualities found in other ANE religions. This lessens the persuasiveness of Milgrom's theory that P conceives of ritual 'impurity' as a metaphysical force, released by (demonic) humans when they kill animals.

A Concern to 'Conserve Life' as the Ethical Basis of Israel's 'Dietary System'?

What are we to make of Milgrom's inference, from other elements of Israel's 'dietary system', that a 'respect for life' is the ethical basis of Leviticus 11? First, there is a methodological problem with this inference. The text of Leviticus, and the entire OT, gives no indication that the 'blood prohibition' (Lev. 17.10-14; Gen. 9.3-6), 'instructions for ritual slaughter', the 'kid prohibition' (Exod. 23.19; 34.26; Deut. 14.21) and the 'prohibited animals' (Leviticus 11) comprise a 'dietary system'. This observation does not rule out the possibility that these texts reflect a unified dietary system. However, it would seem that one is required to demonstrate that Leviticus 11 presupposes these texts as important for its interpretation, in the way Milgrom suggests, before so much is assumed. Without such a demonstration it seems somewhat

---

71. For example, see Kenton Sparks's documentation of the similarities between 'J's' primeval history and the literary shape of Eridu Genesis and Atrahasis (Kenton L. Sparks, *Ancient Texts for the Study of the Hebrew Bible: A guide to the Background Literature* (Peabody, MA: Hendrickson Publishers, 2005], p. 339).

72. This observation does not imply that P's ritual texts do not serve some other polemical purpose.

speculative to claim that they are based upon a common ethical concern to conserve life so that the inference Milgrom draws concerning the ethical basis of Leviticus 11 should be treated cautiously.

Second, it is not certain that an ethical concern for the conservation of life is foundational for the 'blood prohibition' and 'ritual slaughter' components of Milgrom's 'dietary system'. His insistence on the humane nature of Israel's method of ritual slaughter is subjective, relying on what one considers a humane method of animal slaughter.[73] Although Milgrom is certain that this method is chosen because it constitutes a humane procedure of slaughter, it is possibly selected to facilitate the collection of sacrificial blood in bowls (Exod. 27.3l; Num. 4.14). Milgrom himself considers that '...it seems that the only way that this could happen was to slit the animal's throat so that the blood vessels could quickly drain from the cut into a vessel'.[74] Thus, even if שחט does represent the Levitical procedure for ritual slaughter, it hardly constitutes evidence that a desire to conserve animal life is uppermost in the legislator's mind.

With regard to the blood prohibition, it is not clear that the motive for not eating blood (Lev. 17.11) is to inculcate an ethical 'respect for life'.[75] Kiuchi identifies three difficulties with Milgrom's interpretation of this verse. First, even if the threat of the כרת penalty in Lev. 17.10 applies narrowly to those who eat the blood of the 'peace offering' this does not imply that the interest of v. 11 is limited to this offering. As Kiuchi points out,

> v. 11, being a motive clause, may well speak of a general principle underlying the prohibition of blood consumption. And indeed all three parts of v. 11 are couched in highly general language. It seems then that 'the blood' in v. 11 could apply to the blood of all sacrifices.[76]

As further evidence that v. 11 has *all* sacrificial blood in view, Jay Sklar cites the prohibition against eating '*any* blood' (כל־דם) in v. 10. 'Verse 10 is thus a general prohibition against eating blood; it is not limited to the peace offering alone.'[77]

73. Milgrom, possibly following the view of traditional rabbinic exegesis which regards this as a humane method of slaughter, describes this particular method of slaughter as 'painless'! (Milgrom, *Leviticus 1–16*, p. 46).

74. Milgrom, *Leviticus 1–16*, p. 716.

75. Against Milgrom's suggestion that the blood prohibition stands at the centre of Leviticus 11, Liss observes that blood is not even mentioned in this chapter whereas it is in other purity regulations (Hanna Liss, 'Ritual Purity and the Construction of Identity – the Literary Function of the Laws of Purity in the Book of Leviticus', in T. Römer [ed.], *The Books of Leviticus and Numbers* [Colloquium biblicum lovaniense, 55; Leuven: Peeters, 2008), pp. 329-54.

76. Kiuchi, *The Purification Offering*, p. 102.

77. Sklar also provides a counter-argument to Milgrom's difficulties with the traditional view of Lev. 17.11 (*Sin, Impurity, Sacrifice, Atonement: The Priestly Conceptions*, pp.

The second problem Kiuchi identifies with Milgrom's interpretation of Lev. 17.11 is that it requires an 'artificial and forced' link between vv. 3-4 and v. 11.[78] Though vv. 3-4 indicate that the slaughter of an animal at a place other than the altar is viewed as murder, they 'do not imply any capital offence to be expiated, and there is no reason to mention the fact that blood may not be consumed'.[79] In addition to this, 'if the offerer brought a sacrificial animal to the sanctuary and slaughtered it, this act would constitute a totally legitimate act. It is not a sin; he has not committed a murder.'[80] Milgrom responds to this criticism as follows:

> In answer, one has to keep in mind that all sacrifices, save the well-being offering, become the property of God...Thus the life blood of the animal reverts to its creator, and therefore no crime has been committed. The well-being offering, though, is solely for the benefit of its offerer. He kills it for its flesh. For an Israelite, it is a capital crime, unless he returns its life force, the blood to its creator via an authorized altar.[81]

But to contend that it is a crime to kill the 'peace offering' Milgrom must assume what he is trying to prove, namely that the motive for not eating blood is to atone for taking an animal's life by delivering its life to God's altar. As Kiuchi points out, Leviticus 17 does not otherwise indicate that it is a crime to kill an animal at the altar. A further weakness in Milgrom's response has to do with his suggestion that the 'peace offering' is the only offering that does not become the property of God. If he is right, we should expect that the only part of this offering left at the altar should be the blood to atone for its murder. However, the fat, liver, and kidneys are collectively burnt on the altar, producing a 'pleasing aroma to Yahweh' (Lev. 3.3-5, 9-11, 14-16).[82] In agreement with Kiuchi and Sklar we may conclude that no compelling reason exists to view vv. 3-4 as the interpretative context for the motive clause in v. 11.

The final criticism Kiuchi makes of Milgrom's interpretation of Lev. 17.11 relates to the latter's equation of the purpose of the clause לכפר על־נפשׁתיכם ('to make כפר for your lives'), in v. 11, with the contextual

177-79). See Roy Gane's similar criticism of Milgrom's interpretation of Lev. 17.11 (*Cult and Character: Purification Offerings, Day of Atonement, and Theodicy* [Winona Lake, IN: Eisenbrauns, 2005], p. 171).

78. Kiuchi, *The Purification Offering*, p. 102.
79. Kiuchi, *The Purification Offering*, p. 103.
80. Kiuchi, *The Purification Offering*, pp. 102-103.
81. Milgrom, *Leviticus 17–22*, p. 1475.
82. Milgrom himself acknowledges that these things are 'reserved for the deity', so it is unclear how he comes to the conclusion that Yahweh does not in some way benefit from the offering (*Leviticus 1–16*, pp. 207-208).

meaning of the same clause in Exod. 30.11-16.[83] Observing that, within Exod. 30.11-16 and Num. 31.48, this clause occurs within a legal context that threatens an outbreak of divine wrath against the Israelites if they do not pay 'ransom' (כֹּפֶר) money for holding a census, Milgrom infers that the clause must imply just as much in Lev. 17.11. But Kiuchi rightly concludes that

> It is one thing to argue that *kipper* has the same sense in both sections, but quite another to argue that the extra-linguistic situation of כפר על נפשיכם is also alike or identical in both sections. As for the latter there is no support in the context of Lev. 17.[84]

Taking these criticisms of Milgrom's interpretation of Lev. 17.11 into account, it appears that a desire to 'conserve life' does not form the ethical rationale for Israel's blood prohibition.[85]

---

83. And, it should be added, Num. 31.48. Milgrom's argument in this regard is set out in Milgrom, *Leviticus 1–16*, pp. 707-708.

84. Kiuchi, *The Purification Offering*, p. 103.

85. Contra Milgrom and others it is questionable whether vegetarianism is affirmed in Gen. 1.29-30 and Gen. 9.1-7 *for the express purpose of limiting the slaughter of animals*. Two passages, which testify to the wilful killing of animals prior to the flood narrative, suggest that it is not. The first concerns God's provision of 'tunics' for Adam and Eve made from animal skins (Gen. 3.21) and the second narrates Abel's offering of an animal sacrifice (Gen. 4.4). The latter's offering is accepted by Yahweh whereas he 'did not have regard' (לֹא שעה) for his brother Cain's 'cereal offering' (מנחה, Gen. 4.5). How is one to avoid the conclusion that the wilful slaughter of animals recorded in these passages contradicts vegetarianism? The answer lies in that it was the eating of animals rather than the slaughter of animals that was denied to the first humans. This approach is taken by Umberto Cassuto. In relation to Abel's animal offering (Gen. 4.4) he points out that the 'offering of animal sacrifices does not point to the custom of eating flesh… On the contrary, it will be noted that the fat and the blood go to the altar, yet they may not be eaten!' (U. Cassuto, *A Commentary on the Book of Genesis I* [Jerusalem: Magnes Press, 1964], p. 206). And in connection with God's provision of animal skin 'tunics' for Adam and Eve (Gen. 3.21) he contends that 'there is no contradiction here to the principle of vegetarianism implied both in the previous section (i 29) and the present (iii 17-19), for there is no necessity to suppose that the verse refers specifically to skins of cattle that had been slaughtered for the purpose of eating their flesh' (Cassuto, *Commentary on Genesis I*, p. 171). If he is correct, it may imply that the concern of Genesis 1–11 lies not in the unethical killing of animals, which would seemingly contradict Gen. 3.21 and 4.4, but on preserving the symbolic value of their blood (i.e. life). This symbolic meaning is reaffirmed in Gen. 9.1-7 by God's prohibition against eating the blood.

One may argue that the declaration that animals would 'fear and dread' humans, in the post-flood world, would seem unnecessary if they were killed by humans before this time. But the nature of the claims made by this text must be kept in mind. Few scholars may suggest that they are historical, as though there was a historical moment before which humans were vegetarian or before which rainbows did not exist. Just as the narrator has adopted the naturally occurring rainbow as a symbolic reminder of God's

Third, Milgrom's contention that Leviticus 11 reflects the legislator's ethical concern to conserve life is negated by the framing of the food prohibitions
themselves. In relation to the negative description of the prohibited animals
as טמא and שקץ, David Wright observes that '[t]his negative characteriza-
tion of non-permitted animals seems to me not to support a desire to inculcate
a reverence for animal life'.[86] Moreover, in response to Milgrom's contention
that no legislation is required to limit the number of animals slaughtered
because the average Israelite could not afford to eat meat often, Houston
points out that if this were true, on the one hand, an average Israelite did not
require the laws of Leviticus 11, yet, on the other hand, there still remained
no limitation to the number of animals that could be slaughtered by the
wealthy.[87] We may also ask, with Jonathan Klawans, why God requires
animal sacrifice if he is concerned to limit the loss of animal life?[88]

covenant to preserve humankind (Gen. 9.9-18), it seems that he has utilized the naturally
occurring 'fear and dread' animals have of humans as a symbol of the latter's rule over
the creation. Perhaps this explanation can be most clearly understood when the polemic
function the Noachide narratives served against certain ANE traditions is taken into
account. For example, Sarna comments that the 'climax to the biblical Flood story
affords an illuminating contrast to its Mesopotamian counterpart. The heroes of both are
recipients of divine blessings, but whereas Utnapishtim and his wife are granted immortality and are removed from human society, God's blessing to Noah and his family is
socially oriented. They are not to withdraw from the world but to be fertile and to utilize
the resources of nature [i.e. now including animal flesh] for humanities [*sic*] benefit'
(Sarna, *Genesis*, 60). No doubt the 'fear and dread' animals have of humans is presented
as stemming from their awareness that the latter will henceforth eat them, but the thrust
of the passage would still seem to encourage the eating of animals rather than dissuade
such a practice. For another critique of the view that these texts promote vegetarianism
see Edwin Firmage, 'The Biblical Dietary Laws', pp. 196-97.
    86. D.P. Wright, 'Observations on the Ethical Foundations of the Biblical Dietary
Laws: A Response to Jacob Milgrom', in *Religion and Law: Biblical–Judaic and Islamic
Perspectives* (Winona Lake, IN: Eisenbrauns, 1999), pp. 193-98 (197).
    87. Houston, *Purity and Monotheism*, p. 77. Admittedly the persuasiveness of Hous-
ton's argument is contingent on the nature of Israelite law. If the law does not reflect the
ideal but rather points toward an ideal this may make it possible for the food laws to
encourage a reverence for life without preventing an unlimited slaughter of permitted
animals. As argued by Wenham, it is impossible to legislate for a perfect society which
means that some actions may still be permitted which remain at odds with the ideal. He
contends that the ideal, which surpasses legislation, is that which is affirmed by the
narrator within narratives (i.e. the 'ceiling of ethics'). Alternatively by despising certain
behaviour a narrator may indicate that which is contrary to the ideal, yet permitted by
law (e.g. bigamy). This last insight may provide indirect support for Houston's argument
because there are no occasions in which a narrator appears to disapprove an individual's
offering of numerous animal sacrifices. Gordon J. Wenham, *Story as Torah. Reading
Old Testament Narrative Ethically* (Grand Rapids: Baker Academic, 2000), p. 80.
    88. For example, if Milgrom is correct it would seem strange that the narrator appears
to affirm Solomon's offering of 142000 animals in 1 Kgs 18.63.

> While few scholars deny the importance of death-avoidance to the biblical purity system, some questions remain. One question concerns the relationship between death-avoidance and sex-avoidance. A second question concerns sacrifice. Indeed, the centrality of death to the ritual purity system brings us to a riddle at the heart of our concerns. Why, if the ritual purity system is concerned with keeping death out of the sanctuary, does the sacrificial system involve precisely the opposite: the killing of animals, in the sanctuary?[89]

In conclusion, Milgrom's appeal to elements of Israel's so-called 'dietary system' to establish an ethical basis to the food prohibitions of Leviticus 11 is not entirely persuasive. Though it is not disputed that the concept of death is important for the meaning of Leviticus 11, his argument that a restriction on the death of animals is this legislation's ethical goal does not receive strong textual support.

The Conceptual Relationship among the Terms קדש, חל, טהר, *and* טמא

Milgrom's attempt to identify the ethical basis of the food prohibitions, by appealing to the conceptual and semantic relationships between קדש, חל, טהר, and טמא in Lev. 10.10, is similarly problematic. First, he argues that Lev. 10.10 belongs to H, and this means that he cannot be certain that the conceptual relations between impurity and holiness in this verse represent how they are conceptualized by P.[90] This uncertainty particularly attaches to Milgrom because he regards these two sources as advocating ideas of holiness that stand in 'flat contradiction' to one another.[91]

Second, Milgrom overreaches the textual evidence when he defines טמא as the *exact* antonym of קדש, thereby claiming that they are opposing metaphysical forces. He bases this definition on his assumption that whereas חל may come into contact with what is קדש, the latter may not contact what is טמא without incurring death (e.g. Lev. 7.20-21; 22.3).[92] Thus, '...whereas the common may be either pure or impure the sacred may not be impure'.[93]

---

89. Klawans adds, in connection with his claim that death-avoidance does not explain sex-avoidance, 'it remains unclear whether or not the fear of death really explains why sex and birth *always* defile, even when no mishap occurs. Moreover, why is it that the only substances that flow from the body and defile are sexual or genital in nature? Even blood flowing from the veins of a dying person is not ritually defiling. A number of scholars have convincingly argued, against Milgrom, that the overarching concern with death-avoidance does not fully explain the particular concern with genital discharges' (Klawans, *Purity, Sacrifice, and the Temple*, p. 57).

90. Milgrom, *Leviticus 1–16*, p. 617.

91. Milgrom, *Leviticus 1–16*, p. 694.

92. Milgrom, *Leviticus 1–16*, pp. 731-32.

93. Milgrom, *Leviticus 1–16*, p. 616. Milgrom uses this argument as evidence that חל is not an antonym of קדש. Milgrom, *Leviticus 1–16*, p. 733.

This assumption leads him to the conclusion that קדשׁ and טמא are exact antonyms, cultic representations of the 'forces of life' and the 'forces of death' respectively.[94] But though these terms share a partial antonymous relationship, the contention that they are exact antonyms possibly goes too far. To begin with, what is holy can become טמא without incurring death. For example, Leviticus 1–16 implies the regular defilement of a consecrated priest (Leviticus 8) because he could marry and have children (Lev. 20.13-15), even though sexual intercourse made people טמא (Lev. 15.16-18).[102] Richard Averbeck draws the following conclusions in this regard.

> On the one hand, becoming unclean did not change the status of a priest from holy to common—he did not need to go through another set of (re)conse-cration procedures in order to function as a priest after he was cleansed from his uncleanness. On the other hand, if he entered the tabernacle in an unclean condition, he would thereby defile the tabernacle and become responsible to bring a sin-offering for his defilement of the tabernacle presence of God... Again, on the one hand, his unclean *condition* did not affect his *status* as a holy priest.[96]

Evidently, Averbeck distinguishes between holy and common as *states* and clean and unclean as *conditions*. This interpretation is supported by a closer examination of the interrelationship between the relevant terms in Lev. 10.10.

ולהבדיל בין הקדש ובין החל ובין הטמא ובין הטהור

Implied are the existence of antonymous relations between, on the one hand, קדשׁ and חל, and, on the other hand, טמא and טהר. The antonymous relationship between קדשׁ and חל is evident when the following implications, drawn from the observation that a consecrated priest could become טמא, are considered:

---

94.   Milgrom's conceptual argument necessitates his assignment of Lev. 10.10 to H because this verse charges the priests with the responsibility of enlarging the realm of holiness. Milgrom, *Leviticus 1–16*, p. 616.

95.   Though certain kinds of uncleanness prevent a priest from partaking in the eating of the 'holy things' (קדשׁים, Lev. 22.4a) this is restricted to some of the most serious forms of defilement, namely the disease called צרעת and a chronic flow (זב) from the sexual organs. There is no indication that lighter forms of defilement prevented one from eating the offerings. For a further example of permission being granted for priests to become defiled see Lev. 21.2-3.

96.   Richard Averbeck, 'Clean and Unclean', in *NIDOTE*. II (ed. W.A. VanGemeren; Grand Rapids: Zondervan , 1997), pp. 477-86 (482). Robert Kugler also points out that 'in spite of the popular belief that uncleanness in P is thought to endanger the holy, contact between the sanctified and impurity never actually damages the holy in Leviticus 1–16' (R.A. Kugler, 'Holiness, Purity, the Blood and Society: The Evidence for Theo-logical Conflict in Leviticus', *JSOT* 76 [1997], pp. 3-27 [15]).

i. A קדש priest may be either טמא or טהר, but not חל.
ii. A חל person may be either טמא or טהר, but not קדש.

One may conclude that though Milgrom correctly points out that the chiastic structure of v. 10 (i.e. בין...ובין/ובין...ובין) focuses attention on the concepts of קדש and טמא, it is simplistic to conclude that the two terms are *exact* semantic opposites, albeit opposing forces.[97] To conclude that קדש exhibits polysemic antonymous relations with חל and טמא within Lev. 10.10 seems more accurate. This observation cautions against Milgrom's suggestion that קדש and טמא are opposing metaphysical forces, since according to the same logic we could conclude that חל is another opposing force of קדש. Yet what would this conclusion mean?

The interrelationships of these four terms can be accounted for in another way. To begin with, the antonymous concepts of קדש and חל appear to be *states* that may vary in their ritual *condition*. That is, they become טמא or טהר by defilement or purification respectively. When approached from this polysemic perspective, it is not apparent that the concepts of טמא and קדש are opposing forces, and if they are not locked in a kind of metaphysical battle then Milgrom's theory that 'uncleanness' is a force eviscerated of the demonic loses some of its persuasiveness.

The above difficulties with Milgrom's claim, that 'uncleanness' is *indirectly* related to the life of the Israelite by the threat it poses to the sanctuary, have further implications for his cultic view of 'uncleanness'. First, the lack of evidence for his assumption that 'uncleanness' has only cultic significance for the sanctuary invites a re-examination of the effect which the incursion of impurity has. Before it is assumed that 'uncleanness' has no direct significance for the Israelites themselves, the following questions relating to its occurrence in Leviticus 11 require consideration. First, what is the symbolic meaning of a person becoming 'unclean until evening' (Lev. 11.24, 25, 28, 39, 40)? If it is not just to protect the sanctuary, what other function might this have? Second, why are no prescriptions for the purification of unclean persons given in Leviticus 11? This omission seems strange if the importance of the impurity laws is to guard the sanctuary from impurity.[98] Third, why must the Israelite emotionally detest (שקץ) those things that could make him unclean (Lev. 11.9-23; 41-42)?[99] Does this reflect a concern to protect the sanctuary or oneself, or both?

---

97. Milgrom, *Leviticus 1–16*, p. 616.

98. Admittedly prescriptions for the washing of clothes are given in vv. 25 and 40. Nevertheless, this observation may simply highlight the point being made here. That is, despite reference being made to the washing of clothes there is *still* no prescription given for the purification of the person.

99. Douglas translates שקץ to mean 'to utterly reject' in preference to its traditional

Second, though Milgrom's view of death's relationship to the concept of
טמא seems unsatisfactory, it does appear that death forms a semantic element of this concept within Leviticus 11. On the one hand animals may make
a person unclean only after they *die*. On the other hand, there is some consensus that the criterion that distinguishes the unclean birds of Leviticus 11 is
that they ingest *dead* animals. If the relationship between uncleanness and
death does not reflect a desire to conserve animal life, what is its significance? Milgrom may have too quickly attempted to interpret the relationship
between 'uncleanness' and death in terms of modern ecological ethics. Other
explanations for the association between death and 'uncleanness' require
consideration.

The preceding evaluation has found several difficulties with Milgrom's
proposal that the ethical principle underlying Leviticus 11 is a desire to
conserve animal life. In the absence of evidence for the kind of ethical basis
Milgrom proposes for the food laws of Leviticus 11, two issues need addressing. First, Milgrom has demonstrated that P is concerned with ethics
(contra Knohl). This makes it possible, though not certain, that P has an
ethical rationale for the dietary regulations of Leviticus 11. Since an ethical
concern to conserve life is not necessarily present in Leviticus 11 we are
invited to examine what other ethical impetus this legislation may serve.

Second, since the relationship Milgrom proposes to exist between טמא
and death is unsatisfactory, there is a need to reinvestigate what significance
death has for the concept of טמא in Leviticus 11. Given that the relationship
between 'uncleanness' and death may function on a symbolic dimension in
some cases, it seems advisable that the present study investigate whether
there is a larger symbolic dimension to these laws. It remains possible that
such a dimension is intended to encourage ethical obedience of the kind
implied in the command to 'be holy' in Lev. 11.44-45.

These two issues are possibly related. That is, the symbolic meaning of
these regulations may encourage the Israelites to avoid what is symbolized by
טמא (death?). If this is the case it may invite us to ask how this concept of
טמא relates to the dynamic concept of holiness in Lev. 11.43-45, which
scholars commonly describe as foreign to the concept of cultic טמא. However, before I make my own exegetical observations of the occurrence of the
term טמא and its related terms, namely מות, שקץ and קדש, a brief summary
and evaluation of Douglas's attempt to account for an ethical basis to
Leviticus 11 will be provided.

rendering 'to detest'. This rendering has significance for the interpretation of Leviticus
11 and it will therefore be dealt with below. See Mary Douglas, *Leviticus as Literature*
(Oxford: Oxford University Press, 1999), pp. 166-69.

Mary Douglas

Douglas, like Milgrom, proposes a different ethical basis for Leviticus 11 from that which characterizes H's view of holiness. Before I can proceed to argue that the ethical concern of Leviticus 11 is in fact comparable to that which H subsumes under its idea of holiness, the validity of Douglas's proposal requires assessment.[100]

Since publishing *Purity and Danger* (1966), a work that is seminal to many subsequent anthropological studies of the biblical purity texts,[101] Douglas has modified her proposal that the purity regulations of Leviticus reflect a general tendency in human societies to exclude those things that do not conform to what is accepted as normal.[102] Her original argument views 'impurity' as matter 'out of place', and the role of an impurity system is to define what does not fit within a given society.[103] But, in her words, this approach failed because

> [o]ver time...the analogy between biblical uncleanness and other systems of pollution began to break down. The main weakness of my attempt to naturalize and generalize purity concepts is that local definitions of pollution are the negative aspect of specific normative schemes of the world. I knew that the negative side cannot be compared across the board without also comparing the positive side.[104]

100. The earlier work of Douglas is adequately summarized and critiqued elsewhere so that we may confine our attention to her most recent material that deals with the ethical basis of Leviticus 11. My interaction with Douglas is confined to Douglas, *Jacob's Tears* (2004) and Mary Douglas, 'The Forbidden Animals in Leviticus', *JSOT* 59 (1993), pp. 3-23. A thorough review and evaluation of Douglas's earlier theories of Israel's purity regulations is provided in Houston, *Purity and Monotheism*, pp. 93-114. For a review of how Douglas's renewed assessment of Israel's purity regulations compares to her original work consult Jonathan Klawans, *Impurity and Sin in Ancient Judaism* (Oxford: Oxford University Press, 2000), pp. 7-10, 18-19.

101. Wenham, *Leviticus* (1979); Levine, *Leviticus* (1989); Milgrom, *Leviticus 1–16* (1991); Hartley, *Leviticus* (1992); Phillip Jenson, *Graded Holiness* (JSOTSup, 106; Sheffield: JSOT Press, 1992); Samuel E. Balentine, *Leviticus* (Louisville, KY: John Knox Press, 2002).

102. That is, she has nuanced her view that the purity laws represent 'the manifestation of a general cognitive bias, rejection of whatever does not fit the positive system of categories' (Mary Douglas, *Jacob's Tears. The Priestly Work of Reconciliation* [Oxford: Oxford University Press, 2004], p. 124).

103. Developed in Mary Douglas, *Natural Symbols: Explorations in Cosmology* (London: Barrie & Rockliffe, 1970).

104. Douglas, *Jacob's Tears*, p. 124. 'No one has levelled the main and obvious objection [i.e. to her prior explantion], the lack of equivalence between taboo as understood in the rest of the world and the rules of Leviticus. Everywhere else taboo is specifically tied to behaviour in such a way as to protect valued social and moral

In other words, to understand Israel's purity system one must begin by defining the positive social values of this particular people group. For this reason, in her latest work Douglas begins with the ethical ideals of Israelite society before considering how its purity system may facilitate an individual's adoption of these values.

The general ethical purpose Douglas assigns to P's purity regulations is as follows.

> The rules of purification and avoiding uncleanness offer to the people of Israel a chance to live by the principles that undergird the cosmos; they uphold the action of the Creator by their own enactment of the law.[105]

The motivation for keeping these laws, and thereby the attainment of an ethical lifestyle, is the threat Israel's 'uncleanness' poses to God's residence in the sanctuary. In this regard, Douglas assumes Milgrom's view of 'uncleanness' as a metaphysical force.

> The divine presence explains the scrupulous care that has to be taken to avoid impurity affecting a tabernacle which houses God. 'Why the urgency to purge the tabernacle? The answer lies in this postulate: the God of Israel will not abide in a polluted sanctuary. The merciful God will tolerate a modicum of pollution. But there is a point of no return. If the pollution continues to accumulate, the end is inexorable...'[106]

Nevertheless, Douglas's interpretation departs sharply from Milgrom's in that she presupposes that Leviticus was composed in Exile.[107] She proposes that its material is composed in a way that leads a temple-less exilic reader around an imaginary tabernacle:[108] Leviticus 1–16 represents the outer court where sacrifices take place; Chapters 17–24 'correspond to the sanctuary where the priests have access, and where the altar of showbread and menorah (candelabra) are placed';[109] and Leviticus 25–27 deals with God's covenant

---

standards. The connection with danger allows ideas to organize society by persuading, justifying, warning, mustering moral pressure. Yet the unclean animals in Leviticus do not serve these uses. No danger is attached to contact with them. The person who has had contact with a carcass does not have to make atonement, he or she only has to wash and wait until evening to be clean. This is merely a minor ritual disability. The rules make no engagement whatsoever with social life' (Douglas, 'The Forbidden Animals in Leviticus', p. 7).

105. Douglas, *Jacob's Tears*, p. 169.

106. Douglas, *Jacob's Tears*, p. 168. Quotation is from Milgrom, *Leviticus 1–16*, p. 258.

107. Douglas, *Leviticus as Literature*, pp. 6-12; Douglas, *Jacob's Tears*, p. 154. Chapter 1 pointed out that Milgrom argues that P and H were largely composed in pre-exilic times.

108. Douglas, *Jacob's Tears*, p. 154. This idea is first argued in Douglas, *Leviticus as Literature*.

109. Douglas, *Jacob's Tears*, p. 149.

with Israel, 'in the innermost recesses of the tabernacle [i.e. 'the most holy place'] is the container in which the covenant document is supposed to be placed'.[110] Within the exile's imaginary tabernacle Douglas suggests that the dietary laws of Leviticus 11 have 'the function of developing the analogy between the altar and the body'.[111] According to her, there is

> a lot about bodily impurity and sacrificed animal bodies in the first section [i.e. Lev. 1–16]. I shorten the exposition by saying that the human body is assimilated to the altar. Within the sense of the microcosm, as the tabernacle is equivalent to Mount Sinai, so is the body equivalent to the tabernacle. It must be kept pure, like the altar. No meat can be taken into the body and consumed as food that may not be laid on the altar and consumed by fire. The same rules for each.[112]

Thus, the dietary regulations are accurately interpreted by asking, in the first place, how they serve to enhance the analogy between the body and the altar. Presumably an individual's conscious embodiment of the altar within exile promotes an ethical way of life. But before we can assess her argument in this regard, a more detailed explanation of how Douglas arrives at this position is in order.

To begin with, Douglas argues that the analogous relationship between body and altar is suggested by the fact that the two principles governing what is 'consumed' (אכל) on the altar are determinative for what the Israelites may eat in Leviticus 11. First, reflecting what is true of the altar, she says that 'we get the impression that the only meat that the Israelites are allowed to eat must come from their flocks or herds'.[113] Second, the prohibition against eating carnivorous birds (Lev. 11.13-19) is analogous to the fact that blood is not burnt on the altar.[114] She concludes that the sharing of these principles implies that Israel's diet is limited to what is consumed by the altar's fire.

In support of this conclusion, Douglas contends that the Israelites may use only those animals that are part of the covenant.[115] She suggests that

> [t]he covenant, whose text is kept in the tabernacle, covers both humans and their livestock. The work animals must rest on the Sabbath (Exod. 20. 10; 23. 12, Deut. 5. 14), like their masters, and the firstborn of all the animals of the flocks and herds must be presented to the Lord, like the firstborn of their

110. Douglas, *Jacob's Tears*, p. 149.
111. Douglas, *Jacob's Tears*, p. 170.
112. Douglas, *Jacob's Tears*, pp. 149-50.
113. Douglas, *Jacob's Tears*, p. 170.
114. 'Blood is not offered or burnt on the altar. Whatever the reason given for not eating blood (it is a doctrine of respect for life, 7.26-7; 17.14), the upshot of the law is that blood is not to be consumed (same word) either by the mouth or by flames on the altar' (Douglas, *Jacob's Tears*, p. 170).
115. Douglas, *Jacob's Tears*, p. 170; cf. Douglas, *Purity and Danger*, p. 54.

masters (Exod. 13. 2, 12; 22. 22.29; 34. 19). This endows the sheep, cattle, and goats with special ritual status and entitles them to the dignity of a consecrated death.[116]

Thus, what is good for the tabernacle, in this case animals raised within the covenant, is good for Israelite food.

Assuming that the 'rules of purification and avoiding uncleanness offer to the people of Israel a chance to live by the principles that undergird the cosmos',[117] Douglas proceeds to identify what she thinks are the ethical objectives of the analogy created between body and altar in Leviticus 11.

First, following Milgrom, she accepts that the dietary regulations benefit the unclean animals. 'They can flourish without fear of the hunter or trapper because their carcasses convey uncleanness on contact. Something important is being said about taking life.'[118] Douglas thinks that the exclusion of predatory animals from Israel's diet as 'unclean' corroborates this conclusion.

Second, Douglas suggests that certain animals are assigned an unclean status because they resemble the vulnerable in society. On the one hand, she considers that some of these are included because they bear the likeness of humans who are 'lamed, maimed or otherwise disfigured'.[119] On the other hand, the fish without scales and fins (Lev. 11.10-12) represent those people who are vulnerable because of their youthfulness. This argument assumes that a lack of scales and fins is intended to exclude young fish from the Israelite diet. She infers that it is

> their vulnerable youthfulness that would be symbolized by absence of scaly covering. Fishes hatch out naked, their fins and scales grow on them, so shoals of baby fishes, minnows, whitebait and larvae of insects, the orphans of the water world, would be forbidden by this rule.[120]

116. Douglas, *Jacob's Tears*, p. 170.
117. Douglas, *Jacob's Tears*, p. 169.
118. Douglas, *Jacob's Tears*, p. 172.
119. Douglas, 'The Forbidden Animals in Leviticus', p. 22. Douglas does not mention this ethical purpose of the dietary regulations in *Jacob's Tears*. Though she may have altered her thinking to a certain extent, the following extract from her book *Leviticus as Literature* indicates that she has not completely abandoned this part of her argument found in the article cited here. 'Interpreting the law as a mark of respect for these creatures would mean that God protects swarming water animals from being preyed upon by his people. Scaly covering is a protective armour, fins guide locomotion, being without them is a disadvantage... Reading the text again, the prohibited water creatures...are all swarmers, blessed to bring forth abundantly. In some species absence of fins and scales exposes bare skin and assimilates the whole species into the class of foetus and young. Water-swarmers excite compassion as well as signify fertility, they are vulnerable' (Douglas, *Leviticus as Literature*, pp. 168-69). However, it is acknowledged that in *Leviticus as Literature* Douglas subordinates this view to her new idea that the animals permitted for food fall within the covenant.
120. Douglas, 'The Forbidden Animals in Leviticus', p. 22.

The path by which Douglas arrives at this conclusion is not straightforward. To begin with, she identifies those morphological features by which the legislator identifies animals as 'unclean' in Leviticus 11 as analogous to the 'blemishes' (מום) that disqualify priests and sacrificial animals from serving and being offered on the altar, respectively (Leviticus 21–22). This analogy is not derived exegetically, but from Douglas's observation that one could liken the morphological features that make an animal unclean with the blemishes that disqualify priests and animals from the altar on the basis of a 'something lacking'/'something superfluous' principle. She interprets this principle as that which is reflected by the list of blemishes for priests and animals in Leviticus 21–22.[121]

And, by assuming that Leviticus has the 'ring structure' she assigns it, Douglas identifies the symbolic meaning of the 'blemishes', and the features that qualify an animal as 'unclean', as signs of vulnerability.[122] On the one hand, she infers this from what she thinks is the mid-turn of the ring (i.e. Leviticus 19) which emphasizes the need for the Israelites to uphold matters of justice in their dealings with others. On the other hand, she places importance on the fact that the term 'blemish' is used to describe the result of an injustice done to another person in Lev. 24.19-20.

> The statements on blemish connect it with inequitable dealings. It would now appear that the forbidden species which are not covered by the law against eating blood, either have something lacking (like joints, legs, fins or scales) or something superfluous (like a burden on their backs) and that their disfigurement has something to do with injustice.[123]

According to Douglas, this view of the ethical foundation of Leviticus 11 makes sense of the command to be holy in Lev. 11.44-45:

> Holiness is incompatible with predatory behaviour. The command to be holy is fulfilled by respecting blood, the symbol of violent predation, and respecting the symbolic victims of predation. The forbidden animals in this perspective represent the endangered categories for whom Isaiah spoke, the oppressed, the fatherless, the widow (Isa. 1.17). Respect for them is a way of remembering the difference between the clean and unclean, the holy and the unholy.[124]

The inclusion of a command to be (ethically) holy is, Douglas thinks, in keeping with the ethical thrust of the preceding dietary regulations. This proposal appears to avoid the inconsistency in Milgrom's proposal in which

---

121. Douglas, 'The Forbidden Animals in Leviticus', p. 20.

122. For Douglas's proposal that Leviticus has a 'ring structure' see Douglas, 'The Forbidden Animals in Leviticus', p. 11.

123. Douglas, 'The Forbidden Animals in Leviticus', p. 20.

124. Douglas also finds it telling that Leviticus 19 begins with the same injunction to be holy that concludes Leviticus 11 ('The Forbidden Animals in Leviticus', pp. 20, 22-23).

he at one and the same time rejects the notion that P has an ethical view of holiness yet cites this view of holiness as the rationale for the food laws. Nevertheless, I shall argue below that Douglas's interpretation of Leviticus 11 suffers from a similar inconsistency in her use of literary sources.

Evaluation. Though Douglas's attempt to interpret the dietary regulations as facilitating the attainment of an ethical lifestyle is commendable, several of her exegetical arguments make her theory implausible. First, her attempt to show that the dietary regulations establish a relationship between the individual and the altar is unpersuasive. Most devastating for this idea is the fact that Leviticus 11 permits for food more than what is burnt on the altar. At the very least this is true of the consumption of fish (Lev. 11.9). Douglas attempts to avoid this plain reading of the text by appealing to Milgrom's idea that the fish are not considered 'unclean' but 'detestable' (שֶׁקֶץ).[125] Putting aside the fact that Milgrom's distinction between 'unclean' and 'detestable' is debatable (see see pp. 81-86) it is not clear how this argument avoids the fact that P permits the eating of fish. Moreover, that fish are included in Israel's diet undermines Douglas's suggestion that Israel's diet is limited to those animals raised within the covenant.

Douglas's appeal to the blood prohibition to establish an analogous relationship between the altar and the body is similarly unsatisfactory. Blood is not mentioned in Leviticus 11 and the prohibition against eating carnivorous birds seems to resonate with the emphasis in Leviticus 11 on the need to avoid death rather than blood. Even if it is possible that other passages imply a relationship between the blood prohibition and the fact that blood is not burnt on the altar (Lev. 7.26-27; 17.10-13), such an inference does not indicate that this idea is uppermost in the legislator's mind in Leviticus 11.[126]

---

125. 'Leviticus does not count those that swarm in the waters and in the air as unclean, they are merely abominable' (Douglas, *Jacob's Tears*, p. 173).

126. Douglas thinks that the idea of the blood prohibition is implied by the use of the verb אכל ('to consume') in Leviticus 11. 'Blood is not offered or burnt on the altar...the upshot of the law is that blood is not to be consumed (same word) either by the mouth or by flames on the altar' (Douglas, *Jacob's Tears*, p. 170). But it is not apparent that the verb אכל is used to establish a relationship between a prohibition against burning blood on the altar and against the consumption of blood by the Israelites. On one hand, in a chapter concerned with diet, this verb is required for practical rather than theological reasons. On the other hand, there *is no* explicit prohibition against the altar's 'consumption' of blood in Leviticus 1–7 that could be echoed in the legislation of Leviticus 11. Appendix 2 argues that the use of the verb אכל, with reference to the consumption of offerings on the altar, establishes a symbolic connection between the latter and the priests who 'consume' (אכל) parts of these offerings. Douglas herself admits this connection ('The Forbidden Animals of Leviticus', p. 19).

Second, the attempt to interpret those morphological characteristics, used to identify unclean animals, as symbolic of the vulnerable of society is shot through with difficulties. (1) The comparisons Douglas makes between 'blemishes' and 'injustice' rely on her proposed 'ring-structure' for Leviticus. However a recent critique of this structure makes its existence seem doubtful,[127] undermining the use of Leviticus 19 (i.e. the 'mid-turn of the ring') as the interpretative key for Leviticus 11 and Leviticus 21–22. (2) It is not evident that the principle of 'something lacking/something superfluous' is operative in all the cases of unclean animals in Leviticus 11 that are not explained by the 'blood prohibition'. This limitation in Douglas's argument is reflected in her appeal to morphological features that are not mentioned in relation to the eight creatures identified as 'unclean' in Lev. 11.29-30: 'Consider the list, especially the swarming insects, the chameleon with its lumpy face, the high humped tortoise and beetle, and the ants labouring under their huge loads.'[128] With the exception of 'swarming' (שרץ) these things are not mentioned. (3) It would seem inconsistent for the legislator to aim at inculcating respect for the vulnerable yet at the same time have the Israelites 'detest' (שקץ) those animals that symbolize them.[129] (4) Leviticus 11 exhibits no distinction between unclean animals that symbolize predatory behaviour and those that symbolize the vulnerable. How is one to determine when one animal teaches the avoidance of injustice (predatory behaviour) and another animal the need to love one's vulnerable neighbour?[130] (5) the context in which 'blemish' is

---

127. See Nihan, *From Priestly Torah to Pentateuch*, pp. 114-18. See also Watts, *Ritual and Rhetoric in Leviticus*, pp. 21-22; Trevaskis, 'The Purpose of Leviticus 24 within its Literary Context', 297.

128. Douglas, 'The Forbidden Animals of Leviticus', p. 22.

129. Douglas renders תשקץ as 'you shall utterly reject' in preference to the emotional overtones associated with the traditional rendering 'to abominate' or 'to detest'. She cites the absence of any use of 'vivid Hebrew pejoratives' for the שקץ animals. By translating the term to mean 'to shun', Douglas appears concerned to overcome the seemingly insurmountable problem that an animal created by God could be called abominable. For her, this problem disappears if one is simply 'to shun' these particular animals as being merely out of bounds to Israelites, rather than as something abominable *per se*. However, there are two problems with Douglas's reasoning. First, there is no textual evidence for rendering שקץ 'you shall utterly reject', that is, as an idiosyncratic use of this root. Second, the problem regarding how one of God's creatures could be termed 'abominable' is resolved if the said animals are symbolic of something that should be regarded as abominable. Below it is argued that this 'something' is the prospect of a life lived outside of Yahweh's immediate presence. See Douglas, *Leviticus as Literature*, pp. 166-69. See also Houston's critique of Douglas's rendering of שקץ in this way (Houston, 'Towards an Integrated Reading', p. 155).

130. Maccoby makes a similar criticism of Douglas in this regard. 'To be forbidden has in one case a negative connotation, and in the other a positive one, but this does not matter as long as some moral lesson can be drawn' (Maccoby, *Ritual and Morality*, p. 204).

used to refer to the result of an injustice done to another person (Lev. 24.16-22) does not support the symbolic interpretation Douglas gives this term. Rather, 'blemish' is a general term which describes the physical damage one may cause another person.

Third, Douglas's attempt to equate the underlying ethical concern of Leviticus 11 with the command to 'be holy' in Lev. 11.44-45 is liable to the same criticism of inconsistency applicable to Milgrom. In attempting to avoid the conclusion that some fish are considered 'unclean', she adopts Milgrom's source-critical analysis of Leviticus 11 by maintaining that P understood 'unclean' and 'detestable' animals as belonging to two different cultic categories, the latter not being viewed as 'unclean'.[131] But this forces Douglas to admit, with Milgrom, that Lev. 11.43-45 belongs to H since the terms 'unclean' and 'detestable' are used as synonyms. This has implications for her argument that the dietary regulations of Leviticus 11 are concerned with the maintenance of justice. Douglas contends that these regulations have something to do with this concern, because '[e]ncouragingly, 19.2 starts with the injunction to be holy, in the same way that ch. 11 ends'. But, if according to her Lev. 11.43-45 are written by H, the comparison she draws between Leviticus 11 (P) and Leviticus 19 (H) breaks down.

Finally, Douglas's theory of what ethical concerns underlie Israel's dietary regulations is vulnerable to many of the same criticisms levelled against Milgrom's explanation. To summarize, first, it is not possible to use Lev. 17.11 as evidence that Leviticus 11 is intended to inculcate a respect for animal life. Second, the restriction of Israel's diet to the clean animals does not imply that fewer animals are killed. Should we not expect that if the Israelites have an appetite for meat they will soon breed enough domestic clean animals to satisfy it? Milgrom attempts to counter this argument by claiming that an Israelite would not wish to deplete his livestock.[132] But why would Israel not produce more domestic animals? Moreover, Leviticus 11 does not prohibit the slaughter of unclean animals and one would think that a family would choose to exterminate animals that could otherwise make clean food and cooking utensils unclean (Lev. 11.29-38).[133]

---

131. A summary and evaluation of the distinction Milgrom makes between 'unclean' (טמא) and 'detestable' (שקץ) animals is offered on pages 83-87.

132. Milgrom, *Leviticus 1–16*, p. 735.

133. Against this possibility Douglas reasons that 'the verb to touch has also the idea of harming, damaging, laying hands upon as if to steal or strike'. While it is true that the root נגע can sometimes have the senses Douglas suggests, to automatically assume that it carries this general meaning in Leviticus 11 is to perform what Barr refers to as 'illegitimate totality transfer' (see Chapter 2). Several observations concerning how this verb is *used* within the present context prevent the conclusion Douglas makes. First, prior to Leviticus 11, the verb *may* carry a sense of violence only when its object is a human being. Second, in 12 of the 14 times the verb is used with an inanimate object it

In conclusion, the proposals made by Milgrom and Douglas concerning the ethical basis of Leviticus 11 seem unsatisfactory. This permits an examination of what other ethical rationale may underly this legislation. In contrast to the theories of Milgrom and Douglas, I shall ask whether the ethical concern of Leviticus 11 has to do with the observance of ethical commandments. Such a concern characterizes H's view of holiness and, if it is arguably present in Leviticus 11, this will increase the likelihood that H's command to 'be holy' in Lev. 11.43-45 makes explicit what is implicit within the preceding regulations. However, before an exegetical study of Leviticus 11 is undertaken I shall point out how my interpretative approach is different from that used by Milgrom and Douglas.

A Proposal for Reading the Ethics from, rather than beyond, the Text of Leviticus 11
The interpretative approach of Milgrom and Douglas tends to infer the underlying ethical concerns of Leviticus 11 from *beyond* the text. They reach beyond the text by seeking to infer the ethical intention of Leviticus 11 from what the enactment of the dietary regulations meant within the original socio-historical setting. In this regard, their methodology compares to that used in Gorman's study of ritual texts.[134] This observation is particularly true for Douglas. For example, in line with her assumption that impurity (pollution) must be understood against the 'normative scheme' of Israel's world, she proceeds to reconstruct this ideal ethic and then ask questions about how the regulations of Leviticus 11 may have served to facilitate Israel's adoption of this ethic. With regard to the latter, she often assumes that the text presupposes more than it does. For example, how does she know that certain animals are intended to recall the blemished priests and sacrifices of Leviticus 21–22? As argued above, this requires imagination rather than exegesis.

Similarly, Milgrom infers from texts outside Leviticus 11 that it is intended to inculcate an ethical respect for life and then attempts to explain how the dietary regulations may have contributed to Israel's adoption of this concern. The importance Milgrom attaches to conceptualizing 'what happened' is evident in his use of parallel texts to identify 'missing data'. For

---

occurs as part of a warning directed at the potential subject of the verb (Gen. 3.3; Exod. 19.12 [×2]; 29.37; 30.29; Lev. 5.2, 3, 7; 6.11, 20; 7.19, 21). The remaining two occurrences carry the neutral sense of physical touch (Gen. 28.2; Exod. 12.22). Third, it is argued below that נגע is a paradigmatic relation of שקץ in Leviticus 11 and this relationship suggests that it most likely carries the notion of warning rather than of doing harm to something. See Douglas, *Leviticus as Literature*, p. 142.

134. See Chapter 2.

example, though nothing is mentioned about the need for unclean persons to wash themselves in Leviticus 11, he argues that this is expected since this is the case in Lev. 17.15; 22.6.[135] This observation touches on the difficulty with the approach taken by Milgrom and Douglas to the text of Leviticus 11. Both scholars attempt to recover how the dietary regulations worked in practice in an effort to understand how they were understood. Chapter 2 argued that this approach fails to deal with the form these ritual prescriptions come to us, namely as a text. By contrast, the present study seeks to interpret the dietary regulations on the premise that they *are* literature. The difference is significant, since whereas Milgrom and Douglas attempt to infer what is missing in this text from elsewhere, the present study asks why the legislator chose to make no reference to certain things and why he emphasizes others. It assumes that an interfusion exists between the ethics and theology of Leviticus 11 and this text's literary art (see Chapter 2).[136]

An Examination of the Meaning of טמא *in Leviticus 11*

Although not explicitly stated as such in Leviticus 11, scholars typically classify its content as 'food/dietary laws'.[137] However, though dietary considerations comprise a significant part of this material, the chapter places emphasis on matters other than diet. For example, the prohibited animals, which include clean animals that die of natural causes (Lev. 11.31-32), defile not only by ingestion. Their carcasses convey 'uncleanness' when touched,[138] carried,[139] and via the defilement of items used for cooking otherwise clean food.[140] Moreover, matters such as the length of time one remains 'unclean',[141] and the purification/disposal of defiled clothes (vv. 25, 40) and vessels (vv. 32, 33, 35), are also dealt with. For this reason, the classification of Leviticus 11 as 'food/dietary laws' is potentially misleading. With this qualification in mind, I shall survey the structure and contents of Leviticus 11, paying close attention to the occurrence of the term טמא. After this, I shall suggest a possible symbolic meaning for this term and consider whether a possible ethical concern within these regulations anticipates H's call to 'be holy' in vv. 43-45.

---

135. Milgrom, *Leviticus 1–16*, p. 667.
136. Cf. Alter, *The Art of Biblical Narrative*, pp. 18-20.
137. Keil, *The Pentateuch*, p. 358; R.K. Harrison, *Leviticus* (Leicester: IVP, 1980), p. 120; Levine, *Leviticus*, p. 63; Gerstenberger, *Leviticus*, p. 131; Balentine, *Leviticus*, p. 94.
138. Verses 24, 26, 27, 28, 31, 36, 39.
139. Verses 28, 40.
140. Verses 32, 33, 34, 35, 38.
141. Verses 24, 25, 28, 31, 39, 40.

Structure and Content of Leviticus 11

Two explanations are commonly given for the significance of the structural units typically identified in Leviticus 11.[142] Some maintain that they reflect a slow process of development and that vv. 24-40, 43-45 and 46-47 are later insertions.[143] By contrast, other scholars argue that the respective units are arranged according to various categories of animals,[144] or seemingly arbitrary topics that relate to an individual's relationship to the creation and the covenant.[145] However, my aim is to ascertain the symbolic meaning of 'uncleanness', and whether there is an ethical concern associated with this, through inferences drawn from cases of deliberate rhetorical progression in Leviticus 11 (see Chapter 2).[146] That is, I shall assume that 'uncleanness' is a concept whose (symbolic?) significance for the individual is clarified as the chapter progresses from a general notion of unclean animals (Lev. 11.1-23) to the precise meaning and significance it has for the Israelites (Lev. 11.43-45). For reasons that will become clear in exegesis, I depart from the consensus and propose that Leviticus 11 comprises five structural units: vv. 1-23, which are unanimously agreed as relating to the identification of prohibited animals; the consequences associated with becoming 'unclean' are given in vv. 24-28; the symbolic significance of these consequences is revealed in vv. 29-42; the climactic vv. 43-45 provide a rationale for why one should avoid becoming 'unclean' and instead continue on in holiness, vv. 46-47 are a post-script to Leviticus 11.

Identification of the Prohibited Animals (Lev. 11.1-23)

Lev. 11.1-23 is concerned with the identification of clean and unclean animals and is further divisible according to the habitat of the specified creatures. The first sub-unit relates to animals that live on the land (vv. 2-8),

---

142. Verses 1-23, 24-40, 41-45, 46-47.

143. A. Bertholet, *Leviticus* (Tübingen: J.C.B. Mohr, 1901), p. 33; K. Elliger, *Leviticus* (Tübingen: J.C.B. Mohr, 1966), pp. 140-48; Milgrom, *Leviticus 1–16*, pp. 691-98; Gerstenberger, *Leviticus*, p. 132; In addition to these verses Houston regards vv. 41-42 as part of the H redaction (*Purity and Monotheism*, pp. 27, 33, 65).

144. Harrison, *Leviticus*, pp. 120-33; John H. Sailhamer, *The Pentateuch as Narrative* (Grand Rapids: Zondervan , 1992), p. 335.

145. Allen, P. Ross, *Holiness to the Lord: A Guide to the Exposition of the Book of Leviticus* (Grand Rapids: Baker Academic, 2002), pp. 258-59.

146. For literary progression as a rhetorical device, see Amit, 'Progression as a Rhetorical Device in Biblical Literature', pp. 3-32. To my knowledge Wenham is the only scholar to suggest that there is an element of thematic progression in Leviticus 11. He suggests that Lev. 11.24-45 answers questions that may have arisen out of the content of Lev. 11.1-23 (Gordon J. Wenham, *The Book of Leviticus* [Grand Rapids: Eerdmans, 1979], p. 176).

the second to creatures that 'swarm' (שרץ)[147] in the seas and streams
(vv. 9-12), the third to birds of the air (vv. 13-19), and the fourth to insects
that 'swarm' (שרץ) in the skies (vv. 20-23). These units prescribe what
animal carcasses from each respective habitat may not be 'eaten' (לא
תאכלו) or 'touched' (לא תגעו).[148] The classification of these species
according to the four categories employed in Genesis 1 is seen as significant
below.[149]

Nevertheless, the first unit (vv. 1-8) is distinguishable from the others in
vv. 1-23 by its unique description of the prohibited animals as 'They are
unclean for you' (טמא [טמאה] הוא לכם, vv. 4, 5, 6, 7, 8). By contrast, in
referring to any of the prohibited animals of vv. 9-23 the legislator says 'It is
detestable for you' (שקץ הוא לכם, vv. 12, 20) or 'They are detestable for
you' (שקץ הם לכם, vv. 10, 42).[150]

Milgrom attempts to identify the rationale underlying this transition from
'unclean' (טמא) to 'detestable' (שקץ),[151] arguing that it reflects a previously
unrecognized gradation in biblical impurity.[152] Moreover, he concludes that

---

147. שרץ is a collective noun including 'all small creatures that go about in shoals and
swarms, insects that fly in clouds, such as gnats and flies generally' (Snaith, *Leviticus
and Numbers*, p. 63).

148. Houston, following traditional Rabbinic exegesis (e.g. Rashi), assumes that the
prohibition against touching (vv. 8-40) has in mind an original festival setting, 'when it
was necessary for the ordinary Israelite to enter the sacred courts, and it would be a
serious offence to do so in a state of uncleanness'. He contends that a daily prohibition
against touching the carcasses of unclean animals 'would be wholly impractical; there
are many occasions in the ordinary course of life when it is necessary to touch and
indeed to carry the dead bodies of 'unclean' animals, for example to bury a dead donkey,
or to remove a dead mouse from the larder' (Houston, *Purity and Monotheism*, p. 39).
However, the impracticalities Houston and the rabbis suggest are easily surmountable
(i.e. 'There is more than one way to skin a cat'). One can tie a rope around a dead
donkey's hock and drag it away with a couple of live ones and a shovel would suffice for
removing a dead mouse from within one's home.

149. For the relationship between the animal categories of Leviticus 11 and Genesis 1
see Douglas, 'The Forbidden Animals in Leviticus', p. 16; Samuel E. Balentine, *The
Torah's Vision of Worship* (Minneapolis: Fortress Press, 1999), pp. 159-60.

150. 'They are detestable' (שקץ הם) is found in v. 13.

151. The root שקץ means to 'make detestable' and is associated with the feeling of
revulsion toward something. Michael A. Grisanti, 'שקץ', in *NIDOTTE*, I. (ed. W.A.
VanGemeren; Grand Rapids: Zondervan, 1997), pp. 243-46 (243-44). Snaith says that
שקץ refers to creatures that are ritually unclean and unfit for food, which have
something nasty about them. Snaith, *Leviticus and Numbers*, p. 63. Noordtzij notes that
elsewhere the term refers to things connected with the worship of foreign gods (Isa.
66.17 and Ezek. 8.10) (*Leviticus*, p. 124).

152. Milgrom, *Leviticus 1–16*, p. 659. This theory is not original to Milgrom. David
Hoffmann, following Rabbinic tradition makes the following conclusion concerning the
cultic status of שקץ animals. 'In Pesachim 23a wird aus letzterem Satze die Lehre gefolgert,

the synonymous use of the two terms in Lev. 11.43-45 is further evidence that these verses derive from H. This conclusion rests on his supposition that the blurring of terminological distinctions maintained in P is a characteristic trait of this source.[153] Before I can argue that the transition from טמא to שקץ reflects the use of literary art to achieve a symbolic purpose, Milgrom's suggestion, that it reflects different cultic categories, needs to be examined at some length.

The carcasses of animals that are טמא defile by ingestion or direct contact (Lev. 11.1-8; 24-40; 46-47). By contrast, a carcass of an animal labelled as שקץ makes one טמא only by ingestion. The evidence Milgrom offers as proof for this distinction in P is summarized and evaluated below.

First, outside of Lev. 11.43-45, Milgrom observes that the status of 'unclean' is restricted to animals that may make a person *ritually* unclean when their carcasses are either eaten or touched (v. 8). He claims that the same is not true of animals described as שקץ, because these are described as defiling by ingestion, not touch.[154] However, does the absence of the verb 'to touch' (נגע) in passages where the prohibited animals are described as שקץ necessarily imply that they do not make one unclean by touch? A consideration of the syntactical similarities between vv. 8 and 11, which relate to animals described as טמא and שקץ respectively, negates such a conclusion.

מבשרם לא תאכלו ובנבלתם לא תגעו[Lev. 11.8]

מבשרם לא תאכלו ואת־נבלתם תשקצו[Lev. 11.11]

The significant difference in syntax between these two verses is the replacement of ובנבלתם לא תגעו with ואת־נבלתם תשקצו in v. 11.[155] Given that each verse begins with a prohibition against eating the animals regarded as either טמא (v. 8) or שקץ (v. 11), and that the verbs תגעו (v. 8) and תשקצו (v. 11) share the same object (i.e. נבלה), it seems reasonable to assume that 'do not touch' (v. 8) and 'detest' (v. 11) are closely related in meaning.[156] Indeed, the emotional revulsion conveyed by the more forceful

---

dass man mit verbotenen Speisen auch keinen Handel treiben darf. Nur wenn die zufällig in unsern Besitz kommen (במזדמן), dürfen wir sie verkaufen.—ואת נבלתם תשקצו könnte einmal negative aussagen wollen, dass selbst die נבלה nur שקץ, aber nicht טמא ist' (David Z. Hoffmann, *Das Buch Leviticus.* I [Berlin: Poppelauer, 1905–1906], p. 333).

153. Milgrom, *Leviticus 17–22*, pp. 1327-30.

154. That is, with the exception of Lev. 11.43-44 (H), the verb נגע does not occur in passages where animals are described as שקץ (Milgrom, *Leviticus 1–16*, p. 656).

155. The use of the direct object marker in v. 11 does not diminish the similarity of these verses. For example, see the same phenomenon in relation to the root נפש in vv. 43-44. These verses are clearly parallel in meaning as argued by Milgrom, *Leviticus 1–16*, p. 683.

156. In a more technical sense they are *paradigmatic relations*. Though Noth assumes

שֶׁקֶץ appears to be a deliberate intensification of what is implied by the command לֹא תִגַּע. The urgent repetition of שֶׁקֶץ in v. 11 would also seem to add weight to this conclusion.[157] Thus, 'Not only must you refrain from touching (vv. 1-8), but absolutely detest these animals', possibly reflects the intention of this transition.[158] The significance this intensification has for a possible symbolic meaning of טָמֵא requires investigation. However, Milgrom's proposal for the underlying rationale of a distinction between שֶׁקֶץ and טָמֵא still requires some more assessment.

The rationale Milgrom offers for why the שֶׁקֶץ fish and birds are unable to defile by touch is their apparent marine origin. This conclusion is arrived at by way of the law given in v. 36:

> A spring or cistern in which water is collected shall remain pure, however, but whoever touches [in it] such a carcass shall be impure.[159]

In light of this verse, which indicates that water can convey impurity (vv. 34, 38) while its source remains pure, Milgrom suggests that since both fish and birds (i.e. שָׁרַץ) are created from the waters (cf. Gen. 1.20) then like the

---

that v. 11 refers to touching, he regards the verse as an interpolation owing to the repetition of the root שֶׁקֶץ. As I shall argue below, this repetition was a deliberate and emphatic intensification of the need to refrain from eating or touching unclean animals. See Noth, *Leviticus*, p. 93.

157. Milgrom himself notes the urgency conveyed by the repetition of שֶׁקֶץ in Lev. 11.11 (*Leviticus 1–16*, p. 656). The present final form interpretation of the transition from טָמֵא to שֶׁקֶץ in vv. 8-12 makes Houston's suggestion that v. 11 is a later insertion, on the basis that 'there is awkward repetition of the end of v. 10 at the beginning of the verse, but also the resumptive repetition in v. 12 of the substance of v. 10', unnecessary. These things appear to add to the intensification of the legislator's prohibition against even touching these animal carcasses. See Houston, *Purity and Monotheism*, p. 43.

158. Perhaps noteworthy, in this regard, is Firmage's explanation for why a prohibition against touching occurs in Lev. 11.8. In arguing that the laws concerning carcass contamination via contact are 'typologically speaking radically separable, and arise from different concerns', Firmage explains the presence of a command not to touch unclean animals in v. 8 as functioning to 'stress the absoluteness of the prohibition against eating'. I am contending, in a similar vein, that the requirement that the Israelites 'detest' these animals represents an intensification in the legislator's attempt to dissuade them from eating these animals. See Firmage, 'The Biblical Dietary Laws', p. 207.

159. Milgrom identifies this verse as seminal to the mishnaic ruling: 'all (utensils made from the skin of creatures) that are in the sea are pure' (*m. Kelim* 17.13; cf. *t. Kelim B Mes.* 7.4; *Sipra*, Shemini par. 6.9). However, the purpose of the rabbis seems more likely to have been to sanction the use of the skin of טָמֵא marine animals for the making of various utensils. To infer more from this ruling, as Milgrom does, seems speculative (Milgrom, *Leviticus 1–16*, p. 657).

waters they do not contaminate by touch.[160] But Milgrom is engaging in some special pleading here, for Gen. 1.20 does not identify water as the element from which fish or birds were created.

First, there are syntactical observations that negate Milgrom's claim that birds originated from the waters in Gen. 1.20.[161] Instead of taking יעופף as a jussive *polel* (i.e. 'let fly to and fro'), Milgrom translates the second verb as a relative clause:[162]

> God said, 'Let the waters bring forth swarms of living creatures, and birds
> that fly above the earth across the expanse of the sky.'

But this translation ignores the deliberate chiasmus of this verse (cf. Gen. 1.5, 10):

ישרצו המים שרץ נפש היה   Clause A

ועוף יעופף על־הארץ על־פני רקיע השמים   Clause B

In clause A the verb is followed by habitat (water), then the category of creature (swarming things) and finally a qualification of these creatures (living creatures). This order is reversed in clause B where the category of creature (winged creatures) is followed by the verb, then the habitat (sky) and finally a qualification of this habitat (firmament of the heavens). The placing of habitat first and last in clauses A and B, respectively, reflects the author's intention to emphasize that the creational acts (i.e. the jussive verbs), by which these habitats were filled, are distinctive yet simultaneous.[163] The following translation captures this intention:

> God said, 'Let the seas swarm with swarmers, living creatures and let birds
> fly to and fro above the earth across the firmament of the heaven.'

Translated in this way it is not possible to argue that 'birds were created out of water'.

Second, the claim that fish are created *out of* water in Gen. 1.20, in the same way that man is created '*from* dust of the ground (עפר מן־האדמה)' (Gen. 2.7), is unwarranted. Rather, המים as the subject of ישרצו simply

---

160. Milgrom, *Leviticus 1–16*, p. 658. Milgrom is followed by Klawans, *Impurity and Sin in Ancient Judaism*, p. 31.

161. Milgrom's contention that birds were created from המים is supported by John Calvin, *Genesis* (trans. John King; Grand Rapids: Eerdmans, 1948), p. 88; E.A. Speiser, *Genesis* (New York: Doubleday, 1964), p. 6; Nahum M. Sarna, *Genesis* (Philadelphia: Jewish Publication Society of America, 1989), p. 10.

162. Keil suggests that the tendency among scholars to translate v. 20 in this way follows the LXX rendering 'and with birds that fly (πετεινὰ πετόμενα)' (Keil, *The Pentateuch*, p. 60).

163. Gordon J. Wenham, *Genesis 1–15* (WBC, 1; Dallas: Word Books, 1987), p. 4. Wenham notes that the same use of chiasmus is evident in Gen. 1.5, 10.

means that God said 'let the sea swarm with swarmers, living creatures
(ישרצו המים שרץ נפש היה)'. The possibility that the waters are to
generate fish is excluded. In this regard, Claus Westermann favourably
quotes W.H. Schmidt:

> 'V. 20a is not stating that the sea is to generate the water animals, but merely
> that these animals are to swarm in the water, that is to be present there.'
> Nothing more than this is intended.[164]

Thus Milgrom's claim that fish are created *out of* water is not supported by
Gen. 1.20 and this is further evidence for viewing the rationale he offers for
what he argues is a cultic distinction between שקץ animals and those called
טמא as implausible.

Having rejected the distinction Milgrom makes between the terms טמא
and שקץ, we can return to the observation that שקץ represents an intensification of the command לא תגעו in Lev. 11.8. This observation may suggest that there is more to the regulations of Lev. 11.1-23 than food, for the
progression from 'do not touch a carcass of an טמא animal' (vv. 1-8) to
'detest such a carcass' (vv. 9-23) would not seem to leave a reader satisfied in
knowing what animals they may/may not eat. Surely it raises the question of
what threat is posed by the carcass of an 'unclean' animal that they should
'detest' it. As God's creatures (Genesis 1) it seems improbable that there is
anything innately detestable about them. It remains possible that the intended
reader would ask questions about what these animals symbolize that makes
them 'detestable'. For my purposes, this use of literary progression as a
deliberate rhetorical device within vv. 1-23 suggests that we may find the
answer to what is symbolized in the material that follows. To anticipate, I
shall argue that the legislator addresses the consequences of eating/touching
the prohibited animals in vv. 24-28.[165] However, what is symbolized by

---

164. Claus Westermann, *Genesis 1–11* (London: SPCK, 1984), p. 136. Similarly,
Leupold states that 'here the situation is not analogous to the work of the third day,
where "the earth brought forth." Here it is not the waters that bring forth... The optative
of the verb *šaraṣ* followed by the cognate object *šereṣ* here must mean: "Let the waters
swarm with swarms." ...We simply do not know from what source fish and birds sprang.
They are simply bidden to people in their respective domains' (H.C. Leupold, *Exposition
of Genesis* [London: The Wartburg Press, 1942], p. 78).

165. Approached in this way, vv. 24-40 do not appear to be a later insertion (*pace*
Noordtzij, *Leviticus*, p. 126; Milgrom, *Leviticus 1–16*, p. 667). Noordtzij concludes they
are an insertion because, whereas they relate to contact with unclean carcasses and
associated consequences, the rest of the chapter is preoccupied with distinguishing
between animals. However, surely distinguishing between animals will raise the question as to why a distinction needs to be made. Moreover, there is a progression across
the chapter that has gone unnoticed by scholars.

'uncleanness' and its associated consequences is not explicitly answered until vv. 29-38.[166]

The Consequences Associated with Becoming טמא (Lev. 11.24-28)[167]
In the second literary unit (Lev. 11.24-28), the consequence of touching an 'unclean' animal carcass is revealed and this provides the rationale for why one should 'detest' (שקץ) such animals (cf. vv. 9-23).[168] Three observations signify that this is the purpose of this pericope. First, contra what might be expected if the threat of טמא is limited to the sanctuary, only its effect on the person is mentioned in these verses. The legislator explains that upon eating or touching the carcass of an 'unclean' animal, a person becomes 'unclean' (יטמא, vv. 24, 25, 26, 27, 28).[169] Second, the transition to the objectively phrased third person in these verses should not be missed.[170] This similarly indicates that the legislator's interest has shifted from the identity of 'unclean' animals to the effect that they have on an individual. Third, the root שקץ does not occur, which also appears to reflect a shift of emphasis from the source of 'uncleanness', which they must 'detest', to its consequences.[171] The root שקץ does not recur until vv. 41-42 where the emphasis returns to the avoidance of the source of 'uncleanness'.

The consequence of becoming 'unclean' is disclosed within this unit (i.e. vv. 24-28): a person would 'become unclean until evening' (יטמא עד־הערב, vv. 24, 25, 28). Since this is the only penalty associated with

166. Thus, note the use of progression as a rhetorical device in Leviticus 11. This observation cautions against the view that Leviticus 11 is composite. For an exception to this consensus see Wilfried Warning, *Literary Artistry in Leviticus* (Leiden: E.J. Brill, 1999), pp. 49-56.

167. It is my conviction that a change in emphasis, to the indirect means of becoming טמא and its association with מות, warrants viewing vv. 24-28 and 29-42 as distinct literary units. This view runs contrary to the general approach of scholars who argue that vv. 24-40 represent a single (and later) literary unit.

168. Houston recognizes the change in emphasis in vv. 24-40 but concludes that they have in mind the regular impracticalities arising from the 'do not touch' law. 'The eventualities in mind are probably only such regular domestic problems as the death of the old donkey, or the removal of dead dogs from the yard or dead mice from the storeroom' (Houston, *Purity and Monotheism*, pp. 49-50). But this explanation does not account for the progression from the consequence (you will become unclean) to eight particular animals that threaten to make clean food unclean (vv. 29-38), and then clean food that becomes unclean (vv. 39-42).

169. Indeed, in v. 26b the object of תגעו is not even mentioned. This observation provides further evidence that it is the actions, and their associated consequences, of the individual that are of interest to the legislator in this pericope.

170. Observed by Noth, *Leviticus*, p. 94.

171. The legislator does not indicate that a person can become שקץ until v. 43, after the full significance of its symbolic meaning is revealed (vv. 29-42).

becoming 'unclean' in Leviticus 11, it seems reasonable to assume that what is symbolized by יטמא עד־הערב is what necessitates one to 'detest' unclean animals (cf. vv. 9-23).[172] This possibility gains persuasiveness in view of the omission of purification rites for people in Leviticus 11. Despite Martin Noth's claim that no such procedures are required for this kind of impurity, the requirement for such ablutions is implied from elsewhere (Lev. 17.15).[173] Indeed, their omission becomes striking when it is recognized that purificatory rites are included for clothes (vv. 28, 40) and cooking utensils (v. 32), but not people. Given that this omission is probably deliberate, we must ask what it reveals about the legislator's purpose.

Negatively, the omission of purificatory rites possibly prevents the conclusion that the laws narrowly serve the cultic purpose of protecting the sanctuary from an accumulation of טמא. It seems likely that these rites would be included if that were the case.[174]

Positively, the omission of purificatory rites indicates that the legislator wishes to stress the consequence of becoming 'unclean', namely the individual remains טמא *'until evening'*. But the real significance of this penalty lies behind what it means to be unclean 'until evening'. A period of uncleanness is associated with a period of exclusion from the sanctuary (Lev. 12.4b). Thus, Milgrom is right in suggesting that the omission of purificatory rites serves to make the person's exclusion from the holy sanctuary until after evening emphatic. In other words the the implication of becoming 'unclean'

---

172. Milgrom suggests that there are no penalties associated with becoming טמא in Leviticus 11 unless the purificatory ablutions were neglected. However, this claim that there is no penalty associated with becoming טמא in Leviticus11 appears to be negated by the revulsion an Israelite was to exhibit toward these animals and the fact that the legislator focuses his attention on the consequences for the individual rather than the sanctuary. See Milgrom, *Leviticus 1–16*, p. 653.

173. As pointed out by Milgrom, there is an obvious omission of any instructions for purification in these verses. The non-mention of ablutions indicates that it is the actual consequence of defilement that is emphasized (i.e. exclusion from Yahweh's immediate presence). That they are implied is pointed out by Milgrom (i.e. Lev. 17.15; 22.6). He also observes that the purification of utensils and laundering of clothes implies how much more a person would need to undergo ablutions (vv. 25, 28, 40b. cf. Lev. 15.5, 6, 7, 8, 10, 11, 13 etc.). See Milgrom, *Leviticus 1–16*, p. 667. Similarly, Keil assumes ablutions were necessary after evening (*The Pentateuch*, p. 368). Snaith departs from the consensus by suggesting that these verses refer to a secondary uncleanness not requiring ablutions. But, if so, why the emotional שקץ? See Snaith, *Leviticus and Numbers*, p. 66.

174. Milgrom himself argues that the only reason that a חטאת was to be brought for a person who had become defiled in the way anticipated by Lev. 5.2-4 was because they had failed to undergo the required purificatory rites (*Leviticus 1–16*, pp. 297-99, 310-14). For a critique of Milgrom's argument see Kiuchi, *The Ḥāṭā' and Ḥaṭṭā't*, pp. 13-14.

is that one is excluded from the sanctuary until evening.[175] Yet what could be the significance of such exclusion that it requires one to שקץ the source (i.e. טמא) of exclusion (cf. vv. 9-23)? I have already rejected Milgrom's cultic view that it is a preventative measure taken to protect the sanctuary from the 'forces of death'. We seem justified in enquiring what this exclusion symbolizes that made it so abhorrent to the Israelites.

The symbolism of an 'unclean' person's exclusion from the sanctuary is arguably revealed in the next section of Leviticus 11, namely vv. 29-40. The next section argues that this person's experience is symbolic of the penalty of 'death' (מות) experienced by Adam and Eve upon eating the fruit of the tree of good and evil (Genesis 3). In this sense, *the status of* טמא *would symbolize the consequence of rebelling against Yahweh, namely exclusion from His immediate presence.*[176] Since the reader is persuaded to avoid such exclusion, presumably by observing Yahweh's cultic *and* ethical commandments, this would imply that these regulations have an ethical concern.[177] Moreover, this ethical concern would seem comparable with that which characterizes H's view of holiness.

The Symbolic Significance of טמא *(Lev. 11.29-42)*
Verses 29-42 comprise the third literary unit of Leviticus 11. They are unified by the legislator's concern to dissuade the Israelites from becoming 'unclean' by means of clean food that has become defiled. However, this unit divides further into material dealing with the defilement of clean food by the dead

175. '[D]efiled means disqualified for approaching the tabernacle' (Douglas, *Jacob's Tears*, p. 169).
176. It is necessary to qualify the nature of the divine presence lost as 'immediate' because Yahweh continues to relate to people after Adam and Eve's expulsion from the Garden and this implies a degree of presence. Nevertheless, that the qualitative aspect of divine presence diminishes after the expulsion of Adam and Eve seems to be assumed in the rest of the Pentateuch. For example, below I shall argue that a parallel is drawn between Yahweh's presence in the Garden of Eden and the Tabernacle. If this argument is accepted then the prohibition against all people, with the exception of the priest on the Day of Atonement (cf. Leviticus 16), from entering the most holy place where Yahweh is visibly present above the ark would seem to emphasize that the Israelites enjoy only a restricted access to Yahweh's presence.
177. One may ask why I presume that it is 'cultic and ethical commandments' that the Israelites must keep. It is because, elsewhere in the Pentateuch, exile (i.e. exclusion from God's immediate presence) represents the fate of Israel if it disobeys Yahweh's cultic and ethical commandments (e.g. Leviticus 26).
The present study is not in disagreement with Klawans's suggestion that the impurity arising from cultic and ethical transgressions must be thought of as two distinctive categories. However, where my proposal differs from Klawans is that I argue that Israel's cultic impurity system was intended to persuade the Israelites to observe both cultic *and* ethical commandments. See Klawans, *Impurity and Sin in Ancient Judaism*, pp. 43-60.

carcasses of eight specified animals that שרץ on the ground (vv. 29-38; 41-42) or by natural death itself (vv. 39-40). As observed for vv. 24-28, the root שקץ does not occur in vv. 29-38 or 39-40 either.[178] This is probably because the emphasis is on the need for the Israelites to avoid becoming טמא (i.e. excluded from the sanctuary), by association with clean food that becomes defiled, rather than on specific unclean animals.[179] However, the root does occur again in vv. 41-42 where the direct danger posed by eating prohibited animals that שרץ on the ground is again of interest.

Lev. 11.29-40 continues the literary progression, so far seen to be characteristic of Chapter 11, and reveals that the symbolic meaning of טמא overlaps with the meaning of מות ('death', vv. 31, 32, 39). First, the eight טמא creatures listed in v. 29 defile people or cooking utensils only 'when dead' (במתם, vv. 31, 32).[180] Thus, when one of these animals is מֵת it threatens to make the source of food and water 'unclean' (vv. 31, 32, 33, 34, 35,[181] 38[182]).[183] The masculine noun מות refers to a state opposite to life (Deut.

---

178. Nevertheless, Liss has made the stimulating speculation that the use of שקץ in this chapter may be related to the term used to describe reptiles etc (i.e. שרץ). Thus, though the former term does not occur in this section, perhaps the sound of שרץ is still intended to evoke feelings of revulsion towards these animals. See Hanna Liss, 'Ritual Purity and the Construction of Identity', p. 9.

179. As pointed out by scholars, given the small size and relatively large numbers of the eight named animals mentioned in v. 29, it is difficult to imagine the kind of defilement described in vv. 32-38 being completely preventable. What scholars seem to have overlooked is that this observation may indicate that the emphasis is on the individual's need to avoid *food* which has come from these unclean sources.

180. Milgrom, on Lev. 11.31, suggests that the reference to the animals as 'dead' is required because these things were so repulsive that one might have thought touching them alive would have made one unclean. Therefore, the legislator underlines that the problem occurs when they are 'dead'. He proposes that the use of במתם rather than 'carcasses' (בנבלתם) might be because במתם occurs in v. 32. Moreover, he claims that its use in v. 32, in preference to בנבלתם (cf. v. 24b) served to emphasize that these animals need not be dead the moment that they fall into the vessel in order to defile (*Leviticus 1–16*, pp. 672-73; cf. Wenham, *Leviticus*, pp. 178-79). The plausibility of this suggestion is undermined by two observations. First, there is no reason why the legislator should establish that one of these animals could defile after dying *within* in a vessel. Would not the use of בנבלתם still warn an Israelite off eating food made in a vessel in which one of these animals fell into and later died? Second, as is argued below, it ignores the significance of the use of במתם within this context, namely in its description of an animal's rather than a human's death.

181. Note that in the case of vv. 35-38 the carcass is of a שרץ animal that has died.

182. I assume that water 'put on the seed' may imply that this seed was destined to grow crops for eating.

183. Of importance are the parenthetical remarks that whereas water taken from an unclean vessel is itself unclean (v. 34), the source of water remains clean (v. 36). Verse 36 serves to guarantee that purification from uncleanness is always available.

30.15, 19, 2 Sam. 15.21) which is brought about by either natural or violent means.[184] Since מות is predominantly used of humans in the OT its reference to animal carcasses in vv. 31 and 32 is striking. In fact, whereas the noun occurs numerous times with reference to human death, it is used with reference to animals only in Lev. 11.31-32 and Eccl. 10.1.[185] Elsewhere, animals that die of natural causes are referred to as נבלה (Lev. 7.24; 17.15; 22.8; Deut. 14.21;[186] Job. 42.8; Ezek. 44.31).[187] Ezek. 44.31 even distinguishes between those animals that have נבלה (i.e. of natural causes) and those that have been torn by wild animals. Thus, the legislator's use of מות in Leviticus 11 is possibly a deliberate attempt to imply what it means to become 'unclean' and why one's exclusion from the sanctuary is undesirable.[188] That is, one's status as 'unclean' is in some way connected with the concept of מות. This suggestion becomes more plausible when the occurrence of the verb ימות in Lev. 11.39 is considered.

Despite the fact that the verb ימות is used elsewhere of animals in the OT, albeit rarely,[189] its occurrence in v. 39 has even more significance than the

---

184. F. Brown, S.R. Driver and C.A. Briggs, *A Hebrew and English Lexicon of the Old Testament* (Oxford: Clarendon Press, 1929), p. 559; Koehler and Baumgartner, *The Hebrew and Aramaic Lexicon of the Old Testament.* II, pp. 563-64.

185. With regard to Eccl. 10.1, Michael Fox argues that זבובי מות means 'deadly' or 'doomed' flies, rather than 'dead flies'. Yet he suggests that since flies are not deadly, it is better to redivide זבובי מות to read זבוב ימות. This re-division of the text would result in Eccl. 10.1 reading 'no sooner does a fly die than it decays and spoils the ointment' (Michael V. Fox, *A Time to Tear Down and a Time to Build Up: A Rereading of Ecclesiastes* [Grand Rapids: Eerdmans, 1999], p. 301). If Fox is correct, the use of the noun מות to describe the state of a dead animal is restricted to Leviticus 11.

186. The use of נבלה rather than במתם in the dietary laws of Deut. 14.3-21 merits special mention because scholars have long debated the historical relationship between the two passages. However, the different terminology used of death may suggest that other differences in these laws reflect a difference in authorial purpose.

187. Milgrom notes that the term נבלה is generally defined as the carcass of an animal that was neither killed nor slaughtered but died naturally (*Leviticus 1–16*, p. 653). The term is sometimes used to describe humans who have died as a result of judgment: slaughtered men (Gen. 34.27); a women stoned to death (Deut. 22.21); a person executed by fire (Josh. 7.15).

188. It does not appear to be a reference to the prohibition against eating animals which have become the prey of other animals (cf. Exod. 22.30). As Harrington points out, 'Exodus forbids eating prey but says nothing about an animal which has died of old age (Exod. 22.30)' (Hannah Harrington, *The Purity Texts* [London: T. & T. Clark, 2004], p. 84).

189. The verb is elsewhere used of the death of cattle (Gen. 33.13), fish (Exod. 7.18; Ps. 105.29), frogs (Exod. 8.9), lions (Eccl. 9.4), worms (Isa. 66.24) and dogs (1 Sam. 24.15). By comparison, it is used with reference to human death more than 700 times (Koehler and Baumgartner, *The Hebrew and Aramaic Lexicon of the Old Testament.* I, pp. 562-63).

occurrence of the noun in vv. 31-32; for whereas מות is presented as the *indirect* agent of defilement in vv. 29-30 (i.e. the 'dead' [מות] *animals* are the *direct* means by which otherwise clean food is made 'unclean'), vv. 39-40 identify death as the direct agent by which the carcasses of clean animals are defiled. As if to emphasize this point, the clean animal is identified as a clean quadruped (i.e. 'from a beast that is for you to eat' [מן־הבהמה אשר־היא לכם לאכלה], v. 39a). Thus, the clean quadruped, the animal sacrificed and eaten by the Israelites, becomes a meal of 'uncleanness' through its direct association with מות. When they 'die' (מות), these animals may still look deceptively 'good and pleasing to the eye' for food, but they are dangerous to eat or touch because they render one 'unclean'—excluded from the sanctuary.[190]

The persuasiveness of this suggestion increases when it is observed that without מות having theological significance in vv. 39-40 the prohibition against touching dead (נבלה) animals in vv. 24-28 becomes redundant. As Houston observes,

> if the dead bodies of animals pollute, unless correctly slaughtered for food, which unclean animals cannot be, there is nothing distinctive to be said about unclean animals in this connection and hence no connection between the subjects of diet and contact pollution.[191]

Houston concludes that 'it seems likely that vv. 39-40 is secondary in relation to vv. 24ff., adding a reference to a subject dealt with at greater length in ch. 17'.[192] However, since it is not clear to me why 'it seems likely' that these verses are secondary, it seems safer to rely on a final form interpretation. This does not pose any problems to exegesis when the uniqueness of the use of מות in connection with an animal is taken into account: when a clean animal 'dies' (מות), it makes those who eat it unclean. In this way the legislator makes a connection between the notions of מות and טמא.

But why should an animal's 'death' (מות) render one 'unclean' and what does this indicate about the abhorrence of exclusion from the sanctuary? In my view the deliberate use of מות, instead of נבלה, in vv. 31, 32 and 39, is meant to recall the first מות experienced by mankind, namely that described in Genesis 3. It is perhaps significant that the root מות first occurs within the Garden of Eden narrative (Gen. 2.17; 3.3, 4). However, before linking what is symbolized by מות in Genesis 3 with what is symbolized by טמא in

---

190. Against Milgrom, who considers vv. 39-40 as fitting 'into no sequence, either in the bloc [i.e. vv 24-40] or in the rest of the chapter', the position of this pericope dealing with quadrupeds is meaningful when approached in this way. Note that בהמה means quadruped since it is specified as such in Lev. 11.2-3 (Milgrom, *Leviticus 1–16*, p. 692).

191. Houston, *Purity and Monotheism*, p. 52.

192. Houston, *Purity and Monotheism*, p. 52.

Leviticus 11, it is essential to provide evidence that Genesis 2–3 is assumed by Leviticus 11.[193] This is especially the case since scholars generally view Genesis 2 and 3 as part of the source J rather than P.[194]

EXCURSUSES

Evidence Suggesting Intertextuality between Genesis 2–3 and Leviticus 11

In making a case for viewing Genesis 2–3 as important for the interpretation of Leviticus 11, I shall begin by arguing that the Garden of Eden narrative contains sanctuary symbolism. This argument aims to establish that exclusion from the sanctuary may symbolize Adam and Eve's exclusion from the Garden. After this I shall examine whether certain literary features of Leviticus 11 may allude to the Garden narrative in Genesis.

Sanctuary Symbolism in the Garden of Eden Narrative (Genesis 2–3)

Wenham argues that 'sanctuary symbolism' permeates the Garden of Eden narrative (Genesis 2–3), identifying eight such symbols.[195] First, the term used to describe the divine presence in the tabernacle (הִתְהַלֵּךְ) is also used of Yahweh walking in the garden (Gen. 3.8; Lev. 26.12; Deut. 23.15; 2 Sam. 7.6-7). Indeed, even without this verb the presence of God within both the Garden (Gen. 2.15, 19, 21) and sanctuary would seem enough to establish a relationship between them.[196] Second, entrance to both garden and sanctuary

---

193. It is true that allusions to creation motifs and a sanctuary, both of which are common to ANE literature, are not necessarily allusions to a body of literature about creation or a sanctuary. However, if one takes a synchronic approach to the Pentateuch the probability that an allusion to Genesis 1–3 is made must surely increase. Thus, the present argument proceeds on the assumption that the implied Israelite reader of Leviticus 11 would probably make specific connections with Genesis 1–3 in addition to general ANE notions of creation and sanctuary.

194. E.g. Herman Gunkel, *Genesis* (1901; Macon, GA: Mercer University Press, 1997), pp. 4-15; Speiser, *Genesis*.

195. Gordon J. Wenham, 'Sanctuary Symbolism in the Garden of Eden Story', in *Proceedings of the Ninth World Congress of Jewish Studies, Division A: The Period of the Bible* (Jerusalem: World Union of Jewish Studies, 1986), pp. 19-25. See also D.W. Parry, 'Garden of Eden: Prototype of Sanctuary', in *Temples of the Ancient World* (ed. D.W. Parry and S.D. Ricks; Salt Lake City: Deseret, 1994), pp. 126-52; Kiuchi, *Leviticus*, pp. 29-30.

196. David P. Wright, 'Holiness, Sex, and Death in the Garden of Eden', *Biblica* 77 (1996), pp. 305-29 (307).

is restricted to the east (Gen. 3.24; Ezek. 10.19; 11.1; 43.1-4).[197] Third, he cites the work of Carol Meyers who claims that the 'menorah' (מנרה) of the tabernacle (Exod. 25.31-35) is stylized on the Tree of Life (Gen. 2.17; 3.22).[198] Fourth, the description of Adam's job 'to serve and to keep' (לעבדה ולשמרה, Gen. 2.15) is elsewhere used to describe the Levites's guarding and ministering duties in the sanctuary (Num. 3.7-8, 8.26, 18.5-6).[199] Wenham adds to this apparent priestly role of Adam the observation that Yahweh clothed (לבש) Adam and Eve (Gen. 3.21) as Moses clothed (לבש) Aaron and his sons (Exod. 28.41, 29.8, 40.14; Lev. 8.13). Fifth, it is suggested that the rivers of Genesis 2 resonate with Ezekiel's vision of rivers flowing from the temple in Ezek. 47.1-12. Sixth, the precious stones found within the rivers of Genesis 2 are attached to the priestly garments (Exod. 25.7; 28.9-14, 20).[200] Seventh, God's emplacement of Cherubim (כרבים) to guard (לשמר) the eastern access to the Garden (Gen. 3.24) is recalled by the use of Cherubim as a decorative feature of sanctuaries.[201] Finally, he draws a

197. Wenham, 'Sanctuary Symbolism', p. 21.

198. Carol L. Meyers, *The Tabernacle Menorah* (Missoula, MT: Scholars Press, 1976). Wright questions whether the botanical features of the menorah are convincing enough to make it symbolic of the Tree of Life in Genesis 2–3. However, he does not indicate why, nor does he interact with Meyers. See Wright, 'Holiness, Sex, and Death in the Garden of Eden', p. 312. More recently, Andreas Ruwe has suggested that the menorah may not only reflect the Garden of Eden narrative, but may also allude to the seven-fold structure of Genesis 1. See Andreas Ruwe, *'Heiligkeitsgesetz' und 'Priesterschrift': literaturgeschichtliche und rechtssystematische Untersuchungen zu Leviticus 17:1–26:2* (Tübingen: J.C.B. Mohr [Paul Siebeck], 1999), pp. 324-25.

199. Wright adds that '[s]upport for this interpretation of the verb *šāmar* comes from the end of the Garden story where duties of working and guarding are reiterated. The man is to continue his working (*ʿābôd*), but now outside of the garden: "God Yahweh sent him from the Garden of Eden to work (*la ʿābôd*) the land from which he was taken" (3.23). The duty of guarding (*šāmar*) is also repeated, but is reassigned to the *kĕrubîm*. They are to protect the garden from encroachment: "(Yahweh) stationed *kĕrubîm*, and the flame of the whirling sword on the east of the Garden of Eden to guard (*lišmor*) the way of the tree of life" (3.24)' (Wright, 'Holiness, Sex, and Death in the Garden of Eden', p. 308).

200. Wenham, 'Sanctuary Symbolism', pp. 400-404. Wright's suggestion that these are less convincing than the other data Wenham uses in arguing that there is sanctuary symbolism in Genesis 2–3 is only of concern if the overall argument is not persuasive which does not seem to be the case. See Wright, 'Holiness, Sex, and Death in the Garden of Eden', p. 312.

201. Exod. 25.18-22; 26.1, 31; 36.8, 35; 37.7-9; Num. 7.89; 1 Kgs 7.29; 8.6-7; 2 Chron. 3.7, 10-14; 5.7-8. See Wenham 'Sanctuary Symbolism', p. 21. In this connection, Stordalen comments that '[t]he frequent occurrence of cherubs in cultic setting [*sic*] corresponds to the apprehension of the shrine as a door to heaven' (T. Stordalen, *Echoes of Eden: Genesis 2–3 and Symbolism of the Eden Garden in Biblical Hebrew Literature*

parallel between the threats posed by the fruit of the tree of the knowledge of good and evil, in the Garden (Gen. 2.9, 3.6), and the ark of the covenant, in the holy of holies. The former, while 'pleasant to the sight, good for food and to be desired to make one wise', would cause one 'to die' (מות) when eaten (Gen. 3.4). Death is also the penalty associated with touching the latter (Exod. 25.16, Deut. 31.26).

We may cite two additional arguments in favour of the view that a literary connection exists between the Garden of Eden and Israel's cultic sanctuary. The first, suggested by Calum Carmichael, is a common concern to avoid an awareness of nakedness in both places. According to Carmichael, the law which prohibits a priest from showing his nakedness within the sanctuary (Exod. 20.26) draws attention to the shame associated with Adam and Eve's awareness of their nakedness in the Garden (Exod. 20.26; cf. Gen. 3.7).

> The rule [i.e. Exod. 20.26] should be read as a symbolic reminder. Human beings had provoked the deity by their awareness of nakedness in their first encounter ever with God in the garden. Therefore, at times when man attempts to approach God at an altar, he should take measures to keep himself from becoming aware of nakedness in order to avoid repeating Adam and Eve's provocation.[202]

Second, a parallel threat is arguably posed to post-Garden humans who would attempt to approach either Garden or sanctuary. In the Garden this is a 'flaming sword' (להט החרב, Gen. 3.24) and in the sanctuary it is consumption by divine fire (Lev. 10.1-3).[203]

Thus, there appears to be enough evidence to suggest that there is a symbolic relationship between the tabernacle and the Garden of Eden. It remains for me to demonstrate that this relationship is alluded to within the prescriptions of Leviticus 11. This will help to strengthen the proposal that a period of 'uncleanness' symbolizes Adam and Eve's 'death' after rebelling against Yahweh in Genesis 3.

[Leuven: Peeters, 2000], p. 293). In support of his argument Stordalen cites E. Brovarski, 'The Doors of Heaven', *Orientalia* 46 (1977), pp. 107-15, and Claus Westermann, *Genesis 12–36* (Minneapolis: Augsburg, 1985), pp. 456-57.

202. Carmichael views the exposure of nakedness as provocative to God in the sense that it reflected that humans had attempted to become godlike (Calum M. Carmichael, *The Origins of Biblical Law: The Decalogues and the Book of the Covenant* [Ithaca, NY: Cornell University Press, 1992], p. 77). Contra Wright, if this insight is correct it supports Wenham's suggestion that the shared vocabulary concerning the clothing of Adam and Even and the priests is significant. See Wright, 'Holiness, Sex and Death in the Garden of Eden', p. 313.

203. Perhaps the need to approach the sanctuary with sacrificial blood is an additional sign of the threat the sanctuary poses to post-Garden humans?

Allusions to the Garden of Eden Narrative in Leviticus 11

Inferences Drawn from the Structural Arrangement of Leviticus 11–15
That Leviticus 11 alludes to Genesis 2–3 is possibly inferred from an investigation into the rationale governing the arrangement of purity topics in
Leviticus 11–15. Two attempts have been made to understand the arrangement of this material in terms of its reference to Genesis 1–3. First, John
Sailhamer suggests that the legislator's use of the four creational categories
of animal classification in Leviticus 11 (i.e. land animals, birds, water creatures and 'small creeping things') is a deliberate allusion to Genesis 1.[204]
Moreover, the topic of the unclean parturient (Leviticus 12) alludes to the
problems women would have bearing children after humankind's exclusion
from the Garden (Gen. 3.16) and the purification of individuals suffering with
a particular skin disease (צרעת, Leviticus 13–14) is related to God's covering of man's nakedness (Gen. 3.21). Unfortunately, he does not explain how
the uncleanness associated with genital discharges (Leviticus 15) fits into
such a schema.

Second, Kiuchi has similarly argued that these chapters (Leviticus 11–15)
relate directly to the narrative of Genesis 2–3. Beginning with his existential
translation of טמא as meaning 'a state of hiding oneself' (i.e. an allusion to
the hiding of Adam and Eve in the Garden of Eden)[205] Kiuchi makes the following inferences regarding the arrangement of Leviticus 11–15 in relation to
Genesis 2–3. First, he suggests that the unclean animals of Leviticus 11
exhibit feature(s) of the serpent (Genesis 3).[206] Second, the 'unclean' parturient of Leviticus 12 is thought to assume the pain of childbirth associated with
God's judgment (Gen. 3.16a).[207] Third, he suggests that the sections dealing
with menstrual blood (Leviticus 12; 15.19-30) and semen (Lev. 15.1-18)
allude to the hiding of Adam and Eve since they relate to the most *hidden*

204. Sailhamer, *The Pentateuch as Narrative*, pp. 332-35. Douglas appears to be the
first scholar to have taken the Genesis 1 background to Leviticus 11 seriously in
interpretation. See Douglas, *Purity and Danger*, p. 54. Milgrom also assumes 'that Lev
11 is rooted in Gen 1' (Milgrom, *Leviticus 1–16*, p. 47).

205. Kiuchi, *A Study of Ḥāṭā' and Ḥaṭṭā't*, pp. 67-68.

206. He refers to the occurrence of גחן ('belly') in Lev. 11.42, the only occurrence of
this root outside of Gen. 3.16, as the strongest evidence for this possibility. However, he
lists other serpent-like features as follows: 'swarming on the ground (thus, direct contact
with the ground is also suggested), amphibious, having no leg to walk by…hiding itself
in dark places, being unable to move straight, swallowing food, its tongue being split'
(the latter two are argued to be the opposite of chewing the cud and divided-hoofs
respectively). According to Kiuchi, creatures having features that are remote from the
features of the serpent are called 'clean' (*A Study of Ḥāṭā' and Ḥaṭṭā't*, p. 105).

207. Presumably Kiuchi means that the parturient is deemed טמאה because she is
symbolic of life under God's judgment outside of the Garden of Eden.

parts of the human body. Finally, he similarly proposes that the condition of צרעת in Leviticus 13–14 refers to Adam and Eve's 'hiding' in the Garden. This is in line with his contention that the purpose of this particular law is to force a טמא (read 'hiding') person to uncover himself before the priests.[208]

Though one may not agree that Leviticus 11–15 is structured according to the narrative of Genesis 2–3, and despite the obvious lack of agreement between these two theories, these scholars do appear to have identified some deliberate allusions to Genesis 1–3 in Leviticus 11–15. However, an even stronger case can be made with respect to Leviticus 11.

Allusions to Genesis 2–3 within Leviticus 11

The material of Leviticus 11 makes a number of allusions to the creation account of Genesis 1 and the Garden of Eden narrative (Genesis 2–3). First, most commentators acknowledge that the author of Leviticus 11 has classified animals according to the same categories mentioned in the account of creation, namely 'swarming' (שרץ) water creatures (Gen. 1.20; Lev. 11.10); 'birds' (עוף) of the sky (Gen. 1.20; Lev. 11.13); 'living creatures' (נפש היה) that live upon the earth (Gen. 1.24; Lev. 11.2) and 'creeping things' (רמש, Gen. 1.24; Lev. 11.20, 44[209]).[210]

Second, within the narrative of the Pentateuch, Leviticus 11 records the third time in which God's assignment 'of all' (מכל) a particular food source to humans is accompanied by a prohibited food source (לא תאכל, Gen. 2.16-17; 9.3-4; cf. Lev. 11.4, 8). That both Gen. 2.16-17 and 9.3-4 come within creational contexts is significant given our observation that Leviticus 11 classifies animals in accordance with how this is done in the creation account of Genesis 1.[211] Thus, it would appear that the concept of 'food

---

208. Kiuchi maintains that the 'seeing' of the priests is representative of the 'seeing' of God. See N. Kiuchi, 'A Paradox of the Skin Disease', *ZAW* 113 (2001), pp. 505-14.

209. Although רמש does not occur in Lev. 11.20, שרץ is widely regarded as its synonym.

210. Many scholars acknowledge a correspondence between the classification of animals in Genesis 1 and Leviticus 11 without arguing that the latter alludes to the former. So Wenham, *Leviticus*, pp. 165, 170; Gerstenberger, *Leviticus*, p. 132; Houston, *Purity and Monotheism*, pp. 33-35; Balentine, *Leviticus*, p. 95; Balentine, *The Torah's Vision of Worship*, pp. 159-60; Kiuchi, *Leviticus*, p. 210. Though Milgrom does not specifically say that the categorization of animals in Leviticus 11 alludes to that found in Genesis 1, he does say 'that Lev 11 is rooted in Gen 1' (Milgrom, *Leviticus 1–16*, p. 47).

211. For the symbolism of new creation in Genesis 9 see Wenham, *Genesis 1–15*, pp. 206-207. Erhard Blum shows an awareness of the relationship between these food prohibitions when he makes the following comment. 'Der hier und in Lev 11 so betonte Sinn gerade der Speisegebote als Aspekt der privilegierenden Heiligung »für« Jhwh lenkt aber insbesondere den Blick zurück auf die Bedeutung der Speisegebote in einem früheren Zusammenhang, Gen 1 und 9: *Markierte dort die Freigabe tierischer Nahrung*

prohibition' in Leviticus 11 is meant to invoke the idea that Israel is experiencing a new beginning in God's immediate presence, a point not previously observed by scholars.

Third, as pointed out by Douglas, Milgrom and Kiuchi, the Hebrew term גחון ('belly'), which occurs in Lev. 11.42, is used elsewhere in the OT only of the serpent in Gen. 3.14. The possibility that this term's occurrence in Leviticus 11 is a deliberate allusion to the serpent seems to increase with the use of the verbs הלך ('to go') and אכל ('to eat') in both Lev. 11.42 and Gen. 3.14, and perhaps even the (unexpected?) absence of the serpent from Leviticus 11.[212] Although I do not entirely agree with Kiuchi's claim that serpent-like features are exhibited by all the unclean animals in Leviticus 11, this seems possible for the eight animals mentioned in Lev. 11.29-30.[213] In addition to the fact that these animals שרץ on the ground, two more observations suggest that the choice of the eight animals that 'swarm on the ground' is an intentional allusion to the serpent of Genesis 3.[214] First, rather than described as an unclean source of food, these animals are described as a *means* of defilement for clean food.[215] This characteristic of these animals resonates with the presentation of the serpent as the *means* by which Eve was tempted to eat the forbidden fruit (Gen. 3.1-6). Second, the statement concerning these animals in Lev. 11.29a that '[t]hese for you are unclean, of swarmers that swarm upon the earth (וזה לכם הטמא בשרץ השרץ על־ארץ)' should also be taken into account. In view of the fact that these eight animals do not comprise the only שרץ animals that were considered

(nach dem ursprünglich strikten Verbot) *die Distanzierung Gottes gegenüber seiner Schöpfungswelt, so ist hier seine erneute (partielle) Zuwendung verbunden mit einer Einschränkung der tierischen Nahrung*' (Erhard Blum, *Studien zur Komposition des Pentateuch* [Berlin: W. de Gruyter, 1990], pp. 323-24).

212. Kiuchi, *A Study of Ḥāṭā' and Ḥaṭṭā't*, p. 105.

213. See also the comments made by Keil, *The Pentateuch*, p. 372. It may not matter that a 'mouse' does not share the anatomical features of the serpent. We are dealing with literature, and the principles around which these eight creatures cohere seem to be the notions of moving on the ground and their particular ability to exclude a person from God's presence. Both of these things may encourage a comparison of these animals with the serpent of Genesis 2–3.

214. One might ask, 'Why, if this material is intended to allude to the serpent, is the serpent itself not mentioned?' In answering, I would suggest that to do so may have 'short-circuited' the rhetorical progression that characterizes this text. Moreover, I would ask why one should expect it to be made explicit?

215. Contra Milgrom, it should be noted that it is possibly this characteristic of these animals which excludes them from being referred to as שקץ. That is, the emphasis of this passage is on avoiding the food these animals defile, rather than avoidance of these animals *per se* (although see vv. 31, 36). Milgrom argues that they do not fall into the so-called category of שקץ because they were the רמש made on the land (Gen. 1.24) rather than from the sea (i.e. Gen. 1.20) (*Leviticus 1–16*, p. 658).

טמא (Lev. 11.41),[216] how should we understand the comparative force of
בשרץ? I would tentatively suggest that these eight 'serpent-like' animals are
singled out as those the Israelites must watch more carefully than the other
unclean שרץ: 'Watch them, they are cunning! They have the ability to have
you excluded from the sanctuary via their ability to defile food that is good
and pleasing to the eye.'[217]

Finally, the penalty associated with eating or touching 'unclean' carcasses
in Leviticus 11 is one's exclusion from the sanctuary 'until evening'. This
consequence possibly alludes to the penalty experienced by Adam and Eve
upon eating the forbidden fruit, namely *their exclusion from Yahweh's immediate presence* (Gen. 3.23-24), an exclusion which turned out to be the symbolic meaning of מות (cf. Gen. 3.4). However, the assumption that מות
carries this symbolic meaning requires some defense in view of Barr's
contention that 'death' does not represent divine punishment in Genesis 2–
3.[218] He contributes two arguments in support of this interpretation.[219]

First, he argues that the phrase 'on the day' (Gen. 2.17b) implies that the
couple should have physically died on the day they ate the prohibited fruit if
'death' is divine punishment. Second, on the day Adam and Eve ate the fruit
Barr contends that the resultant punishment is confined to the realm of work.

> His punishment is that the ground is put under a curse…it is pain and failure
> in work, toil and frustration in toil, and the final frustration is death, the final
> proof, far off in the future, that all this work will get him nowhere. On the
> contrary, his death will mean his own returning to that same refractory soil
> which has made his life so bitter. His death is not the punishment, but is only
> the mode in which the final stage of punishment works out.[220]

Yet Barr does not consult an article by R.W.L. Moberly which accounts for
both of these observations in a way that indicates that 'death' is the divine
punishment experienced by Adam and Eve in Genesis 3.[221]

---

216. I have already argued above that 'detestable' (שקץ) animals were regarded as
'unclean' (טמא). It makes no difference whether v. 41 is the work of H, as proposed by
Houston, since even if it is conceded that H confused P's terminology scholars do not
suggest that it also added to the stock of unclean animals that 'swarm on the earth'. Thus,
we may assume that P was aware of unclean animals that 'swarm on the earth' in addition
to the eight mentioned in vv. 29-30. See Houston, *Purity and Monotheism*, p. 65.

217. As Keil points out, more fear was associated with these animals because they
could more easily defile (by dying and falling on something) than other unclean animals
(*The Pentateuch*, p. 370).

218. James Barr, *The Garden of Eden and the Hope of Immortality* (London: SCM
Press, 1992), pp. 8-11.

219. Barr, *The Garden of Eden*, p. 8.

220. Barr, *The Garden of Eden*, p. 9.

221. R.W.L. Moberly, 'Did the Serpent Get It Right?' *JTS* 39 (1988), pp. 1-27. Barr
acknowledges this article in a more recent response to Moberly's criticism of his

First, with regard to the prepositional phrase ביום, Moberly proposes that it possibly refers to 'when' rather than a literal day.[222] He likewise observes that thoughtביום אכלך may be translated as 'on *the* day', this rendering is not absolutely required by the Hebrew. Moreover, 'if a writer wished unambiguously to ensure the sense "on *the* day", it would be necessary to use the definite article with יום and employ a different construction, for example, 'ביום אשר תאכל.[223] Thus, contra Barr, there may be no reason to expect that Adam and Eve should physically die on the very day they ate the forbidden fruit.

Second, Moberly points out that it is unnecessary to expect that the promise 'you will surely die' has in mind physical death. The term מות may be used as a metaphor.

> The justification for such an approach is the fact that 'death' and 'life' are both terms that in religious and moral contexts are inherently suggestive of metaphorical senses in which they apply to the quality of human life, rather than its mere presence or absence. Such metaphorical, qualitative usage is well attested elsewhere in the Old Testament. In Deuteronomy, for example, life and death are set before Israel (Deut. 30.15, 19), and while their meaning no doubt includes the literal sense of existence and non-existence, the primary concern of the text is the quality of life that will characterize Israel's occupation of the land. The fact that 'life' is linked with good and blessing, and 'death' with evil and curse, makes this clear.[224]

In defense of this non-literal reading of 'death' in Genesis 2–3, Moberly points out that it is 'the Hebrew understanding of life under Torah, as classically expressed in Deuteronomy, that has set the context for Genesis 3, in Gen. 2.15-17'.[225]

---

interpretation of Genesis 2–3, but he does not develop his argument, in this regard, any further. See Barr, 'Is God a Liar? (Genesis 2–3)—and Related Matters', *JTS* 57 (2006), pp. 1-22.

222. He observes that it carries such a meaning in Gen. 2.4; 5.1-2; Exod. 32.34; Num. 3.1; 2 Sam. 22.1; Isa. 11.16.

223. Moberly, 'Did the Serpent Get It Right?', p. 14.

224. He adds that a similar view of life and death is present in Proverbs (Moberly, 'Did the Serpent Get It Right?', p. 16).

225. Moberly, 'Did the Serpent Get It Right?' p. 16; cf. pp. 4-5 where he argues that 'death as a result of disobedience to Torah, such as in Deut. 30.15, 19, may also be present in the Genesis narrative'. Barr is scathing in his criticism of Moberly's proposal that 'you will surely die' refers to an accursed life, saying '[o]f course the nouns "death" and "life" are found in religious and moral contexts that apply to the quality of human life. But this cannot be taken up and transferred to apply to God's words "you will surely die" spoken to Adam and Eve in Gen. 2.17. That God, speaking to the primitive pair about the dangers from the tree, was saying to them "in the day you eat of it you will surely suffer a serious diminution of the quality of life" will not be taken seriously in the

Moberly's assessment of what 'death' means in Genesis 2–3 seems to make more sense of the plain reading of this narrative than Barr's. Moreover, it stands in continuity with the punitive function ascribed to death in this passage within the scholarly tradition. Thus, we may put aside Barr's interpretation and continue with our exegesis on the assumption that 'death' is a punishment experienced by Adam and Eve after they rebel against God in the Garden. The death in view is a life lived in exclusion from God's immediate presence, a kind of living death, and includes the termination of life in which people return to the dust from which they are made.

In conclusion, our investigation makes it seem likely that the legislator deliberately alludes to the creation account of Genesis 1 and the narrative of the Garden of Eden (Genesis 2–3) in Leviticus 11. It seems reasonable to assume that the root מות is employed in vv. 31, 32 and 39 to indicate the symbolic meaning of טמא, namely a punitive '*exclusion from Yahweh's immediate presence*'. This interpretation implies that the purpose of these regulations extends into an ethical realm because to avoid the reality symbolized by 'uncleanness' (i.e. 'death') one would be encouraged to observe both the cultic and ethical commandments.[226] In the event that טמא is found to mean more than 'cultic/ritual uncleanness', we are invited to ask how this concept may relate to the dynamic concept of קדש in Lev. 11.44-45. This task is made especially urgent considering that the ethical concern I have assigned to Leviticus 11 (P) would seem comparable with that which characterizes H's view of holiness. To this task we now turn by way of exegesis of Lev. 11.43-45.

Exegesis of Leviticus 11 Continued

A Rationale for Being קדש rather than Becoming טמא (Lev. 11.43-45)
The hortatory style of Lev. 11.43-45, which includes a command for the Israelites to 'be holy', is unique within Leviticus 1–16. Some scholars attempt

---

scholarly world. The proposal might at the most be included among the many marginal possibilities that have been put forward, but as the definite and correct answer it has no chance of acceptance' (Barr, 'Is God a Liar?', p. 12). But in response to Barr one might point out that the threat of suffering 'a serious diminution of the quality of life' in the form of exile from Canaan was to be taken seriously by the Israelites (Lev. 26.14-46; Deut. 28.15-69). Scholars are aware of an analogous relationship between Adam and Eve's expulsion from the Garden and the threat that Yahweh would exile Israel from (the Garden of) Canaan so that it might not be as difficult to accept Moberly's proposal as Barr thinks.

226. The possibility that this interpretation is correct increases if one accepts Moberly's suggestion that the nature of Adam and Eve's 'death' is similar to that associated with 'disobedience to Torah'.

to reconcile the requirement to be קדש with the dietary regulations by suggesting that God requires the Israelites to display *cultic* holiness.[227] That is, the Israelites were to be a ritually 'clean' group of people among the 'unclean' nations.[228] Conversely, other scholars, while often concurring that these verses expected Israel to be ritually different from the nations, conclude that the hithpael התקדש, and the associated command to הייתם קדשים, are simply a reflection of H's view of holiness.[229]

However, both these positions result from an interpretation of טמא as meaning no more than 'cultic/ritual uncleanness', that overlooks the possible symbolic meaning this term has in Leviticus 11. The present study argues that the status of טמא represents a person's punitive 'exclusion from Yahweh immediate presence'. We are now in a position to reconsider how the call to be קדש in Lev. 11.43-45 relates to the instructions on טמא in Leviticus 11.

That Lev. 11.43-44 are climactic to Leviticus 11 is inferred from their deliberate 'symmetric, introverted structure', identified by Milgrom:

Verse 43	A	You shall not make yourselves (נפשתיכם) detestable with any creature that swarms.
	B1	You shall not make yourselves unclean therewith and thus become unclean
Verse 44	B2	For I Yahweh am your God.
	B'1	You shall sanctify yourselves and be holy,
	B'2	for I am holy.
	A'	You shall not defile yourselves (את־נפשתיכם) with any swarming creature that moves upon the earth.

---

227. Ross, *Holiness to the Lord*, pp. 250-51; Wenham, *Leviticus*, pp. 170, 180; Houston comments that the use of holiness terminology in the context of vv. 44-45 'extends the ritual situation to the continuous life of the people, rather than implying an ethical reference, as in the Holiness code itself' (Houston, *Purity and Monotheism*, p. 248).

228. Though foreign land and food are called טמא (Am. 7.17; Hos. 9.3), it is possibly noteworthy that this term is never applied to foreign peoples in the OT and, recently, Christine Hayes has argued that there is no developed notion of inherent Gentile impurity within the OT and the Second Temple Period. Of particular significance is her suggestion that, within the Pentateuch, the impurity of Gentiles is contingent upon their engagement in immoral acts. See Christine E. Hayes, *Gentile Impurities and Jewish Identities* (Oxford: Oxford University Press, 2002), pp. 20-24.

229. Milgrom argues that 'The separation of the animals into the pure and the impure is both a model and a lesson for Israel to separate itself from the nations. The latter have defiled themselves by their idolatry and their immorality. Israel must, therefore, refrain from partaking of their practices and, thereby, become eligible for a life of holiness—the way and nature of its God' (*Leviticus 1–16*, p. 689). Likewise Snaith claims that the holiness of vv. 44-45 is ritual holiness, rather than moral holiness (*Leviticus and Numbers*, p. 67; cf. Houston, *Purity and Monotheism*, pp. 237-38, 248).

The intensity of these climactic verses is also underscored by the first use of שקץ to describe what a person would become upon defilement. There appears no reason not to think that this transition reflects a deliberate intensification as was earlier demonstrated for the replacement of לא נגע with שקץ (cf. vv. 8 and 11).[230]

Two observations regarding vv. 43-44 will facilitate our understanding of how the command to be קדש relates to the instructions concerning טמא. First, with regard to the use of 'you shall not make yourselves detestable' (אל־תשקצו, v. 43), we must ask to whom the Israelites will become detestable (שקץ)? In view of my contention that the concept of טמא is related to God's expulsion of Adam and Eve from the garden, are we not to conclude that the defiled person is likewise shunned as repulsive by God? Thus, lines A and A' demand Israel not to act in a way that will result in God's exclusion of them from his immediate presence. Such a demand implies that they presently enjoy this quality of divine presence.

Second, a deliberate intensification in these verses is evident from the provision of 'your persons' (נפשתיכם, vv. 43, 44) as the object of שקץ and טמא respectively. Milgrom chooses to translate נפש to mean 'throat' on the grounds that defilement by eating is clearly on view.[231] While the root נפש can sometimes mean 'throat',[232] however, Milgrom overlooks that elsewhere in Leviticus it means strictly 'person' or 'life'.[233] Nevertheless, 'throat' and 'life' are closely related by 'breath', a core semantic element of נפש,[234] so that a word-play is possibly made on the root: by eating טמא food, the Israelites would at once defile their 'throats' *and* have their 'persons' excluded from Yahweh's immediate presence.

These points suggest that the main purpose of the preceding instructions pertaining to טמא are aimed at warning Israel against having themselves excluded from God's immediate presence as Adam and Eve were before them. The call to be קדש (vv. 44-45) must be understood against this background. The two כי clauses (B2, B'2) are pivotal to such an understanding because they provide rationales for the immediately preceding statements (B1, B'1).[235] Since God is קדש, the Israelites must not live in such a way that will exclude them from his presence, but be קדש. Viewed in this way, the command to be קדש should be understood as a command to remain in his קדש

---

230. See pages 86-87.

231. Milgrom, *Leviticus 1–16*, p. 684.

232. H. Seebass, 'נֶפֶשׁ', in *TDOT*, IX (ed. G.J. Botterweck and H. Ringgren; Grand Rapids: Eerdmans, 1975), pp. 497-519 (505).

233. Lev. 2.1; 4.2; 5.1, 4; 7.20, 27; 15.17; 17.11; 22.11.

234. D.C. Fredericks, 'נֶפֶשׁ', in *NIDOTTE*, III (ed. W.A. VanGemeren; Grand Rapids: Zondervan, 1997), pp. 133-34 (133).

235. Milgrom, *Leviticus 1–16*, p. 684.

presence. This finding is corroborated by the additional rationale given for being קדש in v. 45a: 'I am Yahweh who brought you up out of Egypt to be your God'. The loss of presence experienced by Adam and Eve is regained through Israel's redemption from Egypt. This renewed divine presence is apparently the underlying rationale for the prescriptions concerning טמא in Leviticus 11.[236] The food prohibitions allude to humankind's creation in God's presence. The significance of this allusion would not have been missed. Their ancestors's eating forbidden fruit was in fact an eating of death: they were excluded from Yahweh's immediate presence. Leviticus 11 asks them not to make the same mistake of eating themselves out of Yahweh's immediate presence. This time the forbidden fruit is unclean animals, yet the taking and eating of them represented the same offence Adam and Eve commit against God. For this reason, the commands to התקדש and היתם קדשים should not be viewed as a command of initiation, but of continuation. They are to continue on in their holiness. But this is a provocative statement, since most scholars regard only the sanctuary, its equipment and the priests as holy in Leviticus 1–16. Thus, Chapter 5 will inquire to what extent the text of Leviticus 1–16 presents the Israelites as קדש in the sense that has been argued here.

The present study should not be understood as denying that the food laws made a distinction between 'holy' Israel and the 'unholy' nations.[237] The point

---

236. The importance of God's liberation of Israel from Egypt for understanding the rationale underlying this legislation is probably underscored by an *inclusio* in Leviticus 11 formed by the use of the root עלה. Gary Rendsburg observes that the use of the participle המעלה ('the one who brought up') is the only time in the Pentateuch where the root עלה occurs in the first person to describe God's redemption of Israel from Egypt. Apart from this occurrence the term הוציא is used. Rendsburg concludes that the rare use of המעלה in Lev. 11.45 is explained by the frequent use of the root עלה to describe the 'bringing up' of ingested food by ruminants in vv. 3, 4 (×2), 5 and 6. See Gary A. Rendsburg, 'The *Inclusio* in Lev. xi', *VT* 43 (1993), pp. 418-21.

237. My conclusion is not mutually exclusive of the common view that clean/unclean animals represent Israel/non-Israel. The following statement by Wenham is representative of this view. 'The division into clean (edible) foods and unclean (inedible) foods corresponded to the division between holy Israel and the Gentile world. Among those animals that were clean there were a few types that could be offered in sacrifice. Similarly there was a group of men within Israel who could offer sacrifice, namely the priests. Through this system of symbolic laws the Israelites were reminded at every meal of their redemption to be God's people. Their diet was limited to certain meats in imitation of their God, who had restricted his choice among the nations to Israel. It served, too, to bring to mind Israel's responsibilities to be a holy nation' (Wenham, *Leviticus*, p. 170; see similarly Milgrom, *Leviticus 1–16*, pp. 724-25; Lester L. Grabbe, *Leviticus* [Sheffield: JSOT Press, 1993], p. 59). The correspondence Wenham draws attention to receives textual support from Lev. 20.24b-26 for which Milgrom has proposed has the following chiastic structure (Milgrom, *Leviticus 17–22*, pp. 1760-61).

of contention between the present study and the traditional interpretation of Lev. 11.43-45 concerns the nature of the holiness commanded. The latter assumes that the Israelites became cultically holy by observance of the food laws and that it was this that distinguished them from the nations. Only secondarily did this separation from the nations encourage them to be ethically holy. By contrast, my study claims that the nature of holiness commanded is partially ethical. Of course there would be a cultic distinction between Israel and the nations, but this is on the plane of 'clean' *versus* 'unclean'. The real distinction that is encouraged is not only cultic but also ethical (cf. Leviticus 18–20).

A question arising from the present Chapter, concerning the nature of uncleanness in Leviticus 11, is whether the relative loss of divine presence is limited to a practical exclusion from the sanctuary or to a broader experience than this. I shall attempt to answer this question after I have attempted to confirm that the term 'uncleanness' also symbolizes a person's exclusion from Yahweh's immediate presence in Leviticus 12–15. But to anticipate, it would seem that an individual's exclusion from the sanctuary, on account of whatever kind of uncleanness, fulfils an educational function within Israel. The 'death' of Adam and Eve leads to the frustration of the Garden quality of life they lived in God's immediate presence. The 'uncleanness' of a person represents this 'death' as a *threat* to the Hebrew audience: Israel, analogous

A   24bI Yahweh am your God
          who has set you apart (הבדלתי) from all peoples
          B   25aAnd you shall distinguish (הבדלתם) between the clean and
                   the unclean quadrupeds and between the unclean and the clean
                   birds.
          B'   25bYou shall not make yourselves detestable with a quadruped or
                   bird or anything with which the ground swarms, which I have
                   set apart (הבדלתי) for you to treat as unclean.
A'   26You shall be holy to me, for I Yahweh am holy
          and I have set you apart (אבדל) from other peoples to be mine.

Both structure and the fourfold use of the verb 'to separate' (בדל) would seem to forge a correspondence between clean/unclean animals and Israelites/non-Israelites. If so, this means that the dietary laws might have encouraged the Israelites to separate themselves from the 'unclean' non-Israelite peoples.

However, in my opinion, this conclusion does not deny the possibility that the unclean animals of Leviticus 11 represent the temptation to rebel against Yahweh. To the contrary, non-Israelite practices are often presented as a means by which the Israelites may abandon their covenant allegiance. Thus, the food laws probably do both. On the one hand, they encourage the Israelites to separate from non-Israelites. On the other hand, as literature they remind the Israelites not to embrace the customs of the non-Israelites because this will result in death.

to Adam as she is, has the hope of Garden living before them in Canaan.[238]
As Adam and Eve's death is not simply physical but a frustrated experience
of life, so too is Israel's death (i.e. exile from Canaan) viewed as the frustration of living without God's blessing (cf. Leviticus 26). If this interpretation
is correct it may mean that Leviticus 11 (P) aims to persuade the Israelites to
avoid the reality standing behind 'uncleanness' (i.e. exile) by encouraging
them to observe Yahweh's cultic and ethical commandments. Such a concern
would not appear to be very different from the ethical concern which
characterizes H's view of holiness.

Conclusion

The present Chapter has examined Leviticus 11 to see if the explicit command to 'be holy' (vv. 43-45), commonly assigned to H, explicates what was
already implicit within P's 'dietary regulations' (vv. 1-42). It argues that the
legislator used rhetorical progression to direct an audience, familiar with
Genesis 1–3, to the symbolic meaning of these regulations. First, the food
prohibitions recall Yahweh's command that the first humans should not eat
the forbidden fruit: *to eat unclean food represents one's rebellion against
God's will*. Second, the consequence of eating 'unclean' food, namely becoming 'unclean till evening' (טמא עד־הערב), represents the consequence of
'death' (מות) experienced by Adam and Eve after they rebelled against
Yahweh in the Garden: *to become 'unclean till evening' was to be excluded
from Yahweh's immediate presence at the sanctuary on account of the rebellion symbolized by eating or touching what was forbidden*. Though the
relatively short period of uncleanness which prevented one from approaching
the sanctuary may seem insignificant, it symbolized the prospect of exile
from the promised land. Interpreted in this way, the 'dietary regulations' were
intended to dissuade the Israelites from experiencing exile as a consequence
of rebelling against Yahweh's will. This would imply that there is an ethical
concern underlying Leviticus 11. Not a general ethical concern for the Israelites to 'respect life' (*pace* Milgrom and Douglas), but a concern that the
Israelites should live lives of cultic and moral integrity. Since this ethical
concern does not seem different from that which characterizes H's view of
holiness, H's command to 'be holy' in Lev. 11.43-45 may explicate the symbolic meaning of P's 'dietary regulations'. If this suggestion is correct, P's
concern that the Israelites should conform themselves to Yahweh's will may
reflect part of its view of holiness. However, before this hypothesis can be

---

238. For the analogy between the Garden of Eden and the 'promised land' see Magnus
Ottosson, 'Eden and the Land of Promise', in *Congress Volume: Jerusalem 1986* (ed.
J.A. Emerton; Leiden: E.J. Brill, 1988), pp. 177-88.

tested further, Chapter 4 will furnish additional support for the proposal that a period of 'uncleanness' symbolizes one's punitive 'exclusion from Yahweh's immediate presence' by examining the meaning of 'uncleanness' in some of P's remaining purity regulations (Leviticus 12–15).

Chapter 4

MORTAL 'FLESH' (בשר) AS SYMBOLIC SOURCE OF 'UNCLEANNESS' (טמא) IN LEVITICUS 12–15

Introduction

Chapter 3 argued that the command to 'be holy' which concludes Leviticus 11 (vv. 43-45) may explicate P's own view of holiness. My analysis of P's 'dietary regulations' proposed that, as literature, they persuade the Israelites not to rebel against Yahweh as the first humans did in the Garden, urging them to 'be holy' (Lev. 11.43-45). Within this analogy, a person's status as 'unclean' (טמא) symbolizes Adam and Eve's punitive exclusion from Yahweh's Garden presence. However, since this argument departs from the consensus, that P's concept of holiness is devoid of ethical concerns, it is necessary to demonstrate that the symbolic meaning I assigned to 'uncleanness' in Leviticus 11 is consistent with the use of this term in the remaining 'purity regulations' (Leviticus 12–15). This study should add to the persuasiveness of the argument made in Chapter 3 that P has an interest in the ethical lives of the Israelites that is similar to that found in H.

Owing to the large size of Leviticus 12–15, the present study focuses on identifying what rationale may underlie the 'uncleanness' associated with the disease called צרעת in Leviticus 13.[1] Even so, time is still devoted to exam-

---

1. The traditional rendering of the term צרעת as 'leprosy' follows the LXX translation of this term as λεπρα. It is noteworthy that this Greek term does not refer to what modern medicine refers to as leprosy or Hansen's Disease and it is certain that the latter is not the disease diagnosed in Leviticus 13. Indeed, acknowledging that scientists have yet to identify a disease that accounts for the various symptoms, particularly the rapid rate at which צרעת is presumed to spread in Leviticus 13, Milgrom speculates that we are not dealing with a single real disease at all. Rather, we are in the realm of ritual (see similarly *m. Neg.* 3.1; 12.1; Heinisch, *Das Buch Leviticus*, p. 60). This understanding seems correct, especially considering that this disease also infects inanimate objects such as garments (Lev. 13.47-59) and houses (Lev. 14.33-53). We may speculate that the legislator has selected several diseases to draw on their symbolism in much the same way as he has done with animals in Leviticus 11 (see Chapter 3 and Appendix 1). In line with this suggestion, it is argued below that these diseases of skin and inanimate objects are selected and arranged to achieve a theological, rather than medical, purpose. See

ining some of the surrounding purity laws, namely those for the unclean mother (Leviticus 12) and the uncleanness associated with discharges from sexual organs (Leviticus 15), to see if these support my interpretation of Leviticus 13.[2]

The results of Chapter 3 have a bearing on the hermeneutic employed in the present study. First, my exegesis will presuppose that the status of 'unclean' is symbolic for humanity's exclusion from God's immediate presence (cf. Genesis 3).[3] An effective use of symbolic language requires that once a symbolic meaning is assigned to a particular term, this term should retain its symbolic meaning as it recurs throughout the rest of the text.[4] In the event that the same symbolic meaning is not evident for 'uncleanness' in Leviticus 12–15 it will falsify my interpretation of Leviticus 11. Conversely, if there is evidence that it retains the same meaning in these chapters, then the

Milgrom, *Leviticus 1–16*, p. 817. See also John Wilkinson, 'Leprosy and Leviticus: A Problem of Semantics and Translation', *SJT* 31 (1978), pp. 153-66; Levine, *Leviticus*, p. 75; Hartley, *Leviticus*, p. 186; Harrington, *The Purity Texts*, p. 88. In an effort to respect the author's decision to refer to multiple diseases with the one term, the present study will not offer a translation of צרעת. It is my view that scholars who have rendered this term differently according to the nature of the infected object may have detracted from the overall symbolic meaning of Leviticus 13–14. For example, most scholars translate it as 'leprosy' or 'scale disease' when applied to humans, but as 'mildew' when applied to inanimate objects. To my knowledge, only Hoffmann consistently translates צרעת as 'leprosy' (i.e. 'Aussatz') throughout Leviticus 12–15 (Hoffmann, *Das Buch Leviticus*, pp. 357-432). For an investigation into the impact the mistranslation of the term צרעת as 'leprosy' has had on modern sufferers of this disease see Gilbert Lewis, 'A Lesson from Leviticus: Leprosy', *Man* 22 (1987), pp. 593-612.

2. The present study does not examine the prescriptions for the purification of a person healed from צרעת (Lev. 14.1-32) and the צרעת-afflicted house (Lev. 14.33-53). To interact with these texts would not contribute significantly to the argument being made here and would needlessly take up considerable space. Nevertheless, my explanation for the symbolic meaning of the prescriptions in Leviticus 13 has significance for the meaning of כפר in Leviticus 14 and I intend to expand on this subject in a forthcoming article. To anticipate, I argue that by overlooking the symbolic 'moral' dimension of Leviticus 13, scholars have unnecessarily confused the issue of what כפר means within Leviticus 14 by assuming that this chapter is a non-sin context. If I am correct in assuming that the person and house afflicted with צרעת symbolize the experience of divine judgment (see below), then the making of כפר for the healed person (Lev. 14.1-32) and the house (Lev. 14.33-53) may complete the symbolism: rebellious humanity re-enters God's presence and enjoys his favour only via the making of כפר.

3. In this sense, a person's 'uncleanness' is analogous to the 'death' (מות) the first couple experience in Genesis 3 *after they rebelled against the Lord*. Thought of in this way, 'uncleanness' should not be considered as the *cause* of a person's exclusion from Yahweh's immediate presence, but as the *result* of an action that symbolizes rebellion (e.g. the ingestion of unclean food; cf. Chapter 3).

4. See Chapter 2; Jones, *The Symbol of Water in the Gospel of John*, p. 14.

conclusion in Chapter 3, including the contention that Lev. 11.43-45 may reflect what is implicit within the preceding regulations, gains persuasiveness.

Second, the present investigation explores the possibility that Leviticus 13 is characterized by the same use of 'rhetorical progression' as identified in Leviticus 11. That is, it will consider whether the legislator uses an inductive method of communication to impress the full theological message of the laws concerning צרעת upon the readership.[5]

Assessment of Previous Explanations

We begin by looking at previous interpretations of Leviticus 13. There are two main views. First, dating back as far as Qumran, and still held by some modern scholars, there is that which assumes that the disease called צרעת is associated with sinfulness in either a literal or symbolic sense. Second, the consensus view among modern critical scholarship is that the occurrence of this disease is unrelated to the individual's sinfulness. These approaches are summarized and assessed below. I shall draw on some of the insights gained from these approaches for my own interpretation of Leviticus 13.

The Person Afflicted with צרעת as Sinner

Though there are exceptions, some biblical texts (i.e. Num. 12.1-15; 2 Kg. 15.5; 2 Chr. 26.19), the literature from Qumran, medieval rabbinic exegesis and some modern scholars assume that a person's affliction with צרעת is associated with sin.[6] There are three main ways in which scholars have interpreted this association.

---

5.   Further evidence for complexity within the literary arrangement of Leviticus 13 comes from the observation that the repeated reference to three kinds of skin complaints in this chapter reflect a 'certain artistic arrangement'. 'Verse 2 speaks of (1) discoloration of skin, (2) pustule, and (3) inflammation. In the following discussion in vv. 3-17 the terms recur in the order 3, 2, 1. In vv. 18-23 the order is 1, 2, 3, and in vv. 24-28 it is 3, 2, 1' (Stephen K. Sherwood, *Leviticus, Numbers, Deuteronomy* [Berit Olam; Studies in Hebrew Narrative and Poetry; Minnesota: Liturgical Press, 2002], pp. 65-66). This pattern was first identified by M. Fishbane, 'Biblical Colophons, Textual Criticism and Legal Analogies', *CBQ* 42 (1980), pp. 438-49 (443).

6.   One notable exception is the NT which does not explicitly identify people with צרעת, which it translates as λεπρα, as sinful. Similarly, Maccoby observes that 'even the rabbis do not consistently regard "leprosy" as the result of the sin of slander because they sometimes speak of it as the result of infection, as when they advise people not to place themselves in a position where the wind is blowing from the direction of a "leper" (*Lev. R.* 16.3)' (Maccoby, *Ritual and Morality*, p. 121). Nevertheless, it is noteworthy that other infirmities are associated with sin in the NT. See for example the paralysis of the man in Mark 2.

The Disease צרעת *as a Consequence of a Specific Sin*

The view that צרעת is a consequence of an individual's specific sin belongs largely to the sectarians at Qumran and traditional rabbinic exegesis. The most well-known text from Qumran, in this regard, is the Damascus Document (4Q270) which lists a person afflicted with צרעת in a catalogue of transgressors.[7] Similarly, later rabbinic exegesis in Midrash Sifra (*c.* 3rd century CE), *Midrash Leviticus Rabba* (*c.* 5th century CE)[8] and the *Babylonian Talmud* (*c.* 6th century CE)[9] reflects a belief that צרעת results from sin.[10] Their association of צרעת with sin is not arbitrary but derives from the observation that the former is often presented as the consequence of divine judgment in the OT. As Milgrom points out

7. In addition to 4Q270, Harrington quotes several other scrolls that view this disease as the consequence of sin, namely 1QH 1.32, 4Q512 28 viii, and MMT B 73 (Harrington, *The Purity Texts*, pp. 91-92). Other texts, cited by Milgrom, which display a similar view of צרעת include 1QHab 9.9-12; 11.12-16 and 4QOrdb 30.8-9. For 4QOrdb 30.8-9 see M. Baillet, *Qumran Grotte 4 III (40482-40520)* (DJD, 7; Oxford: Clarendon Press, 1982), p. 265. Milgrom, *Leviticus 1-16*, pp. 821-23. See also J.M. Baumgarten, 'The 4QZadokite Fragments on Skin Disease', *JJS* 41 (1990), pp. 153-65 (162).

8. 'For ten things does scale disease come upon the world: (1) idol worship, (2) gross unchastity, (3) bloodshed, (4) the desecration of the Divine Name, (5) blasphemy of the Divine Name, (6) robbing the public, (7) usurping [a dignity] to which one has no right, (8) overweening pride, (9) evil speech (slander), and (10) an evil eye (greed)' (*Midr. Lev. Rab.* 17.3). Further rabbinic references to the relationship between צרעת and sin are found in *t. Neg.* 6.7, *b. Ber.* 5b and, taking into account the rabbinic tradition, Louis Ginzberg makes the following comment regarding the relationship between sin and this disease. 'The law in regard to lepers was particularly severe, for they were denied the right of staying within the camp, whereas the unclean were prohibited merely from staying near the sanctuary. The lepers were the very ones who had worshipped the Golden Calf, and had as a consequence been smitten with this disease, and it was for this reason that God separated them from the community. Thirteen sins are punished with leprosy by God: blasphemy, unchastity, murder, false suspicion, pride, illegal appropriation of the rights of others, slander, theft, perjury, profanation of the Divine Name, idolatry, envy, and contempt of the Torah' (Louis Ginzberg, *The Legends of the Jews*. III. [Philadelphia: Jewish Publication Society of America, 1909–38], pp. 213-14).

9. 'R. Samuel b. Nahman said in the name of R. Yochanan: Because of seven things the plague of scale disease is incurred: slander, the shedding of blood, vain oaths, incest, arrogance, robbery, and envy' (*b. 'Arakin.* 16a; cf. *b. Sebu.* 8a; Midr. Lev. Rab. 18.4; cited in Milgrom, *Leviticus 1–16*, p. 823).

10. Klawans points out that 'there is no explicit articulation of the notion of leprosy as a punishment in the Mishnah' (Klawans, *Impurity and Sin in Ancient Judaism*, pp. 98-99). However, that such an understanding is found earlier at Qumran and later in the 5th and 6th centuries CE make it possible that no 'explicit articulation' of this matter is given in the Mishnah because it is more concerned with the physical identification of the disease, rather than its cause.

many of the biblical narratives concerning *ṣāraʿat* confirm its origin in divine wrath (Miriam, Num. 12.9; Gehazi, 2 Kgs 5.27; Uzziah, 2 Chr. 26.18-21). Thus, analogous to its Mesopotamian counterpart, it is attested in biblical curse formulas, such as 'May the house of Joab never be without someone suffering from discharge or scale disease' (2 Sam. 3.29; cf. 7.14).[11]

And taking into account that a person with צרעת receives harsher treatment than other unclean people (i.e. Lev. 13.45-46),[12] Bamberger concludes that

> the biblical authors did not regard *ṣāraʿat* as just one disease among others. To them it was a *negaʿ*, 'smiting,' the manifestation of extreme divine displeasure. Unlike other forms of defilement, it does not merely exclude the defiled person from the sanctuary—it bars that person from all human society.[13]

Despite this evidence that certain early interpretative communities attributed a punitive function to this disease, such a view is no longer acceptable in a world which understands the natural causes of various skin-diseases. For this reason David P. Wright draws the following contemporary application from the prescriptions concerning צרעת.

> There are many parallels between the Bible's view about those suffering from *ṣāraʿat* and unscientific popular views about those suffering from the serious diseases of modern concern. These popular views grow out of society's fears and attempts to explain evil, and out of its social context. These explanations, while turning chaos to order for some, are sometimes injurious, psychologically if not physically, to the sick… Knowledge about the ancients' symbolic understanding of biblical *ṣāraʿat* and the effects it had upon sufferers in antiquity can serve as an avenue for critiquing our own thinking (or mis-thinking) about modern disease.[14]

But while Wright's remarks may be applicable to the later rabbinic interpretation of צרעת as God's judgment on a *specific* sin, it is not clear that it applies to the intention of Leviticus 13. Those diagnosed with this disease are not accused as sinful. Though צרעת is associated with divine judgment on

---

11. Milgrom, *Leviticus 1–16*, p. 821. Maccoby attempts to avoid the conclusion that there may be a moral aspect to the prescriptions concerning צרעת in Leviticus 13 by claiming that Naaman's affliction with this disease in 2 Kings 5 is unrelated to sin. This claim is not entirely accurate. God heals Naaman from this disease only after he complies with his will, and at the end of this narrative Elisha's servant Gehazi is stricken with צרעת within a sin-context. See Hyam Maccoby, *Ritual and Morality*, p. 120.

12. Bamberger says that the '"leper", adjudged to be under divine displeasure, was completely isolated and had to observe the rules of mourning' (Bernard J. Bamberger, *The Torah: A Modern Commentary. Leviticus* [New York: Union of American Hebrew Congregations, 1979], p. 125).

13. Bamberger, *Leviticus*, p. 116.

14. Published in Milgrom, *Leviticus 1–16*, p. 824.

evil in the narratives referred to above, the assumption that this disease is related to an individual's sin is not the view of Leviticus 13. On the one hand, no connection is made between צרעת and sin in Leviticus 13. On the other hand, though the bringing of a 'sin offering' (חטאת) by a person healed of צרעת (Leviticus 14) suggests a connection between the disease and sin,[15] the verb 'to sin' (חטא) does not occur in connection with this offering as it does in Leviticus 4. In line with this observation, a more general notion of sin, not specific to the healed person, is possibly in view.[16] We may affirm Wright's

15. Moreover, scholars observe certain parallels between the rituals prescribed in Leviticus 14, including the live-bird rite, and those prescribed for the Day of Atonement (Leviticus 16): Hoffmann, *Das Buch Leviticus*, p. 396; Wenham, *Leviticus*, pp. 208-209; Hartley, *Leviticus*, p. 195; Tikva Frymer-Kensky, 'Pollution, Purification, and Purgation in Biblical Israel', in *The Word of the Lord Shall Go Forth: Essays in Honor of David Noel Freedman in Celebration of his Sixtieth Birthday* (ed. Carol L. Myers and M. O'Connor; Winona Lake, IN: Eisenbrauns, 1983), pp. 399-410 (400). Thomas Staubli argues that it is incorrect to draw an analogy between these rituals because, first, there is no reference made to the removal and delivery of 'evil' in Leviticus 14 and, second, birds are commonly associated with human life in the OT and in the ANE and, if this is their significance in Leviticus 14, this would be in keeping with the symbolic meaning of the other ingredients of the ritual in this chapter. In response to Staubli it can be pointed out that one could view the bird rite in Leviticus 14 as performing both symbolic functions. On the one hand it could represent the removal of evil, and on the other hand the new life given to the healed man. See Thomas Staubli, 'Die Symbolik des Vogelrituals bei der Reinigung von Aussätzigen (Lev. 14,4-7)', *Biblica* 83 (2002), pp. 230-37. Boris Ostrer has used statistical analysis to argue that, within the live-bird rite of Leviticus 14, the bird is an analogue of the purified leper rather than a carrier of impurity (Boris S. Ostrer, 'Birds of Leper: Statistical Assessment of Two Commentaries', *ZAW* 115 [2003], pp. 348-61). However, after reading Ostrer's study one cannot help but wonder if his methodology too quickly brackets out the use of one's imagination when interpreting the Leviticus 14 rite within the immediate context of Leviticus 16. Barton's recent defence of the biblical critic's responsibility to utilize both objective and subjective approaches to interpretation is relevant here. After assessing the truthfulness of Andrew Louth's caricature of 'biblical criticism' as having a misguided aim of objectivity Barton makes the following conclusion. 'To my mind the essential nature of biblical criticism is thus a deep and imaginative understanding of the text, not very unlike what Louth himself is calling for. To sink oneself in a text until its meaning becomes lucid involves all the exercise of imagination and intuition that for Louth are the mark of the humanities… It also involves, and I do not wish to deny this, technical skills such as knowledge of languages and the ability to piece together the solutions to puzzles about authorship, date, composition' (John Barton, *The Nature of Biblical Criticism* [Louisville, KY: John Knox Press, 2007], p. 55; cf. Andrew Louth, *Discerning the Mystery: An Essay on the Nature of Theology* [Oxford: Clarendon Press, 1983]). I would also add that Ostrer's view of semantics does not allow for the operation of extra-linguistic factors within the process of interpretation.

16. Hartley contends that the lack of any confession of sin in Leviticus 14 implies that specific sin is not of concern. However, no directive to confess sin is made in Leviticus 4 either. See Hartley, *Leviticus*, p. 200.

criticism of the latter Rabbinic interpretation of people afflicted with צרעת as sinners, but this does not appear to be the viewpoint of Leviticus 13–14.

The Disease צרעת as Symbol of Evil

A more nuanced version of the traditional rabbinic identification of צרעת–afflicted people *as sinners* is found in an alternative approach which views צרעת, rather than the person, as symbolic of evil. The afflicted person is not identified as sinful, but the disease is interpreted as symbolic of a particular kind of sin. This position is most eloquently argued by the conservative Jewish scholar David Z. Hoffmann. To understand his approach a familiarity with his systematic understanding of Levitical impurity is helpful.

Hoffmann assumes that there are two kinds of uncleanness. First, 'bodily uncleanness' includes the cases described in Leviticus 12–15, and some of the food prohibitions in Leviticus 11.[17] Second, there is what Hoffmann identifies as 'uncleanness in conflict with holiness', which he classifies as that resulting from the transgression of ethical laws and the eating of unclean food.[18] Since the first kind of uncleanness is associated with the body, he infers that 'uncleanness in conflict with holiness' is 'pollution of the soul'.[19] Observing that one may be cleansed from 'bodily uncleanness' but not 'pollution of the soul',[20] he concludes that the nature of the former is symbolic while that of the latter is real. More specifically, various sub-categories of 'bodily uncleanness' symbolically correspond to different kinds of sin to serve an ethical function.

> [O]n the whole each impurity is an image of sin, and as Israel distanced itself from the image of sin and carefully separated this from the sanctuary and from the holy, it was always aware of its true task. The observation of the purity laws should lead to the purity of thought and deed.[21]

In line with this understanding, he suggests that צרעת

> appears as a symbol of an evil, which endangers and disadvantages the society that exists for the service of God, and that one is entitled and obliged to expel it from the society.[22]

According to Hoffmann the prescriptions concerning צרעת were to encourage the Israelites to refrain from 'social sins'.[23]

---

17. Namely those instances in which a person comes into contact with 'death' by touching an unclean carcass or eating food that has been defiled by the death of one of the eight creatures identified in Lev. 11.29-38 (Hoffmann, *Das Buch Leviticus*, p. 304).

18. Hoffmann, *Das Buch Leviticus*, p. 303.

19. Hoffmann, *Das Buch Leviticus*, p. 303.

20. Hoffmann, *Das Buch Leviticus*, p. 304.

21. Hoffmann, *Das Buch Leviticus*, p. 318 [translation mine].

22. Hoffmann, *Das Buch Leviticus*, pp. 317-18 [translation mine].

23. Hoffmann, *Das Buch Leviticus*, p. 315 [translation mine].

Though there are some difficulties with Hoffmann's proposal, which I shall deal with in a moment, his suggestion that צרעת is symbolic of a particular kind of 'social sin' as opposed to God's judgment on specific sin is useful. This idea allows him to take seriously the narrative depiction of צרעת as divine punishment without having to argue that Leviticus 13 views a person with this disease as suffering on account of specific sin.

Nevertheless, two difficulties with Hoffmann's proposal caution against adopting the symbolic meaning he attributes to צרעת. First, the disease is not viewed as 'evil' in the OT but as divine judgment.[24] Second, his equation of this disease with 'social evil' appears somewhat arbitrary, and is possibly based on the uncertain assumption that this disease threatened others through physical contact.[25]

The Person with צרעת *as Symbolic 'Sinner' (Kiuchi)*
Kiuchi offers a novel interpretation of the צרעת-afflicted person as symbolic of a 'sinner'. He arrives at this conclusion by way of a literary approach to the prescriptions of Leviticus 13 which assumes that they are intended to teach a spiritual or theological lesson. He states his reasons for this approach by comparing the two hermeneutics one may use in the interpretation of Leviticus 13.

> One is that the text merely presents prescriptions for examining a disease called *ṣāra'at*, and nothing more. Another is that some (spiritual, or theological) message is conveyed by various symptoms and examination procedures. The former approach, though it has been commonly taken, is not satisfying in that it does not take due account of the concepts of cleanness and uncleanness, which…are spiritual…[26] Thus, the section v. 2-46 is not concerned about the healing of *ṣāra'at*, nor simply portraying various manifestations of death by the symptoms. The most suitable approach to the section should explain why the disease of *ṣāra'at* is chosen, and why the person is pronounced clean when he is totally covered by *ṣāra'at*.[27]

Kiuchi concludes that the answers to these questions are interrelated. First, he argues that this disease (i.e. צרעת) is chosen on account of its 'patchy' and 'white' appearance, and its 'latent' nature. Second, the declaration of a

24. That God refers to a time when he will 'put' (נתן) an affliction of צרעת in a house (Lev. 14.34) would seem to make Hoffman's symbolic interpretation difficult. Hoffmann does not comment on this statement.

25. That the disease was not contagious is argued by Milgrom, *Leviticus 1–16*, p. 818.

26. Kiuchi justifies his view of cleanness and uncleanness as symbolic of spiritual states as follows. 'At least, cleanness and uncleanness are states which concern the presence of the Lord. In this priestly legislation it is clear that a clean state enables one to come before the Lord; "cleanness" and "uncleanness" are spiritual matters' (Kiuchi, 'A Paradox of the Skin Disease', p. 511).

27. Kiuchi, 'A Paradox of the Skin Disease', pp. 510-11.

person as clean when completely covered with צרעת (v. 13) fulfils an educational purpose using the symbolic meanings of this disease's characteristics. He reaches the following conclusion concerning the educational purpose of Leviticus 13.

> Our proposal is that an educational purpose of the text is intended by the author, which is that man should not hide his own sinfulness from God. *Ṣāra'at* is the most suitable disease for representing the latent, persistent and hidden nature of human sinfulness. And the Lord is pleased that the uncleanness should be exposed before him.[28]

Since this is a somewhat surprising conclusion to make considering sin is not mentioned in Leviticus 13, I shall explain how he arrives at it before assessing its persuasiveness.

First, Kiuchi argues that there is an emphasis on the latency of צרעת within Leviticus 13. According to him this emphasis is evident from the fact that the text assumes that a person who is pronounced clean may become unclean again (vv. 7, 14, 35).[29] Kiuchi associates this characteristic of the disease with a person's tendency to hide his sinfulness.[30]

Second, he assumes that the whiteness associated with צרעת symbolizes purity.[31] This assumption is based on the observation that 'whiteness' has this meaning in some other OT passages (e.g. Isa. 1.18; Ps. 51.9; Dan. 12.10). For Kiuchi, the 'cleanness' brought to mind by the whiteness of this disease indicates, paradoxically, that the death caused by צרעת brings about life (i.e. cleanness). Thus the white patches on an unclean person point to the hope of gaining life through death.

Third, Kiuchi contends that an alternation between the patch of disease and the person as the object of certain verbs (i.e. טמא, הסגר, ראה) emphasizes that 'the diseased area, though patchy, is the person himself'.[32] He provides Lev. 13.3 as an example of this common tendency to alternate between objects.

וראה הכהן את־הנגע בעור־הבשר ושער בנגע הפך לבן ומראה
הנגע עמק מעור בשרו נגע צרעת הוא וראהו הכהן וטמא אתו:

Noting that while נגע is clearly the object of ראה in v. 33a, and that the object of this same verb in v. 33c is either the affliction or the afflicted person, he suggests that the latter ambiguity is deliberate and is intended to lead the reader to the conclusion that *the affliction is the person*.

---

28. Kiuchi, 'A Paradox of the Skin Disease', p. 514.
29. Kiuchi, 'A Paradox of the Skin Disease', p. 509.
30. Kiuchi, 'A Paradox of the Skin Disease', p. 510.
31. Kiuchi, 'A Paradox of the Skin Disease', p. 507.
32. Kiuchi, 'A Paradox of the Skin Disease', p. 510.

Fourth, he combines these last two observations to reach the following conclusion.

> When the equation of a patchy diseased area with the person is combined with the latent nature of the disease, it could be assumed that there lies an assumption in the text that the person afflicted with *ṣāraʿat* hides himself, and because of this assumption the lawgiver strongly demands the person to make it public by himself.[33]

Finally, based on his first assumption, that the latency of this disease symbolizes a human tendency to hide sinfulness from Yahweh, Kiuchi suggests that

> Lev 13,2-44 appears to describe pathological aspects of *ṣāraʿat* in connection with divine presence (cleanness/uncleanness), but it really focuses on human nature (presumably sinfulness) in general by describing various symptoms and procedures associated with *ṣāraʿat*. To put it another way, the disease of *ṣāraʿat* is chosen because its symptoms are most apt for describing the nature of human sinfulness.[34]

According to him, a person tries to hide a patch of צרעת (as he does his sinfulness) until it becomes so obvious that others bring him before a priest (symbolizing Yahweh's presence).[35] Such a person is declared 'unclean', which Kiuchi elsewhere describes as symbolic for the 'state of hiding oneself from the Lord',[36] and is removed from the camp (symbolic of one's death). However, there are signs that by exposing one's disease (read: sinful nature) before Yahweh one may live (i.e. become clean). This idea is conveyed by the white patches which simultaneously make one unclean yet bring to mind the idea of cleanness by their white colour. When these patches finally cover the entire person, thereby making him white (cf. Lev. 13.13), he is declared clean. Kiuchi concludes that purity is achieved because the person is both dead to his sinful nature and alive to God at the same time.

Assessment. Kiuchi's methodological approach is similar to the one advocated in Chapter 2. He is rightfully critical of those who attempt to explain, rather than interpret, Leviticus 13 by appealing to the field of medicine.[37]

---

33. Kiuchi, 'A Paradox of the Skin Disease', p. 510.

34. Kiuchi, 'A Paradox of the Skin Disease', p. 513.

35. Kiuchi suggests that the use of the hophal הוּבָא ('he shall *be* brought') reflects a person's unwillingness to come to the priest on his own accord. However, this interpretation overlooks the use of the same verb form in Lev. 14.2 in connection with a person who is to be cleansed after being healed of the disease. See Kiuchi, *Leviticus*, p. 230. See similarly Milgrom, *Leviticus 1–16*, p. 776.

36. Kiuchi, *A Study of Ḥāṭāʾ and Ḥaṭṭāʾt*, pp. 101-106.

37. Kiuchi makes the helpful observation that the legislator does not exhibit either an interest to heal or make the afflicted people clean in Leviticus 13. In connection with this case, he notes that most commentators attempt to solve this paradox in medical terms:

However, his interpretation of Leviticus 13 is not acceptable for the following reasons.

First, there is no evidence that the disease צרעת is symbolic of a person's 'hiding' of his sinfulness from Yahweh. The concept of 'hiding', which Kiuchi introduces as important for the interpretation of these prescriptions, appears to derive from his unique translation of חטא as meaning to 'hide oneself existentially from the Lord', rather than from the text of Leviticus 13.[38] His argument that the latent nature of צרעת is suggestive of hiding seems to give unwarranted emphasis to what is a relatively minor aspect of the disease. Indeed, the disease is arguably not viewed as latent in the three verses he mentions (i.e. vv. 7, 14, 35). Though both vv. 7 and 35 assume cases in which a person may or may not have the disease, they provide prescriptions for the diagnosis of the person who definitely has it. In other words, they do not have in mind cases in which people have צרעת only to have it disappear and then return. Verse 13 does not present the disease as latent when the person is declared clean but explicitly states that the person is covered with צרעת.

Even if it is demonstrable that צרעת can remain latent within a person, how does Kiuchi know that latency is symbolic of an existential mode of 'hiding from the Lord?' For the idea of latency to bring to mind that of 'existential hiding' one would need to personify צרעת. Kiuchi explains that the equation of the diseased area with the person, achieved by alternating between these as the object of certain verbs, suggests personification. Thus, if the disease has a latent (i.e. hiding) nature then so has the person. Nevertheless, while the object of the verbs ראה, טמא, and הסגר is sometimes ambiguous, Kiuchi's inference from this that the person is viewed as 'hiding from the Lord' seems doubtful. When it is considered that this aspect of 'hiding' is central to his interpretation of the entire chapter, objective evidence is required for his argument to remain plausible.

Second, that the colour 'white' (לבן) symbolizes 'cleanness' in Leviticus 13 is not clear.[39] Before this symbolic interpretation can be accepted Kiuchi must demonstrate that this semantic domain of 'white' would be accessed by a reader within this context. The association of this colour with uncleanness

---

they equate the cleanness with the healing process (Kiuchi, 'A Paradox of the Skin Disease', p. 506). He cites August Dillmann, *Die Bücher Exodus and Leviticus* (Leipzig: F. Hirzel, 1880), p. 609; E.V. Hulse, 'The Nature of Biblical Leprosy', *PEQ* 107 (1975), pp. 87-105; Wenham, *Leviticus*, p. 195; Harrison, *Leviticus*, p. 142; Levine, *Leviticus*, p. 78; Milgrom, *Leviticus 1–16*, pp. 785-86; R. Péter-Contesse, *Lévitique 1–16* (CAT, 3a; Genéve: Labor & Fides, 1993), p. 206; Hartley, *Leviticus*, p. 191; D.P. Wright and R.N. Jones, 'Leprosy', in *ABD*, IV, pp. 277-82.

38. Kiuchi, *A Study of Ḥāṭā' and Ḥaṭṭā't*, pp. 102-103. For an assessment of Kiuchi's translation which finds it improbable consult Leigh M. Trevaskis, 'On a Recent "Existential" Translation of ḥāṭā'', *VT* 59 (2009), pp. 313-19.

39. Kiuchi, 'A Paradox of the Skin Disease', p. 507.

suggests that it would not. And though he attempts to explain this final observation as a paradox (i.e. the white disease is a latent sign of cleanness in this person's dying), the persuasiveness of his argument requires one to accept his more general theory of 'sin'.[40]

Third, his literary approach to the interpretation of Leviticus 13 is unbalanced by the disproportionate attention he gives to the case in v. 13. While it is important to grapple with the question of why a person covered in צרעת is declared 'clean', Kiuchi does not establish why this case deserves more attention than the other cases. A balanced literary approach would ask questions concerning how the sequence of the cases may contribute to the educational purpose of this Chapter. Rather than refer to texts outside the immediate context to explain why the person in v. 13 is declared clean (as Kiuchi does), a literary interpretation should ask if this can be understood from the context. And, finally, a literary approach should explain why v. 13 occupies a seemingly non-climactic position within Leviticus 13 if it is so important for the chapter's interpretation.

Conclusion

Each of these attempts to interpret the association between the disease צרעת and sin is problematic to some extent. However, for the time being we may acknowledge that the *lasting contribution of the ancient rabbinic interpretation of Leviticus 13, continued in the work of scholars such as Hoffmann, and independently arrived at by Kiuchi, is its recognition of a relationship between* צרעת *and the moral realm.*[41] The present study attempts to provide a more accurate articulation of this relationship. Nevertheless, before we can proceed in this regard, an evaluation of some modern proposals that deny a relationship between the prescriptions concerning צרעת and ethics is required.

A Person's Affliction with צרעת as Unrelated to Sin

Contrary to the views examined in the previous section, most modern scholars reject the notion that affliction with צרעת is related to sin in Leviticus

---

40. Again, see Trevaskis, 'On a Recent "Existential" Translation of *ḥāṭā'*', pp. 313-19.

41. 'Leviticus does not judge the leper morally; but it defines him as one of the categories of persons and things which are ritually impure. As Brody points out (1974: 111-12), although there is no explicit moral condemnation of the man found to be leprous, the terms for moral valuation are all there in the text. Leviticus does not deny that leprosy is punishment for sin; it simply ignores the idea' (Lewis, 'A Lesson from Leviticus: Leprosy', p. 598). I am in agreement with these sentiments in so far as I assume that the biblical authors were aware of a relationship between צרעת and sin. However, below I shall dispute the claim that this idea is ignored within Leviticus 13.

13.[42] These scholars view the uncleanness associated with this disease as symbolic, serving an educational function in relation to more abstract matters of holiness. Since their proposals potentially undermine my proposal, that 'uncleanness' is related to the moral realm on a symbolic dimension, it is necessary for us to assess their validity.

The Person with צרעת as an Antitype of 'Wholeness' (Mary Douglas)
Reacting against a tendency to understand the rationale underlying various kinds of uncleanness in a piecemeal fashion, Douglas attempts to understand the purity laws of Leviticus as a symbolic system.[43] Beginning with her hypothesis that ritual uncleanness is 'dirt out of place' she argues that there is an all-encompassing pattern from which this 'dirt' must be excluded.[44] This pattern is subsequently identified as Israel's concept of holiness:

> Since each of the injunctions is prefaced by the command to be holy, so they must be explained by that command. There must be contrariness between holiness and abomination which will make over-all sense of all the particular restrictions.[45]

Her next move, in her study of the rationale underlying Israel's purity system, is to define what she thinks is Israel's concept of holiness. Accepting that its root (i.e. קדש) means 'set apart',[46] she contends that 'the next idea that emerges is of the Holy as wholeness and completeness'.[47] In defence of this assertion she offers the observation that

> [m]uch of Leviticus is taken up with stating the physical perfection that is required of things presented in the temple and of persons approaching it. The animals offered in sacrifice must be without blemish, women must be purified after childbirth, lepers should be separated and ritually cleansed before being allowed to approach it once they are cured.[48]

42. Milgrom, Balentine, Budd, Gerstenberger, Hartley, Wenham.
43. Douglas's explanation, for why the uncleanness of a person with צרעת is unrelated to ethics, must be understood against her original anthropological approach to P's purity regulations (e.g. Douglas, *Purity and Danger*). Even though she has modified this approach (see Douglas, *Leviticus as Literature*), it is still worth evaluating because many of her conclusions were adopted by subsequent commentators (e.g. Wenham and Milgrom).
44. Douglas, *Purity and Danger*, p. 53.
45. Douglas, *Purity and Danger*, p. 63.
46. Douglas, *Purity and Danger*, p. 63.
47. Douglas, *Purity and Danger*, p. 64.
48. Douglas, *Purity and Danger*, p. 64. This reference to a person with 'leprosy' (i.e. צרעת) is accepted and developed by Wenham. 'When a man shows visible signs of lack of wholeness in a persistent patchy skin condition, he has to be excluded from the covenant community. Temporary deviations from the norm do not attract such treatment,

All these injunctions are prefaced by the general command: 'Be holy, for I am holy.' We can conclude that holiness is exemplified by completeness. Holiness requires that individuals shall conform to the class to which they belong. And holiness requires that different classes of things shall not be confused.[49]

Combining this view of holiness with her assumption that the root קדשׁ essentially means 'to be separate', Douglas contends that ethics forms a subcategory rather than the essence of holiness.

Holiness means keeping distinct the things of creation. It therefore involves correct definition, discrimination and order. Under this head all the rules for sexual morality exemplify the holy. Incest and adultery (Leviticus xviii, 6-20) are against holiness, in the simple sense of right order. Morality does not conflict with holiness, but holiness is more a matter of separating that which should be separated than of protecting the rights of husbands and brothers.[50]

Presumably then, for Douglas, the uncleanness of a person afflicted with צרעת is unrelated to ethics. Instead this person serves as an antitype *to the idea of holiness*, namely physical wholeness. From this perspective, the purpose of Leviticus 13 is to present holiness to Israel as the idea of completeness. Each time a person with צרעת was excluded from the camp Israel was reminded to strive to maintain the boundaries God prescribed for their lives.

In responding to Douglas, one can agree that there is an important association made between physical completeness and the idea of holiness in Leviticus (see Chapters 5 and 6). However, while holiness may be symbolically embodied by physical wholeness, it is not clear that a condition that is less than 'whole' accounts for why a person with צרעת is considered 'unclean'. Milgrom responds to this claim of Douglas's by stating that her explanation

fails to take into account the two pairs of antonyms laid down by the Priestly legislators: holy-common and impure-pure (10.10). A blemished animal or priest is not impure but common (*ḥōl*). As for the prohibition against the blemished in the sanctuary, it only applies to priests officiating in the sanctuary and to animals offered on the altar. By contrast, any blemished Israelite—priest and lay person alike—may enter the sacred precincts and offer his sacrifices. If the holy and the impure are lethal antagonists…then they clash not in the matter of 'wholeness' but on an entirely different plane.[51]

but if the symptoms last for more than two weeks, he must go to live outside the true Israel' (Wenham, *Leviticus*, p. 203).

49. Douglas, *Purity and Danger*, p. 67.
50. Douglas, *Purity and Danger*, pp. 64, 67.
51. Milgrom, *Leviticus 1–16*, pp. 766, 1001.

A further difficulty with Douglas's original explanation relates to her assumption that 'uncleanness' is 'dirt out of place'.[52] Assuming that there 'must be contrariness between holiness and abomination which will make over-all sense of all the particular restrictions', she concludes that holiness must be the equivalent of completeness.[53] But if the status of 'unclean' is symbolic of one's *punitive* exclusion from Yahweh's immediate presence (cf. Chapter 3), it remains possible that the 'contrariness' between holiness and uncleanness is explained on another dimension, namely that of ethics. That is, if an 'unclean' person's exclusion from the community, or from worship at the sanctuary, symbolically represents an experience of divine judgment, the physical factor that renders the person 'unclean' is possibly symbolic of an ethical problem rather than an abstract idea of 'incompleteness'. If this proposal is correct it allows us to retain Douglas's insight that physical wholeness is symbolic of holiness but reject her equation of uncleanness with that which does not conform to the ideal of wholeness. Moreover, approached in this way, the distinction Douglas maintains between the idea of holiness and ethics is weakened. Though physical wholeness may represent holiness, the latter may be best thought of in terms of ethical wholeness if the experience of an 'unclean' person symbolizes a person's punitive exclusion from Yahweh's immediate presence.

Finally, Douglas's identification of the disease as that which is contrary to the pattern of God's holiness is problematic. Elsewhere in the OT, צרעת is a vehicle of divine judgment. If the disease has this symbolic meaning in Leviticus 13, it would seem extraordinary that *it* is what results in these people becoming incomplete (i.e. unholy).[54] Would not we expect divine judgment to fall on those who are already unholy?

For these reasons we may put aside Douglas's interpretation of the uncleanness associated with צרעת as unrelated to the moral realm. It is left for us to evaluate Milgrom's proposal for why uncleanness results from this disease.

The Person with צרעת *as Symbol of Death (Jacob Milgrom)*

Milgrom argues that the rationale for why צרעת makes one unclean is that a person with this disease reflects the realm of death.[55]

> [T]he common denominator of all the skin ailments described in Lev. 13 is
> that the body is wasting away. As the continuation of Aaron's prayer ex-

52. Douglas has changed her view on 'uncleanness' as 'dirt out of place'. See Douglas, *Leviticus as Literature*.

53. Douglas, *Purity and Danger*, p. 63.

54. See especially the statement 'I put an affliction of צרעת in a house of the land of your possession' (Lev. 14.34).

55. He is followed by Hartley, *Leviticus*, pp. 145, 199-200.

pressed it: 'Let her not be like a corpse that emerges from its mother's womb with half its flesh eaten away' (Num 12.12)... Thus it is the visible 'peeling off,' the striking characteristic of the scale diseases listed in Lev. 13—reminders of the disintegration of the corpse and the onset of death—that has led to their impure status and to the banishment of their carriers from the community.[56]

Milgrom offers four observations to defend his claim that a person with צרעת manifests the realm of death.[57] First, Aaron prays that his צרעת-stricken sister Miriam would not 'be like a corpse' (תהי כמת; Num. 12.12). Second, there are similarities between the purification rites for the person with צרעת and the corpse-contaminated person: 'both require aspersion with animal blood that has made contact with cedar, hyssop, and scarlet thread and been diluted in fresh water ([Lev.]14.4-7; Num. 19.1-13)'.[58] Third, unlike all other unclean people, only a corpse and a person with צרעת contaminate others by being under the same roof. Fourth, Milgrom claims that there is an explicit identification of this disease with death in Job. 18.13 which he translates as 'His skin is eaten away by a disease; death's firstborn consumes his limbs' (יאכל בדי עורו יאכל בדיו בכר מות:).

Though Milgrom's final two observations are possibly inconclusive his observation that the person with צרעת is associated with the realm of death seems correct.[59] But even if we accept that people with צרעת symbolize death, does this adequately account for why they are identified as unclean? Several observations suggest that it does not. First, the association between the diseased persons and death, in Leviticus 13, appears limited to the mourning rites they must undergo and their exclusion from the camp (cf. Lev. 13.45-46). In this way the emphasis of Leviticus 13 is on death as the consequence of a person having צרעת rather than on death as the appearance of this person. Second, in view of the findings concerning the meaning of 'death' (מות) in Chapter 3, perhaps we should expect that the death symbolized by a person's exclusion from the camp in Leviticus 13 is more than physical death. In line with this idea, while a person may take on a deathly

56. Milgrom, *Leviticus 1–16*, pp. 819-20.

57. Milgrom, *Leviticus 1–16*, p. 819.

58. Milgrom, *Leviticus 1–16*, p. 819.

59. First, there is no direct evidence that the person with צרעת contaminates others under the same roof (i.e. by 'overhang'). Milgrom claims that contamination by 'overhang' is implied for this type of impurity by the command that such a person 'shall dwell apart' (בדד ישב, Lev. 13.46). He also cites ancient rabbinic interpreters who interpret this kind of uncleanness in the same way. Nevertheless, it is argued below that the directive to 'dwell apart' symbolizes the person's death rather than serves to prevent the defilement of other people. Second, though it is possible that Job's disease is צרעת, this is not certain so that it is not clear that the book of Job forges an intentional relationship between צרעת and death. See Milgrom, *Leviticus 1–16*, p. 805.

appearance (cf. Num. 12.12), something more than this appearance is possibly responsible for his diagnosis as 'unclean'. Third, by simply identifying the rationale underlying Leviticus 13 as 'death', Milgrom does not indicate how this is related to the association between צרעת and divine judgment elsewhere in the OT.[60] Keeping in mind the previous point, it seems worth investigating if the 'death' symbolized by this person's exclusion from Israelite society as unclean is related to some form of divine judgment. Fourth, his argument does not account for why garments and houses stricken with צרעת are considered unclean (cf. Lev. 13.47-59; 14.33-53). Fifth, Kiuchi contends that the declaration that a person is clean does not always coincide with healing. He suggests that

> it is unlikely that the condition of the person with *ṣāra 'at* implies healing even if he is pronounced clean, for there is always the potential that a person, once affected by *ṣāra 'at*, suffers relapses. Such a condition cannot be described by *ṭp*.[61]

In addition to this suggestion, the possibility that the person declared 'clean' in v. 13 may immediately revert to 'uncleanness' is emphasized by the verbless clause which introduces v. 14: 'When live flesh appears on him' (וביום הראות בו בשר חי). The use of the niphal infinitive construct 'appears' (הראות) within this verse may draw the reader's attention to this possibility.[62] Thus, it seems difficult to view the cleansed person in v. 13 as healed.

Sixth, there is no attempt made to understand the rationale for uncleanness associated with צרעת from the text itself. Rather, Milgrom looks elsewhere for evidence that this disease is related to the idea of 'death'.

Conclusion

Our examination of the interpretations of צרעת offered by Douglas and Milgrom has argued that they are unsuccessful in their attempt to explain the uncleanness resulting from this disease without making reference to 'sin'. Nevertheless, Milgrom's insight that a person with this disease may represent 'death' seems reasonable and will be taken into consideration in my interpretation of Leviticus 13 below. Yet it seems noteworthy that, though he arrives at this conclusion on the basis of the narrative texts concerning

60. Though Milgrom observes that there is a relationship between צרעת and divine judgment elsewhere in the OT he does not explore how the two are related within the prescriptions of Leviticus 13.

61. Kiuchi, 'A Paradox of the Skin Disease', p. 507.

62. The only other infinitive constructs that occur in this chapter are in v. 56 (הכבס; *hothpaal*) and the concluding v. 59 (לטהרו לטמאו; both *piel*). Theodor Seidl views the introductory clause of v. 14 as so unusual within this context that it warrants it being assigned to a latter hand (*Tora für den 'Aussatz'-Fall. Literarische Schichten und syntaktische Strukturen in Levitikus 13 und 14* [St Ottilien: EOS Verlag, 1982], p. 33).

צרעת, he seems to overlook that this disease is a consequence of divine judgment in most of these texts. This observation provides further encouragement to assess whether the prescriptions of Leviticus 13 are related to the realm of ethics.

The Rationale of 'Uncleanness' in Leviticus 13

The previous section proposed an association between the prescriptive texts concerning צרעת in Leviticus 13 and the realm of ethics. This association was mainly inferred from how צרעת-afflicted people are presented in narrative-texts. The remainder of this Chapter uses the method of interpretation presented in Chapter 2, and employed in Chapter 3, to see if there is an ethical dimension to Leviticus 13. Of particular interest is whether the term 'unclean' exhibits the same symbolic meaning that was assigned to it in Leviticus 11 (cf. Chapter 3), namely a punitive 'exclusion from Yahweh's immediate presence'.

Structure

Leviticus 13 is divisible into two major units. The first (vv. 1-46) is concerned with the diagnosis of the skin complaint called צרעת. The second (vv. 47-59) prescribes the diagnosis and treatment of garments and vessels afflicted with the same disease. Scholars observe that Lev. 13.47-59 dislocates the logical sequel to Lev. 13.1-46, namely the prescriptions for cleansing a person healed from צרעת (Lev. 14.1-32).[63] Nevertheless, the materials, listed in Lev. 13.47-59, contract the same disease as humans (i.e. צרעת) which encourages one to uncover the rationale for their present location before resorting to diachronic explanations. Indeed, more or less identical introductory formulae delineate this chapter into eight literary sub-units which likewise encourage a final form interpretation:

63. Noordtzij and Noth conclude that vv. 47-49 are a later addition (Noordtzij, *Leviticus*, 142; Noth, *Leviticus*, 104, 106). See also W. Kornfeld, *Das Buch Levitikus* (Die Welt der Bibel; Kleinkommentare zur Heiligen Schrift, 15; Düsseldorf: Patmos, 1972), p. 49; Seidl, *Tora für den 'Aussatz' Fall*, pp. 43, 46. Milgrom and Wenham account for the position of these laws by suggesting that the diseased garments share similarities in appearance with the diseased person. For example, Wenham observes that both 'are abnormal surface conditions that disfigure the outside of the skin or garment. Both cause the surface to flake or peel' (Wenham, *Leviticus*, p. 201; cf. Milgrom, *Leviticus 1–16*, p. 808). Moreover, he suggests that they may further elucidate the diagnostic tests for whether an infection was unclean. In my view, only this second idea possibly explains why a decision was made to interrupt what would appear to be the more logical sequence.

v. 2   אָדָם כִּי־יִהְיֶה בְעוֹר־בְּשָׂרוֹ ('When a human has on the skin of his flesh')

v. 9   נֶגַע צָרַעַת כִּי תִהְיֶה בְּאָדָם ('When there is an affliction of צָרַעַת on a human')[64]

v. 18 וּבָשָׂר כִּי־יִהְיֶה בוֹ־בְעֹרוֹ ('When flesh has on its skin')

v. 24 אוֹ בָשָׂר כִּי־יִהְיֶה בְעֹרוֹ ('Or when flesh has on its skin')

v. 29 וְאִישׁ אוֹ אִשָּׁה כִּי־יִהְיֶה בוֹ ('When a man or a woman has on it')

v. 38 וְאִישׁ אוֹ אִשָּׁה כִּי־יִהְיֶה בְעוֹר־בְּשָׂרָם ('When a man or a woman has on the skin of their flesh')

v. 40 וְאִישׁ כִּי יִמָּרֵט רֹאשׁוֹ ('When a man has his hair fall out of his head')

v. 47 וְהַבֶּגֶד כִּי־יִהְיֶה בוֹ ('When a garment has on it')

Content

The first sub-unit (vv. 2-8), following the general introduction to the chapter ('Yahweh spoke to Moses and Aaron'; יהיה אל־משה ואל־אהרן וידבר לאמר, v. 1), indicates that when a skin infection appears deeper than 'the skin of the flesh' a person is 'unclean'. The second sub-unit (vv. 9-17) designates 'live flesh' (בשר חי)[65] exposed by צרעת as 'unclean'. The third and fourth sub-units (vv. 18-27 and 24-28) stipulate that 'flesh' exposed by צרעת, in the place where there were 'boils' or 'burns', qualifies a person as 'unclean'. The fifth sub-unit (vv. 29-37) deals with cases of צרעת that may afflict the head of a man or woman. The sixth sub-unit (vv. 38-39) describes a situation in which dull white spots 'breaking out' on the skin are considered 'clean' (טהר). The penultimate sub-unit (vv. 40-46) prescribes the diagnosis for צרעת on a man's bald head and what should be done with him, and the final unit (vv. 47-59) deals with various materials that contract צרעת and commands their destruction by fire.

Exegesis of Leviticus 13

The following exegesis of Leviticus 13 aims to identify if there is a symbolic dimension to this material that is continuous with that proposed to exist in Leviticus 11 (cf. Chapter 3). Of particular interest is whether such a dimension reflects an ethical concern associated with the meaning of uncleanness identified in Leviticus 11. The presence of an ethical concern within Leviticus

64. Milgrom incorrectly regards vv. 2-17 as a single literary unit because כי, which is used to introduce a new subject in Leviticus 13, 'does not reappear until v. 18'. But it does in v. 9a (Milgrom, *Leviticus 1–16*, p. 772).

65. Though this phrase literally means 'live flesh', most commentators render it 'raw flesh'. However, the root חיה never occurs with the sense 'raw flesh' elsewhere in the Pentateuch, so I shall retain the literal rendering 'live' in the present work. Hartley's translation of the phrase as 'ulcerated tissue' seems overly interpretative (Wenham, *Leviticus*, p. 189; Milgrom, *Leviticus 1–16*, p. 784; Hartley, *Leviticus*, p. 171).

13 would support my contention that the command to 'be holy' in Lev. 11.43-45 makes explicit what is an underlying expectation in P's ritual texts. This possibility will become even more likely if P's ethical concern is not dissimilar to that which characterizes H's view of holiness.

'Uncleanness' Resulting from a Condition That Is on the 'the Skin of his Flesh' (vv. 2-8)

This introductory case (vv. 2-8) is introduced by the phrase: 'When a human has on the skin of his flesh' (אדם כי יהיה בעור־בשרו).[66] It is concerned with the diagnosis of a skin complaint referred to as צרעת. Many commentators translate והיה בעור־בשרו לנגע צרעת (v. 2b) as '*and it develops into a* צרעת *on his body*'.[67] But because vv. 3-8 allow for the possibility that

---

66. The collocation 'when a human' (אדם כי) occurs as the subject of יהיה once elsewhere in the OT (Lev. 1.2). Scholars assume that 'human' is used as a sex-inclusive term in both instances, which is possible and, if correct, explains why it used instead of 'man' (איש; Levine, *Leviticus*, p. 74; Milgrom, *Leviticus 1–16*, p. 772; Gerstenberger, *Leviticus*, p. 153; Hartley, *Leviticus*, p. 186). But it does not explain why this term is preferred over the more common sex-inclusive term 'person' (נפש). Elsewhere in Leviticus, נפש is used 16 times as the sex-inclusive subject of various case-laws (cf. Lev. 2.1; 4.2, 27; 5.1, 4, 15, 17, 21; 7.21, 25 [inferred from context]; 17.11, 14; 18.29 [inferred from context]; 19.8 [inferred from context]; 23.29; 24.17). By contrast, אדם is used in this way on only two occasions, namely Lev. 1.2 and 13.2. The sex-specific terms איש and אשה occur within such formulas 19 (Lev. 13.29, 38, 40; 15.2, 16; 19.20; 20.9, 27; 21.9, 18; 22.14, 21; 24.15, 17, 19; 25.26, 29; 27.2, 14) and six times (Lev. 12.2; 13.29, 38; 15.19, 25; 20.27) respectively. Milgrom suggests that the use of אדם, rather than נפש, on these occasions reflects the legislator's intention to exclude non-Israelites from the observance of the sacrificial prescriptions (Leviticus 1–7; cf. Lev. 1.2) and the purity laws of Leviticus 13 (he follows the rabbis in this regard [see *m. Neg.* 3.1]). The difficulty with this suggestion, as acknowledged by Milgrom, is that non-Israelites are required to observe many other prohibitions (e.g. Lev. 17.8, 10, 13, 15; 20.2). Nevertheless, observing that these requirements are mostly confined to H, he attempts to defend this argument by speculating that P is less inclusive (Milgrom, *Leviticus 1–16*, pp. 772-73). However, considering that Chapter 3 lessens rather than sharpens the theological distinctiveness of H, to argue that these verses can be overlooked so as to resolve this tension seems unsatisfactory. Moreover, Gordon McConville argues that P shares the same ethnic inclusive concerns exhibited by H (J. Gordon McConville, '"Fellow-Citizens": Israel and Humanity in Leviticus', in McConville and Möller [eds.], *Reading the Law. Essays in Honour of Gordon J. Wenham*, pp. 10-32). Thus, for the moment we may entertain the possibility that something more than sex and nationality governs the legislator's decision to use 'human'. In Chapter 5 I shall argue that the semantic range of this term includes the notion of mortality, and that this is what accounts for its use in this chapter. אדם is recognized as having a theological aspect in Deuteronomy and the Deuteronomistic history, but not in P. See Fritz Maass, 'אָדָם', in *TDOT*, I, pp. 75-87 (79-80).

67. NAS; JPS; Noth, *Leviticus*, p. 102; Wenham, *Leviticus*, p. 189; Milgrom, *Leviticus 1–16*, p. 774; Gerstenberger, *Leviticus*, p. 153.

the person does not have צרעת, the היה of v. 2b is more accurately translated '*may develop* into an affliction of צרעת'.[68] This translation is also supported by the nature of the second case which is more confidently introduced with: 'If there is an affliction of צרעת on a human' (נגע צרעת כי תהיה באדם, v. 9a).[69] In other words, vv. 9-17 deal with a case which the laity recognizes as צרעת before the person is diagnosed by the priest (see discussion below).

Therefore v. 2 anticipates an occasion when the laity observes one of three skin complaints[70] which they consider *might develop* into צרעת.[71] When such a case arises the person is to 'be brought' (והובא) before the priests, apparently by those who notice the skin complaint.

The difference between 'may develop' and 'it develops' is important. The latter would mean that the three skin complaints mentioned in v. 2 are symptoms of an indisputable case of צרעת. But the prescriptions that follow do not identify any of these as a clear sign of the disease. Alternatively, the first, and in my opinion, correct rendering means that these are signs that it *may develop* into the disease. If this interpretation is correct, it would seem

68. As does NIV; Heinisch, *Das Buch Leviticus*, p. 60; J.R. Porter, *Leviticus* (Cambridge: Cambridge University Press, 1976), p. 97; Noordtzij, *Leviticus*, p. 136; Hartley, *Leviticus*, p. 189; John W. Kleinig, *Leviticus* (Saint Louis, MO: Concordia Publishing House, 2003), p. 271; see Paul Joüon and T. Muraoka, *A Grammar of Biblical Hebrew* (Rome: Editrice Pontificio Istituto Biblico, 1996), pp. 357-58. That the priest is required to quarantine such a person to determine if the affliction is צרעת is further confirmation that this skin complaint 'may develop' into this disease. Therefore, even if one translates והיה בעור־בשרו לנגע צרעת (v. 2b) as 'and it develops', a certain level of uncertainty must still be assumed. Though he translates v. 2a 'and it turns into', Wenham at least acknowledges that the first case is one which the layman suspects is 'serious'. This view would be in agreement with the position taken here, namely that the first case is less developed than the one which follows (vv. 9-17). Nevertheless, it should not be inferred that the lay person brings a suspicious case to the priest merely for confirmation from the expert priest. This is because a case follows which is clearly an outbreak of צרעת, yet the lay person must still bring the afflicted subject to the priest. This observation may suggest that the priest's 'looking' (ראה) at the affliction performs a theological function in as much as a physical one. See discussion below, and Wenham, *Leviticus*, p. 197; Noordtzij, *Leviticus*, p. 136.

69. Moreover, the second case does not allow for the possibility that the skin complication is not צרעת. We should also note that the subject of the verb פשה, used to describe the spreading of the disease in the first case (vv. 5, 6, 7 [×2], 8), is only ever a condition which *may develop* wherever else it occurs in the OT. This use of פשה is discussed in more detail below.

70. Namely, a 'discoloration' (שאת), a 'scab' (ספחת), or a 'shiny mark' (בהרת) (v. 2).

71. Thus Kiuchi is misguided when he interprets the outbreak of the disease in v. 7 as evidence of the 'insidious nature of the disease'. That the person had the disease before v. 7 is not certain (Kiuchi, 'A Paradox of the Skin Disease', p. 506).

that the indisputable sign that the skin complaint is צרעת is the exposure of a person's 'flesh' (בשר). Two observations point to this conclusion.

The Recurring Phrase 'the Skin of his Flesh'

The indirect object of יהיה within the first case's introductory formula is the unusual prepositional phrase 'in the skin of his flesh' (בעור־בשרו, v. 2a). This phrase occurs only within this chapter of the OT, and no less than five times in vv. 2-4a, thus we are entitled to ask why the legislator qualifies 'skin' with 'of his flesh' when this qualification is not used elsewhere.[72]

Milgrom assumes that the phrase 'on his flesh' reflects no more than the legislator's desire to exclude the skin of the head.[73] In part, this assumption is possibly correct considering that there is a section dealing with צרעת of the head which closely parallels Lev. 13.2-8 (i.e. vv. 29-37).[74] But it remains likely that the phrase 'the skin of his flesh' has more than practical significance. First, if the phrase has only practical significance, why does the legislator refer four times to 'the skin of his flesh' in the opening two verses? Would it not have been sufficient to mention it once? Observe, for example, v. 2:

72. Other collocations of 'skin' (עור) in the OT are 'Moses's face' (Exod. 34.29, 30, 35), the 'burnt offering' (Lev. 7.8) and rams and goats (Gen. 22.16; Exod. 25.5; 26.14; 35.7, 23; 36.19; 39.34). There is some difference between these and the phrase 'the skin of his flesh' in Leviticus 13. First, when the collocation is an animal (i.e. the burnt offering) the skin is removed. Thus, the collocation simply identifies the source of the skin. Second, 'the skin of Moses's face' is the most similar to 'the skin of his flesh', because both identify the location of the thing of interest. In the case of Moses it was where his skin shone, in the case of the diseased person in Leviticus 13 it is where the complication has arisen. But if 'flesh' simply refers to the person's body, what is achieved by qualifying the person's skin in this way? It would seem that the most plausible explanation is that the legislator is deliberately drawing attention to the term 'flesh'.

73. Regarding 'on his skin' in Lev. 13.29, Rashbam (followed by Hoffmann and Milgrom) suggests that it is not a redundant phrase but allows for the section that follows which deals with the head etc. 'Rashbam's interpretation is opposed to that of Sifra (so also LT) which attributes halakhic significance to the allegedly redundant phrase "on his skin." ...In the Be'ur Wessely labels Rashbam's interpretation as "far-fetched."' See Milgrom, *Leviticus 1–16*, 773; Martin I. Lockshin, *Rashbam's Commentary on Leviticus and Numbers. An Annotated Translation* (ed. and trans. Martin I. Lockshin; Providence, RI: Brown Judaic Studies, 2001), p. 72; Hoffmann, *Das Buch Leviticus*, p. 367.

74. Though is it not possible that the skin complications associated with the head (vv. 29-37) are in addition to those mentioned in vv. 2-17, which may also occur on the head? That the legislator uses בשר as a substitute for the complete person in vv. 18 and 24, and that the skin complications specifically associated with the head do not occur in vv. 2-17, cautions against being overly confident that 'on the skin of his flesh' is simply employed to exclude the head from those particular regulations.

אָדָם כִּי־יִהְיֶה בְעוֹר־בְּשָׂרוֹ שְׂאֵת אוֹ־סַפַּחַת אוֹ בַהֶרֶת וְהָיָה
בְעוֹר־בְּשָׂרוֹ לְנֶגַע צָרָעַת

When a human has *in the skin of his flesh* a swelling or an eruption or a spot,
and it may develop, *in the skin of his flesh*, into an affliction of צרעת.

In addition to this double reference, would it not seem redundant in v. 3, after
specifying that the priest is to look at the affliction 'in the skin of his flesh'
(cf. v. 2), to say 'if the appearance of the affliction is deeper than the skin *of
his flesh*'? There appears to be more emphasis placed on the flesh underlying
the skin than is necessary if only practical concerns are of interest.

Second, interpreting the recurring reference to 'the skin of his flesh' in
purely practical terms overlooks the direct relationship between exposed
'flesh' and the declaration of uncleanness in the next case (vv. 9-17). For
some reason the legislator directly identifies 'flesh' as 'unclean' (v. 15), and
if the purpose of these prescriptions is ritualistic before it is practical, one
may wonder if the flesh has symbolic significance.

Third, in the parallel cases comprised by Lev. 13.18-28, which presumably
apply to diseases of the body *and* head, 'flesh' is used as a substitute for
'person' (vv. 18, 24). If, as Milgrom assumes, 'the skin of the flesh' is used
to identify a particular part of the body, would it not seem unlikely for the
legislator to then use 'flesh' to refer to the entire person?

In conclusion, though it appears that the legislator *may* use the phrase 'the
skin of his flesh' within vv. 2-8 to refer to the skin of a certain part of the
body, there is some evidence that the term 'flesh' has more than practical
significance. For the moment we may assume that it has both practical and
symbolic significance. Below I argue that the legislator deliberately introduces Leviticus 13 with a case dealing with physical flesh so that he may
allude to the symbolic meaning of flesh when he deals with צרעת of the
non-fleshy parts of the body in a later case (i.e. vv. 29-37). We have already
seen that he does something similar in Leviticus 11 which begins with the
practical concerns of diet (Lev. 11.1-8) and progressively moves on to reveal
the symbolic meaning of these regulations.

The Potential Exposure of Flesh by Spreading צרעת
The legislator's concern to identify situations in which the integrity of the
skin covering flesh is threatened by צרעת is further evidence that exposed
'flesh' is the indisputable sign of this disease. If the priest, upon looking at
the 'affliction' (נגע, v. 3a), observes that 'hair in the affliction has turned
white' (ושער בנגע הפך לבן, v. 3b) and 'the affliction appears deeper than
the skin of his flesh' (ומראה הנגע עמק מעור בשרו, v. 3c), he is to conclude that it is צרעת (v. 3d) and 'declare him unclean' (וטמא אתו).[75] The

<hr/>

75. That the issue is whether the skin covering the flesh is threatened by the disease is

phrase 'deeper than the skin of his flesh' *may* imply that the priest sees 'flesh',[76] but even if this is not the case, it certainly indicates that the spread of this disease will ultimately infect the underlying 'flesh'.[77]

The main point of vv. 2-8, then, is that a skin complaint will result in the declaration that a person is 'unclean' *if* it threatens to move beneath the 'skin' covering the 'flesh'. Though the text does not say that the priest sees 'flesh' (cf. Lev. 13.15) the phrase 'deeper than the skin of his flesh' appears to make this a possibility. Moreover, assuming that the legislator is using the literary device of rhetorical progression to induct his reader to the meaning of these laws (cf. Leviticus 11; Chapter 3), we may note that the frequent reference to 'flesh' in the first case possibly raises the reader's interest about what relationship there is between 'flesh' and the diagnosis of a disease that renders one unclean. Below I shall consider some evidence that the term 'flesh' is used with a symbolic meaning within Leviticus 13. First, I shall use a cognitive linguistic analysis to assess whether a competent reader would access a symbolic meaning for this term within this context. Second, I shall discuss a

---

reflected in the sub-case that follows in vv. 4-8. If a 'bright spot' (בהרת) does not appear deeper than the skin and the hair in it has not turned white (v. 4; cf. vv. 5-8), this person is quarantined for two weeks to determine if the 'bright spot' 'spreads' (פשה). The text states what happens if it does not spread (i.e. the priest concludes that it is a 'scab') and what happens if it spreads after the person is pronounced clean. When the latter happens the person is re-examined and pronounced unclean for it is now considered a case of צרעת. Thus, the additional time of quarantine has as its aim to see if the skin is threatened.

76. Milgrom adopts the position of the rabbis who interpret 'appears deeper than the skin' as meaning that it only appears deeper but is not actually deeper. Nevertheless, he is not able to provide any evidence to support this conclusion. Indeed, his statement that '[s]ome medical authorities suggest that this phenomenon is due to the involvement of the dermis, the deeper part of the skin; in effect, a thickening of the skin has occurred' suggests a risen, rather than deeper, appearance (Milgrom, *Leviticus 1–16*, p. 778). That the disease was progressing in a way that threatened to expose the 'flesh' seems to be assumed by Noordtzij. He comments in relation to the case of vv. 9-17 that the diseased person 'had disregarded the initial symptoms of the disease [cf. Lev. 13.2] and allowed it to progress, and the swelling had developed into an open sore' (Noordtzij, *Leviticus*, p. 137).

77. In line with this Bamberger suggests that 'deeper than the skin of his body' 'might mean that the affection is not superficial but extends below the skin' (Bamberger, *Leviticus*, p. 118). However he reminds us that the traditional rabbinic understanding (e.g. Rashi, Rashbam) is that these things only 'appear' to be deeper than the skin as a result of color. Noordtzij also assumes that 'deeper than the skin' refers to a subcutaneous infection (*Leviticus*, p. 136). See A.M. Silbermann (ed.), *Pentateuch with Targum Onkelos, Haphtaroth and Rashi's Commentary: Leviticus* (trans. A. Blashki and L. Joseph; Jerusalem: Silbermann Family, 1932), p. 51; Lockshin, *Rashbam's Commentary on Leviticus and Numbers*, p. 74.

recent study of some Qumran texts which suggests that the term בשׂר was used with an ethical meaning as early as the 3rd century BCE.[78] However, prior to undertaking these two studies an examination of the relationship the idea of 'flesh' bears to that of 'uncleanness' and the disease צרעת within Leviticus 13 is required.

'Live Flesh' as the Source of Uncleanness (vv. 9-17)

Whereas vv. 2-8 identify three skin complaints that *may develop* into צרעת, several observations indicate that the second case (vv. 9-17) assumes that the disease is present in its fully developed form. First, the introductory formula anticipates a situation in which the people who bring this person are confident that it is צרעת (v. 9a).[79] This interpretation is suggested by the fact that, whereas three skin complaints comprise the predicate of the verb יהיה in v. 2, the same verb not only lacks a predicate in v. 9, but these three skin complaints are not even mentioned before it is commanded that the person 'be brought' before the priests (cf. v. 2). Presumably the omission of these complaints reflects that the disease has moved past the stage of suspicious. This understanding is confirmed by the replacement of the subject אדם in v. 2 with נגע צרעת in v. 9. Rather than introducing the case by anticipating a 'human' who has several spots on the skin of his flesh that *may* develop into צרעת, the legislator reveals that he already has the disease by stating 'When there is an affliction of צרעת on a human' (נגע צרעת כי תהיה באדם, v. 9).[80]

Second, when the priest looks at this case he finds that the hair has turned white and that there is 'live flesh' (בשׂר חי) in the afflicted area (v. 10b).[81] For this reason the legislator calls it a צרעת נושנת. Even though the niphal participle נושנת comes from the root ישׁן ('to be old'), Milgrom prefers to render it 'chronic' in the sense that it is a disease that has only recently erupted.[82] He concludes that in this instance

---

78. See pages 138-47.

79. Though Gerstenberger notes that the introductory clause of v. 9 suggests that those who bring this person have already ascertained that this is a case of צרעת, he, inconsistently, concludes that it should be interpreted as meaning 'in the case of a *suspected* malignant eruption' (Gerstenberger, *Leviticus*, p. 162 [emphasis mine]).

80. Even though אדם is removed as the subject of the verb יהיה, it is retained as the indirect object of this verb within the phrase באדם. Thus, as Seidl points out, all of the prescriptions of vv. 9-17 assume the notion of אדם (*Tora für den 'Aussatz' Fall*, p. 153).

81. A literal translation of v. 10b is 'living tissue of live flesh' (מחית בשׂר חי) (Wenham, *Leviticus*, p. 198).

82. Milgrom, *Leviticus 1–16*, p. 785. By contrast, Wenham correctly interprets the use of נושנת as indicating that this is an 'old' infection (*Leviticus*, p. 198).

the sore is not old because it has just erupted (Ehrlich 1908–14). Hence this adjective addresses the future; it is bound to recur and remain, so it is 'chronic'.[83]

Yet the text does not say that this is a recent eruption in the person's skin. Alternatively, translating נושנת as 'old' is in keeping with the observation that the introductory formula (v. 9a) implies that those who brought this person to the priest were already confident that it was a case of צרעת. Presumably they noticed the disease at an advanced, 'old', stage.[84]

Third, whereas the first case introduces the disease as one that 'may develop into צרעת' nothing is said of development in the introduction of this section. It is said 'When there is an affliction of צרעת on a human' (נגע צרעת כי תהיה באדם, v. 9a). And, in contrast to the preceding case (vv. 2-8), this one does not anticipate a situation in which the priest discovers that the complication is not צרעת.[85]

Fourth, the addition of the clause 'He will not quarantine him because he is unclean' (לא יסגרנו כי טמא הוא, v. 11b), after he has already noted that 'live flesh' (v. 10b) is exposed and that this is a case of an 'old צרעת' (v. 11a), seems unnecessary considering that a case which appeared 'deeper than the skin of the flesh' is automatically pronounced unclean without any need for quarantining in v. 3. The only ostensible reason for why this statement is included is that it is intended to indicate that the natural course of 'spreading', identified by a period of quarantine in vv. 2-8, is the exposure of 'living flesh'.[86] The legislator emphasizes that no period of quarantine is necessary because the sight of 'live flesh' is the sign of a *fully developed* case of צרעת.[87]

83. Milgrom, *Leviticus 1–16*, p. 785.

84. See August Dillmann, *Exodus und Leviticus* (2nd edn; Leipzig: F. Hirzel, 1880), p. 509.

85. True, the person is declared 'clean' if the disease completely covers him (vv. 12-13), but the text does not say that he ceases to have צרעת.

86. This is a more persuasive explanation than that provided by Milgrom: 'This warning is essential, for one might argue that if a white shiny spot warrants quarantine (v. 4), so a white discoloration, despite the clear evidence of white hair and raw flesh, should also be quarantined' (Milgrom, *Leviticus 1–16*, p. 785). Would the reader not have understood that the purpose of quarantining in vv. 3-8 was to see if the white shiny spots became deeper than the flesh and turned hair white? If so, it would seem incomprehensible why they might have felt compelled to quarantine the case in vv. 9-17.

87. The reference to 'in the skin of his flesh' in v. 11 would be purely redundant if this phrase is only intended to delineate the part of the body that is of interest. Not only has 'live flesh' just been seen by the priest in v. 10, but within that verse a reference to 'in the skin' is made which, if Milgrom is correct, assumes that the reader is already aware of what part of the body is on view. These observations are further evidence that 'flesh' has more than a physical meaning in this chapter.

The progression from a case in the process of developing (vv. 2-8) to one that is clearly an 'old צרעת' (v. 9) raises the question as to what made those who brought the man in v. 9 so confident that it was such a case. The answer comes in what precedes the declaration that it is צרעת נושנת. First, within the sore there is white hair and, second, the priest sees 'live flesh' (הבשר החי). Three observations indicate that 'live flesh', rather than 'white hair', is the definitive sign of a fully developed case of צרעת.[88] One, though white hair is undoubtedly related to the disease, the exposure of 'flesh' rather than 'white' hair is emphasized in the first case (vv. 2-8). Two, the legislator soon identifies 'raw flesh', not 'white hair', as 'unclean' (v. 15).[89] Three, he goes to great lengths to demonstrate that it is the exposure of 'living flesh' which is important in the last two sub-cases of this section (i.e. vv. 14-15; 16-17).[90] Four, in a latter case 'yellow' (צהב) hair is prescribed as a diagnostic aide rather than 'white hair' (vv. 30, 32, 36). Since the change of colour appears more important than the colour itself, the hair is possibly used to determine if the disease has spread 'deeper than the skin of *the flesh*'.[91]

The legislator achieves at least two things by progressing from a developing case of צרעת (vv. 2-8) to a fully developed case (vv. 9-17). First, the second case interprets the danger of a skin complaint 'spreading' in vv. 2-8: *a 'spreading' disease threatens to move into the 'flesh' so that the latter is seen by the priests*. Second, once attention is drawn to the 'flesh', the second case proceeds to clarify that 'flesh' rather than צרעת is the source of uncleanness (v. 15). This last point is made by the inclusion of a sub-case in which a person is declared clean when the צרעת completely covers the body (vv. 12-13).

Verses 12-13 have generated much speculation as to why a man completely covered with צרעת is pronounced 'clean'.[92] Most commonly, the

---

88. Wenham likewise recognizes that the definitive sign that the skin complication makes a person unclean is the presence of 'raw (living) flesh' in the second case (Wenham, *Leviticus*, p. 198). And Seidl observes that 'flesh' is 'always determinate' as the sign of this disease within Leviticus 13 (*Tora für den 'Aussatz' Fall*, p. 180).

89. Thus, in commenting on the meaning of the phrase הבשר החי טמא Hoffmann says 'This, but not לבן is מטמא' (*Das Buch Leviticus*, p. 376 [translation mine]).

90. This observation cautions against viewing 'live flesh' as no more than a third symptom of צרעת, alongside 'white hair' and 'spreading' (*pace* Milgrom, *Leviticus 1–16*, p. 785). It is better to understand raw flesh as that which the disease in vv. 2-8 was threatening to expose.

91. That is, something must be going on under the skin to change the colour of the hair.

92. Hartley assumes that vv. 12-13 introduce a situation unrelated to the preceding 'old צרעת' (cf. vv. 10-12) so that on view is a case in which scales cover a person's entire body without opening up the skin. However, in Leviticus 13 צרעת occurs with the definite article only within these verses (three times) and this makes it likely that it is

declaration of clean is explained in medical terms.[93] But the literary progression of Leviticus 13 suggests an answer might lie elsewhere than in dermatological studies. Up until this point of the chapter it is not clear if uncleanness is generated by the 'flesh' or the צרעת. It could be either. However, three things in vv. 12-17 clarify that 'flesh' is the source of uncleanness. First, when the person is completely covered with this disease he is pronounced 'clean' (v. 13) which, by implication, means that the צרעת cannot be 'unclean'.

Second, vv. 14-15 emphasize that the person declared clean after being covered with צרעת is unclean the moment 'raw flesh' appears (v. 14a). The use of a nominal clause to introduce this sub-case (i.e. 'When there appears on him raw flesh'; וביום הראות בו בשר חי) seems to draw attention to 'flesh' as the decisive diagnostic factor of uncleanness.[94] Moreover, the replacement of an introductory אם, as is used to introduce other sub-cases of this nature in Leviticus 13, with the preposition ב may convey a sense of urgency in relation to the sudden appearance of flesh which is complemented by the immediate declaration that this person is unclean.[95]

---

the same infection that is referred to in vv. 10-11. That is, the disease which has exposed 'live flesh' has now covered the person in a way that prevents the flesh from showing (Hartley, *Leviticus*, p. 191).

93. For example, Milgrom, following G.R. Driver, ventures that '[h]ealing has occurred by desquamation; the scaly crust peels off, leaving white beneath' (Milgrom, *Leviticus 1–16*, p. 785. cf. G.R. Driver, 'Leprosy', in *Dictionary of the Bible* [2nd rev. edn; ed. J. Hastings, F.C. Grant and H.H. Rowley; New York: Scribners, 1963], pp. 575-78 [576]; Noordtzij, *Leviticus*, pp. 137-38; Dillmann, *Exodus und Leviticus*, p. 509). Maccoby attempts to explain Lev. 13.12 on medical terms. He suggests that 'total whiteness was regarded as a disease of albinism that was distinct from the disease of "leprosy." Even though the patient had been previously declared unclean, the subsequent spread of the whiteness over throughout the body had revealed him to be suffering from albinism, not "leprosy"' (Maccoby, *Ritual and Morality*, p. 124). There are two difficulties with his conclusion. First, albinism does not spread, one is born with it. Second, his explanation does not account for the immediacy with which the disease reappears in the verse which follows 'When raw flesh appears'.

94. The use of such a clause to introduce a case does not occur elsewhere in this chapter.

95. Both Seidl and Elliger argue that vv. 14-15 are a later addition to Leviticus 13. However, the six observations which they assume indicate this may actually support my contention that these verses draw attention to the root-source of uncleanness in Leviticus 13. Seidl observes, first, that there is no introductory אם, instead there is a prepositional connection. In terms of the argument being made here, this syntax may draw attention to the urgency of a situation in which flesh is suddenly exposed. Second, the author establishes uncleanness with a prefixed form of טמא (i.e. יטמא) and, as for the previous point, this may convey the immediacy with which a person becomes unclean once flesh is exposed. Whereas the afflicted person is the subject of the verb on this occasion (i.e.

Third, 'live flesh' is explicitly identified as unclean in vv. 14-15: 'the live flesh *is certainly* unclean' (הבשר החי טמא הוא, v. 15).[96] Most scholars overlook the emphatic nature of this declaration, conveyed by the use of the only tripartite nominal clause within Leviticus 13.[97] Perhaps significantly, the

'he will be unclean'), on other occasions in Leviticus 13 the priest is the subject of the *piel* טמא (perfect) and this implies that some time elapses before a suspicious case is *declared* 'unclean'. Third, whereas the establishment of uncleanness follows the investigation by the priest in the other cases in Leviticus 13, in v. 14 the legislator simply declares that the person is unclean from the moment live flesh appears. Fourth, there is an accumulation of 'unclean-statements' in vv. 14-15 which does not occur elsewhere in the chapter. In addition to these observations Elliger notes that, first, the declaration that the 'flesh', rather than the person, is unclean in v. 15 is at odds with what happens elsewhere in Leviticus 13. Second, he observes a difference in expression: in vv. 14-16 the legislator says בשר חי rather than מחית בשר חי (cf. v. 10). See Seidl, *Tora für den 'Aussatz' Fall*, p. 33; Elliger, *Leviticus*, p. 33.

96. Hartley refers to a person becoming 'afflicted' with בשר חי ('live flesh') in v. 14. However it is misleading to use the term 'affliction' for two reasons. First, נגע ('affliction'), which occurs frequently in this chapter, does not occur in v. 14. Second, the verse simply anticipates the moment when 'live flesh' appears on this person ('When live flesh appears on him' [ובים הראות בו]). In other words, live flesh is a sign rather than an affliction (*Leviticus*, p. 191). The unexpectedness of the statement הבשר החי טמא הוא leads Jastrow to conclude that they are a later 'amplifying gloss' (Morris Jastrow, 'The So-called Leprosy Laws: An Analysis of Leviticus, Chapters 13 and 14', *JQR* 4 [1913–14], pp. 357-418 [364]).

97. T. Muraoka defines a tripartite nominal clause as one in which 'one of the three components is a third-person independent personal pronoun'. Moreover, he identifies the purpose of the pronoun in the type found in v. 15 (i.e. definite noun-phrase-indefinite noun-phrase-pronoun) as giving 'prominence to the preceding constituent' (Takamitsu Muraoka, 'The Tripartite Nominal Clause Revisited', in *The Verbless Clause in Biblical Hebrew. Linguistic Approaches* [ed. Cynthia L. Miller; Linguistic Studies in Ancient West Semitic; Winona Lake, IN: Eisenbrauns, 1999], pp. 187-213 [188, 203]; cf. Takamitsu Muraoka, *Emphatic Words and Structures in Biblical Hebrew* [Leiden: E.J. Brill, 1985]). Unfortunately it is difficult to assess how K. Shimasaki's theory of 'focus structure' applies to this clause structure. Although he deals with instances of extraposition (i.e. *casus pendens*), he does not indicate how his model of interpretation would apply to the 'extraposed element + noun phrase + resumptive pronoun' word order, other than suggest it would constitute one of the following focus structures: (1) 'Argument-Focus Structure'; (2) 'Clause-Focus Structure'. Keeping in mind that Shimasaki excludes the extraposed element (i.e. הבשר החי) from the 'clause domain', which thus becomes טמא הוא, it seems that our clause may fall outside his proposal. This is because this kind of clause (i.e. טמא הוא) has what Shimasaki calls 'Predicate-Focus Structure' which he does not consider applies to the kind of extrapositional case we are dealing with. Therefore, it is not possible to comment on the implications of his work for the translation of this verse. Nevertheless, Shimasaki's idea does not negate Muraoka's approach to this kind of tripartite clause so that the translation offered for this verse above still stands. See Katsuomi Shimasaki, *Focus Structure in Biblical Hebrew: A*

only other tripartite nominal clause in Leviticus also occurs in the immediate context of a reference to בשר: 'When any man has a discharge from *his flesh* (בשרו), his discharge is *certainly* unclean (זובו טמא הוא, Lev. 15.2)'.[98] Thus, Lev. 13.15 seems to clarify that 'live flesh' is the essential criterion for diagnosing a case of uncleanness.[99]

Fourth, the use of the verb 'to see' (ראה) in v. 15 may also suggest that 'flesh' is the source of uncleanness. This verb occurs 28 times within this chapter,[100] twice as often as in any other chapter of the Bible. On every occasion that it has a priest as its subject within Leviticus 13 it is followed by a conditional clause introducing various symptoms that the priest must see before declaring a person unclean.[101] There are two exceptions. The first is when 'flesh' is the direct object of the verb in v. 15. This time, instead of being followed by a conditional clause, the text immediately says 'he will declare him unclean' (יטמא). The appearance of 'flesh' makes further tests unnecessary, presumably because 'the live flesh *is certainly* unclean' (v. 15).

Study of Word Order and Information Structure (Bethesda, MD: CDL Press, 2002), pp. 245-49.

It is noteworthy that nearly all commentators translate this clause as '(the) raw flesh is unclean' (cf. ESV; NAS; NJB; NRS; Noth, *Leviticus*, p. 99; Wenham, *Leviticus*, p. 190; Levine, *Leviticus*, p. 79; Hartley, *Leviticus*, p. 171; Milgrom, *Leviticus 1–16*, p. 769). To my knowledge, the only attempts to translate the pronoun הוא are made by Kornfeld and the NEB. Kornfeld renders the clause 'Das wilde Fleisch ist *etwas* Unreines' (emphasis mine). However, the emphatic use of הוא would appear to be more forceful than 'etwas'. The NEB 'raw flesh is *to be considered* unclean' (emphasis mine) is preferable, but it still falls short of conveying the prominence הוא gives to the fact of the uncleanness of the raw flesh. See Kornfeld, *Levitikus*, p. 50.

98. Milgrom departs from the consensus, altering the Masoretic cantillation so as to include זובו within the clause מבשרו זובו, which he translates 'his discharge being from his member'. Though he acknowledges that one could translate מבשרו as part of the clause that precedes it (i.e. 'when any man has a discharge *from his member*') he contends that then the rest of the verse, namely זובו טמא הוא, 'can only with great difficulty be rendered "his discharge (it) is impure"' (Milgrom, *Leviticus 1–16*, p. 906). But this conclusion is problematic on two counts. First, it overlooks the linguistic phenomenon of the tripartite nominal clause. Second, it ignores that the same type of clause, which he suggests can only be rendered with 'great difficulty', occurs in Lev. 13.15, a verse which Milgrom does not discuss. Elliger's translation of זובו טמא הוא (Lev. 15.2b) as 'so ist sein Ausfluß unrein', but הבשר החי טמא הוא (Lev. 13.15b) as 'Das wilde Fleisch ist unrein', reflects an inconsistent treatment of the tripartite nominal clause. The emphasis he conveys with 'sein' in Lev. 15.2 should be included in Lev. 13.15 (*Leviticus*, pp. 160, 191).

99. As is also suggested by Porter, *Leviticus*, p. 98.

100. A multiple of seven.

101. Lev. 13.3, 6, 17, 25, 27, 30, 31, 32, 34, 43, 50, 51, 55. This is also true of those occasions when the verb, with the priest as subject, is not followed by a direct object.

The second exception is the single occurrence of the verb after the priest has already looked (ראה) and found symptoms that establish that the person has צרעת (v. 3b). This second exception is noteworthy, considering that it occurs in a verse which twice refers to the 'skin of his flesh'. Thus, in both cases, after the priest has seen the flesh (v. 15) and seen the symptoms on the 'skin of his flesh', he immediately 'pronounces him unclean' (וְטִמְּאוֹ). Within the prescriptions of Leviticus 13 a person becomes 'unclean' after a priest pronounces this when he 'sees' the 'flesh' exposed or threatened by צרעת.[102]

Nevertheless, since I have argued that the decisive factor for determining if a case is צרעת is the exposure of 'live flesh' there is a potential problem at this point. How does this understanding account for the fact that v. 12 assumes that it is צרעת that 'breaks out' and 'covers' all of this person's body without the exposure of 'live flesh'? The answer comes in v. 16 which states: 'or *if the live flesh* recovers and turns white again' (או כי ישוב הבשר החי ונהפך ללבן). Combining this legislation with the observation that this case presupposes an 'old צרעת' (cf. v. 9a), it would seem that v. 12 has in mind a situation in which 'live flesh' is turned white by the rapid spreading (i.e. 'it breaks out'; פשה תפשה) of צרעת. It assumes that the disease is initially diagnosed by the priest's observation of 'live flesh', but in time this 'old צרעת' turns white so that, paradoxically, with the disappearance of the 'live flesh' the person is pronounced clean while still having the disease. Though this is a strange case, perhaps it reflects that we are dealing with a ritual rather than a medical text. The legislator may have constructed such a case to make a theological point, namely 'flesh', not צרעת, is 'unclean'. It seems that a connection is made between 'flesh' and 'uncleanness' by the end of this second case (vv. 9-17).

This interpretation raises a question concerning what it is about 'flesh' that makes it (v. 15), and the person upon whom it is found, 'unclean'. Two observations suggest that the symbolic, rather than physical, meaning of 'flesh' accounts for its 'uncleanness' in Leviticus 13.

---

102. We may speculate that, in this regard, the priest's 'seeing' of the flesh and 'declaration' of uncleanness represents God's actions in relation to human rebelliousness. Kiuchi argues that the phrase 'pronounce him unclean' (v. 3) does not mean that 'until the priest pronounces the person unclean the latter is not yet unclean. The hiding nature of the leprous disease is evident. So it is wrong to take the pronouncement as signifying that the case becomes one of a leprous disease only when the priest pronounces so. The priest's pronouncement has the function of officially uncovering the case before God' (Kiuchi, *Leviticus*, p. 230). However, the truthfulness of this statement relies, first, on his presupposition that 'uncleanness' is symbolic of the state of 'hiding oneself against the Lord' and, second, the assumption that the disease is itself 'unclean'. I have already rejected the first presupposition (see above and Trevaskis, 'On a Recent "Existential" Translation of *ḥāṭā'*', pp. 313-19) and below it is argued that צרעת cannot be considered unclean because when it completely covers the person he is pronounced 'clean'.

First, a comparison of the use of בשר in vv. 2-8, 9-17 and the parallel
cases of 18-23 and 24-28 indicates that something more than physical flesh is
on view. In vv. 2-8 the term refers to physical flesh. This understanding is
apparent from the several references made to 'his flesh' (בשרו, vv. 2, 3, 4)
and the phrase 'the priest shall look at the affliction on the skin of *the* flesh'
(וראה הכהן את־הנגע בעור־הבשר, v. 3). However, since the legislator
states that 'the live flesh is certainly unclean' (v. 15b) 'flesh' would seem to
gain a symbolic meaning in vv. 9-17. If the symbolic meaning assigned to
'unclean' in Leviticus 11 is correct its association with 'flesh' in Leviticus 13
may introduce a moral dimension to the latter term. Finally, the use of 'flesh'
as a substitute for a person in vv. 18-28 (see below) seems to be symbolic.

Second, the first two cases forge a parallel relationship between the concepts of 'flesh' (בשר) and 'human' (אדם).[103] First, within the introductory
clauses of vv. 2 and 9, which are parallel in syntax, the phrase 'on the skin of
his flesh' (בעור־בשרו, v. 2) is replaced with 'on a human' (באדם, v. 9).
Second, one can find the same parallel drawn within the second case (vv. 9-
17), namely whereas an 'affliction of צרעת' is '*on a human*' (v. 9), the same
case is soon referred to as 'an old צרעת *on the skin of his flesh*' צרעת
נושנת הוא בעור בשרו, v. 11b). Thus, the terms 'human' and 'flesh'
seem deliberately aligned, and if אדם has more than sex-inclusive significance in Lev. 13.2 (see page 127, footnote 66), this may indicate that 'flesh'
carries a similar symbolic meaning to this term.

To identify the symbolic significance of 'flesh' as it is used in Leviticus 13
a cognitive linguistic study of the term, as it is used in Genesis 1–Leviticus
12 is undertaken in what follows. Following this I shall present evidence that
the Qumran sectarians used the term 'flesh' with an ethical meaning.

A Cognitive Linguistic Study of בשר *in Genesis 1–Leviticus 12*

The term בשר is applied to humans and animals within Genesis 1–Leviticus
12.[104] With regard to its use in relation to humans, it occurs 25 times within
the Pentateuch prior to Leviticus 13, and on only two of these occasions is
the referent clearly limited to physical flesh (Gen. 40.19; Exod. 4.7). For reasons that will become clear below, an examination of the use of the remaining 21 occurrences within their narrative order will be helpful. After this

---

103. Seidl refers to the two terms as synonyms (*Tora für den 'Aussatz' Fall*, p. 156).
104. Observing that texts commonly assigned to P show a relatively greater interest in
'flesh' than other 'sources', Josef Scharbert makes the following comment. 'Gegenüber
den anderen Pentateuchschichten fällt hier aber das offensichtlich große interesse am
„Fleisch" sowohl der Tiere als auch des Menschen auf, das diese Tradition durch die
unverhältnismäßig häufige Verwendung des Begriffes verrät' (Josef Scharbert, *Fleisch,
Geist und Seele im Pentateuch* [Stuttgart: Verlag Katholisches Bibelwerk, 1966], p. 48).

examination, using a cognitive linguistic approach, I shall assess whether the reader of Leviticus 13 is likely to 'access' a symbolic domain of this term's semantic frame when interpreting how it is that 'flesh' is 'unclean' (Lev. 13.15).

Genesis. The term 'flesh' occurs four times within the Garden of Eden narrative (Genesis 2–3), and on each of these occasions it is used to affirm the union between husband and wife.[105] The notion of a husband and wife being 'one flesh' (בשר אחד, Gen. 2.24) already introduces a symbolic dimension to the term 'flesh'.

Domains: *Union between a man and woman in the Garden of Eden narrative.*

The next 15 occurrences of בשר are found within the Noahic narrative (Gen. 6.1-9.29) where the term is used with multiple senses.[106] First, it connotes the mortality of humans: 'Yahweh said, 'My spirit will not contend with humanity (אדם) forever, because he is flesh' (ויאמר יהוה לא־ידון רוחי באדם לעלם בשגם הוא בשר, Gen. 6.3);[107] second, the phrase 'all flesh' (כל־בשר) is a collective reference for humans and animals. In this regard, the narrative qualifies 'all flesh' as having 'corrupted its way upon the earth' (Gen. 6.12), so that God pronounces judgment on 'all flesh', 'for the earth is full of violence because of them' (Gen. 6.13), and will destroy 'all flesh' (Gen. 6.17) with the exception of that portion of 'all flesh' he saves on the ark.[108] After he sends the flood, Yahweh makes a covenant to preserve 'all flesh' from the same form of judgment.[109] Thus, in contrast to the positive symbolism associated with human 'flesh' in Genesis 2–3, the term carries mostly negative connotations within the Noahic narrative: 'all flesh' is a perpetrator of violence and the recipient of divine judgment. In support of this observation Bratsiotis comments that

> [s]ince the negative qualities of human nature are connected with *bāśār* in the OT, *kōl bāśār* normally appears in a derogatory sense. Consequently, men (all of whom are indeed *bāśār*) in their existential situation and in their general relationship to each other, are placed before God in sharp contrast to him. Wherever *kōl bāśār* appears as an idiom (thus with the exception of Lev. 4.11; 13.[1]3; Nu. 8.7; etc.), the idea that the *bāśār* that all men share in

---

105. Gen. 2.21, 23 (×2), 24. 'Here the ideal of marriage as it was understood in ancient Israel is being portrayed, a relationship characterized by harmony and intimacy between the partners' (Wenham, *Genesis 1–15*, p. 69).

106. There is only one reference to literal 'flesh' within this narrative, and that is in the context of eating the 'flesh' of animals (i.e. Gen. 9.4).

107. Wenham, *Genesis 1–15*, p. 142; Sarna, *Genesis*, p. 46.

108. Gen. 6.19; 7.15, 16, 21; 8.17.

109. Gen. 9.11, 13, 16, 17.

common is used to denote their distinction from God and emphasize their distance from him lies behind it more or less clearly. As the almighty Creator and Lord, majestically from above God alone rules, judges, and passes judgment on *kōl bāśār*, 'all flesh,' as his creation.[110]

Moreover, commenting specifically on the occurrence of כל־בשר in Gen. 6.12, he suggests that

> it cannot be denied that in this passage sin is intimately connected with *bāśār*, and that it is also used to denote the ethical aspect of man, in spite of the cosmic dualism between *rûaḥ*, 'the spirit of Yahweh,' and *bāśār* (which is here par. to *'ādām*, 'man'). Moreover, it can be maintained with certainty that *bāśār* as a designation of man (so esp. in Ps. 56.5[4]; 78.39; as well as *kōl bāśār*), and especially as antithesis to God (so Jer. 17.5; Job 10.4; 2 Ch. 32.8), not only emphasizes all the characteristics of *bāśār* that have been mentioned, *but also reflects its ethical inadequacy and inclination to sin as well as its physical nature.*[111]

Domains: *Sinful humanity and animals; recipient of divine judgment.*

The term 'flesh' next occurs six times in Genesis 17. On each occasion it refers to the place where circumcision is performed.[112] Though the term clearly refers to literal flesh, there are some indications that it may have more significance than this. Within the Pentateuch, of the six times 'flesh' appears as a collocation of the verb 'to circumcise' (מול), which occurs 22 times,[113] five of them occur within Genesis 17.[114] Why was it necessary to refer to the 'flesh' in connection with circumcision within this chapter? If it was to identify the location of the practice, why not simply stipulate the 'foreskin' (ערלה, vv. 11, 14, 23, 24, 25)? And why refer to the 'flesh' five times? It is quite possible that its use is idiomatic. However, considering that this narrative emphasizes circumcision as a reminder of the need for covenant faithfulness to Yahweh, it may also be speculated that the repeated directive to make this sign 'in the flesh' carries a symbolic meaning.

Of the three remaining attestations to human 'flesh' in Genesis, on two occasions it symbolizes the union that exists between siblings (Gen. 29.14; 37.27). Its final occurrence refers to the literal 'flesh' that birds strip from a person in Joseph's interpretation of a dream (Gen. 40.19).

---

110. N.P. Bratsiotis, '*Basar*', in *TDOT*, II, pp. 317-32 (327).

111. Bratsiotis, '*Basar*', p. 329 (emphasis mine).

112. Gen. 17.11, 13, 14, 23, 24, 25. See Gordon J. Wenham, *Genesis 16–50* (Nashville: Thomas Nelson, 1994), p. 24.

113. Genesis 17 (×11); 21.4; 34.15, 17, 22 (×2), 24; Exod. 12.44, 48; Lev. 12.3; Deut. 10.16; 30.6.

114. The other occurrence is Lev. 12.3.

Domains: *The flesh removed during the rite of circumcision; its removal is possibly symbolic for covenant faithfulness; union between siblings; flesh.*

Exodus. The term is applied to humans three times in Exodus. Its first occurrence carries a literal sense (i.e. Moses's flesh; Exod. 4.7). However, on the other two occasions it appears to carry an additional symbolic meaning. First, garments must cover a priest's 'naked flesh' (בשר ערוה; Exod. 28.42) so that, 'when they enter the Tent of Meeting or when they approach the altar to serve in the holy place they will not bear their guilt and die' (בבאם אל־אהל מועד או בגשתם אל־המזבח לשרת בקדש ולא־ישאו עון ומתו; Exod. 28.43; cf. 20.26). In this instance 'flesh' would seem to refer, in the first place, to the male genitalia. U. Cassuto considers that the requirement that priests do not officiate naked within the sanctuary may oppose what was practiced among certain peoples in the ancient East.[115] This suggestion may be correct, but it still does not explain why the legislator is opposed to such a practice.[116] Moreover, Exod. 28.42 does not just say 'naked', but 'naked flesh'. Within the narrative of the Pentateuch 'nakedness' carries negative connotations with the exception of Adam and Eve's nakedness before their rebellion in the Garden of Eden.[117] They covered their nakedness after the rebellion (Gen. 3.7). While 'one flesh' lives happily in God's presence within the Garden of Eden, it is the object of divine punishment in Genesis 6–9. Thus, considering that the tabernacle is symbolic of Eden (see Chapter 3) we may speculate that God's immediate presence is no longer accessible to 'naked flesh' in the way it was in the Garden.[118]

115. There are two occasions on which the need to cover a priest's nakedness in the sanctuary is mentioned, namely Exod. 20.26 and the present verse (U. Cassuto, *A Commentary on the Book of Exodus* [Jerusalem: Magnes Press, 1983], p. 257; see similarly, Scharbert, *Fleisch, Geist und Seele im Pentateuch*, p. 50).

116. After all, Israel adopted many other practices of the ancient near Eastern peoples.

117. Gen. 3.7; 10, 11; 9.22; 23 (×2); 42.9, 12 (used metaphorically for the vulnerability of the land).

118. Similarly, Scharbert, in his investigation into the use of the term 'flesh' in the Pentateuch, makes the following conclusion concerning the ability of 'flesh' to live in God's presence: 'Jedenfalls ist das Fleisch eigentlich der Begegnung mit Jahwe unwürdig. Deshalb sieht die Bundesordnung vor, daß die Priester, wenn sie vor Jahwe treten, ihr „Fleisch" sorgsam bedecken. Auch der Gebrauch der Gebetsformel „Gott der Geister für alles Fleisch" bringt die Gefahr zum Bewußtsein, in der sich das unwürdige „Fleisch' vor Gott befindet, weil ihm Gott jederzeit seinen „Geist' entsiehen kann. Wenn aber Israel der Schwäche „allen Fleisches' nachgibt und den Bund bricht, dann wird es im Gericht aus Hunger das „Fleisch der Söhne und Töchter" und heißt nach israelitischer Denkweise sein eigenes Fleisch verzehren. So zeigt also der priesterliche Theologe, wie unwürdig das „Fleisch" gegenüber Gott ist, wie gefährdet es durch seine sittliche Schwäche ist, wie sehr es aber auch durch Gott begnadet werden kann' (Scharbert, *Fleisch, Geist und Seele*, p. 55).

The final application of the term 'flesh' to humans (Exod. 30.32) may convey a similar symbolic meaning. This time Yahweh commands that his 'holy anointing oil' (שמן משחת־קדש) 'upon the flesh of a human shall not be poured' (על־בשר אדם לא ייסך; Exod. 30.32). Cassuto is probably correct in his suggestion that the intention of this law is to prevent this holy oil from being used for secular anointing.[119] But even so, this verse sets up a similar opposition between the notion of 'holy' and human 'flesh' to that found in Exod. 28.42-43.[120] We may also inquire why the legislator felt it necessary to qualify the flesh as 'human'. Presumably it was out of the question to apply this oil to animals, so the animal/human distinction is possibly not at issue. And because there is no indication that the application of this oil is limited to the head (cf. Lev. 8.30), 'flesh' is not used to stipulate a specific part of the body.

Domains: *Human flesh; male genitalia; profane humanity*

Leviticus 1–12. Human 'flesh' is only referred to once in Leviticus, prior to Chapter 13, in connection with the circumcision of a baby boy in Leviticus 12. In addition to its literal sense, we may assume that the symbolic meaning it possibly has in Genesis 17 would be accessed by the intended reader within this context.

Domains: *The material removed during the rite of circumcision; its removal may symbolize covenant faithfulness.*

Summary of the Semantic Frame of בשר

Primary domain: Flesh
In Genesis 1–Leviticus 12, even though the term בשר profiles against the domain of literal 'flesh' on only nine of the *c.* 26 times that it refers to humans, it always profiles against literal 'flesh' when referring to animals (i.e. 33 times). The domain of literal 'flesh' would appear to be the most likely accessed at the 'crystallization point' of interpretation.

Other domains: Union between a man and woman in the Garden of Eden narrative; rebellious humanity and animals; recipient of divine judgment; union between siblings; removal as symbol of covenant faithfulness; profane humanity; male genitalia.

---

119. Casuto, *Exodus*, p. 398. See also Cornelis Houtman, *Exodus* (Leuven: Peeters, 2000), pp. 575-76.
120. Observe also the fronting of the prepositional phrase.

Though it would seem that literal 'flesh' is the first domain accessed at the moment of crystallization, any one of these other domains may be accessed 'post-crystallization'. The likelihood of them being accessed is

> determined by such factors as the immediate literary context, the familiarity of the reader with the context (entrenchment), and the amount of time given to subsequent reflection (i.e. post-crystallization processes).[121]

Worth considering is that, since בשר profiles against something other than 'flesh' more than 70% of the time when it is applied to humans it may not take long to begin accessing other domains post-crystallization.

There are several reasons why it seems reasonable to assume that a reader familiar with the text of Genesis 1–Leviticus 12 would access the symbolic domains of בשר during the post-crystallization interpretative process. First, the literary context of Leviticus 13 (i.e. Leviticus 11–15) appears to assume that both Genesis 1–3 and Genesis 6–9 are significant for its interpretation. The primary domains against which בשר profiles in these passages are symbolic. In Genesis 1–3 it symbolizes the union between Adam and Eve in God's presence before their rebellion. In Genesis 6–9 it is primarily symbolic of the rebellion of humankind and animals against God and his subsequent judgment of them. Genesis 17 possibly also looms large within the interpreter's mind considering that the removal of בשר during the process of circumcision has just been referred to in Leviticus 12. Though the primary domain accessed in the latter passage is no doubt human 'flesh', we cannot rule out the possibility that the removal of this flesh brought to mind the concept of covenant faithfulness. If this possibility is accepted, it seems that the interpreter of Leviticus 13 already has some encouragement to begin accessing the symbolic domains against which בשר profiles in Genesis 1–Leviticus 12.

Second, the apparently redundant repetition of the phrase 'the skin of his flesh'; the parallel relationship established between בשר and אדם; and the use of בשר as a substitute for 'person' in vv. 18 and 24 possibly increase the reader's interest in why בשר is associated with uncleanness. Of particular importance may be that בשר is used as a substitute for humans when it occurs within the Noah narrative where it profiles against the domains of human rebellion and divine judgment on rebellious humans.

Third, if the symbolic meaning Chapter 3 assigned to the status of 'unclean' in Leviticus 11 is correct, the statement that 'raw flesh is certainly unclean' (Lev. 13.15) would seem to encourage a reader to ask how 'flesh' could be 'unclean'. Indeed, this statement may only make sense once it is considered that the term 'unclean' is applied to those things which should be excluded from God's immediate presence.

---

121. Wardlaw, *Conceptualizing Words*, p. 90.

Finally, to a reader with a general knowledge of the Pentateuch, the frequent mention of צרעת is likely to bring to mind the notion of divine judgment. A person may ask how 'flesh' could be the recipient of what symbolizes
divine judgment in Leviticus 13.

*There seems to be reasonable evidence that, though a reader of Leviticus
13 would have first accessed the domain 'human flesh' when interpreting
בשר, familiarity with the relevant texts and the literary context of this
material would encourage the interpreter to access the symbolic domains this
term has in Genesis 1–Leviticus 12. The most likely domain, in this regard,
would be that of 'human rebellion against Yahweh and its divine punishment'.*

This interpretation of the term 'flesh', within Leviticus 13, departs from
the consensus that it has no more than a physical meaning. Yet a recent study
of certain Qumran documents argues that the use of בשר had a similar
negative symbolic meaning to the one I have proposed as early as the 3rd
century BCE.[122] Thus, to increase confidence in my symbolic interpretation of
this term it will be helpful to review this study before returning to our exegesis of Lev. 13.18-28.

The Symbolic Meaning of בשר *at Qumran*
The possibility that there is a symbolic dimension to the meaning of בשר in
Leviticus 13 is also suggested by the use of this term in some Qumran texts.
Several texts from Qumran indicate that this community associated a use of
בשר with morally rebellious humanity. In a study aimed at demonstrating
that Paul's view of σάρξ finds its antecedent in Palestinian Jewish sapiential
traditions, rather than in the theological developments of the Jewish Diaspora,
Jörg Frey concludes that in some Sapiential texts from Qumran,

> [f]lesh [i.e. בשר] is deeply linked with sin and impurity and in some way
> opposed to the spirit of God that gives insight and knowledge. Moreover,
> flesh seems to represent an evil sphere or even power that causes human sin
> and causes the pious to stumble.[123]

He argues that 4QInstruction, which he dates from the late 3rd century to
early 2nd century BCE, already reflects the antithesis Paul later articulates as
existing between 'flesh' (σάρξ) and 'spirit' (πνεῦμα).[124] This symbolic use
of 'flesh' appears to have influenced later writings found at Qumran, speci-

---

122. Jörg Frey, 'The Notion of "Flesh" in 4QInstruction and the Background of Pauline
Usage', in *Sapiential, Liturgical and Poetical Texts from Qumran. Proceedings of the
Third Meeting of the International Organization for Qumran Studies, Oslo 1998* (ed.
Daniel K. Falk, Florentino García Martínez and Eileen M. Schuller; Leiden: E.J. Brill,
2000), pp. 197-226.
123. Frey, '"Flesh" in 4QInstruction and Pauline Usage', p. 209.
124. E.g. Rom. 7.5-6; 8; 1 Cor. 5.5; Gal. 3.3; 4.29; 5-6; Phil. 3.3.

fically some of the communal hymns. For example, in 1QH[a] 5.30-33 the term
בשר is 'characterized in terms of sin, impurity and depravation':[125]

> In the mysteries of your insight
> [you] have apportioned all these things,
> to make your glory known.
> [However, what is] the spirit of flesh (בשר)
> to understand all these matters
> and to have insight in [your woundrous (*sic*)] and great counsel?
> What is someone born of a woman among all your awesome works?
> He is a structure of dust fashioned with water,
> his counsel is the [iniquity] of sin, shame of dishonor and so[urce of] impurity,
> and a depraved spirit rules over him.[126]

It is even more explicitly characterized as sinful in 1QH[a] 12.30f.:

> What is flesh (בשר) compared to this?
> What creature of clay can do wonders?
> He is in sin (בעוון) from his maternal womb
> and in guilty iniquity (באשמת מעל) right to old age.[127]

More stimulating, in terms of my suggestion that בשר is closely associated
with the idea of 'uncleanness' and therefore exclusion from the community,
is a passage from 1QS. This text, of a similar genre to 1QH[a] [i.e. communal
hymn], appears to apply the term 'flesh' to 'those remaining outside the
Essene community', a class of people it associates with the realm of
death:[128]

> However, I belong to evil humankind (ואני לאדם רשעה)
> to the assembly of unfaithful flesh (ולסוד בשר עול);
> my failings (עוונתי), iniquities (פשעי), my sins (חטאתי)
> with the depravities of my heart (עם נעוית לבבי)
> let me belong to the assembly of worms
> and of those who walk in darkness.[129]

Thus, the 'member of the community himself confesses sharing the lot of
sinful humanity, because he is בשר'.[130] And in this connection, the life of
those within the realm of 'flesh' is one of judgment (1QS 11.11f.):

---

125. Frey, '"Flesh" in 4QInstruction and Pauline Usage', p. 203.
126. Frey, '"Flesh" in 4QInstruction and Pauline Usage', pp. 202-203.
127. Frey, '"Flesh" in 4QInstruction and Pauline Usage', p. 205.
128. Frey says it has this meaning in 1QH[a] too ('"Flesh" in 4QInstruction and Pauline
Usage', p. 207).
129. Frey, '"Flesh" in 4QInstruction and Pauline Usage', p. 207.
130. Frey, '"Flesh" in 4QInstruction and Pauline Usage', p. 208.

> As for me, if I stumble,
> the mercies of God shall be my salvation always,
> and if I fall by the sin of the flesh (בעוון בשר),
> in the justice of God which endures eternally, shall my judgment be'[131]

In connection with the use of 'flesh' within this particular passage Frey arrives at the following conclusion.

> The rendering of the phrase בעוון בשר is quite decisive. Many interpreters have tried to weaken the expression in order to keep it close to the biblical [i.e. OT] usage of בשר and the majority of English translations remain unclear. As Jürgen Becker has stated, in the phrase בעוון בשר the word בשר has the function of *genetivus auctoris*: consequently, flesh is the cause of the evil deed and it is the power that provokes evil deeds.[132]

It is not argued here that this use of 'flesh' at Qumran proves my symbolic interpretation of this term within Leviticus 13. But it does make my suggestion more plausible. Frey thinks that the text which is seminal to 1QH[a] and 1QS (i.e. 4QInstruction) is a pre-Essene work associated with people connected and interested in the Temple.[133] If such a community in postexilic times could use 'flesh' in connection with the ideas of sin and judgment, it does not seem unlikely that the author of Leviticus could. Indeed, would not the same reason that motivates Frey to find an antecedent of Paul's use of 'flesh' (σάρξ) in Qumran, motivate one to find the antecedent of Qumran's use of 'flesh' in the OT? Frey does not think so, but this seems to reflect his unawareness of the semantic frame of בשר in the OT, which includes *'human rebellion against Yahweh and its divine punishment'*.

Flesh Exposed by צרעת *in the Place of a 'Boil' or 'Burn Caused by Fire' Makes a Person Unclean (vv. 18-28)*

Immediately following the 'chronic' case of צרעת in vv. 9-17 are two parallel cases that differ only in the location from where the disease may spread.

131. Frey, '"Flesh" in 4QInstruction and Pauline Usage', p. 208.
132. Becker argues that 'Auf alle Fälle macht 11,12 ("wenn ich strauchle durch die Sünde meines Fleisches") deutlich, dass hier בשר die Ursache des Sündigens ist, die Macht, die zur Sünde verführt' (J. Becker, *Das Heil Gottes. Heils- und Sündenbegriffe in den Qumrantexten und im Neuen Testament* [SUNT, 3; Göttingen: Vandenhoeck & Ruprecht; 1964], pp. 111-12), cited in Frey, '"Flesh" in 4QInstruction and Pauline Usage', p. 208).
133. '[L]ike most of the other Sapiential texts from Qumran, the work [4QInstruction] should be classified as a non-Sectarian, or non-Essene, or—more precisely—pre-Essene work. As A. Lange has shown from the treatment of cultic issues, the document seems to have originated in sapiential circles which were connected with and interested in the Temple'. More precisely he thinks that the text probably dates from the end of the 3rd or in the first half of the 2nd century BCE. See Frey, '"Flesh" in 4QInstruction and Pauline Usage', p. 213.

The first section (vv. 18-23) anticipates a case in which צרעת may spread from a 'boil that has healed' (שחין שׁ ונרפא, v. 18) and the second assumes a case in which the disease spreads from the 'burn of a fire' (מכות־אשׁ, v. 24). The conjunctive 'or' (או) links the two cases so that they should be read in parallel.[134] Of particular significance, in terms of their parallel form, is that they share the same introductory formula 'When *flesh* has on its skin' (בשׂר כי־יהיה בעורו, vv. 18, 24). Thus, the concern with 'flesh' in vv. 2-17 gains greater prominence within vv. 18-28 by it being made the subject the verb יהיה.[135] That 'flesh' is used here as a substitute for a person (i.e. symbolic sense) helps to confirm the suggestion that there is a progression from literal flesh in vv. 2-8 to the symbolic dimension of 'flesh' in vv. 9-17.[136] Indeed, the legislator's decision to use בשׂר as a substitute for a human is particularly striking considering the negative connotations this term has just been given in v. 15, namely '*raw flesh is certainly unclean*'.

Having argued that a symbolic meaning of 'human rebellion under divine judgment' is at least part of the intended meaning of בשׂר in Leviticus 13,[137] we may begin to understand why these two sections (i.e. vv. 18-23 and 24-28), which are introduced by 'When flesh has on its skin' (בשׂר כי יהיה בערו), come at this point in the chapter. Both sections deal with the diagnosis of צרעת that may 'break out' from the site of either a 'healed boil' (vv. 18-23) or the 'scar of a burn' (vv. 24-28). It is proposed that, by pre-

---

134. Note that a chiastic reversal of the use of the three diagnostic tools mentioned in Lev. 13.1-8 occurs in these two sections which also serves to draw attention to their parallel relationship. שׂאת (v. 19), פשׂה (v. 22), בהרת (v. 23) are found in reverse order in vv. 24, 27, 28. See Fishbane, 'Biblical Colophons, Textual Criticism and Legal Analogies', p. 443.

135. Seidl notes that the theme of 'live flesh' continues after vv. 14-15 with it being conspicuously prefaced with an introductory כי (*Tora für den 'Aussatz' Fall*, p. 33). Since we are to assume that the subject is 'flesh' (i.e. vv. 18, 24) it does not seem to matter that literal flesh is not mentioned as a diagnostic test in this section. The directive to pronounce the person unclean when the complication is 'deeper than the skin' (vv. 20, 25) may also bring to mind the idea of flesh.

136. Wenham, *Leviticus*, p. 190; Gerstenberger, *Leviticus*, p. 154. Though certain scholars accept that בשׂר can be interpreted as a substitute for 'person' in vv. 18 and 24, they limit its symbolic meaning to it being a general referent to humans and animals. Thus, the legislator employs the noun to acknowledge that animals may suffer from the same disease. For example, in Milgrom's opinion '[t]he text chooses *bāśār* "body, flesh" over *ādām* "person" (vv. 2, 9) or *'îš 'ô 'iššâ* "man or woman" (v 38) because *šĕḥîn* "boils" also afflict animals (e.g., Exod. 9.9, 10), and only *bāśār* comprises both' (*Leviticus 1–16*, p. 787; cf. Hoffmann, *Das Buch Leviticus*, p. 377). But there is no evidence that this prescription is intended for the examination of animals, and so we may put this argument to the side while we look for a more likely explanation for the use of this noun.

137. See pages 138-47.

scribing two parallel cases dealing with צרעת associated with a 'boil' or 'burn' respectively, the legislator intends to identify צרעת as a symbol of *divine judgment*. Within my symbolic understanding of Leviticus 13, this interpretation would mean that 'flesh' represents that which attracts God's judgment (symbol = צרעת), and the consequence of this judgment is the pronouncement of 'uncleanness'.

'Boils' are related to divine judgment elsewhere in the OT. In this regard, Milgrom comments that in other places their occurrence

> in Scripture attest to its being a highly visible and dreaded disease sent by the divinity (e.g., Exod. 9.9, 10, 11; 2 Kgs 20.7; Isa. 38.21; Job 2.7) for the violation of the covenant (Deut. 28.27, 35).[138]

But what is the significance of the case concerning 'a burn of a fire' (מכות־אש, v. 24)? Though the nominal form 'burn' (מכות) occurs only here in the OT, it comes from the nominal root כוה which is used metaphorically of God's judgment in Isa. 43.2.[139] Possibly of greater importance is the source of this burn, namely 'fire' (אש). 'Fire' is often associated with God's judgment within the Pentateuch[140] and it is possibly noteworthy that the reader has witnessed God's wrath manifest itself as a consuming fire within the immediate context of the purity regulations (cf. Lev. 10.2).[141]

We may speculate that the two cases of צרעת, associated with 'boils' and 'burns of fire' in vv. 18-28, are intended to induct the reader into understanding the symbolic meaning of this disease in relation to בשר: *it associates the spreading of* צרעת *with God's judgment on* בשר.[142]

Clarification of the Symbolic Meaning of 'Flesh' (vv. 29-37)

Milgrom points out that this section comes now because it deals with the 'non-fleshy' parts of the body. He seems correct in so far as a later case dealing with the head (vv. 40-46) describes an affliction as having only 'the appearance of צרעת of flesh' (Lev. 13.43). But though vv. 29-37 fall within the category of cases dealing with 'non-fleshy' parts of the body, there may be a literary explanation for why they are included at this point of the

---

138. Milgrom, *Leviticus 1–16*, p. 787.

139. Elsewhere the verbal root is found only in Prov. 6.28.

140. Gen. 19.24; 9.23, 24; Lev. 10.2.

141. From a cognitive linguistic point of view, though fire is also associated with God's 'presence' elsewhere in the Pentateuch (e.g. Gen. 15.17; Exod. 3.2; 13.21; 14.24), it is difficult to see how this sense of its meaning would be accessed within this context.

142. In this regard, notice that it is God who sends the disease in Lev. 14.34: 'When you enter the land of Canaan...and I put an affliction of צרעת in a house of the land of your possession' (כי תבאו אל־ארץ כנען...ונתתי נגע צרעת בבית ארץ אחזתכם).

chapter. This section, we may propose, serves to emphasize the symbolic meaning of 'flesh' that is developed earlier in the chapter. It lends itself to this purpose because the idea of 'flesh' cannot be taken literally. However, can it be argued that the idea of 'flesh' is assumed even though it is not mentioned in this section? Several observations suggest than it can.

First, prior to this section the legislator has already referred to the 'non-fleshy' part of the body as 'flesh'. To start with, the statement 'and if the צרעת covers all his flesh' (והנה כסתה הצרעת את־כל־בשרו, v. 13) is a reference to a person 'from his head to his feet' (מראשו ועד־רגליו, v. 12). And within the section that comes immediately before vv. 29-37 the term 'flesh' is used on two occasions as a substitute for 'human' (vv. 18, 24). Second, assuming that the reader registers that a person is 'flesh', in a symbolic sense, the directive for the priest to examine if the lesion appears deeper than the skin and whether or not the hair has turned yellow (v. 30) suggests that what lies under the skin is still of primary importance.[143] It seems that the idea of 'flesh' would be accessed in this section and that the legislator has not referred to it because it is not literally, but symbolically, present. Thus, if we are still directed to think of what lies below the skin, in the present case of צרעת on the head or beard, the legislator is possibly emphasizing that the problem with 'flesh' lies not in its physical nature but in its symbolic meaning.

Only the 'Breaking Out' of צרעת *Renders a Person Unclean (vv. 38-39)*

These verses deal with a case that is pronounced clean, and interrupt two cases dealing with צרעת of the head. Milgrom explains their present position in terms of the legislator's decision to structure the chapter according to sex.

> The question needs to be asked: Why did not the editor first complete his description of impure cases (vv. 42-44) before describing pure cases? Apparently, he ordered his material according to the subject: men and women together first (vv. 38-39), then men alone (vv. 40-44; *Keter Torah*).[144]

Yet if this explanation is correct why did the legislator choose to include the case of an infection of the beard in vv. 29-37 which presumably relates only

---

143. Since hair of the head or beard turns white naturally it was probably necessary for the legislator to stipulate 'yellow' rather than 'white'. Once again, the change in hair colour may indicate that the disease has penetrated below the skin. Milgrom suggests that the distinction in hair colour, between that associated with צרעת of the body and the head, is what necessitated the separate presentation of this case. But presumably the location of the disease on the person's head was more decisive than this in the present arrangement of the cases. See Milgrom, *Leviticus 1–16*, p. 794.

144. Milgrom, *Leviticus 1–16*, p. 799.

to males?[145] If the material is ordered according to the subject then this ought to have come as part of vv. 40-44 which deal strictly with men.

A better explanation for the position of vv. 38-39 becomes apparent when the rhetorical progression which characterizes this chapter's construction is kept in mind. Two striking aspects to this case emerge when it is compared to the preceding cases. First, whereas every other skin complaint in this chapter has the potential to develop into צרעת, this skin condition does not make a person unclean and this may raise the reader's interest as to why this is so. Second, this is the only case in which a disease other than צרעת is the subject of the verb פרח ('to break out'). Moreover, every other occurrence of this root within Leviticus 13–14 is associated with uncleanness. Below I argue that a combination of these two observations serves to emphasize within the context of Leviticus 13 that it is only when 'flesh' is exposed by צרעת that a person becomes unclean.

In Leviticus 13–14, two different terms for spreading are used for describing the physical spread of disease on a person's skin. The most common term is פשה ('to spread') which occurs 22 times and only here in the OT.[146] The other term is פרח ('to break out'; 'to flower') which occurs only eight times in these chapters. What is the semantic relationship between these terms? Though Milgrom suggests that פרח describes a more rapid process of spreading than פשה, it is not clear how he arrives at this conclusion considering that, as he admits, the etymology of this term is uncertain and it does not occur outside these chapters in the OT.[147] That the legislator did not consider them synonyms which he alternates between for stylistic effect is apparent when close attention is paid to how they are used. The subject of פשה is only ever a skin condition that *may develop* into צרעת. In other words, it occurs only as a process observed prior to the diagnosis of צרעת.[148] By contrast, with the exception of its use in v. 39, the term פרח is only used in definite cases of צרעת in Leviticus 13–14.[149] Thus, this term would seem

145. Hoffman argues that vv. 29-30 are applicable only to males because, first, there is a reference to צרעת of 'the beard' (הזקן) and, second, the preposition with a masculine singular pronominal suffix within the phrase 'When a man or woman has on him' (ואיש או אשה כי־יהיה בו, v. 29a) (*Das Buch Leviticus*, p. 380).

146. Lev. 13.5, 6, 7 (×2), 8, 22 (×2), 23, 27 (×2), 28, 32, 34, 35 (×2), 36, 51, 53, 55; 14.39, 44, 48.

147. Milgrom, *Leviticus 1–16*, p. 781.

148. Lev. 13.5, 7, 22, 27, 35, 36, 51; 14.39, 44. This observation helps to confirm my earlier conclusion that the introductory case (vv. 2-8) is concerned with the diagnosis of a skin complaint that may develop into צרעת. Moreover, it also confirms that the case in vv. 29-37 is a parallel case, concerning the diagnosis of צרעת of the head or beard, to that of vv. 2-8. Only פשה is used to describe the process of spreading in these cases.

149. Lev. 13.12, 20, 25, 39, 42, 57; 14.43. Even though the 'breaking out' of disease in v. 12 results in a state of cleanness, note that this occurs in a case that has already been diagnosed as צרעת.

to convey that there will either be, or already is, a fully developed outbreak of the disease in question. For this reason, it is not used in vv. 2-8 and 29-27 which deal with skin diseases that 'may develop' into צרעת. Even in the parallel cases concerning boils (vv. 18-23) and burns (vv. 24-28), whereas פרח is used to describe the 'breaking out' of צרעת from these wounds (vv. 20, 25) the legislator reverts to the use of סגר when a period of quarantine is prescribed for uncertain cases (vv. 22, 27 // 23, 28).

These observations help to make sense of the case that comes in vv. 38-39. This text is the only occasion in Leviticus 13–14 where a disease other than צרעת occurs as the subject of the root פרח (v. 39). This case seems to have been included at this point to disclose that the notion of פרח leads to a declaration of uncleanness only if it is צרעת that is spreading on the person and ultimately uncovers 'flesh'. It draws attention to the function צרעת has in representing God's judgment on 'flesh' (read: 'human rebellion against Yahweh').

But there is still one question that needs to be answered concerning the location of this case within these laws. Why does the legislator revert to a case dealing with 'the skin of their flesh' rather than continue on with diseases associated with the head? A possible reason is that it provides a contrast with the preceding case in which a person is declared unclean when צרעת inflicts localized areas on the head (i.e. vv. 29-37). In order to emphasize that God's judgment is symbolized by צרעת, not any other skin complaint, the legislator includes a case which, though 'many white spots' have 'broken out' over a person's body, the person remains clean.

By this stage of the laws in Leviticus 13, the reader should understand the following. First, uncleanness associated with צרעת is related to the exposure of 'flesh'. Second, the 'flesh' at issue is not merely physical flesh but the symbolic meaning of 'flesh'. Third, the 'breaking out' of צרעת on a person is symbolic of God's judgment on 'flesh', also conveyed by the priest's 'seeing' of the flesh.

The Fate of the Man Who Has צרעת on his Bald Head (vv. 40-46)

This final case concerning the diagnosis of צרעת on the head of a bald 'man' (איש) concludes with a prescription for what should be done with such a person (vv. 45-46).[150] Other than the location of the disease, namely in the bald area of a man's head, there are two observations that set this case apart from those that precede it. First, the introductory formula is different from the others found in this chapter. Every other case is introduced by the formula Y

---

150. Though nearly all scholars consider vv. 45-46 as a separate section that prescribes the general treatment of anyone diagnosed with צרעת, it is argued below that they specifically refer to the treatment of the man with this disease on a bald area of his head.

X‎כי־יהיה/תהיה‎, where X = subject of verb, and Y = ‎בעור־בשרו‎ (v. 2);
‎בעור־בשרם‎ (v. 9); ‎בו־בערו‎ (v. 18); ‎בערו‎ (v. 24); ‎בו‎ (vv. 29, 47); ‎באדם‎
(v. 38)

By contrast, the case in vv. 40-44 is introduced by ‎ואיש כי ימרט ראשו‎
('When a man's hair falls out of his head', v. 40a). However, it appears as
though the normal formula is present, but interrupted by two cases of
baldness that are declared clean. Once these are dealt with the normal formula is resumed by 'When he has on his bald crown or forehead' (‎וכי־יהיה‎
‎בקרחת או בגבחת‎, v. 42a). This textual structure is illustrated diagram-
matically as follows:

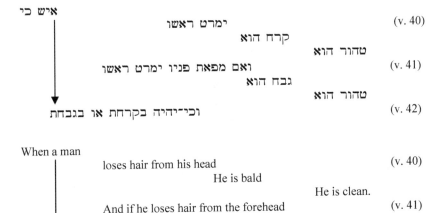

```
איש כי
            ימרט ראשו                                    (v. 40)
                    קרח הוא
                            טהור הוא
            ואם מפאת פניו ימרט ראשו                      (v. 41)
                    גבח הוא
                            טהור הוא
וכי־יהיה בקרחת או בגבחת                                   (v. 42)
```

```
When a man
            loses hair from his head                     (v. 40)
                    He is bald
                            He is clean.
            And if he loses hair from the forehead       (v. 41)
                    He is bald on the forehead
                            He is clean
When [a man; cf. v. 40a] has on his bald crown or forehead.  (v. 42)
```

What function is served by the interruption of the normal introductory formula with two cases concerning 'clean' cases of baldness? It seems as though
this structure serves to create a thematic transition from the 'clean' case that
precedes it (cf. vv. 38-39). Just as the 'many white spots', that had 'broken
out' in the case involving men and women, most probably raised the suspicion of onlookers (vv. 38-39), so might a man's sudden loss of hair. Thus, the
phrase 'he is clean' (‎טהור הוא‎) in v. 39 occasions the legislator's mention
of two kinds of baldness that are pronounced 'clean' (vv. 40b; 41b). But most
importantly this transition continues the legislator's emphasis that it is by the
action of ‎צרעת‎ that a person becomes 'unclean'. And this purpose probably
explains why a final case involving a ‎צרעת‎ afflicted bald area is introduced
by the resumption of the normal introductory formula in v. 42. Though
baldness is not in itself 'unclean', when it has an affliction that is reddish-
white, the legislator says that 'it is a ‎צרעת‎ breaking out' on these areas
(v. 42b). If the priest looks at it and it has an 'appearance like ‎צרעת‎ of skin
of flesh' (v. 43):

> He himself is צרעת, he is unclean, the priest will certainly declare him
> unclean, his affliction is on his head. (v. 44)

The addition of 'his affliction is on his head' is unexpected. Milgrom suggests that this clause may have been added to stress that 'although his
affliction is treated like fleshy-skin scale disease' it should be classified as an
affliction of the head.[151] But surely this would be stating the obvious. More
insightful is Kleinig's conclusion that

> [t]his phrase, 'his infection is on his head,' seems to function as a declaratory
> formula akin to the formula of responsibility for one's own death: 'his blood
> on his head' in Josh 2:19; 1 Ki 2:32; Ezek 33:4. It declares that the whole
> person is totally affected by the disease.[152]

This conclusion is supported by what I have already argued concerning
צרעת as symbolic of divine judgment in this chapter.

The afflicted person is referred to as 'The man himself is diseased'
(איש־צרוע הוא, v. 44a). This is the first use of the passive participle צָרוּעַ
in the Bible,[153] and as noted by Milgrom, it serves as an introduction to the
rules regarding the treatment of a person with צרעת (i.e. 'Now the diseased
who has an affliction on him' [והצרוע אשר־בו הנגע], v. 44a).

Though nearly all commentators regard vv. 45-46 as a new unit that
prescribes what is to be done with any person declared to have been afflicted
with צרעת, it would seem as though they are meant to be read as part of the
case dealing with the disease found in the bald area of a man's head (Lev.
13.40-44).[154] To begin with, the formula that introduces all of the other units
of Leviticus 13 (i.e. Y כי X) is lacking in v. 44. By contrast, it is introduced
with the passive participle צָרוּעַ that first occurs in the previous verse. This
observation suggests a high level of literary cohesion between vv. 40-44 and
vv. 45-46.[155]

As further evidence for this literary cohesion, Kleinig draws attention to
two parallel stylistic devices that encourage the interpretation of vv. 45-46
as a continuation of vv. 40-44.[156] First, he notes that the use of the infinitive

151. Milgrom, *Leviticus 1–16*, p. 802.
152. Kleinig, *Leviticus*, pp. 277-78.
153. Kleinig notes that its use in v. 44 is unexpected because 'from what has gone
before, we have come to expect the certification of the infection rather than the infected
person' (*Leviticus*, p. 279).
154. Kleinig appears to be the only scholar who regards vv. 40-46 as forming a single
unit (*Leviticus*, p. 279).
155. We may view this use of צָרוּעַ as an extraposition (i.e. *casus pendens*) by which
the legislator divulges what is to be done with the man who has an affliction on his head.
156. Kleinig, *Leviticus*, p. 279. I do not find Kleinig's suggestion, that a strong relationship between vv. 40-44 and vv. 45-46 is also suggested by a parallel between the
man having a disease on his head and the command that he dishevel his hair, convincing.

absolute with the verb טמא in v. 44 is matched by the twofold warning of one's uncleanness in v. 45. Second, he suggests that the clause 'his affliction is on his head' (בראשו נגעו, v. 44b) is echoed by the following verse's repeated affirmation that 'the infection is on him' (i.e. 'the צרוע who has the affliction on him' [והצרוע אשר־בו הנגע], v. 45a).[157] This additional clause would seem unnecessary if the legislator were not trying to establish this connection.[158]

Nevertheless, Kleinig goes too far in assuming that the instructions for what should be done with 'the diseased' in vv. 45-46 apply *only* to the person who has an affliction on his head.[159] Just because the instructions concerning what is done with this person come as part of the case of baldness in vv. 40-46 does not preclude the possibility that the same treatment was applicable to those afflicted with צרעת in the preceding cases. In other words, the exclusion of the diseased person in vv. 45-46 is included in this case to achieve a literary purpose, possibly making the case of baldness in Lev. 13.40-46 climactic. The legislator discloses what is to happen to such a person, of which five instructions are given. Together they symbolize this person's exclusion from life in God's immediate presence and entry into the realm of death.

'his clothes shall be torn' (בגדיו יהיו פרמים v. 45)
'his head will be dishevelled' (וראשו יהיה פרוע v. 45)
'he shall cover his upper lip' (ועל־שפם יעטה v. 45)
'he shall call out "unclean, unclean"' (וטמא טמא יקרא v. 45)
'he will dwell outside the camp' (כל־ימי אשר הנגע בו יטמא טמא
הוא בדד ישב מחוץ למחנה מושבו v. 46)

Collectively these five practices symbolize that the afflicted person has entered the realm of death, *exclusion from God's immediate presence*. Elsewhere in the OT the first three are associated with funerary rites (Torn clothes: Gen. 37.34; 2 Sam. 1.11; Lev. 10.6; 21.10;[160] dishevelled hair: Lev. 10.6; 21.10; the covering of one's top lip: Ezek. 24.17, 22).[161] Thus, the

As I shall argue below, the practice of dishevelling one's hair was not to draw attention to an infection on the head but to symbolize this man's sorrow.

157. Kleinig, *Leviticus*, p. 279.

158. However, Milgrom suggests that '[t]his lengthy circumlocution is necessary because the ṣārûaʿ here is no longer the same as the one in the previous verse' (Milgrom, *Leviticus 1–16*, p. 802). But this suggestion does not explain the absence of a normal introductory formula, or why vv. 44 and 45 both refer to the afflicted person as a צרוע.

159. Kleinig, *Leviticus*, p. 286.

160. Note that torn clothes can also be associated with sin and its consequences (Num. 14.6; 2 Kgs 22.11, 19; Ezr. 9.5) and other calamities (2 Kgs 11.14; 19.1). Cf. Wenham, *Leviticus*, p. 200

161. Milgrom, *Leviticus 1–16*, p. 803. Early Jewish exegesis (e.g. Ibn Ezra) interpreted the practice of covering one's upper lip as a measure taken to prevent others from

treatment of this person is meant to symbolize that he is associated with the realm of death.[162] And v. 46 possibly emphasizes that the nature of this death is not that of physical death, but exclusion from God's immediate presence.

With regard to the person's exclusion from the camp, Wenham rightly comments

> The holiest area, where one was closest to God, was the tabernacle. It was here that the holy men, the priests, worked. The tabernacle was surrounded by the camp where Israel the holy people of God lived. This in turn was encircled by the area outside the camp, which was populated by non-Jews, sinners, and the unclean. To live outside the camp was to be cut off from the blessings of the covenant. It was little wonder that when a man was diagnosed as unclean he had to go into mourning. He experienced a living death; his life as a member of God's people experiencing God's blessing came to an end. Gen. 3 presents a similar picture... As Adam and Eve experienced a living death when they were expelled from Eden, so every man who was diagnosed as unclean experienced a similar fate.[163]

However, the symbolic cause of this death is possibly not that assigned by Wenham, following Douglas, who argues that the loss of normality associated with skin disease leads to uncleanness. I have argued that the source of death is what is symbolized by 'flesh' that is under God's judgment (i.e. צרעת).

צרעת *as Symbolic of Yahweh's Judgment on Flesh (vv. 47-59)*

This section is considered by some scholars to be an editorial interpolation.[164] Two pieces of evidence are commonly appealed to in support of this position. First, they observe that this unit has its own conclusion (v. 59), a feature absent from each of the preceding cases. Second, the existence of a passage dealing with fabrics afflicted with צרעת between a passage concerned with

---

catching the disease. This interpretation seems unlikely considering that I have argued that the text elsewhere displays ritual, rather than medical, concerns. In this regard see Hartley, *Leviticus*, p. 193.

162. As anecdotal evidence that the diseased man has entered the realm of death, Frymer-Kensky cites the bird ritual of Leviticus 14. 'The living bird is dipped in the blood of the dead bird, the leper is sprinkled with the blood of the slain bird, and the living bird is let loose in the field. The formal similarity between this ritual and the ritual of the Day of Atonement is apparent: both involve two creatures, one of which is killed and the other set free. In the case of the leper, the symbolism focuses on the living bird who has been in contact with death (dipped in the blood of the killed bird) and is then set free: so too the leper has been set free from his brush with death' (Fryer-Kensky, 'Pollution', p. 400).

163. Wenham, *Leviticus*, p. 201.

164. Noordtzij, *Leviticus*, p. 142; Milgrom, *Leviticus 1–16*, p. 808.

the diagnosis of צרעת afflicted people (Lev. 13.1-46) and the prescribed rites for the purification of such people (Lev. 14.1-32) is considered as disruptive to what should have been the natural literary sequence. Nevertheless, there are two reasons why this passage should be interpreted within its present literary context.

First, the fabrics listed in vv. 47-49 are afflicted with the same disease that humans may have in vv. 1-46, namely צרעת.[165] Second, since a symbolic dimension has already been proposed in connection with צרעת, בשר and טמא in the laws relating to humans, the possibility that those concerning fabrics continue the symbolic teaching of this chapter needs to be explored.

To anticipate, it is argued below that the section on צרעת afflicted fabrics was included to underline the meaning of צרעת as symbolic of God's judgment on rebellious humans (i.e. 'flesh').[166] Four observations make it likely that the fabrics symbolize a human. First, the position of this section between one concerned with humans who contract this disease (Lev. 13.1-46) and the purification of humans who have been purified from this disease (Lev. 14.1-32). Second, a symbolic dimension is also suggested by 'fabric' (הבגד) occurring as the subject of the verb יהיה in the introductory formula for this section (i.e. 'When fabric has an affliction of צרעת upon it' [והבגד כי-יהיה בו נגע צרעת], v. 47a). Given that a person stands as the subject of the same verb elsewhere in this chapter's introductory formulas, with the exception of that in v. 9, then it seems likely that the fabrics and materials in question are personified.

---

165. Milgrom and Hartley suggest that it is called צרעת because it resembles similar diseases on humans. But this suggestion does not explain why the same terminology has to be used, as is reflected in Milgrom's defence of why he translates the term differently in vv. 47-58. 'The term denoting scale disease is now applied to fabrics. Because, however, the affection is due to mold (or fungus), it is here and throughout this pericope rendered "mold disease" [i.e. rather than "scale disease"]' (Milgrom, *Leviticus 1–16*, pp. 808-809). See similarly Hartley's translation of this term as 'grievous mildew' in vv. 47-58 but 'grievous skin disease' elsewhere (*Leviticus*, pp. 173, 193). While I do not deny that the disease of these garments may have borne similar features to that of human skin, these similarities may not account, first, for why these prescriptions interrupt those dealing with humans, and second, for why it is necessary to call them the same name. Hartley's suggestion that the latter may have resulted because there were a lack of definitive terms for describing fungal growths on clothes and walls seems speculative.

166. Maccoby thinks that the non-moral nature of צרעת is reflected by the fact that it infects clothes and houses and that it is unclean because it can contaminate the sanctuary. We may respond to his argument as follows. First, the symbolic function of clothes and houses leaves open the possibility that this disease is symbolic of judgment on immorality. Second, as discussed in relation to Lev. 13.12-15 above, the disease itself is not the source of uncleanness. Third, if the threat of the disease is its contamination of the sanctuary, why is this not reflected in the prescriptions of Leviticus 13–14? Maccoby, *Ritual and Morality*, p. 121.

Third, in v. 55b a strong relationship is established between the diseased fabric and the man who has an affliction of צרעת on a bald part of his head (cf. vv. 40-46). In both cases an affliction of צרעת is found on his/its 'baldness of head' (בקרחתו, vv. 42-43; 55) or on his/its bald forehead (בגבחתו, vv. 42-43, 55). In v. 55, all scholars translate בקרחתו או בגבחתו in terms of the front and back of a garment. On a practical level this translation is warranted.[167] However, within the context of the man suffering with an affliction of צרעת on his baldness (vv. 40-46) it seems possible to interpret this description as the personification of the garment.

Finally, there are other biblical examples of clothes representing those who wear them. These include Saul and Jonathan giving David their clothes (1 Sam. 17.38; 18.4, respectively) and David's cutting off part of Saul's robe (1 Sam. 24.1–7).

Nevertheless, scholars observe two significant differences between the case for fabrics and that for people who contract צרעת. The first, that it appears that fabrics are subjected to a law of greater severity than people, is not altogether certain.[168] In the cases for people (vv. 1-46) a person is generally pronounced 'clean' when symptoms of impurity do not change after a period of quarantine.[169] By contrast, when the infected area of fabric does not change colour or does not 'spread' (פשה) it is pronounced 'unclean' (v. 55). Yet, considering that we have already observed that the terminology for baldness links the case of human baldness (vv. 40-46) with v. 55, it is noteworthy that the case concerning baldness requires no test for change. At the very least, this observation cautions against distinguishing too much between the respective laws for humans and fabrics.

The second difference scholars identify between the laws relating to humans and fabrics is clearly correct and important. Whereas humans are excluded from a life lived in God's immediate presence when they are declared unclean (cf. vv. 45-46), fabrics with צרעת are burnt with fire (vv. 52, 55, 57).[170] Considering that this is the main difference between the two sections, and that the fabrics are personified to some extent, this observation would seem to have significance for the interpretation of the symbolic meaning of the laws concerning fabrics. That they come within the immediate context of the fate of the man who has an affliction of צרעת on the bald area of his head, and just before the prescription for sacrifices that the healed צָרוּעַ ('afflicted') must offer in order to be declared 'clean', suggests that the burning of fabrics afflicted with צרעת is meant to confirm that the latter is

167. Though Wenham discusses the problems associated with this interpretation (*Leviticus*, p. 202).

168. Milgrom, *Leviticus 1–16*, p. 813.

169. Verses 4, 10, 13, 16, 17, 20, 25.

170. The burning of the garment seems to be emphasized by the framing of v. 52 with the word 'burn' (שרף) (Sherwood, *Leviticus, Numbers, Deuteronomy*, p. 66).

symbolic of God's judgment. 'Fire' is often associated with God's presence and judgment throughout the Pentateuch. Moreover, Nadab and Abihu have just experienced God's fire of judgment in Lev. 10.1-3.[171] Thus, the meaning of the man's exclusion from God's immediate presence in vv. 45-46 is interpreted as an experience of divine judgment by the burning of fabrics afflicted with צרעת in vv. 47-59. And just as the ultimate source of a person's exclusion from God's immediate presence is the symbolic meaning of 'flesh', here the exposure of 'flesh' by צרעת and the resulting exclusion from God's immediate presence is interpreted in terms of God's judgment.[172]

Thus, rather than a law that interrupts the logical flow between Lev. 13.1-46 and Leviticus 14, vv. 47-59 provide an essential context for understanding the necessity for 'atonement' (כפר) to be made for the healed person to be able to re-enter God's presence as a 'clean' person (cf. Leviticus 14).[173]

Conclusions Arising from the Exegesis of Leviticus 13

The present examination of the regulations concerning צרעת within Leviticus 13 has arrived at the following conclusions. First, in agreement with traditional Jewish exegesis, the disease צרעת serves a punitive function. Nevertheless, in disagreement with this line of exegesis, those afflicted with this disease are not viewed as 'sinful' or deserving of their punishment. This is because, second, צרעת is viewed as divine punishment of what is symbolized by 'flesh' (בשר). In this regard, it seems possible that the legislator has adopted pre-existing cultic customs and utilized them to make a theological point concerning the relationship between mortal humanity and God. This view of the 'uncleanness' associated with צרעת makes sense of the requirement that a person healed of this disease brings offerings for the priest to make 'atonement' (כפר) for him in Leviticus 14. Mortal humanity may only re-enter God's presence on the basis of כפר.[174] Third, this interpretation of Leviticus 13 affirms the symbolic meaning Chapter 3 attributed to the term 'uncleanness' in Leviticus 11 (i.e. 'exclusion from Yahweh's immediate presence'). Moreover, the decidedly ethical connotations associated with

171. And note the burning of people in Num. 11.1-3 and 16.35.

172. The burning of animals that may be representative of their offerers is possibly further evidence that the burning of these fabrics represents God's fire of judgment on people.

173. The healing of the latter (i.e. Lev. 14.1-32) is actually anticipated by the fabric which is pronounced pure in v. 58.

174. This interpretation has implications for the translation of the term כפר since it makes it conceivable that it retains the same meaning in both 'sin' and 'impurity' contexts. The occurrence of the term כפר in both 'sin' and 'purity' texts has led to an, as yet unresolved, debate concerning how it should be rendered. See works by Sklar, Milgrom and Kiuchi.

'flesh' in Leviticus 13 make it seem even more likely that the command to 'be holy' in Lev. 11.44-45 may explicate what is already implicit within P's dietary regulations Lev. 11.1-42.[175]

In the section that follows I shall attempt to support the conclusions of the present Chapter by arguing that they make sense of some of the remaining purity regulations within Leviticus 11–15.

The Significance of 'Flesh' and 'Uncleanness' in Leviticus 12 and 15

Outside Leviticus 13 there remains the uncleanness associated with childbirth (Leviticus 12); the cleansing of a man who has been healed of צרעת (Lev. 14.1-32); a house in which Yahweh has 'put' (נתן) צרעת (Lev. 14.33-53); and genital discharges (Leviticus 15). The following section briefly investigates if the conclusion arrived at so far, namely that 'flesh' represents human rebellion that attracts divine judgment (symbolized by צרעת), the consequence of which is 'death' (symbolized by a state of 'uncleanness') is the source of uncleanness in Leviticus 12 and 15.[176] This investigation will

175. As acknowledged in Chapter 1, to establish that an ethical concern underlies the legislation of Leviticus 11 does not require one to conclude that P's view of holiness was ethical. Nevertheless, that the ethical concern of Leviticus 11 possibly required the Israelites to observe cultic and moral commandments (see Chapter 3 [especially pages 47-79 and 106-107]) may indicate that H's use of holiness terminology in Lev. 11.43-45 interprets the implicit purpose of Leviticus 11 [P]. This is because the ethical dimension of H's view of holiness also consists in the keeping of cultic and ethical commandments (e.g. Leviticus 19).

176. Owing to limited space, it is not possible to interact with the different explanations scholars have offered for why uncleanness is a consequence of childbirth. The most popular view in recent times was contributed by Wenham. Essentially he argues that the loss of blood at childbirth may have associated the new mother with an 'aura of death'. Since she lacks 'fullness of life' she may not approach the sanctuary. While this interpretation remains possible, it does not account for the main question I seek to answer in the present exegetical study of Leviticus 12, namely why is the woman unclean for only half as long when she has a male child? (Wenham, 'Why Does Sexual Intercourse Defile (Lev 15.18)?', pp. 432-34). For a critique of Wenham's explanation see Richard Whitekettle, 'Leviticus 12 and the Israelite Woman: Ritual Process, Liminality and the Womb', *ZAW* 107 (1995), pp. 393-408. Whitekettle's own explanation for the rationale underlying the new-mother's uncleanness in Leviticus 12 similarly does not answer the question of why the period of defilement is reduced if she has a boy. His proposal is also problematic in so far as it attempts to explain the text by using anthropological insights rather than exegesis *per se*. Finally, Frymer-Kensky has proposed that '[i]t may be that, like the person who has touched death, the person who has experienced birth has been at the boundaries of life/non-life and therefore cannot directly re-enter the community. She therefore must undergo a long period of transition before she can reapproach the sacred' (Frymer-Kensky, 'Pollution, Purification, and Purgation in Biblical Israel', p. 401). But as for both Wenham and Whitekettle, this proposal does not explain

provide further support for the argument made in Chapter 3 concerning the idea of 'uncleanness' in Leviticus 11 and, as a result, the proposal that P required the Israelites to be holy in an ethical sense.

The 'Uncleanness' Associated with Childbirth (Leviticus 12)

Leviticus 13 follows the 'teachings' (תורות) concerning 'uncleanness' associated with childbirth (Leviticus 12). On two occasions this kind of uncleanness presupposes knowledge of a later prescription (i.e. Leviticus 15) concerning uncleanness associated with menstruation ('as in the days of her menstrual illness' [כימי נדת דותה, v. 2]; 'as her menstruation' [כנדתה, v. 5]; cf. Lev. 15.19-24) and this raises the question of why the prescription of Leviticus 12 is located prior to Leviticus 15. Several explanations have been offered.

First, some scholars propose that the chapter is a later supplement to Leviticus 15.[177] But regardless of whether this proposal is correct it does not explain why an editor chose to insert it prior to the legislation it presupposes.[178]

Second, other scholars suggest that the arrangement of topics in Leviticus 11–15 corresponds to the narrative sequence of events in Genesis 2–3.[179] However, this suggestion does not account for all the topics included within Leviticus 11–15. For example, though it acknowledges the allusions made to the food prohibition in the Garden (Genesis 2; cf. Leviticus 11) and the theme of reproduction (Gen. 1.28; cf. Leviticus 12; 15), it does not explain

the difference in the duration of defilement associated with having a boy or girl. It should also be pointed out that there has been a long history of scholars who attempt to explain this difference in physiological terms. See for example, David I. Macht, 'A Scientific Appreciation of Leviticus 12:1-5', *JBL* (1933), pp. 253-60. Macht traces physical explanations for the longer period of 'uncleanness' associated with having a female baby back to the time of Aristotle and Hippocrates. For an adequate response to such an approach consult Philip Peter Jenson, *Graded Holiness: A Key to the Priestly Conception of the World* (Sheffield: JSOT Press, 1992), pp. 75-76.

177. Wellhausen refers to Leviticus 12 as a 'subdivision' (*Unterabteilung*) of Leviticus 15; see *Die Composition des Hexateuchs und der historichen Bücher des Alten Testaments* (1899; Berlin: W. de Gruyter, 1963); cf. Dillmann, *Das Bucher Exodus und Leviticus*, p. 550; Bertholet, *Leviticus*, p. 40; Noth, *Leviticus*, p. 97, Kornfeld, *Levitikus*, p. 48; Elliger, *Leviticus*, p. 157; Péter-Contesse, *Lévitique 1–16*, p. 194.

178. The same applies to Tarja Philip's suggestion that Leviticus 12 could not be incorporated into Leviticus 15, which deals with parallel cases for male and females, because there is no equivalent of childbirth for males. Why could not this material have been positioned adjacent to Leviticus 15 if this was the only reason? (Tarja S. Philip, *Menstruation and Childbirth in the Bible: Fertility and Impurity* [SBL, 88; New York: Peter Lang, 2006], p. 112).

179. Sailhamer, *The Pentateuch as Narrative*, pp. 332-35; Kiuchi, *A Study of Ḥāṭā' and Ḥāṭā't*, pp. 67-68. See discussion in Chapter 3.

the presence of prescriptions concerning צרעת (Leviticus 13–14). Kiuchi argues that these relate to the theme of God's provision of clothing for Adam and Eve after their expulsion from the Garden, but this link appears tenuous on closer analysis.[180] Would not the legislator have referred to 'tunics' (כתנת), as he does in Genesis 3, instead of 'garments' (בגד) if he intended to make a connection between these texts? Moreover, how does the reference to 'anything made of skin' (בכל־מלאכת עור, Lev. 13.48) fit within such a theory? Though this approach, taken by Kiuchi and Sailhamer, is correct in so far as it recognizes echoes of Genesis 1–3 in the purity regulations of Leviticus 11–15, it fails to account for all of the prescriptions included within the latter.

Third, Hartley independently argues that these chapters are arranged according to two related principles.[181]

> The first is an ascending order in the length of time of uncleanness, from a few hours for eating unclean food (chap. 11) to several weeks for parturition (chap. 12) to a possible lifetime for one stricken with a grievous skin disease (chaps. 13-14). The second principle is an *inclusio*. In chaps. 11-14 the length of time that something makes a person unclean ascends; then chap. 15 presents types of uncleanness caused by a discharge from the genitals that correspond to each of the varying lengths of uncleanness.[182]

Nevertheless, this explanation is more descriptive of the arrangement of these chapters than an insight into its underlying rationale. In particular, it seems more reasonable to assume that the different durations of uncleanness in Leviticus 15 reflect the chiastic arrangement of this material rather than the author's desire to conclude Leviticus 11–14 with a number of cases that correspond to the various periods of uncleanness prescribed therein.[183]

My interpretation of Leviticus 13 above suggests another reason for why the prescription concerning childbirth is found before Leviticus 15. To antici-pate, *Leviticus 12 forms an inclusio with Leviticus 15 that directs the reader to inquire about the relationship between 'flesh' and 'uncleanness' within Leviticus 13.*[184] Put simply, the reduction of the woman's period of unclean-ness after the circumcision of the 'flesh' of a male baby (Lev. 12.3) serves to

---

180. Kiuchi, *Leviticus*, pp. 242-44.

181. Hartley, *Leviticus*, p. 139. Similarly, Milgrom thinks these chapters are arranged according to the duration and complexity of the purification process, in descending order. Yet the data he provides seems to fall short of proving that this is the main orga-nizing principle (*Leviticus 1–16*, p. 905).

182. Hartley, *Leviticus*, p. 139.

183. The literary structure of Leviticus 15 is dealt with below.

184. The blood associated with childbirth does not seem to be what is emphasized in this passage. If this were the case then we might have expected it to have come as part of Leviticus 15. Instead, the emphasis of Leviticus 12 seems to be on the sex of the child and the period of the resultant uncleanness.

raise the expectations of a reader concerning the meaning of 'flesh' in Leviticus 13.[185]

Scholars have long debated what accounts for the shorter time a woman is unclean after having a male child in Leviticus 12.[186] However, my proposal that 'flesh' is the symbolic source of 'uncleanness' in Leviticus 13, in the sense that the latter symbolizes the consequence of rebellion against Yahweh, resonates most with Hoffmann's proposal that the rite of male circumcision may cleanse the mother.[187] The legislator says 'And on the eight day the *flesh*

185. In other words, the association between the circumcision of the 'flesh' and a reduction in the duration of uncleanness in Leviticus 12 may be one factor that triggers a reader, during the 'post-crystallization' interpretative process, to access domains of meaning other than 'literal flesh'.

186. M. Kalisch cites older Christian commentators who view her additional defilement after having a girl as resulting from Eve's guilt for the 'fall of man' (Marcus M. Kalisch, *Leviticus*, II [London: Longmans, 1867–72], p. 122). Heinisch suggests that there is possibly a medical reason for this, namely that it takes a longer period for the woman to return to her normal state after having a female baby (*Das Buch Leviticus*, p. 59). Bamberger asks whether it is because the birth of a daughter who would one day menstruate makes her birth doubly defiling (*The Torah. A Modern Commentary. Leviticus*, p. 112). Jonathan Magonet proposes a modified version of that argued by Bamberger. He suggests that the longer period of uncleanness that accompanies the birth of a baby girl is to be explained in terms of a physiological phenomenon. Noting that there may be a certain amount of vaginal bleeding in a small number of newborn girls, he speculates that the 'one flesh' principle of Gen. 2.24 may have encouraged the legislator to provide for the situation in which 'with the birth of a baby girl we have the equivalent of two "women", each with an actual or potential vaginal discharge, to be accounted for. Since this uncleanness has to be ritually dealt with and the baby cannot do so, the mother with whom the child was formerly united and from whom she has emerged, symbolically bears the uncleanness so that the period is doubled' (Jonathan Magonet, '"But if it is a girl she is unclean for twice seven days…" The Riddle of Leviticus 12.5', in *Reading Leviticus: A Conversation with Mary Douglas* (ed. J.F.A. Sawyer; JSOTSup, 227; Sheffield: Sheffield Academic Press, 1996), pp. 144-52 [152]). But there are some difficulties with this proposal. First, it is not certain that the Israelites were aware of this medical phenomenon. Second, if the Israelites were aware of this phenomenon, why were they not able to judge cases of 'double-uncleanness' on a case by case basis? Third, why is it assumed that the woman's uncleanness is doubled after the birth of a girl instead of halved after that of a boy? Fourth, it is not clear whether the baby also experiences a period of uncleanness. If it does then the uncleanness can 'be ritually dealt with' (i.e. through a period of defilement) by the baby.

187. Hoffmann explains, 'Dass bei der Geburt eines Mädchens die doppelte Anzahl sowohl der Unreinheits- als der Reinheitstage erforderlich ist, wird vielleicht in physischen Gesetzen seinen Grund haben, dass bei dieser Geburt die Frau einer doppelt so grossen Zeit bedarf, um ihren normalen Zustand wieder zu erlangen (vgl. Nidda 30b). Möglich aber auch, dass die טומאה-Tage bei der Geburt eines Knaben deshalb auf sieben reducirt wurden, damit die Wöchnerin am Beschneidungstage schon rein sei. Dann aber mag der Act der Beschneidung auch die reinigende Wirkung haben, dass

of his foreskin shall be circumcised' (וביום השמיני ימול בשר ערלתו),
Lev. 12.3).[188] Nevertheless, Milgrom argues that this conclusion is inconceiv-
able for four reasons.[189] First, a mother's period of uncleanness is shorter
after having a boy compared with a girl in other ANE cultures.[190] Second, 'it
is hardly conceivable that the rite performed on the boy could in any way
affect the ritual status of the mother'. Third, a newborn child is not considered 'unclean'. Fourth, because the female is not circumcised the mother
would never become clean. However, these arguments do not seem to falsify
Hoffmann's explanation for the following reasons.

First, though it is accepted that the prescriptions of Leviticus 11–15 have
precursors in other cultures, this does not prevent a legislator from offering
his own interpretation of these customs (see Chapter 2 and Appendix 1). If it
were customary for a woman to be unclean for half as long when she had a
boy, the legislator may have used this tradition to teach a theological principle concerning the relationship between 'flesh' and 'uncleanness'.

Second, the possibility that circumcision may impinge on the ritual status
of a child's mother is suggested by the continuity established between mother
and child in v. 2. The case concerning the birth of a male child is introduced
with the verb 'to produce seed' (תזריע) which is followed immediately by
'and she brings forth a male' (וילדה זכר).[191] What is the relationship
between the two verbs 'to produce seed' and 'to bring forth'? Most commentators attempt to avoid the potential redundancy of the second verb by rendering the verb תזריע as 'to conceive'.[192] Thus, 'When a woman conceives, and
brings forth a male/female'. But Milgrom seems right in arguing that the
sense of this verb is most likely 'to produce seed' rather than 'to conceive'.[193]
He proceeds to translate אשה כי תזריע וילד זכר as 'When a woman *at
childbirth* bears a male', attributing an adverbial function to the verb תזריע.[194]
Yet even if this translation is correct, what is achieved by stipulating 'at
childbirth?' Hoffmann proposes that the verb may allude to the use of the

dadurch auch die Tage bis zur vollständigen Reinheit um die Hälfte vermindert werden
konnten' (Hoffmann, *Das Buch Leviticus*, p. 361). Frymer-Kensky similarly notes that
the rite of circumcision may be responsible for reducing the time of uncleanness, but
concludes that this still would not account for why the birth of a female should contaminate for 14 days (Frymer-Kensky, 'Pollution', pp. 400-401).

188. Hoffmann overlooks the reference to 'flesh'. Elliger observes that the phrase בשר
ערלה occurs elsewhere only in Genesis 17 (*Leviticus*, p. 157).

189. Milgrom, *Leviticus 1–16*, p. 744.

190. Milgrom, *Leviticus 1–16*, pp. 763-65.

191. It is perhaps noteworthy that the root זרע also occurs in Leviticus 15 with which
Leviticus 12 forms a literary frame (Lev. 15.16, 17, 18, 32).

192. Ibn Ezra, Hartley, Noordtzij, Wenham.

193. Milgrom, *Leviticus 1–16*, p. 743; see also Kleinig, *Leviticus*, p. 263.

194. Milgrom, *Leviticus 1–16*, p. 742.

same root in Genesis 1, where it refers to the process by which plants produce their *own kind*.[195] If Genesis 1–3 has the same importance for the
interpretation of Leviticus 12 as it does for Leviticus 11 and 13 (see above),
it remains possible that the legislator uses the seemingly redundant תזריע
to emphasize the continuity between the woman and her child: *they are of
the same kind*. This possibility means that it is not 'hardly conceivable' that
the child's circumcision affects the ritual status of his mother. Elsewhere the
relationship established between a person and a sacrificial animal through
the action of 'hand-leaning' (סמך) allows the sacrifice of that animal to
affect its offerer's ritual status.[196] Thus, it may not be so difficult to imagine
that the relationship between a woman and her seed acts as the conduit by
which a rite performed on her child alters her ritual status.

Third, to view the newborn as 'unclean' is not necessary for Hoffmann's
suggestion to be valid.[197] If the legislator has adopted a received custom, then
it is possible that he has introduced the circumcision of 'flesh' as an interpretative key for the symbolic meaning of the woman's uncleanness. The rite
does not imply that the newborn is unclean anymore than the sacrificial death
of an animal implies that the animal is sinful. Both occasions reflect something about the main participant (i.e. the new mother and offerer respectively).

Fourth, the argument that the mother of a girl would never be cleansed is
weak because it overlooks that the period of exclusion contributes in some
way to her purification. Not only is this the case in the previous chapter
('unclean till evening', Lev. 11.24ff.), but even the mother of a male child
must endure a period of uncleanness before she is regarded as 'clean' (Lev.
12.4).

There are two additional arguments that can be made in support of Hoffmann's suggestion that circumcision reduces the mother's period of uncleanness. First, the genitalia of the respective sexes occupy the foreground in this
prescription which would appear to emphasize the role of circumcision. The
legislator initially refers to the two children as 'male' (זכר, v. 2) and
'female' (נקבה, v. 5) rather than 'son' (בן) or 'daughter' (בת).[198] Two explanations have been given for the emphasis on sex, both of which seem
unsatisfactory. On the one hand, Rabbinic interpreters claim that the newborn
is not referred to as a 'son' or 'daughter' so that the law applies also to
women who have stillborn babies.[199] Against this, Milgrom points out that

---

195. Hoffmann, *Das Buch Leviticus*, p. 358. See similarly Milgrom, *Leviticus 1–16*,
p. 743.

196. See Chapter 5.

197. It would not seem to make any difference if the baby were 'unclean'.

198. Only later in v. 6 are they referred to in familial terms, namely as a 'son' (בן) or a
'daughter' (בת).

199. *Sipra*, Tazria' par. 1:5; Hoffmann, *Das Buch Leviticus*, p. 358.

this understanding does not explain why the terms 'son' and 'daughter' appear in v. 6.[200] On the other hand, Milgrom suggests that the sex of the child is referred to because 'at birth the only way to tell the gender is by the sexual organ'.[201] This is true, but it still does not explain why the legislator gives prominence to the sex of the child within the prescription. It seems that the sexual organs remain in the foreground to draw attention to the means by which the woman may have her period of uncleanness reduced, namely *though the circumcision of the flesh of a male's foreskin* ('The flesh of his foreskin shall be circumcised'; ימול בשר ערלתו, v. 3).

Second, Hoffmann's proposal is also supported by my exegetical study of Leviticus 13 which argued that 'flesh' is identified as the source of 'uncleanness'.[202] Moreover, below it is suggested that 'flesh' is the source of 'uncleanness' in Leviticus 15. Given that Leviticus 12 and Leviticus 15 form an *inclusio*, it is possible that 'flesh' has the same symbolic meaning in the prescription for the new mother: the woman becomes unclean in connection with her 'flesh' in Leviticus 15 and the circumcision of her 'seed's' flesh reduces her period of defilement in Leviticus 12.

It seems plausible to argue that the woman's period of uncleanness is related to the removal of 'flesh'.[203] The following section argues that Leviticus 12 cooperates with Leviticus 15 as an *inclusio* that directs the reader to inquire whether there is a connection between 'flesh' and 'uncleanness'. The answer for which is found in Leviticus 13–14.[204]

The 'Uncleanness' Associated with Genital Discharges (Leviticus 15)
The relationship between 'flesh' and 'uncleanness' in Leviticus 12–13 is also apparent within the prescriptions concerning genital discharges in Leviticus 15, the interpretation of which must take into account its chiastic structure.[205]

200. Milgrom, *Leviticus 1–16*, p. 744.

201. Milgrom, *Leviticus 1–16*, p. 744; he follows N.H. Wessely, *Netivot Ha-shalom*. III. *Leviticus* (ed. M. Mendelssohn; Vienna: von Schmid und Busch, 1846).

202. Hoffmann is unaware of a symbolic meaning of 'flesh' in Leviticus 12–15.

203. The present argument does not identify the woman's uncleanness as the consequence of sinfulness. That a specific sin is not on view is possibly suggested by that the 'sin offering' is only small and smaller than the burnt offering (v. 6). Rather it is argued here that 'flesh' is symbolic of human mortality and rebellion (cf. Heinisch, *Das Buch Leviticus*, p. 59).

204. Nihan similarly views the present arrangement of Leviticus 12 and 15 as a literary device that is meant to frame Leviticus 13–14. He suggests that this is because Leviticus 13–14 comprises 'the most severe form of impurity' (Nihan, *From Priestly Torah to Pentateuch*, pp. 308-309). But does this really explain why these chapters require a literary frame? The present argument, that Leviticus 12 and 15 raise a question that is answered within Leviticus 13–14, seems more likely.

205. Identified by Wenham, *Leviticus*, p. 217; cf. Milgrom, *Leviticus 1–16*, p. 905.

A   Introduction (vv. 1-2a)

    B   Abnormal male discharges (vv. 2b-15)

        C   Normal male discharges (vv. 16-17)

            X   Marital intercourse (v. 18)

        C' Normal female discharges (vv. 19-24)

    B' Abnormal female discharges (vv. 25-30)

[Motive (v. 31)]

A'   Summary (vv. 32-33)

Milgrom considers the case concerning marital intercourse (v. 18) to be an 'introverted hinge' which forms the very centre of the chiasm. He cites several observations in support of this view.[206] First, even though the uncleanness of this case appears to be linked to an emission of semen, thereby linking it to rules concerning normal male discharges in vv. 16-17, v. 18 is introduced by אשה rather than איש (cf. v. 16a). Thus, the verse anticipates the succeeding topic of normal female discharges (vv. 19-24). Conversely the verse finishes by making reference to the normal male discharge, thereby linking it with what precedes (cf. vv. 16-17). Second, the legislator has used אשר rather than כי (cf. vv. 2, 16, 19, 25) to indicate the transition to a new category within the same unit of thought.[207]

In assessing the significance of this verse forming an 'inverted hinge' within the chapter, Milgrom concludes

> Thus v 18 is indeed a separate law case whose distinctiveness...is based on the equality of the responsibility in the sexual act, on being the only case of impurity that is under the complete control of the individuals involved, and on representing in literary form the unification of man and his wife as '*one flesh*' (Gen. 2.24).[208]

---

206. Milgrom, *Leviticus 1–16*, p. 931.

207. Milgrom, *Leviticus 1–16*, p. 931. For further evidence that v. 18 is the central verse of this chapter's chiastic arrangement see Richard Whitekettle, 'Leviticus 15.18 Reconsidered: Chiasm, Spatial Structure and the Body', *JSOT* 49 (1991), pp. 31-45 (34-37).

208. Milgrom, *Leviticus 1–16*, p. 931 (emphasis mine). The allusion to the 'one flesh' of the Garden of Eden is also independently identified by Whitekettle who similarly argues that v. 18 is of central importance to unlocking the rationale underlying uncleanness in these prescriptions. He summarizes his argument as follows: 'The organizing principle behind this structure [i.e. the chiastic arrangement of Lev. 15] is a homologous relationship between the reproductive system and the tabernacle. The tabernacle is conceptualized as a pure center, over against the impure, peripheral wilderness. The "center" of reproductive physiology is sexual intercourse (v. 18), with non-generative/waste discharges (A/A') comprising the reproductive system's "periphery". If sexual intercourse is the reproductive "center", why is impurity associated with it? The penis is the instrument of both urination and copulation/ejaculation. This functional ambiguity brings an aspect

This insight is significant considering my findings regarding the relationship between 'flesh' and 'uncleanness' elsewhere in Leviticus 12–13. Here at the centre of a chiasm dealing with unclean discharges the 'one flesh' of Genesis 2 is now 'unclean'. In other words, the 'one flesh' that walked with God in the Garden is now 'excluded from God's immediate presence'. Yet Milgrom's suggestion that this verse alludes to the first 'one flesh' becomes even more poignant when it is observed that the term 'flesh' is explicitly related to the cases of uncleanness elsewhere in this chapter.

First, the genitals of both the men and women in this chapter are referred to as 'flesh'.[209] And the legislator identifies 'flesh' as the common source of discharges that result in uncleanness by using a parallel introductory formula for the first male and female cases.[210]

Verse 2b   איש איש כי יהיה זב מבשרו זובו
'When any man has a discharge, his discharge is from his flesh'

Verse 19   ואשה כי־תהיה זבה דם יהיה זבה בבשרה
'When a woman has a discharge, her discharge is blood from her flesh'[211]

of the "periphery" (waste) to the reproductive "center" ' (Whitekettle, 'Leviticus 15.18 Reconsidered', pp. 31-45). I shall briefly indicate some difficulties with Whitekettle's proposal. The most problematic argument he makes is that the use of the penis in urination introduces an element of impurity into sexual intercourse. First, urine, or for that matter faeces, are not identified as 'unclean' within Leviticus 11–15. Even in Deut. 23.12-15, where instructions are given to defecate outside the camp so that Yahweh may not see 'among you a naked thing' (בך ערות דבר, v. 15), the legislation does not seem aimed at preventing the transfer of 'uncleanness'. Second, would not his conceptual argument have made the 'one flesh' 'unclean' within the Garden? A further difficulty with Whitekettle's approach to Leviticus 15 is his assumption that this legislation is concerned with 'sexual physiology'. It is not apparent from Leviticus 15 that this is of concern to the legislator. One, the sexual organs are not mentioned but are instead referred to as 'flesh'. Two, he has not convincingly demonstrated that the legislator is concerned with pathological problems over against the duration of a discharge. That is, though Whitekettle argues that the outer parts of the chiastic arrangement are concerned with abnormal discharges as opposed to the normal discharges treated within the inner parts, his correct observations are actually confounded with the duration of the respective discharges. Thus, it remains possible that the legislator arranged discharges according to how long they lasted to improve the effect of his chiastic structure. If this understanding is correct, his suggestion that 'uncleanness' in Lev. 15.18 is related to the extent to which a discharge departs from the norm is unfounded.

209. Lev. 15.2, 3 (×2), 19. It may not matter that the literal referent of this kind of 'flesh' is physiologically different from that on view in Leviticus 13. While at the 'moment of crystallization' the specific kind of 'flesh' may come to mind, during the 'post-crystallization' process the reader is likely to access the same symbolic meaning regardless of what kind of physical 'flesh' is on view.

210. As argued by Milgrom, *Leviticus 1–16*, p. 934.

211. This verse would seem to caution against assuming that references to blood in Leviticus 12 imply that blood, as opposed to 'flesh', is the source of uncleanness.

In the case of vv. 2-15, the 'flesh' is emphasized by the double reference to it in v. 3. Though the same introductory formula is not used for the other two cases involving men and women (cf. vv. 16, 25), this is possibly because the reader is meant to assume that the source of the discharge is the 'flesh'.

Second, another occurrence of 'flesh' in this chapter may suggest that it is the source of 'uncleanness'. In v. 7 the legislator says 'Whoever touches *the flesh* of the one with the discharge' (והנגע בבשר הזב) will become unclean till the evening. Regardless of the literal reference of 'flesh' on this occasion, that the legislator indicates that touching the 'flesh' of this person makes one unclean seems noteworthy.[212] Why not say 'Whoever touches the one with the discharge' (והנגע בזב) or 'Whoever touches him' (והנגע בו); cf. 'Whoever touches her' [וכל־הנגע בה], Lev. 15.19)? Considering what I have already argued concerning the meaning of 'flesh' in Leviticus 13, it seems reasonable to speculate that this occurrence of the term focuses attention on its symbolic significance.

Finally, it is noteworthy that the term 'flesh' occurs *seven* times in Leviticus 15.[213] When there is evidence that it has not come about by accident, the sevenfold repetition of a term is often used to underscore its significance.[214] Given the importance I have argued the term 'flesh' has in Leviticus 12–13, and Milgrom's suggestion that the idea is implicit within the central verse of Leviticus 15, it would seem difficult to conclude that the sevenfold repetition of 'flesh' within this chapter is accidental. This repetition may be further evidence that the legislator has drawn attention to 'flesh' as the source of 'uncleanness' in Leviticus 15.

---

212. Some scholars suggest that 'flesh' must refer to the man's genitals for three reasons. First, this is its referent in vv. 2 and 19. Second, the legislator could have simply said 'Whoever touches the one with the discharge (i.e. בזב)'. Third, they argue that if the referent here is 'body' the rule in v. 11 would become redundant. Milgrom sufficiently responds to the third argument by observing that v. 11 is not made redundant by translating בשר as 'body' because it speaks of the reverse process. The first argument is weak, because vv. 2 and 19 are introductory formulas that literally describe the origin of the discharge, namely the genitals. The second argument requires more attention. Milgrom explains that 'flesh' is used to distinguish between the consequences of touching the person's body as opposed to his clothing. But even if this were the case, there is no evidence for this distinction being made in the text. Perhaps the ambiguity surrounding the use of 'flesh' on this occasion reflects that the legislator uses it with its symbolic meaning in mind (see Milgrom, *Leviticus 1–16*, p. 914).

213. Lev. 15.2, 3 (×2), 7, 13, 16, 19.

214. Jacob Milgrom, *Numbers* (Philadelphia: Jewish Publication Society of America, 1990), p. xxxi. Another example of the 'septenary' use of a term within Leviticus 12–15 relates to the occurrence of the root חי ('living') in Lev. 14.1-8. The context, in which the healed person re-enters the community, suggests that the sevenfold recurrence of this term is not an accident but emphasizes the new life gained by this man.

This section has argued that the symbolic meaning assigned to בשׂר in Leviticus 13 is suited to the use of this term in Leviticus 12 and 15. It seems that the common interest the *inclusio* of Leviticus 12 and Leviticus 15 has in relating 'flesh' to 'uncleanness' may serve to raise the question of why they are related. My contention is that this question is answered in the prescriptions of Leviticus 13: 'flesh' symbolizes human rebellion against Yahweh and 'uncleanness' represents the consequence of this rebellion, namely exclusion from God's immediate presence.

Conclusion

Chapter 3 argued that the command to 'be holy' in Lev. 11.43-45 may explicate the symbolic meaning of P's preceding 'dietary regulations' (vv. 1-42). It proposed that these laws were aimed at dissuading the Israelites from experiencing the reality symbolized by 'uncleanness', namely 'exclusion from Yahweh's immediate presence' (i.e. exile from the Land), which would eventuate if they rebelled against his will. This aim seemed to imply that P required the Israelites to observe cultic and ethical laws, a requirement which is similar to H's concept of holiness.

The present Chapter has sought to confirm that a person's 'uncleanness' is symbolic of 'exclusion from Yahweh's immediate presence'. It proposed that, within Leviticus 12–15, human 'uncleanness' (טמא) is related to the concept of 'flesh' (בשׂר) and that the latter is partially symbolic of humanity's rebellion against Yahweh (cf. Genesis 6–9).[215] Central to this proposal is my interpretation of Leviticus 13, in which I argued that the disease called צרעת represents divine judgment on 'flesh'. It is not suggested that צרעת-afflicted people suffered on account of specific sin, or sinfulness, but that their skin conditions were used for an educational function: sinful humanity (בשׂר) stands under God's judgment (צרעת).[216] This provides further evidence for the view that Leviticus 11 sought to dissuade Israel from rebelling against Yahweh and to instead conform themselves to his will. This conclusion would seem to increase the persuasiveness of my suggestion that Lev. 11.43-

---

215. When it is recognised that 'flesh' carries this symbolic meaning it is unnecessary to conclude with Scharbert that 'Diese Bestimmungen zeugen zweifellos von einer religiösen Abwertung des „Fleisches", zumindest soweit es sich um die Geschlechtsorgane handelt' (Scharbert, *Fleisch, Geist und Seele im Pentateuch*, p. 50). It is argued here that the legislator draws attention to the negative symbolic meaning of 'flesh' rather than making a judgment on the value of the human body and its parts.

216. Though I did not interpret Leviticus 14, I would propose that the educational purpose of uncleanness associated with צרעת is completed by the requirement that 'atonement' (כפר) be made for a person healed from this disease (i.e. Lev. 14.1-32). Thus, rebellious humanity (i.e. בשׂר) may only re-enter God's presence on the basis of כפר.

45 makes explicit what is present on a symbolic plane within P's 'dietary regulations' (cf. Chapter 3). However, a weakness in my proposal that P's view of holiness has an ethical dimension is that the holiness terminology in Leviticus 11 is confined to those verses which scholars assign to H (i.e. vv. 43-45). To address this situation, the next Chapter turns to P's prescription for the 'burnt offering' (עלה, Leviticus 1), a text in which scholars assume that P's concept of holiness is implicit, to see if it implies that the laity were required to be holy. If this possibility can be established it will provide further support for the argument made in Chapter 3 that H's command to be holy in Lev. 11.43-45 explicates an ethical view of holiness that is implicit within P's dietary regulations.

Chapter 5

'A MALE WITHOUT DEFECT' (תמים זכר): תמים AS AN ASPECT OF קדש IN THE 'BURNT OFFERING' OF LEVITICUS 1

Introduction

In the wider context of P, the use of the root קדש ('holiness') is restricted to describing the divine presence (Lev. 10.3) and the status of inanimate objects or priests, who gain this status via unction with oil and sacrificial blood (Lev. 8.12, 30). This observation constitutes yet another reason for why scholars regard P's 'holiness' terminology as 'cultic', no more than a label attached to the deity's property.[1] However, the possible symbolic dimension to Leviticus 11 (Chapter 3) cautions against a simple cultic reading of P and invites an investigation into whether H's explicit call to 'be holy' in Lev. 11.44-45 is already anticipated, on a symbolic dimension, in P's prescriptions of Leviticus 1–10. Such a finding will provide further evidence that there is a dynamic, and possibly ethical, aspect to P's view of holiness.

Since, in P, occurrences of the root קדש are never explicitly applied to the laity outside Leviticus 11, the present Chapter examines if there is such a relationship in passages where the concept of קדש is implicit. The latter appears to be the case in the prescription for the 'burnt offering' (עלה, Leviticus 1), where even though the term קדש is absent, the Mishnah,[2] and most modern commentators,[3] assume that this offering was קדש קדשים, a superlative genitive meaning 'most holy'.[4] Yet though this offering possibly symbolized the essence of P's concept of 'holiness', by its complete relinquishment to Yahweh (see Appendix 2), previous interpretations of Leviticus

---

1. For example, see Baruch J. Schwartz, 'Israel's Holiness: The Torah Traditions', p. 53.

2. *m. Zebah.* 5.1; 6.1.

3. Keil, *The Pentateuch*, p. 293; Rendtorff, *Leviticus*, p. 102; Levine, *In the Presence of the Lord*, p. 73; Milgrom, *Leviticus 1–16*, p. 183; Wright, 'Holiness', p. 239; Kiuchi, *Leviticus*, pp. 63-64. Snaith, Noordtzij, and Hartley are three exceptions to this consensus since they assume that the expression merely qualifies those parts of offerings that belong to the priests. A response is made to this claim in Appendix 2. See Noordtzij, *Leviticus*, p. 44; Norman H. Snaith, 'A Note on Numbers xviii 9', *VT* 23 (1973), pp. 373-75; Hartley, *Leviticus*, p. 30.

4. A defence of this assumption is provided in Appendix 2.

I have not examined whether this aspect of the 'burnt offering' may indicate that P desired the offerer to 'be holy'.[5]

An obvious limitation of this study needs to be acknowledged. In the absence of 'holiness' terminology, it would be rash to claim that P was commanding the offerer of the 'burnt offering' to 'be holy'. Rather, I shall argue, via an analysis of the relationship established between the 'male without blemish' (זכר תמים) and the offerer by the gesture of hand-leaning (סמך, Lev. 1.4a), and an analysis of the means by which the 'burnt offering' makes 'atonement' (כפר) for its offerer, that Leviticus 1 implies that God desired the offerer to be 'without blemish' (תמים; cf. Deut. 18.13) in an, at least partially, ethical sense.[6] Such a finding would be a significant step for my attempt to see if the explicit call to 'be holy' (Lev. 11.43-45) is already adumbrated by the rituals of Leviticus 1–10. This is because, though the term תמים is viewed as having a purely cultic meaning when applied to animals in P (i.e. 'without physical blemish'),[7] most scholars regard it as an ethical term in H.[8] Indeed, Douglas claims that it constitutes the essence of 'holiness' in this material.[9] If it can be demonstrated that תמים has this same meaning in Lev. 1.3, albeit on a symbolic dimension, its occurrence within a prescription for an implicitly 'most holy' offering possibly points to an ethical concept of 'holiness' in P.[10] However, before we examine this possibility within the pre-

5. This is with the exception of Kiuchi. However, though Kiuchi similarly argues that the 'burnt offering' implies that P required the Israelites to 'be holy' we conceptualize what this means in different ways. Put simply, whereas I shall argue that this holiness is ethical Kiuchi argues that it is an existential concept (see Kiuchi, *Leviticus*, pp. 40-46, 60-65).

6. So much was explicitly commanded of the Israelites in Deut. 18.13. The root תמם means physical 'completion' or 'integrity' within cultic contexts, and when it is applied to humans B. Kedar-Kopfstein observes that it 'denotes conduct that is right, benign, upstanding, and just, whether expressed in a single act or in a general way of life' (B. Kedar-Kopfstein, 'תמם', in *TDOT*, XV, pp. 699-711 [707]; see also Koehler and Baumgartner, *HALOT*. IV. pp. 1748-51). Since the idea of 'integrity' seems to be common to both cultic and moral contexts, I shall qualify the translation 'integrity' with the adjective 'human' (i.e. human 'integrity') when I think a human quality is in view. The argument that תמים has a symbolic ethical dimension within Leviticus 1 is given later in this chapter.

7. Noth, *Leviticus*, p. 22; Milgrom, *Leviticus 1–16*, p. 147; Knierim, *Text and Concept*, p. 23.

8. Hoffmann, *Das Buch Leviticus*, p. 117; Douglas, *Purity and Danger*, pp. 51-52; Wenham, *Genesis 1–15*, p. 170; Sarna, *Genesis*, p. 50; Milgrom, *Leviticus 17–22*, p. 1873.

9. Douglas, *Purity and Danger*, pp. 51-52; Mary Douglas, 'Deciphering a Meal', *Daedalus* 101 (1972), pp. 61-81 (76-77), cited affirmatively by Milgrom, *Leviticus 1–16*, p. 1873.

10. So long as this argument is plausible (and hopefully persuasive), further support

scription for the 'burnt offering', it will be helpful to summarize and assess how scholars have understood the 'burnt offering', because some of their insights anticipate the argument that will be made here.

Previous Interpretations of the 'Burnt Offering' in Leviticus 1[11]

Source-Critical

Though the present investigation is interested in the final form of Leviticus, engagement with the source-critical interpretation of the 'burnt offering' may assist in identifying some unique features of the prescription in Leviticus 1. We can then ask whether these features might have a literary purpose that sheds light on the prescription's theological meaning.

Most scholars regard the 'burnt offering', along with the 'cereal offering' (Leviticus 2) and the 'peace offering' (Leviticus 3), as of greater antiquity in Israel than the remaining offerings of Leviticus 1–7 (i.e. the 'sin' and 'guilt' offerings).[12] The following three arguments have been offered in support of this assumption.

First, the offerings of Leviticus 1–3 are found in what are traditionally considered the earliest sources (i.e. the 'Jahwist' source ['J']).[13] Since the 'sin offering' and 'guilt offering' are not mentioned in J they must have developed at a later time.

Second, what appear to be the antecedents of the 'burnt offering' within ANE cultures are expiatory.[14] In line with this observation, Milgrom suggests

may be found for it by demonstrating that H applies the term תמים, with the same symbolic meaning, to sacrificial animals. This will be done by looking at the parallel drawn between the קדש priests and תמים sacrificial animals in Leviticus 21–22 in Chapter 6. Kiuchi is the only scholar who has proposed that תמים retains the meaning it has when applied to humans on a symbolic dimension when applied to sacrificial animals and that it partially represents P's view of holiness. It is hoped that the present study will contribute more evidence that this is indeed the case. See Kiuchi, *Leviticus*, pp. 41, 46, 55, 63-64.

11. For a recent interpretation which does not easily fit within either 'source-critical' or 'theological' interpretative categories of the 'burnt offering' see Gilders, *Blood Ritual and the Hebrew Bible*. For a critique of Gilders's argument see Leigh M. Trevaskis, review of *Blood Ritual and the Hebrew Bible*, by William K. Gilders, in *EJT* 17 (2008), pp. 184-85.

12. Milgrom, *Leviticus 1–16*, p. 176. Dillmann regards the 'burnt offering' as the oldest of Israel's offerings. Dillmann, *Exodus und Leviticus*, p. 388.

13. For an overview of these passages see Milgrom, *Leviticus 1–16*, p. 174; Dillmann, *Exodus und Leviticus*, pp. 388-89.

14. For an overview of the 'pre-history' of Israel's 'burnt offering' within the ANE see Leonhard Rost, 'Erwägungen zum israelitischen Brandopfer', in *Vom Ugarit nach Qumran: Festscrift O. Eissfeldt* (BZAW, 77; Berlin: W. de Gruyter, 1958), pp. 177-83; Milgrom, *Leviticus 1–16*, pp. 172-75.

that the expiatory function assigned to the 'burnt offering' in Lev. 1.4, and a limited number of other 'cultic' passages,[15] is a remnant of an older tradition that was 'usurped' by the introduction of the expiatory 'sin offering' (Lev. 4.1-5.13) and 'guilt offering' (Lev. 5.14-26 [Eng. 5.14-6.7]).[16]

Finally, Milgrom thinks that the lack of prescribed cases for why one should offer the עלה, מנחה and שלמים offerings prescribed in Leviticus 1–3 suggests that the motivations for bringing them were taken for granted. By contrast, the more recently introduced 'sin offering' and 'guilt offering' required the priests to explain when these ought to be offered.[17]

Even though the diachronic explanation for these observations is not of interest to the present synchronic study, there is one problem I would like to point out concerning it. The first and second points would appear to be contradictory. If the 'burnt offering' originally had an expiatory function within Israel why is this not recorded in J but P, which is commonly regarded as the later text?[18] Thus, for the time being it seems prudent to assume that, for the final editor of Leviticus, the כפר-function was as essential to the function of the 'burnt offering' as it was to the 'sin offering' and 'guilt offering'. Moreover, the nature of the occasions at hand, rather than historical developments, possibly accounts for why people sometimes offer the 'burnt offering' rather than 'sin offerings' and 'guilt offerings' in J.

Apart from these difficulties, the source-critical approach to Leviticus 1 raises some questions that may aid in the 'final form' interpretation of this material. First, what is the nature of the כפר made by the 'burnt offering', especially considering that other offerings (cf. Leviticus 4–5) provide כפר for specific sin? Moreover, if Milgrom's diachronic explanation for this observation is misguided, why is it mentioned so rarely in connection with the 'burnt offering'? Second, why are cases established for when one should offer the 'sin offering' and 'guilt offering' but not the offerings found in Leviticus 1–3? In what way might such an ommission reflect the purpose of

15. Lev. 9.7, 14.20; 16.24, Job 1.5; 42.8.

16. Milgrom, *Leviticus 1–16*, p. 176.

17. Milgrom, *Leviticus 1–16*, p. 176.

18. Indeed, the current confusion concerning not only the dating, but also the existence, of these putative sources cannot help but undermine the persuasiveness of Milgrom's argument in this regard (see especially Rolf Rendtorff, 'What Happened to the 'Yahwist'? Reflections after Thirty Years' [paper at International SBL Meeting, Edinburgh, 2006]). Another difficulty with Milgrom's diachronic appraisal of the 'burnt offering' is his contention that the verb כפר means 'to expiate' within Leviticus 1. This position contradicts his contention that the abstract notion of 'expiation' became associated with this term only at a later stage in Israel's history. If the 'burnt offering's' כפר-function reflects a very early stage within Israel's history, should not Milgrom conclude that the verb means 'to ransom', since this is the meaning he argues the verb initially had in Israel? See Milgrom, *Leviticus 1–16*, pp. 1082-1083.

the latter prescriptions? I shall attempt to answer these questions within my exegesis of Lev. 1.1-9.

Theological

Two theological purposes are assigned to the 'burnt offering' which are not mutually exclusive. The first is that the 'burnt offering' is a 'gift of entreaty'.[19] Levine, the main proponent of this view, considers that

> [t]he *ōlāh* was a signal to God that His worshippers desire to bring their needs to His attention; its purpose was to secure an initial response from Him. (God is perceived as breathing the aromatic smoke of the *ōlāh* and responding favorably to the overtures of His devotees). Frequently, the *ōlāh* was the first sacrifice in rites that included other offerings as well, which supports this suggestion about its purpose.[20]

He employs two arguments in support of this proposal. On the one hand, he claims that the fact that only the 'burnt offering' is used to attract God's attention within the biblical narratives is evidence that it was intended to attract the attention of the deity.[21] On the other hand, Levine observes that the 'burnt offering' normally precedes the offering of the 'peace offering' (שלמים).[22] He infers from this observation that

> [t]he *ōlāh* was normally utilized for the purpose of invoking the deity preparatory to joining with him in a fellowship of sacrifice, which was the context for petition and thanksgiving, and for the expression of other religious attitudes of this character.[23]

But though these observations seem to confirm that the 'burnt offering' served as a preliminary rite aimed at securing God's favourable attention, there are problems with the narrow definition of it as a 'gift of entreaty'. These problems are evident from Levine's own interpretation of what it means for the 'burnt offering' to make כפר for its offerer. As we shall see below, he argues that, as a valuable gift, it 'ransoms' (כפר) the offerer's life from God's wrathful disposition towards him.[24] This argument in itself suggests that the theol-

19. Milgrom, *Leviticus 1–16*, p. 175; Levine, *In the Presence of the Lord*; W.C. Kaiser, 'The Book of Leviticus', in *The New Interpreter's Bible*, IV (ed. L. Keck; Nashville: Abingdon Press, 1994), pp. 985-1119 (1010); Hartley, *Leviticus*, pp. 22-23.

20. Levine, *Leviticus*, pp. 5-6. cf. Dillmann, *Exodus und Leviticus*, p. 389.

21. Num. 23.1-6; 1 Kgs 18; Judg. 6, 13; 2 Kgs 3. Cf. Levine, *In the Presence of the Lord*, pp. 23-25.

22. Levine, *In the Presence of the Lord*, pp. 25-26.

23. Levine, *In the Presence of the Lord*, p. 26.

24. Levine, *Leviticus*, p. 7. Blum likewise contends that, owing to the presence of both Lev. 1.4b and 1.9bβ, one must hold the two functions of 'gift' (Gabe) and 'atonement' (Sühne) together when interpreting the prescription of the burnt offering (*Studien zur Komposition des Pentateuch*, p. 317).

ogy of the burnt offering extends beyond 'entreaty'. Moreover, Levine's contention that the initial literary position of the 'burnt offering' prescription (i.e. Leviticus 1) indicates that it was the 'gift of entreaty', that was offered prior to other offerings, is not completely persuasive. As James Watts points out,

[i]t is unlikely…that every *šĕlāmîm* could have been preceded by an *'ōlāh*. In times and places where any slaughter of livestock from herd or flock was regarded as an offering to be shared with the deity (so Lev. 7.1-9), the cost would have been prohibitive.[25]

This observation does not imply that the 'burnt offering' did not attract God's attention and achieve the offerer's acceptance, but it may suggest that its function is more nuanced than the idea of 'entreaty'.

The second theological function assigned to the 'burnt offering' is that it symbolizes a 'religious ideal'.[26] Scholars infer that the offering has this purpose from its use within narrative texts. For example, in defending this interpretation of the 'burnt offering', Watts remarks that it

is underscored by biblical stories of human sacrifice. The stories of Abraham and Isaac (Genesis 22), Jephthah and his daughter (Judg 11.31), and King Mesha of Moab and his son (2 Kgs 3.27) all describe the offering of one's child as an *'ōlāh*. Though the stories' evaluations of such acts are mixed, they underscore the idea that to offer an *'ōlāh* is to give up something of great value. The prominence of the *'ōlāh* in biblical rhetoric emphasizes this ideal of self-denial, even though it prohibits the specific act of child sacrifice (Exod. 13.13; Lev. 17.21; 20.3-5; Deut .18.10). The child sacrifice stories suggest that offering an *'ōlāh* indicates a willingness to give God much more than just an animal.[27]

---

25. Watts, *Ritual as Rhetoric in Leviticus*, p. 70.

26. That this view may be held in conjunction with the first view (i.e. 'gift of entreaty') is apparent in the work of Milgrom. Though he regards 'entreaty' as the 'manifest purpose' of this offering he suggests that 'when the sacrifices are prescribed they are listed in order of their sanctity (i.e. importance), and therefore the ubiquitous and venerable *'ōlāh*, burnt in its entirety as a total gift to God, comes first' (Milgrom, *Leviticus 1–16*, pp. 175, 488). Watts understands this suggestion to imply that Milgrom views this offering 'as most representative of Israel's worship, as best expressing the proper worship of God' (James W. Watts, "*'Ōlāh*: The Rhetoric of Burnt Offerings', *VT* 56 [2006], pp. 125-37 [132]). Rendtorff's understanding of the burnt offering as a gift of restitution to Yahweh, taken from what the latter has provided for the offerer within the Land, may also be placed under the definition of the offering as a 'religious ideal'. 'Es ist Gabe an Gott, was auch der Begriff אשה ausdrückt (1,9b.13b.17b). Genauer gesagt: es ist Rückgabe dessen, was der Opfernde zuvor von Gott empfangen hat' (Rendtorff, *Leviticus*, pp. 67-68, 79; see similarly Heinisch, *Das Buch Leviticus*, p. 22). This conclusion relates to Rendtorff's translation of אשה as a 'gift'.

27. Watts, *Rhetoric as Ritual in Leviticus*, p. 71. See similarly Wenham, *Leviticus*, pp. 58-59; Hartley intuits the same function from the prescription within Leviticus 1 (*Leviticus*, p. 24).

With this function in mind, Watts suggests that the prescription for the 'burnt offering' is positioned before those for the other sacrifices in Leviticus 1–7 to establish 'selfless devotion as the religious ideal'.[28]

Ironically, the view that the 'burnt offering' symbolizes a 'religious ideal' has not encouraged its proponents to investigate whether this symbolism may have encouraged the offerer to manifest this ideal in the way he lived (i.e. ethically).[29] Yet if this were part of its function, the prescription for this offering may anticipate the command to 'be holy' in Lev. 11.44-45. This possibility seems strengthened by the 'most holy' nature of the 'burnt offering' (see Appendix 2). Thus, in what follows an attempt is made to extend the work of these scholars by examining the relationship that exists between the offerer and his 'most holy' offering. After this examination, I shall explore what symbolic dimension this relationship may have had and whether it was of such a nature that the offerer understood that he was expected to embody the religious ideal of the 'burnt offering'.[30]

The Nature of the Relationship between the 'Burnt Offering' and its Offerer

To investigate if the ritual for the 'burnt offering' (Leviticus 1) adumbrates the explicit application of 'holiness' terminology to the laity in Lev. 11.44-45, the nature of the relationship between the offerer and the 'burnt offering' needs to be established. The position taken on the nature of this relationship largely depends on how Lev. 1.3-4 is interpreted. These verses read:

אם־עלה קרבנו מן־הבקר זכר תמים יקריבנו אל־פתח אהל
מועד יקריב אתו לרצנו לפני יהוה: ⁴וסמך ידו על ראש העלה
ונרצה לו לכפר עליו:

28. Watts, *Rhetoric as Ritual in Leviticus*, p. 78.

29. An exception is the interpretation offered by Kiuchi. However, though Kiuchi argues that the 'burnt offering' requires that its offerer 'be holy' he denies that the latter is an ethical concept (*Leviticus*, p. 63).

30. The present inquiry is limited to the question of whether this relationship reflects P's desire for the offerer to be holy. It does not attempt to answer the question of whether the offerer was expected to 'be holy' *so that* he could offer the 'burnt offering' or, alternatively, whether sacrificing the 'burnt offering' obliged him to 'be holy'. The later possibility assumes that after making an offering a person would come to the realization that the life God finds acceptable is one lived like the ideal of the 'burnt offering'. Nevertheless, we are dealing with a prescriptive text so that the question can be limited to whether by *reading* Leviticus 1 a person would come to the realization that he was meant to be holy.

Of crucial importance is what kind of relationship is established by the act of 'hand leaning' (סמך)[31] *'so that*[32] it will be accepted on his behalf to make atonement for him' (ונרצה לו לכפר עליו, v. 4a).[33] As pointed out by Sklar,

> the hand-leaning rite results in the animal being accepted for the worshipper (ונרצה לו) in order to make atonement for him (לכפר עליו), i.e., in this regard, the hand-leaning rite has established some type of relationship between offerer and sacrifice such that this sacrifice, which is now accepted for the offerer, is able to effect atonement for him.[34]

Moreover, conceptually, most exegetes regard לרצנו לפני יהוה (v. 3b) as a statement of purpose, revealing the offerer's motive for bringing the 'burnt offering', that precedes a statement of its actualization (i.e. ונרצה לו לכפר עליו, v. 4b).[35] On this reading, essential to the actualization of לרצנו is the pressing down of a hand in v. 4a, indicating that some kind of relationship is established by hand-leaning that allows the offering to make כפר for the offerer.[36] But, Knierim has rejected this traditional interpretation of the relationship between the two occurrences of the root רצה and the act of hand-leaning in Lev. 1.3-4.[37] He argues that לרצנו (v. 3b) and נרצה (v. 4b) refer to two different stages of divine acceptance, of two different actions.[38] Since his argument impacts directly on the hypothesis that hand-leaning establishes a relationship between offerer and offering it requires some consideration.[39]

Knierim rejects the traditional view that the רצה in vv. 3-4 refers to the acceptance of the animal as either a substitute,[40] or an item of worth,[41] 'to

---

31. A.M, Rodriguez, *Substitution in the Hebrew Cultus and in Cultic-Related Texts* (PhD dissertation, Andrews University, 1980), p. 194.

32. For the translation of the *waw* as a consequential consecutive, see Wenham, *Leviticus*, 55.

33. נרצה לו (v. 4bα) should be translated 'it (sacrifice) will be accepted *on his behalf*' because the meaning of its parallel form in Lev. 22.25 (i.e. לא ירצו לכם) is the same as that of לא לרצון יהיה לכם in Lev. 22.20 (Kiuchi, *The Purification Offering*, p. 117).

34. Sklar, *Sin, Impurity, Sacrifice and Atonement* (PhD dissertation), p. 189. Citations are made to Sklar's PhD dissertation on occasions when the material referred to was not included in its publication.

35. See Kiuchi, *The Purification Offering*, pp. 117-18.

36. Wenham, *Leviticus*, p. 55; Milgrom, *Leviticus 1–16*, pp. 150-53.

37. Knierim, *Text and Concept*, p. 36.

38. Knierim, *Text and Concept*, p. 36.

39. Surprisingly, Knierim's proposal in this regard has gone largely unnoticed in the literature since its publication in 1992. See, however, Gane, *Cult and Conscience*.

40. Noth, *Leviticus*, p. 22; Noordtzij, *Leviticus*, p. 33; Kiuchi, *The Purification Offering*, pp. 117-18.

make atonement for him' (לכפר עליו, v. 4b).[42] Pointing out that such a
view presupposes that לרצונו לפני יהוה (v. 3b) and ונרצה לו (v. 4b) are
correlated as a statement of purpose and a statement of actualization,[43]
Knierim claims that this unnecessarily isolates these two clauses from their
main clauses, namely 'to the entrance of the tent of meeting, he shall offer it'
(אל־פתח אהל מועד יקריב אתו, v. 3b) and 'he shall lean his hand on the
head of the burnt offering' (וסמך ידו על ראש העלה, v. 4a).[44] Considering that these two main clauses represent two different acts, and that the
subsequent qualification of each clause is different (i.e. לפני יהוה in v.3bβ
and לכפר עליו in v. 4bα), Knierim concludes that

> [t]hese factors give cause to assume two actions or stages expressed in the
> two main clauses in vv. 3 and 4 for which the offerer needs and/or receives
> favor.[45]

For Knierim, the first 'accepted' act is that of bringing the animal 'to the
entrance of the tent of meeting' (אל־פתח אהל מועד, v. 3bα). As a result
of this act, rather than what happens in the following verse (i.e. hand-
leaning), the offerer becomes the recipient of Yahweh's רצון.[46] The second
act that receives Yahweh's רצון is prescribed as 'he shall lean his hand upon
the head of the burnt offering' (העלה סמך ידו על ראש, v. 4a).[47] Knierim
interprets this act as the legal relinquishment of the animal to a sacrificial
death.[48] Thus, in v. 4, what is accepted is the offerer's decision to commit the
animal to a sacrificial death. In sum, with regard to the two occurrences of
the root רצה in vv. 3-4, he concludes that

> it is to the offerer's favor that his two identified acts are met with positive,
> delightful approval, apparently as a precondition for what follows.[49]

41. E.g. Milgrom, Wright, Snaith.
42. Knierim, *Text and Concept*, p. 36.
43. Knierim, *Text and Concept*, p. 36.
44. Knierim, *Text and Concept*, p. 36.
45. With regard to Knierim's claim that לרצנו and לפני יהוה each refer to separate
preceding acts, he follows Rendtorff who comments: 'Two aspects are stressed thereby:
1. The victim must be perfectly constituted, so that it can serve as acceptance for the
offerer…2. The Offering must be brought to the correct place, so that it can be brought
before Yahweh' (see Rendtorff, *Leviticus*, p. 30-32 [translation mine]; cf. Knierim, *Text
and Concept*, p. 36).
46. That is, with the consensus view Knierim takes the antecedent of the pronominal
suffix of לרצן as a datival reference to the offerer.
47. In this regard, Knierim largely follows Rendtorff, *Leviticus*, pp. 30-32. See
Knierim, *Text and Concept*, pp. 35-37.
48. Knierim, *Text and Concept*, pp. 39-40.
49. Namely, the transfer of the offering to Yahweh by its burning (Knierim, *Text and
Concept*, p. 36).

Though there are commendable aspects to Knierim's analysis of Lev. 1.3-4, the position of the clause לכפר עליו (v. 4bβ) is problematical for his conclusion that two acts are the recipients of Yahweh's רצון in these verses. To conclude that the subject of נרצה (v. 4b) is the act of hand-leaning, Knierim must propose that לכפר עליו (v. 4b) is a later addition. Otherwise, he would be forced to make the conclusion that the act of hand-leaning is the agent of כפר in v. 4b, a notion foreign to the OT.[50] While he makes the parenthetical remark that the secondary nature of לכפר עליו is 'generally accepted', no substantiation for this is given apart from that it is 'generally accepted'.[51] In the absence of evidence that לכפר עליו is of a secondary nature, it seems safest to put aside Knierim's claim that the act of hand-leaning is the subject of נרצה. Instead, a plain reading of the text supports the traditional view that the 'burnt offering' is the most likely subject of נרצה. In support of this view, it should be noted that sacrificial animals are the predominant subject of the niphal form of רצה elsewhere in the OT (Lev. 19.7b; 22.23, 25).[52]

Nevertheless, this problem in Knierim's argument does not undermine his more central suggestion that the two occurrences of the root רצה refer to two stages of divine acceptance. Considering that they both follow independent main clauses and that they are both followed by different qualifications (i.e. לפני יהוה in v. 3b and לכפר עליו in v. 4b respectively), the assumption that they each refer to the same stage of acceptance does not seem as likely. Nevertheless, this conclusion does not mean that no continuity of subject pertains in the two stages of acceptance. Indeed, the idea of continuity may be what is hinted at by the fact that the purpose phrase in v. 3b (i.e. לרצנו) and the statement of actualization in v. 4bα (i.e. נרצה) share the same root. In other words, the double occurrence of the root רצה possibly reflects that, though there is not a single act of acceptance, the same thing is accepted twice. Thus, for the moment Knierim's proposal that Lev. 1.3-4 reflects two stages of divine acceptance is preferred.

But what is accepted on each occasion? It is doubtful that it is the two actions suggested by Knierim, namely the offerer's bringing the animal to the

50. As noted by Kiuchi, *The Purification Offering*, p. 117; Sklar, *Sin, Impurity, Sacrifice and Atonement* [PhD dissertation], p. 189.
51. Knierim, *Text and Concept*, p. 38. To my knowledge, Rendtorff is the only other scholar who refers to Lev. 1.4b as secondary. He suggests that clauses within Lev. 1.2-4 that are not written in the 2nd person indicate that at an earlier stage in the rite's (oral) history Leviticus 1 was used for directing the performance of the ritual. Thus, similarly to Knierim, its secondary nature is assumed by Rendtorff (*Die Gesetze in der Priesterschrift*, p. 23). However, it is noteworthy that in his later commentary on Leviticus 1 Rendtorff makes no reference to v. 4b as a secondary addition (Rendtorff, *Leviticus*).
52. The offerer (המקריב) and guilt (עון) are the subjects of the niphal form in Lev. 7.18 and Isa. 40.2 respectively.

'tent of meeting' (מוֹעֵד אֹהֶל, v. 3b) and the offerer's firm pressing down of his hand (v. 4a).[53] First, in relation to לרצנו, the contextual evidence points strongly to the offering as the antecedent of the pronominal suffix of לרצנו, rather than the offerer (see below).[54] A more accurate rendering is 'for *its* acceptance'.[55] Second, with regard to נרצה, Knierim's suggestion would mean that the act of hand-leaning makes כפר for the offerer. Since the first point departs from the traditional view it requires some comment.

In Lev. 1.3, nearly all exegetes assume that the offerer brings his offering 'for *his* רצון',[56] rather than for 'its [i.e. the offering's] רצון'.[57] This consensus relies on the observation that this is the case in five of the six uses of the noun רצון elsewhere in Leviticus.[58] Moreover, an analogy between לרצנכם (Lev. 22.19) and לא לרצון יהיה לכם (Lev. 22.20), is sometimes cited as further proof that the pronominal suffix of לרצנו is a datival reference to the offerer rather than the offering.[59] Conformably, לרצנו is rendered 'for acceptance *on his behalf*'. On this reading, two interpretations of vv. 3 and 4 are commonly offered. The offerer may bring the 'burnt offering' to the entrance of the tabernacle for *his* acceptance which will be actualized after the imposition of a hand in v. 4 (most commentators). Alternatively, the offerer's *action* in bringing the animal to the tabernacle may be accepted as prerequisite to his subsequent act done for acceptance, namely the imposition of a hand in v. 4a (Knierim).[60] The first, traditional, interpretation has already been argued as depending on a possibly inappropriate correlation drawn between the notion of רצון, in לרצנו (v. 3b), with its actualization in נרצה לו (v. 4b). The

53. Knierim, *Text and Concept*, p. 36.

54. See Hartley, *Leviticus*, p. 13.

55. Nevertheless, this understanding does not exclude the possibility that the offerer is a secondary referent of the pronominal suffix. This could be the case if the animal symbolizes its, or an aspect of its, offerer.

56. Porter, *Leviticus*, p. 17; Noth, *Leviticus*, p. 19; Noordtzij, *Leviticus*, p. 31; Wenham, *Leviticus*, p. 48; Rendtorff, *Leviticus*, p. 31; Levine, *Leviticus*, p. 6; Milgrom, *Leviticus 1–16*, p. 149; Knierim, *Text and Concept*, p. 34; Péter-Contesse, *Lévitique 1–16*, p. 42.

57. Hartley, *Leviticus*, pp. 12-13.

58. Lev. 19.5; 22.19, 20, 29; 23.11. The sixth instance does not specify to whom it refers (Lev. 22.21). Cf. Sklar, *Sin, Impurity, Sacrifice and Atonement* [PhD dissertation], p. 187. Exod. 28.38 is possibly an important analogy to Lev. 1.3. See also Jer. 6.20 and Isa. 56.7. In view of Milgrom's contention that '[t]he subject of *lirṣōnō* is the sacrifice, the object, the offerer, and is so always (Lev 19.5; 22.19, 20)', my observation that the animal occurs as the object in Lev. 1.3 may be particularly significant. It could favour my argument that the 'burnt offering' symbolizes a particular human quality (see Milgrom, *Leviticus 1–16*, p. 149).

59. Kiuchi, *The Purification Offering*, p. 116; Milgrom, *Leviticus 1–16*, p. 149; Sklar, *Sin, Impurity, Sacrifice and Atonement* [PhD dissertation], pp. 187-88.

60. Knierim, *Text and Concept*, p. 36.

second view, Knierim's, is only possible so long as the pronominal suffix of לרצנו is in fact a datival reference to the offerer. Yet, as will be argued below, this interpretation is also unlikely. A third option seems worthy of consideration, namely that the first stage refers to the acceptance of the sacrificial animal, and that the second stage refers to the acceptance of this *acceptable* animal to make כפר on behalf of the offerer after the imposition of a hand.[61]

Only Hartley has argued that the antecedent to the pronominal suffix of לרצנו is the offering.[62] Though he concludes this on the basis that the offering is the subject of the verb נרצה in v. 4, this does not on its own constitute adequate evidence.[63] A more persuasive case can be made from that it is the offering, not the offerer, which is in the foreground in v. 3. For example, v. 3a identifies the antecedent of the pronominal suffix of יקריבנו ('he will bring it') as קרבנו ('his offering') which is subsequently qualified in detail as a 'burnt offering' consisting of a זכר תמים ('a male without defect') taken מן־הבקר ('from the herd', v. 3a). As if to go out of his way to indicate that the offering is of primary concern in v. 3, the legislator finally requires that 'he will bring *it*' (יקריב אתו, v. 3b). Since the same verb appears with a pronominal suffix in v. 3a (i.e. יקריבנו), the appearance of אתו in v. 3b could reflect an attempt to keep the offering in the foreground prior to לרצנו. Negatively, it may be added, that though many commentators appeal to the fact that the offerer is the referent of רצון elsewhere in P, as the grounds for translating לרצנו as 'for acceptance *on his behalf*', this is not necessarily always the case. The referent of the noun is unclear in Exod. 28.38 and Lev. 22.21.[64] Thus, contextually, the argument for identifying the offering with what is accepted by Yahweh is plausible.[65]

---

61. Perhaps it is more accurate to describe what happens as there being one item accepted (i.e. the offering), but from two different perspectives. The first is the acceptance of the animal to fulfil its purpose, and the second is the acceptance of it in fulfilling its purpose. It should also be kept in mind that a close relationship between the destiny of the offering and its offerer may result in there being some ambiguity in the identification of what is accepted in v. 3. That is, though it is essential for the offering to be accepted, it may not be possible to think of this without anticipating its offerer's acceptance in v. 4. Nevertheless, as I shall argue below, I would still maintain that the offering is the primary antecedent of the pronominal suffix in v. 3.

62. Snaith, noting that the pronoun may stand for either the offerer or offering, suggests that it doesn't matter. 'In any case, the meaning is that God shall accept both sacrifice and offerer so that there shall be *rāṣôn* (goodwill, acceptance) between God and man' (Snaith, *Leviticus*, p. 29; cf. Hartley, *Leviticus*, p. 13). But this conclusion prematurely assumes that לרצנו (v. 3) is a purpose statement that is actualized in v. 4.

63. Considering Knierim argues that it is the act of hand-leaning.

64. Note that Milgrom takes Exod. 28.38 as a reference to the offerings (*Leviticus 1–16*, p. 512).

65. Though as pointed out in footnote 62, a level of ambiguity remains regarding the

If the subject of the first stage of acceptance is most likely the offering, as argued above, what is prerequisite for its acceptance? Since the offering is passive in its movement 'to the entrance of the tent of meeting' (אל־פתח אהל מועד, v. 3bα) it is unlikely that it is the act of being brought to the sanctuary (*pace* Knierim). By a process of elimination it would seem that the 'cultic' legitimacy of the animal is singularly determinative of its acceptance.[66] In this regard, v. 3 refers to the species (מן־בקר), sex (זכר) and physical 'integrity' (תמים) of the sacrificial animal. The species does not seem of primary importance for the animal's acceptance because it comes as part of the conditional clause 'If his offering is a burnt offering from the herd' (אם־עלה קרבנו מן־הבקר, v. 3a). That is, רצון is also granted to animals taken 'from the flock' (מן־הצאן, v. 10a) and 'from the birds' (מן־העוף, v. 14a). It seems reasonable to conclude that the main prerequisite for the offering's 'acceptance' in v. 3 is that it is זכר תמים (v. 3aβ).[67] Considering that I have argued that לרצנו and נרצה represent two stages of the same object's acceptance, it is apparently the 'male without defect' (זכר תמים) nature of the animal which is the subject of נרצה in Lev. 1.4a.

The foregoing investigation of the terms לרצנו and נרצה indicates that they reflect two stages of acceptance in Lev. 1.3-4. First, לרצנו (v. 3b) refers to the offerer's motive in bringing an offering. He brings it for *its* acceptance. Prerequisite to this acceptance is that the bull is זכר תמים (v. 3). Second, נרצה (v. 4bα) describes Yahweh's acceptance of the acceptable offering (cf. v. 3) *on behalf* of its offerer (לו) to make כפר for him (v. 4bβ). Prerequisite to נרצה לו is the offerer's act of leaning his hand upon the head of the offering (v. 4a). This understanding assumes that some kind of relationship is established by this action that allows the pre-accepted זכר תמים offering 'to make כפר for him' (לכפר עליו, v. 4b). Of crucial importance in determining what relationship exists between the offerer and the 'most holy' status of the 'burnt offering' are the following questions. First, how may the nature of this relationship established by hand-leaning be conceptualized? Second, what does לכפר עליו mean?

---

antecedent of לרצנו. Although the subject of נרצה (v. 4a) is clearly the offering, the offering is certainly 'accepted on his [i.e. the offerer's] behalf' (נרצה לו). Thus, rather than clarify the antecedent of לרצנו as *either* the offerer *or* the offering, v. 4 allows it to refer to *both*. However, even if both are brought to mind by לרצנו, the above argument would seem to favour the offering as that which is primarily intended.

66. Sklar, *Sin, Impurity, Sacrifice and Atonement* [PhD dissertation], p. 188.

67. In support of this claim, Hoffmann argues that אתו within the clause יקריב אתו (v. 3a) refers to the cultic quality 'a male without defect' (זכר תמים). 'Auffallend ist die Wiederholung יקריב אותו, nachdem das Prädikat יקריבנו bereits gesetzt wurde... Das object, Suffix נו des vorigen Satzes, nachdem bereits das Object זכר תמים dabei gesetzt ist, verlangt jedoch, das er es, nämlich das geweihte Ganzopfer als Solches darbringen soll' (Hoffmann, *Das Buch Leviticus*, p. 117).

With regard to the first question, there are many suggestions for how the relationship implied by v. 4, between a person and his offering, should be conceptualized.[68] We may limit our study to those which fall within the broad categories of *consecration*; *transference*; and *identification*. The last category of identification is divisible into two further sub-categories of *substitution* and *ownership*. Since the answer to the second question is dependent on the relationship between the offerer and animal I shall attempt to answer it in the process of addressing the first question. By defining the nature of this relationship we may be able to assess whether the 'most holy' status of the offering is somehow related to the offerer.

סמך יד *as a Symbolic Act of Consecration*

There are some scholars who suggest that the gesture of hand-leaning served to consecrate or dedicate an offering as a gift to Yahweh.[69] Levine is representative of this approach, suggesting that the rite of hand-leaning was a symbolic act that

> [a]ssured that sacrifices intended for specific rites would be used solely for that purpose. Once assigned in this way, the offering was *sacred and belonged to God.*[70]

Such an interpretation conceptualizes a relationship of complete separation between offering and offerer at the moment of hand-leaning. Indeed, according to Levine, the 'most holy' nature of the 'burnt offering' is a consequence of hand-leaning.[71] That is, 'most holy' merely describes the status of an

---

68. For a discussion of how scholars have understood this relationship consult Rodriguez, *Substitution in the Hebrew Cultus*, pp. 201-208; Bernd Janowski, *Sühne als Heiligeschehen* (Neukirchen–Vluyn: Neukirchener Verlag, 1982), pp. 199-221; Rendtorff, *Leviticus*, pp. 32-48.

69. A comprehensive list of these is provided in David P. Wright, 'The Gesture of Hand Placement in the Hebrew Bible and in Hittite Literature', *JAOS* 106 (1986), pp. 433-46 (437).

70. Levine, *Leviticus*, 6 (emphasis mine).

71. Levine, *Leviticus*, p. 6. Knierim offers a more nuanced understanding of the hand leaning gesture as signifying separation. With regard to its meaning within the prescription of the 'burnt offering', Knierim comments that '[t]he main notion of the act of pressing the hand down concerns...the subjection of the animal to its impending fate of death, literally symbolized by the pressing down firmly of the offerer's hand... This subjection is not a magical but a legal act. It symbolizes the legality of his killing of the animal, not on the substitution for the offerer by the animal or on the flow of substance from the offerer to the animal' (Knierim, *Text and Concept*, p. 39). Knierim departs from Levine's view, that the act simply consecrates the offering to a specific sacrificial purpose, because the same hand-leaning gesture is used for various sacrificial rites. Conversely, Knierim argues that the positioning of the rite immediately before the act of slaughtering suggests that its meaning must be related to the latter (Knierim, *Text and*

offering completely separated from its offerer to fulfil a specific purpose (i.e.
as a עלה, שלמים or חטאת). This interpretation, which regards the phrase
'most holy' as no more than a label of God's property, has implications for
my hypothesis that the holiness of the 'burnt offering' may imply that P
desired the offerer to 'be holy'. Some assessment of whether it is sufficient
to interpret the gesture of hand-leaning simply as an act of consecration is
required. Two observations suggest that it is not.

First, the concept of 'most holy' is applicable to offerings prior to the act
of hand-leaning (see Appendix 2). An offering's 'most holy' status appears to
apply from the moment a decision was made to offer it to Yahweh. The
legislator used the phrase to ensure that the offering was not profaned from a
much earlier stage than the hand-leaning gesture.[72] Thus, the offering was
probably viewed as 'most holy' from the moment the offerer decided to relinquish it to Yahweh.

The second, and more significant, problem with the theory of separation or
consecration is that it does not take into account the intimate relationship
established between the offerer and offering by the act of hand-leaning.[73]
While this phenomenon has already been argued in relation to the subordination of the clause 'and it will be accepted on his behalf' (ונרצה לו) to 'and
he shall lean his hand on the head of the burnt offering' (וסמך ידו על
ראש העלה) in Lev. 1.4, Lev. 7.18 also reflects a relationship that is more
than one of 'separation' or 'consecration'.

Lev. 7.18 comes within the instructions given to the laity concerning its
handling of the 'peace offering' meat (Lev. 7.11-21). It reads

ואם האכל יאכל מבשר־זבח שלמיו ביום השלישי לא ירצה
המקריב אתו לא יחשב לו פגול יהיה והנפש האכלת ממנו עונה
תשא

Concept, p. 38). However, this position overlooks the fact that לכפר עליו is positioned
between וסמך ידו על ראש עלה (v. 4) and ושחט את־בן הבקר (v. 5). As mentioned above, Knierim attempts to overcome this difficulty by suggesting that the clause
לכפר עליו is a later interpolation. Since I have already rejected this claim it can be
concluded that this aspect of Knierim's argument is improbable (see Knierim, *Text and
Concept*, p. 38).

72. See Appendix 2.

73. Wright does not completely reject the claim that the gesture indicates that a
transfer of property or separation has taken place. Yet he does not say why he prefers the
theory of ownership summarized below. I presume that it is because of what is noted
here, namely that while a transfer of property has obviously taken place the theory fails
to take into account the benefits that accrue to the offerer. See Wright, 'The Gesture of
Hand Placement in the Hebrew Bible and in Hittite Literature', p. 437.

Sklar observes that this verse records what will lead to the offerer's non-acceptance.[74] Of importance to the present investigation is the explication of 'the one who offers it shall not be accepted' (לא ירצה המקריב אתו) by the phrase 'it will not *be credited to him*' (לא יחשב לו). Since, in Lev. 7.18, לא יחשב לו would seem to be a partial antonym of ירצה, it is not unlikely that the concept of חשב is present in Lev. 1.3-4.[75] This verse implies that the value of the offering somehow accrues to the offerer, presumably in relation to the gesture of hand-leaning. Needless to say, this kind of relationship goes unaccounted for by the theory of consecration.

סמך יד *as Symbolic of Transference*

Transference theories assume that the imposition of a hand, within sacrificial contexts, results in the transference of the offerer's 'sin' (חטאת), 'guilt' (עון), or personality, to the animal.[76] As a consequence of this transference the animal dies as the offerer's substitute.[77] Thus, a vicarious relationship is proposed to exist between the two parties, whereby the animal's penal sacrificial death is credited to the sinful offerer.

Theories of transference within sacrificial rituals are based solely on Lev. 16.21, though they receive some indirect support from non-sacrificial passages such as Num. 27.18-23 and Deut. 34.9. Lev. 16.21ab reads:

74. Sklar, *Sin, Impurity, Atonement and Sacrifice* [PhD dissertation], p. 190.

75. Contra Bernd Janowski, with Rendtorff, who claims that the concept is not present because the root does not occur in these verses (Janowski, *Sühne als Heiligeschehen*, p. 216; Rendtorff, *Leviticus*, p. 36). Knierim criticizes their conclusion suggesting that it 'surrenders more than is necessary and allowable. Whether or not רצון connotes imputation depends neither on the presence or absence of the root חשב, nor on a spoken declaration, nor on the fact that it approves of an offerer's act' (Knierim, *Text and Concept*, p. 42).

76. Gerstenberger, *Leviticus*, pp. 26-27. Positions differ on whether sin is materially or notionally transferred. See Rodriguez, *Substitution in the Hebrew Cultus*, p. 201.

77. Some scholars claim that the offerer's personality transfers to the animal. This theory divides between those who claim that the animal suffers a substitutionary death in the offerer's place (M. Bernoulli, *Vocabulaire biblique* [Neuchâtel: Delachaux & Niestlé, 1954], p. 130; J.A. MacCulloch, 'Hand', in *Encyclopedia of Religion and Ethics* [ed. J. Hastings; New York: Charles Scribner's Sons, 1951], pp. 492-99 (494); Noth, *Das dritte Buch Mose* [Göttingen: Vandenhoeck & Ruprecht, 1962], p. 13, cited by Wright, 'The Gesture of Hand Placement in the Hebrew Bible and in Hittite Literature', p. 437) and those who argue that the animal becomes the vehicle by which the offerer offers him/herself as a gift to God (Elliger, *Leviticus*, p. 34; Bertholet, *Leviticus*, pp. 2-3; Janowski, *Sühne*, pp. 218-21; all are cited by Wright, 'The Gesture of Hand Placement in the Hebrew Bible and in Hittite Literature', p. 437). The view that the offerer's personality transfers to the animal will not be examined here. First, there is no clear textual support for this position. Second, as pointed out by Milgrom, it is 'alien to biblical thought both because it is magical and because it presupposes the belief that death brings one close to God' (Milgrom, *Leviticus 1–16*, p. 151).

וסמך אהרן את־שתי ידו על ראש השעיר החי והתודה עליו
את־כל־עונת בני ישראל ואת־כל־פשעיהם לכל־חטאתם ונתן
אתם על־ראש השעיר

Almost without exception, scholars accept that some kind of transfer, result-ing from the imposition of Aaron's hands, is assumed by this verse.[78] Of importance to the present inquiry is whether or not this is the case when a hand is imposed within the prescription for the 'burnt offering'. If the gesture symbolizes the transference of the offerer's sin to the animal, it would seem difficult to argue that the relationship between the offerer and the 'burnt offering' was such that the holiness of the latter implies that the former was expected to 'be holy'.

Since various arguments for how one should interpret the transference which occurs in Lev. 16.21 have been frequently documented, the discussion which follows is limited to why I do not consider that this verse implies that sin is transferred as a result of hand-leaning in Lev. 1.4.[79] A corollary of this discussion is that the root כפר more likely connotes 'ransom' than 'expia-tion' within Leviticus 1.

There are at least two observations which caution against using Lev. 16.21 as evidence that sin is transferred via the hand-leaning gesture in Leviticus 1. First, the transference of guilt in Lev. 16.21 occurs within the context of a larger performance not mentioned in Leviticus 1.[80] That is the hand-leaning rite is accompanied by the confession of what is transferred, namely 'all the guilt of the Israelites' (כל־עונת בני ישראל).[81] Significantly, no confession of 'sin' or 'guilt' is recorded in the prescription for the 'burnt offering'.[82] This observation possibly discourages an interpretation that these things were transferred in Lev. 1.4.

---

78. Wright, who argues that nothing is transferred, is the exception ('The Gesture of Hand Placement', p. 436). Sklar adequately responds to Wright's idea (*Sin, Impurity, Sacrifice and Atonement* [PhD dissertation], pp. 183-84).

79. See especially René Péter, 'L'imposition des mains dans l'Ancien Testament', *VT* 27 (1977), pp. 48-55; Rodriguez, *Substitution in the Hebrew Cultus*, pp. 201-208; Rendtorff, *Leviticus*, pp. 32-48; Sklar, *Sin, Impurity, Sacrifice, and Atonement*, pp. 183-87 [PhD dissertation].

80. Kiuchi, *The Purification Offering*, p. 118.

81. An ongoing debate surrounds whether 'sin' and 'rebelliousness' are viewed as subcategories of 'guilt' (i.e. Kiuchi) or independent categories of evil within this verse (i.e. Milgrom, Gane). See Kiuchi, *The Purification Offering*, pp. 153-56; Milgrom, *Leviticus 1–16*, pp. 1035, 1043-1044; Gane, *Cult and Character*, pp. 285-91.

82. Wenham suggests that it was unlikely that the sacrificial ritual was performed in silence and that the hand-leaning rite was most probably accompanied by an explanation for why it was being offered. However, there is no evidence of such an oral procedure in the text. It seems reasonable to assume that the purpose of the offering was understood by the symbolic meaning of the various rites. Wenham, *Leviticus*, p. 53. Hartley likewise considers that the offerer confessed sin when pressing on the animal's head. Hartley, *Leviticus*, p. 21.

Second, the transference of guilt described in Lev. 16.21 occurs within a different context, namely as part of the Day of Atonement ritual. The difference seems to be significant considering that this occasion presupposes Israel's need to have its guilt and sin removed via the Azazel goat. By contrast, the gesture of hand-leaning in Lev. 1.4 comes within a context where the terms חטאת, חטא and עון are not mentioned. Related to this, Knierim, who also contends that 'sin' is not presupposed by Leviticus 1,[83] argues that the pronominal suffix on לכפר עליו refers to 'him' as the substantive subject of כפר, not to his 'sin'.[84]

Nevertheless, despite the non-mention of sin or guilt within Leviticus 1, some scholars maintain that the presence of the root כפר within this chapter refers to the expiation of sin from the offerer.[85] Representative of this approach is Hartley who suggests that, in the absence of any reference to specific 'sin', 'expiation' is made for the general sinfulness of the offerer.[86] Thus, he concludes that the Israelite who offered a 'burnt offering'

> recognized both his complete sinfulness and God's total claim on his life, for the whole offering (i.e. עלה) was completely given to God... This offering granted a person forgiveness for human sinfulness in general.[87]

Yet does the text allow a conceptualization of לכפר עליו in terms of the expiation of the offerer's sin? Or, alternatively, does it refer to the appeasement of God's wrath as a 'ransom' (כֹּפֶר)? If the former, then it remains possible, but not certain, that the act of hand-leaning transfers sin to the sacrificial animal. But if the offering makes 'ransom' for the offerer the transference of sin would seem less likely. Levine proposes two reasons for why it would seem that כפר means 'ransom' within Leviticus 1.

First, the syntax of לכפר עליו suggests that כפר means 'to ransom' (כֹּפֶר) within this context. Levine follows Ibn Ezra's suggestion that לכפר

---

83. Knierim, *Text and Concept*, p. 37.

84. Knierim, *Text and Concept*, p. 38.

85. Rendtorff, following Janowski, argues that the כפר referred to in Lev. 1.4 is achieved only in connection with the offering of a 'sin offering'. Milgrom responds to this suggestion with the observation that the 'burnt offering' makes כפר on its own in Lev. 16.24. See Janowski, *Sühne*, p. 192; Rendtorff, *Leviticus*, p. 38; Milgrom, *Leviticus 1–16*, p. 153.

86. Hartley, *Leviticus*, p. 19. See also Porter, *Leviticus*, p. 20; Noth, *Leviticus*, p. 22; Noordtzij, *Leviticus*, p. 33; Wenham, *Leviticus*, p. 57; Gerstenberger, *Leviticus*, pp. 27-28; Milgrom, *Leviticus 1–16*, p. 1083.

87. Hartley, *Leviticus*, 24. Rabbinic interpreters similarly assume that the 'burnt offering' expiated for a broader range of sins not dealt with by the חטאת and אשם offerings. These sins were normally identified as the transgressions of 'positive' or 'performative' commandments. See Silbermann, *Pentateuch with Rashi's Commentary*, p. 3a; Ibn Ezra, *Leviticus*, p. 3. *t. Menaḥ* 10.2; *Sipra*, Nedaba 4.8; *Midr. Tanḥ.* B 3.9a; *Midr. Lev. Rab.* 7.3, 11; Hoffmann, *Das Buch Leviticus*, p. 123; Milgrom, *Leviticus 1–16*, p. 175.

עליו is an abbreviation of לכפר על־נפשתיכם ('to serve as a ransom for your lives').[88] In support of his approach, Levine draws attention to the fact that the 'burnt offering' 'was not occasioned by any offence that would have placed the offender in need of expiation'.[89]

Second, assuming that לכפר עליו is an abbreviated form of לכפר על־נפשתיכם, Levine surmises that Lev. 17.11 indicates that blood was a symbolic substitute for the נפש of the offerer. This verse reads

כי נפש הבשר בדם הוא ואני נתתיו לכם על־המזבח לכפר
על־נפשתכם כי־הדם הוא בנפש יכפר

Taking this verse as an indication that 'blood can substitute for life to the extent required to ransom it, redeem it',[90] Levine concludes that in the case of Lev. 1.4, the blood ransomed the life of the offerer by protecting him from God's wrath.

> Proximity to God was inherently dangerous for both the worshipper and the priests, even if there had been no particular offence to anger Him. The favorable acceptance of the *ōlāh* signalled God's willingness to be approached and served as a kind of ransom, or redemption, from divine wrath.[91]

Levine's suggestion that כפר means 'to ransom' within the context of Lev. 1.4 seems appropriate, though it may require some modification in view of the subject and object of כפר in this verse.[92]

88. Levine, *Leviticus*, p. 7.

89. Levine, *Leviticus*, p. 6. Levine does not provide a reference for where this is argued by Ibn Ezra.

90. Levine, *In the Presence*, p. 68.

91. Levine, *Leviticus*, p. 7. Knierim responds to Levine's suggestion, that the 'burnt offering' redeems a person from God's wrath, by asking why an offerer would have considered bringing an offering before the tent if it was dangerous. He suggests that '[t]he עלה is not offered for redemption from wrath necessitated by proximity to God. If anything, it is offered, at least in this case, to overcome God's distance from the offerer and to bring the offerer into God's proximity' (Knierim, *Text and Concept*, pp. 77-78). But there are two problems with Knierim's line of argument. First, within the narrative of the Pentateuch, proximity to God has been dangerous ever since Adam and Eve's expulsion from the Garden. Indeed, after the completion of the tent of meeting (Exodus 40), which is itself a symbolic representation of the Garden the humans were expelled from (see below and Chapter 3), one can understand why Moses was unable to enter this structure after God filled it with his glory (cf. Exod. 40.35). Second, Knierim does not seem to have considered that an Israelite might have desired to approach the 'tent of meeting' (אהל מועד) on account of what it symbolized: God was present and accessible to Israel. Could it be that the statement that 'Moses was not able to enter the tent of meeting' (ולא־יכל משה לבוא אל־אהל מועד; Exod. 40.35) implies that he would have desired to enter?

92. Wenham is likewise of the opinion that the 'burnt offering' was regarded as a 'ransom payment' (*Leviticus*, pp. 59-61).

First, the subject of לכפר עליו is clearly not the offering's blood, but the 'burnt offering'. On the one hand, this observation supports Levine's proposal that כפר means 'to ransom',[93] but on the other hand, it cautions against concluding that the ransom *is* the blood. It seems to be the whole sacrificial animal.[94] Averbeck might be closest to the truth when he suggests that the 'burnt offering' is itself an *atonement gift*.

> [T]he burnt offering made atonement not by means of blood manipulation but as a gift that would have the same effect on God as, for example, Jacob's gifts to Esau in Gen 32:20[21], 'For he (Jacob) thought, 'I will pacify (kipper) him (lit., his faces) with these gifts I am sending on ahead; later, when I see him, perhaps he will receive me'… The burnt offering carried an atoning effect as a gift that appeased or entreated God rather than as a literal cleansing procedure.[95]

However, in view of my earlier suggestion that the antecedent of the pronominal suffix of לרצנו (v. 3) and subject of נרצה (v. 4a) was more narrowly the divinely acceptable זכר תמים aspect of the sacrificial animal, one may speculate that it is specifically this which 'ransoms' the 'human' (אדם) who offers the 'burnt offering', rather than the general 'burnt offering' itself.

Second, though Levine is correct in pointing out that לכפר, followed by the preposition על and then a personal object, is more likely to mean 'to ransom',[96] he may go too far in assuming that the pronominal suffix of עליו

---

93. 'If the agent of לכפר is the sacrifice…then it might be more appropriate to translate כפר "ransom" rather than "make atonement"' (Kiuchi, *The Purification Offering*, p. 181).

94. Janowski also notices that it is the complete offering that makes כפר for the offerer (*Sühne*, pp. 191-92).

95. Averbeck, 'עֹלָה', pp. 410-11.

96. In support of Levine's interpretation of this clause we may cite the following statement by Gane. 'While *kipper ʿal* in purification-offering formulas refers to removal/purgation, it does not have this meaning with other kinds of sacrifices. Only in purification-offering formulas is *kipper ʿal* colored by the additional privative idea: *kipper ʿal* …(*min*). Since the privative sense of removal is an addition indicated by the explicit or implied presence of *min*, it seems obvious that the most fundamental sense of *kipper ʿal* does not include the concept of removal/purgation; instead, *kipper ʿal … (min)* is subsumed under basic *kipper ʿal*. In other words, although the basic force of *kipper ʿal* can remain consistent, its usage with purification offerings is unique. We cannot pursue the fundamental sense of *kipper ʿal* here, but it would probably look something like "make amends on behalf of…"' (Gane, *Cult and Conscience*, pp. 139-140). Gane's observation concerning what he argues is the 'fundamental sense' of this collocation provides an adequate response to Gilders's criticism of Levine. Gilders contends that Levine's interpretation of לכפר על as meaning 'to make ransom for' 'requires us to believe that a formula, which appears repeatedly throughout priestly (P and H) texts, has a different meaning in one verse from its meaning everywhere else' (Gilders, *Blood Ritual in the Hebrew Bible*, p. 77). This is not necessarily a persuasive criticism if Gane is correct.

refers to a נפש. Indeed, the reason why the legislator chose not to mention נפש is possibly because the antecedent of the pronominal suffix of עליו is in fact a 'human' (אדם) rather than a נפש (cf. Lev. 1.2). The legislator does not use the term נפש to refer to the offerer until Leviticus 2. That the object of לכפר עליו is אדם rather than נפש may be important considering that Lev. 17.11 established that blood is given to ransom a נפש. If there is a significant difference in the legislator's use of the terms אדם and נפש, this may suggest that something other than the blood 'makes ransom' for the 'human' offerer in Leviticus 1. I shall investigate the meaning of אדם within this context further below.

   The foregoing examination of the term לכפר in v. 4 would seem to exclude the suggestion that the 'burnt offering' functioned to 'expiate' sin from the offerer.[97] In addition to the different performances and contexts which accompany the hand-leaning rites of Lev. 1.4 and Lev. 16.21, this observation suggests that transference of sin does not occur within the former passage.

סמך־יד *as an Act Establishing a Relationship of Substitution ('This Is Me')*[98]

Some scholars interpret the imposition of a hand as establishing a relationship of identification between the offerer and offering.[99] More specifically, the offering becomes its offerer's substitute by taking the latter's place in the ritual. However, this type of substitution is distinguishable from that envisaged by transference theories insofar as no 'material', whether sin/guilt or the offerer's personality, is transferred to the animal. By contrast, identification theories consider that the imposition of a hand simply designates the offering as taking the offerer's place in the ritual, normally so that it can be put to death as the offerer's substitute.[100]

---

   97. The claim that the 'burnt offering' did not expiate sin from the offerer may raise the question of why Yahweh requires appeasement when approached in this way. An attempt is made to answer this question after I have investigated the symbolic meaning of this prescription. However, to anticipate, the 'burnt offering' appeases Yahweh's wrath by its symbolic value as the *life* that is acceptable to Yahweh.

   98.   For example, see Hoffmann, *Das Buch Leviticus*, p. 122; Péter, 'L'imposition des mains dans l'Ancien Testament', pp. 51-52; Kiuchi, *Purification Offering*, p. 117.

   99.   Janowski, *Sühne*, pp. 220-21; H. Gese, *Essays in Biblical Theology* (trans. K. Crim; Minneapolis: Augsburg, 1981), pp. 104-108; Kiuchi, *The Purification Offering*, p. 118. See Hartley for an explanation of how these two scholars differ in their view of how 'substitution' achieves כפר for the offerer (Hartley, *Leviticus*, pp. 20-21).

   100. See Noth, *Leviticus*, p. 22; Janowski, *Sühne*, p. 210. Noordtzij, *Leviticus*, p. 33. Hoffmann comments on the meaning of the rite as follows. 'Durch die סמיכה wird nun das Thier von dem Opfernden selbst zum Repräsentanten dieser Seite seiner Persönlichkeit feierlich ernannt. Die סמיכה ist nicht unbedingt nöthig, sie ist nicht מעכב, weil

The most robust argument for the theory of substitution has been contributed by Kiuchi. Kiuchi rejects the problematical notion that the offering
achieves כפר for its offerer by its *substitutionary death*.[101] First, he remarks
that 'in Lev. 1.4 the idea of 'substitution', which could be the symbolic meaning of the imposition of a hand, is unlikely to include that of "atonement"'.[102]
Second, syntactically, the expression נרצה לו is not directly related to the
act of slaughtering in v. 5.[103] Nevertheless, Kiuchi contends that the notion of
substitution is still intended by the gesture of hand-leaning, though it symbolizes the offerer's indication that 'the animal is taking his place within the
ritual'.[104] He reaches this conclusion via the following observations. First,
observing that the offering 'will be accepted *on his behalf*' (נרצה לו, v. 4bα),
he infers that substitution is intended by noting that the non-acceptance of an
offerer is closely associated with the rejection of an offering in Lev. 7.18.[105]
Second, he suggests that the positioning of סמך יד between לרצנו לפני
יהוה (v. 3b) and נרצה לו (v. 4bα) demonstrates that the meaning of hand-
leaning is implied in the latter (i.e. 'it will be accepted *on his behalf*').[106]
Thus, he concludes that the imposition of a hand indicates that the animal
takes the offerer's place in the ritual.[107]

However, Kiuchi's assumption that '*on his behalf*' connotes substitution is
possibly misguided. As Knierim points out,

> the fact that this act 'will be accepted on *his* behalf' does not necessitate the
> conclusion that 'on *his* behalf'…qualifies the act of pressing down as sub-
> stitution. If that were so, the exegetical crux should not have existed.[108]

This criticism does not disprove Kiuchi's argument, but it does seem to
remove the possibility of knowing with certainty whether the gesture of
hand-leaning symbolizes substitution. Nevertheless, what is gained from

---

das Opfer an sich schon durch die Weihung (הקדשה) die symbolische Bezeichnung
dessen ist, wozu es durch die סמיכה gewissermassen die Vollmacht erhält; aber sie ist
dennoch מצוה, damit der Opfernde dadurch die Bedeutung des Opfers im Heiligthum
vor Gott selbst durch seine eigene That ausdrücke' (Hoffmann, *Das Buch Leviticus*,
p. 122).

101. Janowski is representative of scholars who regard the act of 'hand-leaning' as
identifying the animal as the offerer's substitute which will achieve his substitutionary
death. See Janowski, *Sühne*, p. 210; Kiuchi, *The Purification Offering*, p. 118.

102. Kiuchi, *The Purification Offering*, p. 118.

103. Kiuchi, *The Purification Offering*, p. 118.

104. Kiuchi, *The Purification Offering*, p. 118.

105. Kiuchi, *The Purification Offering*, p. 117.

106. Kiuchi, *The Purification Offering*, p. 117.

107. Kiuchi does not really explain how this does not necessitate the animal experiencing death as the offerer's substitute (*The Purification Offering*, p. 118).

108. Knierim, *Text and Concept*, p. 37.

Kiuchi's work is a more narrowly defined concept of what kind of substitution is possible. If substitution is symbolized by the imposition of a hand, it is unlikely to refer specifically to *substitutionary death*. Though, as Kiuchi notes, this 'is not to say that such a concept may not be expressed by other parts of the sacrificial ritual'.[109] This conclusion leaves open the possibility that the hand-leaning gesture symbolizes the substitution of something other than 'death'. This possibility may be significant considering my argument that the offering accepted on behalf of the offerer in v. 4 is that already accepted on account of it being a 'male without blemish' (זכר תמים) in v. 3. To anticipate, what is symbolized by a 'male without blemish' becomes the offerer's substitute, and thereby 'makes ransom' for him.

סמך־יד *as an Act that Establishes a Relationship of Ownership*

This approach understands that the hand-leaning gesture indicates ownership.[110] As for the arguments for consecration or separation, the ownership understanding conceives of the offering as a 'gift'. However, rather than symbolizing the offerer's relinquishment of the gift, it establishes ownership (i.e. 'this is mine'), thereby ensuring that the benefits of the offering *accrue* to its owner. The essential meaning of the gesture is summed up by Roland de Vaux as follows.

> In placing his hand on the animal's head, the offerer attests that this victim is *his* indeed, that the sacrifice that is about to be presented by the priest is offered in his name, and that the benefits accruing from it will return to *him*.[111]

Conceptually, the accrual of the benefits associated with the offering to the offerer's favour makes sense of the observation that an intimate relationship is established between the two by the imposition of a hand (cf. Lev. 1.4; 7.18).

Despite the objections made concerning this theory by Knierm and Rodriguez,[112] it seems almost natural to assume that the hand-leaning gesture plays some role in establishing ownership.[113] As I shall argue below, this

109. Kiuchi, *The Purification Offering*, p. 118.

110. Snaith, *Leviticus*, p. 29; Rendtorff, *Leviticus*, p. 47; Wright, 'The Gesture of Hand Placement in the Hebrew Bible and in Hittite Literature', pp. 438-39; Milgrom, *Leviticus 1–16*, pp. 151-52.

111. Roland de Vaux, *Studies in Old Testament Sacrifice* (Cardiff: University of Wales Press, 1964), pp. 28-29.

112. Knierim, *Text and Concept*, p. 37; Rodriguez, *Substitution in the Hebrew Cultus*, p. 207.

113. For a defence of the view that hand-leaning establishes ownership consult Milgrom, *Leviticus 1–16*, pp. 151-52, 163 and Wright, 'The Gesture of Hand Placement in the Hebrew Bible and in Hittite Literature', p. 439. Criticism of their arguments is offered by Sklar, *Sin, Impurity, Sacrifice and Atonement* [PhD dissertation], pp. 191-92 and Rodriguez, *Substitution in the Hebrew Cultus*, p. 195.

view does not exclude the possibility that hand-leaning also identifies an animal as a substitute.

Nevertheless, there is one area in which the ownership theory is deficient and this relates to what it perceives as the item of worth that is credited to the offerer. It commonly assumes that the item of worth which accrues to the offerer is the blood (i.e. 'life'; cf. Lev. 17.11) because the offering of the 'burnt offering' makes כפר for the offerer.[114] But there are two problems with this assumption. First, it gives disproportionate emphasis to what is a relatively insignificant part of the ritual for the 'burnt offering'.[115] For example, whereas the blood rites of the 'sin offering' ritual involve the sprinkling and/or daubing of the blood on the altar (Lev. 4.7, 18, 25, 30, 34) or פרכת (Lev. 4.6, 17), the prescription for the 'burnt offering' simply requires that the priests shall 'throw the blood against sides of the altar' (וזרקו את־הדם על־המזבח סביב, Lev. 1.5bα). Though this observation is not conclusive evidence against the possibility that the item of worth associated with the 'burnt offering' was its blood, it raises the question of why so little emphasis is placed on this aspect of the sacrifice if it is singularly responsible for gaining the offerer's divine acceptance.

Second, the most serious problem with viewing the blood of the 'burnt offering' as the item of worth credited to the offerer is that it is not the subject of כפר in the clause לכפר עליו (Lev. 1.4b).[116] In this regard, Kiuchi has emphasized that the subject of כפר in this verse is the sacrifice. In the other offerings prescribed in Leviticus 1–7 the subject is always the priest and it is assumed that the 'blood' makes כפר on these occasions (cf. Lev. 17.11).[117] However, considering that the blood-rite is relatively minor in Leviticus 1 and that the animal is the subject of כפר, and in view of my contention that v. 3 stresses the animal's acceptance on the basis that it was a 'male without defect' (זכר תמים), it seems possible that this 'cultic' requirement is the subject of כפר. This possibility may weaken the distinction

114. This interpretation goes back at least as far as Ibn Ezra who argued that the blood was used 'to be a ransom payment [kōper] for whatever punishment he deserves' (cited by Gilders, *Blood Ritual in the Hebrew Bible*, p. 73). See also the discussion in Sklar, *Sin, Impurity, Sacrifice and Atonement* [PhD dissertation], Chapter 6.

115. This is the main weakness with Gilders's interpretation of the prescription for the 'burnt offering' in Leviticus 1. According to him, the meaning of the offering is inseparable from the blood rite. However, though he is within his rights to ask what significance blood manipulation has in this prescription the relatively minimal attention given to this part of the ritual suggests that it may not be central to this offering's meaning. See Gilders, *Blood Ritual in the Hebrew Bible*, pp. 78-82.

116. For this reason, Sklar's attempt to decide between the theories of ownership and substitution on the basis of Lev. 17.11 is misguided (*Sin, Impurity, Sacrifice and Atonement* [PhD dissertation], pp. 195-97).

117. Kiuchi, *The Purification Offering*, p. 181.

drawn between substitution and ownership theories, because both may simply be attempting to describe how the זכר תמים aspect of the sacrificial animal becomes related to its offerer via hand-leaning. For example, the theory of substitution would suggest that it is accepted in place of what the offerer was not. This is what appeases Yahweh.[118] Alternatively, the theory of ownership would assume that what is meant by זכר תמים is credited to the animal's owner. On account of this Yahweh's wrath is appeased. For the purposes of the present study, which aims to examine if the prescription for the 'burnt offering' implies that the offerer was expected to 'be holy', it seems unnecessary to decide between these two theories. Both suggest that what is meant by זכר תמים is intimately related to the life of the offerer. As we shall see below, this insight has significant implications for the hypothesis that Leviticus 1 implies that P desired the offerer to 'be holy'.

The 'Burnt Offering' as Symbol of Human 'Integrity'

The previous section argued that it was unlikely that either the death or blood of the sacrificial animal made 'ransom' (כפר) for the offerer.[119] Alternatively, it suggested that it is the 'burnt offering', and perhaps more specifically what is meant by זכר תמים, that is presented as the agent of כפר. In view of this argument it seems reasonable to assume that the 'burnt offering' as a whole represented an item of worth that was able to make כפר for its offerer. It is proposed here that it is what the 'burnt offering' symbolized which makes כפר. Several observations make a symbolic interpretation of the 'burnt offering' seem plausible.

First, we may ask 'why not'? If it is acceptable for scholars to argue that there is a symbolic meaning to Israel's purity regulations (Leviticus 11–15) is it out of the question that we might find a symbolic dimension to the sacrificial ritual texts? Klawans has made this point.

> Why is it that some of the very same scholars who look at the food laws and the purity regulations, and see the need to find a key to unlock a complex symbolic system, look at sacrifice as a fossilized vestige, one that is finally bereft of whatever foolish meanings it once had? If the ritual purity system— the prerequisite for sacrifice—can be understood as symbolic, does it not stand to reason that the sacrificial system(s) also might be?[120]

---

118. This argument assumes that Leviticus 1 presupposes that the one who approaches the sanctuary is initially the object of God's wrath. See Kiuchi, 'The Concept of Holiness in the Sacrificial Context', pp. 1-27; Levine, *In the Presence of the Lord*.

119. This is not to say that death or blood do not make כפר for the offerer in other kinds of offerings in Leviticus 1–7.

120. Klawans, *Purity, Sacrifice, and the Temple*, p. 38; cf. Jonathan Klawans, 'Pure Violence: Sacrifice and Defilement in Ancient Israel', *HTR* 94 (2001), pp. 135-57.

To be sure, some scholars already attribute symbolic meaning to sacrificial prescriptions, but they do this in piecemeal fashion. For example, the gesture of hand-leaning in v. 4a is almost unanimously accepted as symbolic.[121] However, if this assumption is true, it seems possible that the 'burnt offering' has a symbolic meaning.

Second, Leviticus 1 invites the reader to interpret it within the symbolic context of Exodus 25–40.[122] At least two observations indicate that Exodus 25–40 is presupposed as important for the interpretation of Leviticus 1. On the one hand, Leviticus 1 begins with a *wayyqtl* form (ויקרא) that invariably points to a connection with the text which precedes it canonically. In this regard, Bruce Waltke and Michael O'Connor comment that

> *Wayyqtl* apart from וַיְהִי introduces the books of Leviticus, Numbers, 2 Kings, and 2 Chronicles, but these are best regarded as secondary beginnings; that is, the books have a connection with the ones that precede them.[123]

That this is the case in Lev. 1.1 is suggested by the lack of a nominative subject for ויקרא so that the verb's subject must be inferred from Exod. 40.35, namely Yahweh.[124] On the other hand, the significance of the 'tent of meeting' (אהל מועד, Lev. 1.1b, 3, 5) must likewise be gained from Exod. 40.34-35, though in actual fact, this structure is only completely understood from a consideration of the divine instructions for its manufacture (Exodus 25–31) and the report of its construction (Exodus 35–40). Several observations suggest that these passages present the 'tent of meeting' as a symbol of the creation that existed prior to the expulsion of the humans from the Garden.

First, the instructions for its construction (Exodus 25–31) are arranged in six addresses that open with 'and Yahweh spoke to Moses saying' (וידבר יהוה אל־משה לאמר; Exod. 25.1; 30.11, 17, 22; 31.1) or 'And Yahweh said to Moses' (ויאמר יהוה אל־משה; Exod. 30.34). Combined with the fact that the seventh address (ויאמר יהוה אל־משה לאמר; Exod. 31.12)

---

121. Noth, *Leviticus*, p. 22; Rodriguez, *Substitution in the Hebrew Cultus*, pp. 192-208; Kiuchi, *The Purification Offering*, pp. 116-19; Knierim, *Text and Concept*, p. 39; Hartley, *Leviticus*, p. 21.

122. Noting the unusual syntax, Rashbam suggested that this opening verse takes up where Exod. 40.34-35 leaves off. And Levine notes that this links Leviticus sequentially to Exodus (*Leviticus*, p. 4). Another indication that Leviticus may continue the symbolic interests of the end of Exodus is the deliberate parallel drawn between the two literary units. Related to this is Rendtorff's observation that '[t]he parallel between Exod. 24.15f + 25.1 and Lev. 1.1 shows that, in the entire construction of the Sinai pericope the offering instructions in Lev. 1ff form the second great complex after the instructions for the building of the sanctuary in Exod. 25ff' (*Leviticus*, p. 22 [translation mine]).

123. Bruce K. Waltke and Michael P. O'Connor, *An Introduction to Biblical Hebrew Syntax* (Winona Lake, IN: Eisenbrauns, 1990), p. 554.

124. Admittedly this inference could also be made from Lev. 1.1b.

introduces a command to keep the 'sabbath' (שבת; Exod. 31.12-18)[125] many scholars suggest that the author deliberately likens the construction of the tabernacle to the six days of creation.[126]

Second, though the account of the building of the tabernacle (Exodus 35–40) is not structured according to the creation account, it contains many phrases and expressions which provide 'unmistakable echoes' of the Genesis creation story.[127] For example, 'Moses saw all the work, and they had done it, as Yahweh had commanded so they had done it' (וירא משה את־כל־המלאכה והנה עשו אתה כאשר צוה יהוה כן עשו ויברך אתם משה; Exod. 39.43; cf. Gen. 1.31; 2.3);[128] 'and all of the work of the tabernacle of the tent of meeting was finished' (ותכל כל־עבדת משכן אהל מועד; Exod. 39.32; cf. Gen. 2.1);[129] and finally 'Moses completed the work' (ויכל משה את־המלאכה; Exod. 40.33b; cf. Gen. 2.2).[130]

---

125. Cassuto notes that expressions derived from the root שבת occur seven times in Exod. 31.12-17 (*A Commentary on the Book of Exodus*, p. 405).

126. Brevard S. Childs, *Exodus* (London: SCM Press, 1974), p. 541; Nahum M. Sarna, *Exploring Exodus: The Origins of Biblical Israel* (New York: Shocken Books, 1986), p. 213; See also Cassuto, *Exodus*, p. 476; P.J. Kearny, 'Creation and Liturgy: The P Redaction of Exodus 25:40', *ZAW* 89 (1977), pp. 375-87; Joseph Blenkinsopp, *Prophecy and Canon* (Notre Dame: University of Notre Dame Press, 1977), pp. 57, 60-66; Moshe Weinfeld, 'Sabbath, Temple and the Enthronement of the Lord: The Problem of the Sitz im Leben of Gen. 1:1–2:3', in *Mélanges bibliques et orientaux en l'honneur de M. Henri Cazelles* (AOAT, 212; Kevelaer: Butzon & Bercker; Neukirchen–Vluyn: Neukirchener Verlag, 1981), pp. 501-512. The absence of such a literary device in the account of the tabernacle's *construction* (Exodus 25–40) seems logical given that it is not God who speaks but Moses.

127. Sarna, *Exodus*, pp. 213-14; F. Rosenzweig, 'Das Formgeheimnis der biblischen Erzählungen', in *Die Schrift und ihre Verdeutschung* (ed. M. Buber and F. Rosenzweig; Berlin: Schocken Books, 1936), pp. 239-61 (254); Benjamin Sommer suggests that the 'extensive verbal parallels between Genesis 1:1–2:4a and Exodus 39–40 (which several scholars have noted) form an *inclusio*, indicating that world creation and tabernacle-construction belong to a single narrative that culminates in the latter' (Benjamin D. Sommer, 'Conflicting Constructions of Divine Presence in the Priestly Tabernacle', *Int* 9 [2001], pp. 41-63 [43]. cf. Peter Schäfer, *Studien zur Geschichte und Theologie des rabbinischen Judentums* [Leiden: E.J. Brill, 1978], pp. 131-33 [cited by Sommer]). Moreover, he observes that this *inclusio* had already been studied by the ancient rabbis. For more general parallels between the Genesis creation narratives and Israel's tabernacle see also Benjamin Sommer, 'Expulsion as Initiation: Displacement, Divine Presence, and Divine Exile in the Torah', in *Beginning/Again: Towards a Hermeneutics of Jewish Texts* (ed. Aryeh Cohen and Shaul Magid; New York: Seven Bridges Press, 2002), pp. 23-48.

128. Sarna suggests that this 'blessing' of the work is an emulation 'of God's culminating, sanctifying, act after he finished his creative work' (Sarna, *Exodus*, p. 214).

129. The language of Exod. 39.32 recalls the conclusion of the creation story (Cassuto, *Exodus*, p. 476).

130. Sarna, *Exodus*, pp. 213-14.

Nevertheless, the symbolism of the tabernacle extends beyond the account of creation described in Gen. 1.1–2.3 because there is some evidence that it also reflects the Edenic Garden (cf. Gen. 2.4–3.24).[131] Of particular significance in this regard are the references to the 'Cherubim' (כרבים) positioned within the tabernacle (Exod. 25.18-22; 37.7-9), which recall the positioning of Cherubim to guard the entrance to the Garden after the expulsion of Adam and Eve (Gen. 2.24), and to the tabernacle Menorah which may be intended to resemble the Edenic Tree of Life (Exod. 25.32; 37.18).[132] Finally, the statement that 'the glory of Yahweh filled the tabernacle' (וכבוד יהוה מלא את־המשכן; Exod. 40.35b) would seem to recall that God was present in the Garden of Eden. In view of the many allusions to the Genesis creation account and the Garden of Eden narrative, Peter Enns seems correct to conclude that

> [i]n the midst of a fallen world, in exile from the Garden of Eden—the original 'heaven and earth'—God undertakes another act of creation, a building project that is nothing less than a return to pre-Fall splendor.[133]

Moreover, he suggests that

> the tabernacle is a microcosm of the created order, a parcel of edenic splendor established amid the chaos of the world. The Sabbath is not just a reminder of the original creation in Genesis 1 and 2, but a reminder of God's re-creation of the cosmos in the tabernacle.[134]

On the basis of these observations I shall assume that the literary context of Leviticus 1 is highly symbolic. It presents the 'tent of meeting' as symbolic of the Garden of Eden from which the first 'human' (אדם) was excluded. Thus, the reader of Leviticus 1 may be entitled to think of the 'tent of meeting', from which Yahweh calls out to Moses (Lev. 1.1), and to which the 'human from among you' (אדם...מכם) brings his 'burnt offering' (Lev. 1.2), as laden with creation, and Edenic Garden, symbolism. Yet though many exegetes recognize this symbolism at the end of Exodus, the significance this symbolic context has for the opening chapter of Leviticus has not yet been explored.[135]

131. For a more comprehensive presentation of the tabernacle's creation-symbolism see pages 93-101.

132. Carol L. Meyers, 'Lampstand', in *ABD*, IV, pp. 141-43 (142).

133. Peter Enns, *Exodus* (Grand Rapids: Zondervan, 2000), p. 521.

134. Enns, *Exodus*, pp. 544-45. Similarly, Sarna comments that the 'Tabernacle... represented, as it were, a microcosm in which the macro-cosmic universe was reflected' (Sarna, *Exodus*, p. 214).

135. Milgrom notes that Leviticus 1–7 are the first divine pronouncement made from the newly erected sanctuary (Exodus 40), 'a fact which underscores their paramount importance', but he overlooks the significance of this context (*Leviticus 1–16*, p. 134). Kiuchi discusses the ideological relationship Leviticus has with Exodus but he does not treat the literary connection between these two texts (Kiuchi, *Leviticus*, pp. 27-28).

Finally, in view of the symbolism attached to the 'tent of meeting', symbolic significance may attach to the offerer's description as אדם...מכם ('a
human from among you', v. 2a). The plausibility of this proposal increases
when one takes the uniqueness of this way of referring to an individual
Israelite into account.[136] The term אדם occurs only seven times in Leviticus
(Lev. 1.2; 5.3; 7.21; 13.2; 16.17; 24.17, 21) compared to the much more
frequent use of נפש (24 times) and איש (52 times). However, its use in v. 2
becomes even more striking when it is considered that אדם falls within the
main statement of a legal text introduced by כי on only two occasions.[137]
Otherwise, in Leviticus, אדם refers to the danger that the 'uncleanness' of a
'human' poses to a 'person' (נפש, Lev. 5.3; 7.21); the requirement that no
'human' be in the tent of meeting on the Day of Atonement (Lev. 16.17),
and the consequences associated with the taking of the life of a 'human'
(Lev. 24.17, 21).[138] The rareness of the term within Leviticus, and its deliberate positioning within a context that is reminiscent of the Garden of Eden
might suggest that it is a deliberate allusion to the first 'human' who was
excluded from this setting. This idea may even be more plausible than
previous suggestions that the term is simply used for sex-inclusive purposes.[139] For example, Hartley suggests in relation to the occurrence of אדם
that

> [i]ts use establishes a tie with Gen. 1.26-27, which says that God created
> אדם in his own image, male and female he created them (cf. Gen. 5.2). The
> use of אדם calls attention to the exalted worth humans have. It is because
> humans bear the image of God that they may worship him and may be

---

136. Rashi appears to have recognised this uniqueness and consequently understood
the use of אדם in Lev. 1.2 as an allusion to the first Adam. He suggests that the legislator made this allusion to the first Adam to ensure that the offerer did not bring a stolen
animal for his offering. 'Since אדם also means Adam, its use suggests the following
comparison: what was the characteristic of the first man (אדם הראשון)? He did not
offer sacrifice of anything acquired by way of robbery, since everything was his! So you,
too, shall not offer anything acquired by way of robbery' (Silbermann [ed.], *Pentateuch
with Targum Onkelos, Haphtaroth and Rashi's Commentary: Leviticus*, p. 2b). Though
there appears to be no textual support for Rashi's symbolic interpretation of the term, it
is significant that he felt compelled to note that the term is possibly an allusion to the
first Adam. Richard Friedman has also drawn attention to the creational significance of
the term אדם within Lev. 1.2. He observes that the order of appearance of the terms
אדם (Lev. 1.2); נפש (Lev. 2.1) and איש (Lev. 7.28) within Leviticus 1–7 parallels the
order these terms are introduced in the creation narratives (see Gen. 1.26; 2.7, 2.23). See
Richard E. Friedman, *Commentary on the Torah* (San Francisco: Harper, 2001), p. 317.
137. i.e. See אדם כי־יהיה בעור־בשרו ('When a human has on the skin of his
body', Lev. 13.2). See the discussion of this clause on pages 127-29.
138. i.e. the one responsible must 'die' (מות).
139. Milgrom, *Leviticus 1–16*, p. 145; Hartley, *Leviticus*, pp. 9, 11; Balentine, *Leviticus*, p. 21.

forgiven and blessed by him. Moreover, אדם includes both males and females.[140]

Hartley goes on to say that the use of אדם and נפש reflects the legislator's desire to frame the legislation in non-sexist, inclusive language,[141] and that אדם, being a racially inclusive term, opened up the possibility for aliens to offer sacrifices to Yahweh.[142]

But Hartley's dependence on Gen. 1.27-28 and 5.2 to establish the sex-inclusive function of אדם in Leviticus 1 may not take the complete symbolic context of Exodus 25–40 into account.[143] Though this material alludes to Genesis 1, it may also presuppose Genesis 2–3 as important for its interpretation (see above). Thus, from a cognitive linguistic point of view, the term אדם is likely to encourage reflection upon humankind as excluded from God's immediate presence, on account of its rebellion, just as much as it recalls it as made in God's image.

Increasing the likelihood that a reader would access the domain of meaning associated with אדם in Genesis 2–3 is the fact that the 'human' on view is probably a male individual. The use of third person singular masculine verbs in Leviticus 1 and possibly the condition that the sacrificial animal be a 'male' (זכר) makes this interpretation apparent.[144] Moreover, the use of the unarticulated אדם also seems to detract from the likelihood that it is used as a sex-inclusive reference to humanity.[145] In this regard, Kiuchi notes that

[i]n Leviticus, 'ādām prefixed by the article appears in 5:4, 6:3 [5:22], 18:5 and 27:29. These passages show that hā'ādām means humanity, man with corporeal aspects, more general than 'ādām alone.[146]

Rather than a simple sex-inclusive reference to humanity, אדם...מכם (Lev. 1.2) possibly has symbolic meaning. In view of the Edenic symbolism of Exodus 25–40, it can be speculated that it is a symbolic reference to either the first Adam or to the human condition outside the Garden.[147]

---

140. Hartley, *Leviticus*, p. 9.
141. Hartley, *Leviticus*, p. 11.
142. Hartley, *Leviticus*, p. 11. See similarly Hoffmann, *Das Buch Leviticus*, p. 117; Balentine, *Leviticus*, p. 21.
143. We may also point out that there is a sense in which his decision to appeal to Genesis 1 and 5 for the meaning of אדם is arbitrary. Why not appeal to Genesis 2–3?
144. See Kiuchi, *Leviticus*, p. 55.
145. Admittedly, one may respond to this suggestion by arguing that the use of the unarticulated noun in Lev. 1.2 is necessitated by the reference to a single indefinite individual. However, this argument would only raise the question of why the legislator did not use the term נפש, which he frequently uses elsewhere when referring to an indefinite individual within ritual texts (e.g. Lev. 2.1; 4.2, 27; 5.1, 4, 15, 17; 7.21).
146. Kiuchi, *Leviticus*, p. 101.
147. Kiuchi suggests that '[t]he agent offering the burnt offering is specified as 'ādām,

Considering what is possibly a highly symbolic context for the prescription for the 'burnt offering', it seems appropriate to examine whether the requirement that it consist of a 'male without blemish' (זכר תמים, v. 3a) has symbolic meaning. To begin with this requirement possibly had the practical function of ensuring that the sacrificial animal was of great value to its offerer.[148] Yet the stipulation that it had to be תמים may have symbolic importance. Within 'cultic' material this term is commonly rendered 'without [physical] blemish' or 'without [physical] defect'.[149] This translation is appropriate considering the list of 'defects' (מום) listed in Leviticus 22 that disqualify an animal as תמים. However, when P applies this term to humans it is unanimously assumed as having ethical significance and is rendered 'morally blameless', 'wholehearted' (Gen. 6.9; 17.1; Deut. 18.13) or, as in the present study, human 'integrity'.[150]

which, in distinction from *nepeš* (see 'Comment' on 2.1), refers to the sinful earthly existence of humans *since the fall*' (Kiuchi, *Leviticus*, p. 61). This symbolic interpretation of the term אדם in Lev. 1.2 may explain the absence of explicit cases for the offerings prescribed in Leviticus 1–3 which Milgrom claims is evidence that these offerings originated earlier in Israel's history. From a literary point of view, one may ask whether the rationale for offering what is prescribed in Leviticus 1–3 is implied in the symbolic dimension of the statement 'When a human from among you brings an offering to Yahweh'. That is, perhaps there is a tension implicit within the possibility of a 'human' (אדם) approaching Yahweh that is not present when a 'person' (נפש) is required to bring a particular offering on account of his sin in Leviticus 4–5.

148. Rendtorff points out that though no explanation is ever given for why animal offerings were commonly males, the greater value of male animals appears to be reflected in the stipulation that a 'leader' (נשיא) must bring a male goat for his 'sin offering' (Lev. 4.22-26) whereas the layperson brings a female goat (Lev. 4.27-35). It may also be significant that in the prescription for the 'guilt offering' the legislator stipulates that one must bring a 'ram without defect' (איל תמים, Lev. 5.15, 18, 25 [Eng. 6.6]). In an offering which emphasizes the need for restitution, the requirement that the animal be not only a male but also mature was possibly intended to ensure that the offerer did not escape cheaply (Rendtorff, *Leviticus*, p. 29; see also Wenham, *Leviticus*, p. 55). The discussion concerning what sex was more valuable among the sacrifical animals has not taken into account the possibility that the Israelites may not have been required to offer their breeding stock. Among such animals the females were probably the most valuable, as they tend to be in modern times. However, not all animals are kept for breeding and these, which are used for meat, would be ranked on value according to their size. Within this class of animals a young bull is more valuable than a young heifer. That a mature male is required for a 'guilt offering' (Leviticus 5) does not suggest that they were more valuable than a ewe. It possibly means that the offering was to be more expensive, not the most expensive, in comparison to the young animals.

149. Milgrom says that this is true for the Priestly writings (i.e. P and H) (*Leviticus 1–16*, 147).

150. Milgrom, *Leviticus 17–22*, p. 1874. See also Wenham, *Genesis 1–15*, p. 170; Sarna, *Genesis*, p. 50. As mentioned in this Chapter's introduction, I shall translate

But there are some indications that תמים carries this same meaning, on a symbolic level, when applied to animals in Leviticus 1.[151] First, while the concept of תמים occurs in relation to other offerings,[152] it is arguably a prominent aspect of the ritual for the 'burnt offering'. This is because the whole animal is emphasized in this prescription. Whereas in other prescriptions the blood ('sin offering') or flesh ('peace offering') remains in the foreground, in Leviticus 1 the תמים 'burnt offering' itself is depicted as making כפר for its offerer and being completely burnt. If the תמים quality of the animal is emphasized in Leviticus 1, it is possibly this quality which serves to 'ransom' (כפר) the offerer. This suggestion opens up the possibility that it is what is symbolized by תמים that makes כפר.

Second, the absence of a list of criteria for establishing what is a תמים animal in Leviticus 1 may also reflect that it is used with a symbolic meaning.[153] Various scholars claim that the absence of such a list reflects that it was the job of the priests, and not the laity, to establish if an animal was תמים.[154] Yet on the one hand, would it not seem essential for an offerer to know what counted as תמים prior to his bringing an animal to the sanctuary? On the other hand, the term תמים does not occur within the section addressed to the priests in Leviticus 6. In fact, no definition of what constitutes a תמים animal is given until Leviticus 22. Though various explanations are given for this observation,[155] it seems possible that, as part of the larger narrative of the Pentateuch, the omission of what physically constitutes a תמים animal, allows the reader to reflect on what it symbolizes Hoffmann

תמים as 'human "integrity"' when it has a human quality in view. I assume that at least part of what it means for a human to be תמים includes the idea of 'ethical behaviour'.

151. Interestingly, though Milgrom concedes that תמים is 'symbolic' of 'the quality of completeness that characterizes YHWH', in relation to Lev. 22.17-25, he does not make this connection in relation to the term's occurrence in Leviticus 1–16 (*Leviticus 17–22*, p. 1873).

152. Lev. 3.1, 6; 4.3, 23; 5.15, 18, 25.

153. Douglas similarly views the recurring stipulation that sacrificial animals must be 'without blemish', without an accompanying definition of what constitutes such animals, as an indication that it has symbolic meaning. '[I]t is frequently repeated that an animal with a blemish is not allowed to be offered for sacrifice. Again, why not? And again, no definition of "blemish", and no reason is given in the first four chapters. The easy answer, that a spoilt gift is unworthy of the altar, is an uplifting thought but not theologically acute' (Douglas, 'The Forbidden Animals in Leviticus', p. 18).

154. Milgrom, *Leviticus 17–22*, p. 1873.

155. Knierim comments that '[t]he text's silence about the meaning of תמים…means only that it emphasizes the activities. But it assumes at the same time that the lay person knows the kind of bull that meets the prescribed criteria when selecting it' (Knierim, *Text and Concept*, p. 23). However, in response to Knierim it may be asked why the legislator included the list of defects that disqualified an animal from being regarded as 'without blemish' in Leviticus 22.

appears to entertain this possibility when he makes the following remark concerning the requirement that the 'burnt offering' be a 'male and without blemish'.

> The adjective תמים is used both of physical perfection, as here [i.e. Lev. 1:3], and of moral integrity (Ps. 15:2; הולך תמים ופועל צדק ['He who walks blamelessly, who makes righteousness']). In the עולה ['burnt offering'], which is זכר and תמים, the fulfilment of the commands: תמים תהיה עם ד' (['You shall be blameless before the Lord your God'] Deut. 18:13) or התהלך לפני והיה תמים (['Walk before me and be blameless'] Gen. 17:1) is to be expressed.[156]

We may add to Hoffmann's citation of Gen. 17.1 and Deut. 18.13 the observation that Noah was תמים (Gen. 17.1). Nevertheless, Hoffmann's interpretation is somewhat arbitrary and a cognitive linguistic approach to the meaning of the term תמים in Lev. 1.3 may yield a more objective result. Prior to Lev. 1.3 it is found just four times (Gen. 6.9; 17.1; Exod. 12.5; 29.1).[157] It occurs with the same sense when describing Noah's blameless character (Gen. 6.9) and within the command for Abraham to 'be blameless' (Gen. 6.9). The remaining two occurrences describe animals 'without physical blemish' (Exod. 12.5; 29.1). Thus, as commonly observed, the semantic frame of this term comprises both the notions of human 'integrity' and physical perfection.

But it seems likely that the idea of human 'integrity' would be accessed by a competent reader of Leviticus 1. Since human 'integrity' is not normally associated with animals the primary domain accessed in this context would be 'without physical blemish'.[158] However, there are several contextual reasons why a person may begin to access the domain of human 'integrity' in the period of post-crystallization interpretation. Two observations suggest that the text of Leviticus 1 may presuppose the Noahic and Abrahamic narratives as important for its interpretation.[159]

First, the only two people who offer a 'burnt offering' prior to Leviticus are Noah (Gen. 8.20-21) and Abraham (Gen. 22.2-13). Moreover, that both of these occasions occur within 'non-sin' contexts (cf. Leviticus 1) is possibly significant.

Second, the 'burnt offering' taken 'from the birds' (מן־העוף, Lev. 1.14-17) may also encourage one to think of the Noahic and Abrahamic narra-

156. Hoffmann, *Das Buch Leviticus*, pp. 116-17 (translation mine).

157. There is another form of the adjective (i.e. תם), which occurs four times prior to this chapter (Gen. 25.27; Exod. 26.24; 28.30; 36.29).

158. Though see discussion regarding the possibility that animals are viewed as having ethical responsibility in the Pentateuch in Chapter 6.

159. To my knowledge Kiuchi is the only other scholar who argues that the requirement that an animal be תמים presupposes these narratives as important for its interpretation (Kiuchi, *Leviticus*, pp. 63-64).

tives. Since 'birds' are not mentioned as part of the general heading in Lev. 1.3, the inclusion of a 'burnt offering' for birds within this prescription is somewhat surprising. Furthermore, the prescription for the 'burnt offering' of a bird lacks the requirement that the animal be תמים (cf. Lev. 1.3, 10).[160] Though these apparent anomalies lead many exegetes to assume that the pericope was a later insertion,[161] it could be that there are literary reasons for its inclusion in Leviticus 1 and for the non-mention of תמים. Rather than doubt the authenticity of the prescription for the bird 'burnt offering' it seems possible that the implied reader was expected to recall that there were two precedents for the sacrifice of birds. First, Noah is recorded as having offered a 'burnt offering' of birds (Gen. 8.20-21) and, second, Abram performs a rite which includes birds in Genesis 15.[162] On the latter occasion, Abram did not cut the birds in two ('do not cut in half' [לא בתר], Gen. 15.10) as is commanded in Leviticus 1: 'do not separate' (לא יבדיל, Lev. 1.17). It may also be significant that though different terms are used for the birds sacrificed in the Noahic and Abrahamic accounts (i.e. היונה in Gen. 8.9; עוף in Gen. 8.20, and תר in Gen. 15.9) these terms occur together in Lev. 1.14 (מן־העוף...הקריב מן־התרים או מן־בני היונה). These observations do not prove that Genesis 8 and 15 are presupposed by Lev. 1.14-17, but they certainly suggest that this is possible.

Considering these observations, it is arguable that, in the process of reading Leviticus 1, a reader would access the human 'integrity' aspect of meaning תמים has when used in connection with Noah and Abraham. If this argument is correct, then it can be proposed that the *item of worth* that ransoms the offerer in Leviticus 1 is what is symbolized by תמים, namely human 'integrity'. By implication, if such a ransom was required to appease

---

160. Scholars commonly draw attention to the missing gesture of hand-leaning in the bird pericope. Yet they overlook that this gesture is missing in that for sheep and goats also. Thus, we may presume that there was a hand-leaning rite associated with birds. With regard to the absence of the term תמים in the עלה for birds, Milgrom says that the תמים and sex requirements were not specified because they were waived for the sake of the poor. Alternatively, he suggests that it may be because it is difficult to determine the sex of a bird and that not even the poor would have thought to have offered a cheap blemished bird (*Leviticus 1–16*, p. 167). However, these explanations are inconclusive. First, the sex of a bird was possibly not difficult to determine for those familiar with the farming of domestic birds. Second, could it not be as easily argued that the תמים condition should not have been required for sheep or goats because a rich person would not have considered offering a blemished one?

161. Though many scholars regard the bird offering as a later addition, this does not explain why a reference to birds was not added to the introductory formula of Lev. 1.2.

162. That the lack of an altar in Genesis 15 makes it unlikely that this was a sacrificial rite does not undermine the argument being made here. It is enough for a reader to gather that when Abram was commanded to cut animals in half he refrained from doing this with the birds.

Yahweh it suggests that the text of Leviticus 1 assumes that the offerer should be תמים.[163] In other words, he or she could probably not help but come to the conclusion that the life God finds acceptable is one that is תמים.

Since the 'burnt offering' does not appear to presuppose 'sin' it seems that Yahweh's wrath is directed against something else. This is probably the rebellious *disposition* of humanity, a condition which is at odds with what is meant by תמים. In other words, though this disposition is generative of the 'sin' for which the Israelites must offer their 'sin' and 'guilt' offerings (Leviticus 4–5), Leviticus 1 is primarily concerned with overcoming the threat God's wrath poses when a 'human', who lacks 'integrity', approaches him to be 'accepted' in the way Adam was before his expulsion. By Yahweh's acceptance of the 'burnt offering', as a symbol of human 'integrity', the offerer's life is 'ransomed' (כפר) so that he may enjoy Yahweh's favourable presence. In this regard, it seems that the 'burnt offering' effects 'ransom' as either the offerer's substitute or as an item of worth credited to him on account of the rite of 'hand-leaning'.

Of significance for the present study is that if תמים is symbolic of what the same term means when applied to humans, then it is possible that it is also the partial essence of P's concept of 'holiness', as Milgrom and Douglas claim is the case in H.[164] This idea is made even more likely by the fact that the 'burnt offering' is possibly to be regarded as P's 'most holy' offering *par excellence* (see Appendix 2).

Conclusion

Chapters 3 and 4 argued that P's 'purity regulations' (Leviticus 11–15) were intended to persuade the Israelites to remain faithful to Yahweh. In relation to my larger aim to ascertain if there is an ethical aspect to P's view of holiness, these findings strengthen my initial hypothesis that the command to 'be holy' in Lev. 11.43-45 (H) may make P's intention, in this regard, explicit. However, since the holiness terminology in Leviticus 11 is confined to a text scholars assign to H it was necessary to investigate if a similar concern for the Israelites to obey Yahweh is present in the prescription for the 'burnt offering' (Leviticus 1) which most scholars view as P's 'most holy' offering *par excellence* (see Appendix 2). This investigation proposed that P's prescription for the 'burnt offering' implies that its offerer was required to have 'integrity' (תמים). This proposal derives from an analysis of the symbolic meaning of this prescription which concluded that the 'without defect' (תמים) character of the 'burnt offering' represented the human 'integrity' (תמים) exhibited in the life of Noah (Genesis 6) and commanded of Abraham

163. Indeed, so much is commanded in Deut. 18.13.
164. Douglas, *Purity and Danger*, pp. 51-52; Milgrom, *Leviticus 1–16*, p. 1873.

(Genesis 17). Moreover, this offering 'ransomed' (כפר) the life of its offerer from Yahweh's wrath. Such a 'ransom' was necessitated by the offerer's identity as 'a human...from among you' [אדם...מכם, Lev. 1.2]). Within the context of Exodus 25–40, which scholars assume is symbolic of the first creation, Yahweh would be displeased at a post-Garden human's (i.e. אדם; cf. Genesis 3) presence.[165] However, by leaning his hand on the head of his offering, the symbolic value of the animal is credited to the offerer so that Yahweh's wrath is appeased. If this interpretation is correct it would mean that P affirms that a life of 'integrity' (תמים) is acceptable to Yahweh. And, since the 'burnt offering' was P's 'most holy' offering *par excellence* (see Appendix 2), it was speculated that the concept of תמים may represent one aspect of P's view of holiness. That is, P may have expected the Israelites to 'be holy' by acting with 'integrity'. Although this conclusion suggests that P's concept of holiness contained an ethical dimension, holiness terminology does not occur in Leviticus 1 so that it remains necessary to establish that the term תמים can be used to symbolize human 'integrity', as an aspect of holiness, within a cultic context. For this reason Chapter 6 examines whether such a relationship exists between תמים and קדש within the parallel lists of 'blemishes' (מום) for priests and animals in Leviticus 21–22. This text represents an opportunity to study this relationship because whereas the priests are referred to as קדש (Leviticus 21) the parallel sacrificial animals are called תמים (Leviticus 22).

165. I presuppose that the 'fall' of humanity is not a strictly NT idea but can be inferred from the text of Genesis 1–11. See Gordon J. Wenham, 'Original Sin in Genesis 1–11', *Churchman* 104 (1990), pp. 309-28.

Chapter 6

THE USE OF תמים TO DENOTE AN ASPECT OF 'HOLINESS' (קדש) WHEN APPLIED TO ANIMALS IN H

The previous Chapter argued that the תמים character of the 'burnt offering' (Leviticus 1) is what 'ransoms' (כפר) its offerer as a prerequisite to receiving divine 'acceptance' (רצון). Since it seemed that the תמים aspect of the 'burnt offering' represented human 'integrity' on a symbolic plane, it was hypothesized that P affirms this human quality as that which is 'acceptable' to Yahweh. Moreover, I proposed that this symbolic meaning of תמים (i.e. human 'integrity') represents one aspect of 'holiness' (קדש) in P.[1] Since 'holiness' (קדש) is not explicitly mentioned in Leviticus 1, the present Chapter attempts to strengthen the argument made in Chapter 5 that when תמים is used of animals it may symbolize an aspect of the holiness expected of humans. It will do this by looking at how תמים is used in the list of 'blemishes' (מום) that disqualify animals from the altar (Lev. 22.17-25). This passage presents an opportunity to examine the relationship between the terms תמים and קדש for two reasons. First, the list of animal blemishes (Lev. 22.17-25) parallels a list of blemishes that disqualify 'holy' (קדש) priests from certain duties (Lev. 21.16-24).[2] Second, these lists promote the

---

1. This proposal may shed some light on what it means for Yahweh to say, 'You shall be holy for I Yahweh your God am holy' (Lev. 19.2). Moses introduces his song about Yahweh in Deuteronomy 32 with the statement that 'his works are תמים' (תמים פעלו, v. 4a) and he justifies this claim with the clause 'for all his ways are justice' (כי כל־דרכיו משפט). That the author of Deuteronomy 32 is conscious of the cultic background of the term תמים can be inferred from his subsequent assessment of Israel's treatment of Yahweh: 'They have dealt corruptly with him; [they are] not his descendents [for] they are *blemished*' (שחת לו לא בניו מומם, v. 5a). Elsewhere the term מום refers to a physical, rather than moral, blemish. See also 2 Sam. 22.31, where God's walk is 'blameless' and Ps. 15.2, where the person who can dwell in the sanctuary is the one whose 'walk is blameless'.

2. That is, offering Israel's sacrifices at the altar (Lev. 21.17, 21, 23). However, that these priests are still permitted to eat 'holy' food (Lev. 21.22) indicates that they retain the status of 'holy'. That it is the physical appearance of the priests that is closely related to their 'holiness' seems implied by the fact that they cannot fulfil the public duty of making offerings.

physical appearance of 'holy' priests and תמים animals as representative of God's 'holiness'. If an examination of these lists suggests that a semantic overlap exists between תמים and קדש, which extends into an ethical dimension, it will strengthen the argument that the תמים quality of the 'burnt offering' symbolizes one aspect of what is meant by קדש in P. From this examination it may also emerge that there is more coherence between the concepts of 'holiness' in P and H than is commonly assumed (cf. Chapter 1). It does not seem problematic to compare the use of תמים in Leviticus 21–22 (H) and in Leviticus 1 (P) because the consensus among scholars is that P and H use the term תמים in the same way of animals.[3] Indeed, those that hold that H is later than P generally assume that H composed the list of blemishes in Leviticus 22 to clarify what P understood as a תמים animal. Thus, I am interested in whether תמים can symbolize human 'integrity', as an aspect of holiness, when used of animals in a cultic context.

A word is in order regarding how my hypothesis, concerning what תמים means in H, differs from that proposed by some other scholars. Both Douglas and Milgrom assume that תמים is the essence of קדש in P and H.[4] More specifically they suggest that תמים means 'ethical perfection'. But the difference with the case I shall make here is that they confine this meaning of the term to those occasions when it is applied to humans. When it is applied to animals they assume that its meaning is limited to 'without (physical) defect'.[5] My contention is that they overdraw the distinction between the meaning of תמים when it is applied to humans and animals respectively, because they do not take into account that sacrificial animals symbolize humans.[6] Thus my proposal differs from theirs by suggesting that, in addition to denoting physical normality, תמים has the symbolic meaning of human 'integrity' when used of animals because they represent what is required of their offerers for divine 'acceptance' (i.e. 'integrity'; cf. Chapter 5).

Finally, since Chapter 2 argued that there is an interfusion between the meaning of ritual texts and their literary-art, this study begins by examining the literary-composition of the parallel lists of 'blemishes' (מום) in Leviticus 21–22. After this examination we shall investigate if this relationship, and the

3. Milgrom, *Leviticus 1–16*, p. 147. To my knowledge no scholar has argued any differently from this.
4. Douglas, *Purity and Danger*, pp. 51-52; Milgrom, *Leviticus 17–22*, p. 1873.
5. 'In the priestly writings, *tāmîm* only [*sic*] refers to physical perfection of (sacrificial) animals (except for 23.15; 25.30, referring to time)' (Milgrom, *Leviticus 1–16*, p. 147).
6. Of course, both Douglas and Milgrom do assign a symbolic role to the sacrificial animals. They argue that these animals represent the Israelites within Israel's putative tripartite systematization of humans and animals. But, they have not enquired whether this symbolic relationship may imply that certain attributes of the sacrificial animals are representative of human values.

content of this material, encourages a symbolic interpretation of the term
תמים in Leviticus 22 (vv. 19, 21) which is related to the idea of holiness. For
example, if the holy appearance of the priests in Leviticus 21 is related to an
ethical view of holiness, the parallel relationship will raise the question if the
same is true of the תמים appearance of animals in Leviticus 22.

The Parallel between the Defects (מום)
for Priests and Sacrificial Animals

Though the requirement that sacrificial animals be 'without-defect' (תמים) is
first given in Lev. 1.3, a list of specific 'defects' (מום) disqualifying animals
from this status is not given until Lev. 22.17-25. Knierim interprets this delay
as reflecting that the offerer is already presumed to know what blemishes
disqualify an animal from sacrifice.[7] This may be so, but the list's immediate
positioning after a similar list of blemishes for priests (Lev. 21.16-24) presumably has significance for why the legislator chose to incorporate it at this
stage.[8] As several commentators point out, the close proximity of these two
lists, and their common interest in physical defects, indicates that they ought
to be interpreted in relation to one another.[9] This approach to their interpretation is also suggested by the many literary indications, documented in what
follows, that the legislator deliberately composed a parallel relationship
between them.

First, both passages list twelve 'defects' (מום) that disqualify either a
priest or an animal from access to the altar.[10] Milgrom comments that

> [t]he artificiality of these lists is manifested by…the transparent attempts
> within each list to reach the number twelve, as by listing broken bones twice
> in the priestly list and specifying four kinds of injuries to the testes in the
> animal list.[11]

7. Knierim, *Text and Concept*, p. 31.

8. Indeed, if Knierim's suggestion that the offerer is presumed to already know what
constitutes a 'without-defect' animal is correct, perhaps the intentional relationship
drawn with the list for priests is one reason for the inclusion of these lists within
Leviticus.

9. This would not have been the case had the list of animal blemishes been included
in Leviticus 1 (see Wenham, *Leviticus*, pp. 295-96; Milgrom, *Leviticus 17–22*, pp. 1838-
39; Hartley, *Leviticus*, p. 360; Gerstenberger, *Leviticus*, p. 317; Balentine, *Leviticus*,
p. 171).

10. Milgrom suggests that blemishes are a common denominator for both chapters,
assuming that 'self-alteration', 'marriage with a "defective" woman', and 'partaking of
sacred food while impure' are 'blemishes'. However, these things are not referred to as
מום and to assume that they have this status underplays the very close relationship
shared by the two lists which identify specific מום (Milgrom, *Leviticus 17–22*, p. 1793).

11. Milgrom, *Leviticus 17–22*, p. 1877.

Other aesthetic blemishes that could have been included are not difficult to imagine and, for my purposes, this may indicate that the intended function of these lists is more than a practical catalogue for identifying blemishes.[12] For example, similar lists of blemishes for priests found in the ANE include blemishes such as crossed-eyes, chipped teeth, mutilated fingers and brands upon the skin.[13] Given that the list in Leviticus 21 does not seem to be an exhaustive one, a concern to draw attention to the relationship between priests and animals possibly takes precedence over any practical concern to ensure an accurate identification of the priests and animals that qualify for access to the altar.[14] This possibility is also suggested by the fact that the list was not included where it would have been most practically relevant, namely within Leviticus 1–7.

Second, with the exception of the 'bruised testicle' (מרוך אשך, Lev. 21.20) in the list for priests, all the blemishes are visible to others.[15] Milgrom identifies this exception of the 'bruised testicle' as evidence that the legislator compiled the two lists of blemishes to correspond to one another. That is, both lists conclude with a reference to the testes (Lev. 21.20; 22.24).

> There exists one blemish among the twelve [for priests] that patently cannot be observed: a crushed testicle. This ostensible flaw is, in actuality, proof of the artificiality of the list. Indeed, it does not fit the criterion of appearance. But it had to be chosen in order to correspond to the list of blemished animals, where injured (and exposed) genitals appear in four different forms (22:24).[16]

12. Commenting on the fact that both lists mention 12 blemishes, Gründwaldt is probably correct in concluding that 'Vermutlich soll die Zahl eine Totalität symbolisieren, so daß die aufgelisteten Behinderungen als *pars pro toto* gelten' (Gründwaldt, *Das Heiligkeitsgesetz Leviticus 17–26*, p. 268). This conclusion, in itself, may imply that the lists had other than practical purposes. Heinisch mentions that the rabbis increased the number of blemishes that may disqualify a priest from service to 142 (*Das Buch Leviticus*, p. 99).

13. Snaith, *Leviticus*, p. 144; Gründwaldt, *Das Heiligkeitsgesetz Leviticus 17–26*, pp. 267-71; Milgrom, *Leviticus 17–22*, pp. 1842-43.

14. After all, according to Knierim the offerer is presupposed as knowing this already in Lev. 1.3 (*Text and Concept*, p. 31).

15. Milgrom, *Leviticus 17–22*, p. 1839.

16. Milgrom, *Leviticus 17–22*, p. 1839. In Deuteronomy the stipulation that a bruised testicle prevents a priest from officiating at the altar is extended to the laity: 'He shall not enter, the one whose testicle is bruised or whose male organ is cut off, the assembly of Yahweh' (לא־יבא פצוע־דכא שפכה בקהל יהוה; Deut. 23.2 [Eng. 23.1]). Indeed it was a serious enough matter for the provision of further legislation: 'When men fight with one another, a man and his brother, and the wife of one approaches to rescue her husband from the hand of him who is smiting him and puts out her hand and seizes his private parts, then you shall cut off her hand. Your eye shall have no pity' (כי־ינצרו אנשים יחדו איש ואחיו וקרבו אשת האחד להציל את־אישה מיד מכהו ושלחה

Third, both lists are possibly composed to form a chiastic structure. Hartley comments that,

> [t]he comparison of the grouping of defects in the two catalogues yields a chiastic structure: the defects enumerated in the pattern for a priest are four, two, six, while for an animal the pattern is six, two, four. This chiasm indicates that the unit was composed to tie this speech closely to the speech in chap. 21.[17]

The proposed chiasm has the following structure.

Priestly defects (Lev. 21.16-24)

> A [4 defects] blind, lame, disfigured, an 'overgrown limb' (שָׂרוּעַ) (v. 18)
>> B [2 defects] impaired leg, impaired hand (v. 19)
>>> C [6 defects] hunchback, withered member, a discolouration of the eye, a 'scab' (גָּרָב), 'scurf' (יַלֶּפֶת), damaged testicles (v. 20)

Animal defects (Lev. 22.17-25)

>>> C' [6 defects] blind, broken limb, mutilated, seeping sores, a 'scab' (גָּרָב), a 'scurf' (יַלֶּפֶת, v. 22)
>> B' [2 defects] an 'overgrown limb' (שָׂרוּעַ), a stunted appendage (v. 23)
> A' [4 defects] bruised, crushed, torn, cut-off testicles (v. 24)

Admittedly, Hartley's idea regarding the chiastically arranged groupings of defects is possibly weakened by the fact that only a *sôp̄ pāsûq* separates the group of 2 defects in B from the group of 4 defects in C. Without this *sôp̄ pāsûq* the 'impaired hand' is connected to the 'hunchback' by the connective 'or' (אוֹ, Lev. 21.20a). However, even if one were to reject Hartley's proposed chiastic structure, he also makes the observation that both lists begin with the defect of blindness and conclude with defects concerning the testicles. Thus, one would need to be cautious in denying that the legislator did not intend there to be some kind of structural correspondence between these two lists.[18]

Fourth, the blemishes appear to match in kind so that 'the same blemishes that invalidate officiating priests also invalidate animal sacrifices'.[19] Both

---

יָדָהּ וְהֶחֱזִיקָה בִּמְבֻשָׁיו׃ וְקַצֹּתָה אֶת־כַּפָּהּ לֹא תָחוֹס עֵינֶךָ׃; Deut. 25.11-12). It seems that the physical completeness expected of priests was, to an extent, extended to the laity in Deuteronomy.

17. Hartley, *Leviticus*, pp. 359-60. cf. Milgrom, *Leviticus 17–26*, pp. 1876-77.

18. Hartley, *Leviticus*, p. 359. Since there is some correspondence between the defects they list, perhaps one should view AC', BB' and CA' as 'parallel panels'. For this structural device see S.E. McEvenue, *The Narrative Style of the Priestly Writer* (AnBib, 50. Rome: Biblical Institute Press, 1971).

19. Milgrom, *Leviticus 17–22*, p. 1877.

lists begin with blindness and end with testicular problems. Though several of the blemishes cannot be identified, Milgrom points out that five of the blemishes are identical which encourages one to conclude that the remaining seven are possibly the same, even though different terminology may be used.[20]

Fifth, the restrictions imposed on priests or animals with blemishes are similar. Though he may continue eating his allocation from Israel's offerings, a blemished priest may not offer these at the altar (Lev. 21.17, 21, 23). Likewise, blemished animals are sometimes permitted as food (Lev. 22.23) but they are generally not to be offered to Yahweh on the altar (Lev. 22.20, 22, 24).[21] For either the blemished priest or animal to enter the immediate vicinity of the altar would 'profane' (חלל) Yahweh's holiness (Lev. 21.23; 22.32).

In conclusion, there is sufficient evidence that the legislator composed these two lists so that they would share a parallel relationship. What significance should we attribute to this relationship? Scholars tend to argue that this parallelism reflects a tripartite-systematization of humans and animals in Israel (cf. pages 104-105). Douglas originally proposed this view and it is developed by Wenham and Milgrom.[22] From this perspective the meaning of the parallelism is thought to reside *beyond* the text: the parallel exposes part of a larger system of thought within ancient Israel. This approach is similar to Gorman's attempt to assess 'what happened' when interpreting prescriptive texts so that it is more of an historical, rather than literary, reading of the text.[23] By contrast, though I do not disagree with their results, the present study will take a literary approach when examining why the legislator has drawn attention to the parallelism evident between these lists.[24] If a symbolic

---

20. He identifies the following blemishes as identical: blind, overgrown limb, broken bones, sores, scabs. Only 'overgrown limb' (שרוע), 'scab' (גרב), and 'scurf' (ילפת) share the same terminology. He explains that '[t]he variation in terminology between the two lists may be ascribed to different biological and environmental factors governing each species' (Milgrom, *Leviticus 17–22*, pp. 1876-77).

21. Verse 23 permits the offering of a 'peace offering' made as a 'freewill offering' with an animal that has either an 'extended thigh' or a 'short limb'. The rationale for this concession is most plausibly explained by Milgrom, following Abravanel. '[T]he freewill offering, being the result of a spontaneous declaration, falls on the animal at hand, whether of good or poor quality (but not if it is defective). Under these conditions, a concession is allowed for an extended or shortened limb, the least of the blemishes. (After all, this limb is not inherently defective, but only so in comparison with others.) But the fulfilment of a vow is set in the future, and the offerer has ample time to find an animal of the finest quality for a votive offering. Hence the votive offering is subject to more rigorous standards than the freewill offering' (Milgrom, *Leviticus 17–22*, p. 1879).

22. Wenham, *Leviticus*, p. 170; Milgrom, *Leviticus 1–16*, pp. 724-25.

23. See review of Gorman's methodology for interpreting ritual texts in Chapter 2.

24. Presumably, the literary-artistry may reflect the legislator's literary purpose (cf.

meaning for a word, phrase or ritual-requirement is identified in one list, this parallel relationship may invite a consideration of whether the same is true within the other.[25] Nevertheless, before our analysis can proceed, a particular anomaly within these parallel lists needs to be acknowledged in case it too has importance for their interpretation.

The Omission of the Term תמים *from the List for Priests 'Without* מום *('Defect')'*

If we presume that that the parallel lists of Leviticus 21–22 have the same practical function (i.e. the identification of blemish-free priests and sacrificial animals), it seems striking that different terminology is used to describe the cultic status of physically complete priests and animals respectively. Though the priests are assumed to be 'holy' (קֹדֶשׁ, Lev. 21.6, קָדֹשׁ, Lev. 21.7),[26] the corresponding blemish-free animals are not referred to as 'holy'

Chapter 2). Milgrom is aware of the literary artistry of Leviticus 21 and attempts to demonstrate 'that the alleged redundancies that ostensibly predominate in the chapter are in reality instrumental to the complex sophisticated craftsmanship that characterises the entire chapter so that there cannot be found even one superfluous word in the entire chapter' (*Leviticus 17–22*, p. 1793). My literary approach is encouraged by Nihan's source-critical observation that within Leviticus 21–22 'the material regarded as traditional is so sparse and fragmentary that one should rather accept these chapters as a free composition by the author of H drawing occasionally on some traditional elements rather than on a specific *Vorlage*' (Nihan, *From Priestly Torah to Pentateuch*, p. 448). This observation does not imply that a pre-existing system of thought within Israel is not reflected by this parallel, but it does allow for the possibility that the latter was original to the legislator.

25. Scholars have overlooked the importance the parallelism of these lists has for their interpretation. Instead a distinction is commonly made between the intention of their content and the significance of their parallelism. Admittedly there are some scholars who assume that a parallel requirement that priests and animals be without physical defect is natural. For example, Noordtzij suggests that a 'physical defect in a priest evidently had the same significance as the various defects in potential sacrificial animals, for whoever served at the altar and whatever was placed on it had to be completely sound in body' (Noordtzij, *Leviticus*, p. 221). But this suggestion only raises the question of why those serving at the altar and what was placed on it had to be sound in body.

26. It is not argued that a priest with a 'blemish' is unholy. He clearly is since he is permitted to eat the 'holy' sacrifices (see prohibitions against defiled priests eating the 'holy things' in Lev. 22.1-9). Nevertheless, that priests have their activities limited by the presence of blemishes suggests that the latter may detract from their symbolic holiness. An unclean priest symbolized the realm of death and exclusion from God's immediate presence (cf. the idea of 'uncleanness' in Chapters 3 and 4). By contrast, a priest with a defect merely failed to reflect the holiness of God in his appearance.

but as 'without-defect' (תמים, Lev. 22.19, 21).[27] This difference requires an explanation.

Since the term תמים has 'without defect' as its primary domain of meaning within P and H's ritual texts, there is nothing peculiar about the legislator's use of this term to describe 'defect' free animals. The non-mention of animals as 'holy' is not difficult to explain either. To refer to them in this way would have prevented the laity, who were not permitted to touch holy-things, from handling their own animals. However, the legislator's decision to omit any reference to the blemish-free priests as תמים seems remarkable for two reasons. First, since the list is limited to physical-blemishes (מום), it is not immediately clear why the legislator would refrain from referring to the blemish-free priests as 'without-defect'. Second, the omission of this term in the list for priests runs contrary to the legislator's intention to draw a parallel relationship between these lists, a relationship which would doubtlessly be enhanced by referring to both animals and priests as 'without-defect' (תמים). What might account for this difference within a relationship that the legislator seems to have otherwise gone to great lengths to emphasize as parallel? Moreover, what might this omission reflect in terms of the legislator's literary purpose in Leviticus 21–22?

To begin with, Milgrom's explanation for why the legislator did not call priests תמים seems correct.

> The term *tāmîm* is not used as a criterion for priests, even though they, too, must be without blemish, for the simple reason that *tāmîm* applied to persons implies moral perfection (e.g., Gen 6.9; 17.1 [P]). In fact, in D (and other sources), it denotes nothing but moral perfection (Deut 18.13). This may be the reason why in D's two pericopes that speak of the unblemished requirement of sacrifices, the word *tāmîm* is conspicuously missing (Deut 15:21; 17:1).[28]

I would like to develop Milgrom's insight further by suggesting that the decision to omit the term תמים from this context points to the legislator's literary purpose in Leviticus 21–22. *The legislator refrained from referring to the ethical standard of the priests to restrict the audience's attention to the role of their physical appearance.*[29] In support of this suggestion one may cite the

---

27. The term קדש is used to refer to the remaining parts of sacrifices, including the 'grain offering' in Lev. 22.1-16. Whereas it is commonplace to describe a priest as 'holy' this description is unheard of for animals which are potential candidates for sacrificial offerings. Gerstenberger overlooks the different terminology used to describe the physical completeness of priests and animals when he states that the 'general manner of speaking about an "unblemished condition" is in any case identical in the two chapters' (Gerstenberger, *Leviticus*, p. 323).

28. Milgrom, *Leviticus 17–22*, p. 1874.

29. Since its primary domain of meaning was 'physical integrity' when applied to animals the legislator was still able to use it of the sacrificial animals in Leviticus 22.

absence of moral defects for disqualifying priests from officiating at the altar in Leviticus 21. Though it is elsewhere assumed that moral purity should characterize the priesthood (1 Sam. 3.13, Hos. 4.6-8; Mal. 2.4-7),[30] and though the legislator commanded Israel to be holy in an *ethical* sense within the immediate context of Leviticus 21–22 (cf. Leviticus 18–20), there are no ethical requirements stipulated for the priests in Lev. 21.16-24.[31] The unexpectedness of this omission is reflected by the Qumran sectarians's supplementation of Leviticus 21 with their own list of moral requirements.[32] And, from a comparative religions point of view, when similar ANE lists for priests are taken into consideration, the omission of ethical blemishes from Leviticus 21 is at odds with other cultures which, though they similarly require their priests to be without physical blemish, require them to live by high ethical standards.[33] Thus it seems that both the legislator's ommission of the term תמים and the absence of ethical requirements when describing the priests reflect his intention to draw attention to the physical appearance of the priests and, in parallel with them, the animals in Leviticus 21–22.[34] On the assumption that physical appearance was the legislator's intended emphasis we can proceed to examine what function the legislator may assign to the appearance of these things in Leviticus 21–22. Where appropriate, the parallelism between these lists is consulted within the larger context of Leviticus 21–22 to see if it aids in their interpretation. To anticipate, I shall argue that Leviticus 21–22 was composed to present the (literary) appearance of the 'holy' priests and תמים animals as representative of God's 'holiness' and a means by which the Israelites would be sanctified.

30. Milgrom, *Leviticus 17–22*, p. 1843; Balentine, *Leviticus*, pp. 169-70.

31. It is not disputed that the priests were implicitly expected to observe the ethical commands given to the laity. However, with the heightened cultic requirements imposed on the priesthood in Leviticus 21 should we not have expected higher moral standards as well?

32. Milgrom, *Leviticus 17–22*, p. 1822.

33. Milgrom, *Leviticus 17–22*, p. 1821.

34. Alternatively, Milgrom accounts for the omission of moral defects that would disqualify priests from offering 'the food of his God' in Leviticus 21 by appealing to the parallel relationship between the lists for priests and animals (Milgrom, *Leviticus 17–22*, p. 1821). He argues that since animals do not have moral imperfections '...the compiler of the priestly defects was constrained to limit himself to physical imperfections' (Milgrom, *Leviticus 17–22*, p. 1822). First, Milgrom's claim that animals do not have moral imperfections requires some qualification. In Gen. 6.12-13 the animal kingdom is part of 'all flesh' (כל־בשר) that falls under judgment for its corruption and for filling the earth with violence, and in Exod. 21.28 an Ox is held responsible for goring a human. In addition to this observation Wenham points out that the Israelite animals were expected to rest from work on the sabbath (Exod. 20.10; Wenham, *Leviticus*, p. 170). Second, in making his argument Milgrom has not considered the possibility that the legislator may have omitted ethical imperfections to emphasize the physical appearance of priests and sacrificial animals.

In conclusion, a case has been made for viewing the parallelism between the lists of blemishes in Leviticus 21–22 as of importance for their interpretation. An anomaly within this parallel relationship, namely the non-mention of priests as תמים, possibly reflects the legislator's purpose in composing these lists. He avoids any reference to the ethical behaviour of the priests and thereby focuses our attention on the role of their physical appearance. In what follows the content of Leviticus 21–22 is examined to establish what this role might be and whether it implies that תמים symbolizes of an aspect of קדש.

The Role of Physical Appearance in the Lists of Leviticus 21–22

Putting aside the parallel nature of the lists of blemishes, commentators sometimes propose that the regulations concerning physical appearance in Leviticus 21–22 were to teach the Israelites about holiness.[35] Of significance for the present investigation is that these scholars assign a symbolic meaning to the requirement for physical completeness.[36] Balentine is representative of this view when he states that '[h]oly and unblemished persons (and sacrifices) are external expressions of the requirement to be holy as God is holy'.[37] In other words, the role of the appearance of the priests and animals of Leviticus 21–22 is to express that the Israelites 'ought' to be 'holy'. Similarly, Wenham contends that there 'are indications within Leviticus 21 that physical integrity was viewed as symbolic of moral integrity'.[38] And, in keeping with this view, Hartley attributes a symbolic function to the physical completeness of the animals in Leviticus 22. He suggests that a twofold rationale underlies this requirement. First, it ensures that the sacrifice is costly.[39] Second, 'the animal's

---

35. Hartley comments that 'this knowledge about the rules for a holy priesthood provides the congregation greater insight into the nature of holiness' (Hartley, *Leviticus*, p. 346; cf. Wenham, *Leviticus*, p. 292; Knohl, *The Sanctuary of Silence*, pp. 189-92; Frank H. Gorman, *Divine Presence and Community: A Commentary on the Book of Leviticus* (International Theological Commentary; Grand Rapids: Eerdmans, 1997), p. 121; Balentine, *Leviticus*, p. 169). I shall interact more carefully with Hartley's understanding of the symbolic understanding of these laws below. Though Milgrom views the parallelism between the lists as reflecting Israel's tripartite systematization of human and animal worlds, he does not attribute a symbolic function to the lists of blemishes. According to him they serve the practical function of maintaining the cultic holiness of priests and animals (*Leviticus 17–22*, p. 1793).

36. This symbolic meaning was first argued by Douglas, *Purity and Danger*, pp. 41-57. For a recent assessment of this aspect of her proposal consult Saul M. Olyan, 'Mary Douglas's Holiness/Wholeness Paradigm: Its Potential for Insight and its Limitations', *Journal of Hebrew Scriptures* 8 (2008), pp. 2-9.

37. Balentine, *Leviticus*, p. 169; cf. Harrison, *Leviticus*, p. 213.

38. Wenham, *Leviticus*, p. 297.

39. Hartley, *Leviticus*, p. 18; see also Harrison, *Leviticus*, p. 44.

freedom from any defect accords with the pure, holy character of God'.[40] With regard to his second point, Hartley, without saying so, may indirectly assume that some kind of symbolic relationship exists between the concepts of תמים and קדש.[41] In line with this assumption, he views the requirement that the priest be without physical 'defect' (מום) as reflecting the expectation that the priest's appearance embody the idea of 'holiness'.[42] And he inter-prets the requirement that sacrificial animals be תמים in Leviticus 22 as evidence that

> [a]n imperfect gift indicates that its giver does not comprehend the absolute perfection of the God to whom that person is making the offering.[43]

This interpretation is reached because

> [t]he wholeness of the priest, just like the wholeness of an animal acceptable for sacrifice, *corresponds to and bears witness to* the holiness of the sanctu-ary and the holiness of God.[44]

In this way, Hartley acknowledges that the referent of the 'holy' appearance of the priests and the תמים appearance of sacrificial animals is the same. They both correspond, in some way, to the holiness of God. Moreover, by suggesting that תמים animals correspond, and bear witness, 'to the holiness of the sanctuary and the holiness of God',[45] he attributes a symbolic meaning to the term תמים because it assumes that the 'wholeness' of sacrificial animals represents (i.e. symbolizes) God's holiness to the Israelites.[46]

If these scholars are correct their conclusion would assist in my attempt to test the hypothesis that the תמים character of the animals in Leviticus 22 is related to the 'holiness' expected of the Israelites. However, though I agree with the symbolic meaning these scholars assign to the physical appearance

---

40. Hartley, *Leviticus*, pp. 18-19.

41. Hartley views holiness as 'wholeness' in the same way proposed by Douglas (Hartley, *Leviticus*, p. 349).

42. Hartley, *Leviticus*, p. 349. Similarly, Gorman reasons that '[t]he wholeness of the body is seen as a reflection of the integrity of the holy. Those who draw near to enact the sacrifices must reflect in the flesh the "wholeness" of the holy realm' (Gorman, *Divine Presence*, p. 123).

43. Hartley, *Leviticus*, p. 363.

44. Hartley, *Leviticus*, pp. 349-50 (emphasis mine). Gorman likewise infers that the physical completeness of these animals 'must reflect the holiness of the sacred place' (Gorman, *Divine Presence*, p. 125).

45. Hartley, *Leviticus*, pp. 349-50.

46. This is also true for those scholars who admit that the physical wholeness of sacrificial animals expresses God's holiness. The reason they have not identified the term 'without defect' as symbolizing human 'integrity' seems to be because they have assumed *a priori* that the concept of holiness in Leviticus 21–22 is the abstract idea of wholeness or normality.

of priests and sacrificial animals, it is noteworthy that they seem to have argued from a conceptual, rather than exegetical, basis.[47] For example, Balentine's proposal derives from his presupposition that in

> Israel's priestly system the concern for the wholeness and integrity of the physical body is an extension of the understanding that God's holiness is perfect and complete.[48]

In the same way, the 'indications' that Wenham suggests point to a symbolic meaning of 'physical integrity' seem to be those things which point to an underlying idea of 'wholeness' in this chapter.[49] Following Douglas, he argues that both cultic and ethical holiness cohere around the concept of 'wholeness':[50] 'wholeness' is the conduit through which cultic holiness (i.e. the physical appearance of priests) points towards 'moral integrity'.

> Various bodily deformities, not all of which can be identified with certainty, preclude a priest from officiating in the sanctuary. The idea emerges clearly that holiness finds physical expression in wholeness and normality.[51]

Since the idea of 'wholeness' appears common to the ideas of holiness and ethics elsewhere in Leviticus a conceptual approach such as this is acceptable.[52] Moreover, Wenham's conclusion that the referent of cultic holiness in Leviticus 21 is moral integrity is encouraged by the predominantly ethical nature of holiness in the immediate context (Leviticus 18–20).[53] However, the limitation of the conceptual approach used by these scholars is that it overlooks certain literary features which would yield more robust results concerning the purpose of these prescriptions.[54] For this reason the proposals made by Balentine, Wenham and Hartley are difficult to defend against the view of those scholars who, confining their interpretation to what is explicitly

47. Knohl is an exception to this and I shall draw on his exegetical observations below (*The Sanctuary of Silence*, pp. 189-92).

48. Balentine, *Leviticus*, p. 169. He derives this presupposition, which is also operative in the commentaries of Wenham and Hartley, from the work of Douglas.

49. Wenham may also have in mind the prohibitions against priests marrying immoral women (Lev. 21.7, 13-14).

50. Wenham, *Leviticus*, pp. 23-25.

51. Wenham, *Leviticus*, p. 292.

52. For the idea of 'wholeness' as basic to cultic and ethical holiness, see Douglas, *Purity and Danger*, pp. 53-54; Wenham, *Leviticus*, pp. 23-25.

53. Even when obedience to cultic commands is viewed as part of what it means to 'be holy' in Leviticus 19–20 these come within an ethical context.

54. Nihan has made a similar argument regarding the need to understand the logic underlying the structure of this material. 'The decisive issue, then, is that of the logic connecting the four units composing Lev 21-22. A major obstacle to understanding this problem has been the failure to perceive that these various rules of conduct for the priests define together a specific conception of holiness, this time not of the community as in ch. 18-20 but of the *sanctuary*' (Nihan, *From Priestly Torah to Pentateuch*, p. 448).

stated in the text, argue that the concern of these chapters is limited to the maintenance of cultic holiness.[55] With this possible criticism in mind, before I can assume that Leviticus 21–22 had the purpose of presenting the 'holy' priests and 'without defect' animals to Israel as 'expressions of the requirement to be holy as God is holy', some exegetical support is required and, in this regard, I offer the following three observations. These will provide an exegetical basis from which I can argue for a symbolic interpretation of תמים as human 'integrity'.

The Sanctuary, Including the Priests and Offerings, Represents the Holiness of God

Some evidence suggests that the holiness of priests, sacrifices, and the sanctuary itself, represent the holiness of God. The consequence of 'profaning' (חלל) these things was the 'profanation' (חלל) of God's 'holy name'.[56] For example, when priests were defiled through contact with death they would become 'profaned' (Lev. 21.4b) and, simultaneously, 'they will profane the name of their God' (יחללו שם אלהיהם, Lev. 21.6). Similarly, when defiled priests compromise the holiness of the offerings Yahweh declares that 'they shall profane my holy name' (יחללו את־שם קדשי, Lev. 22.2). These examples suggest that God's holy reputation (i.e. 'my holy name') is made unholy (i.e. 'profaned') when the priests and the sacrifices are profaned. *The implication is that God's holy presence is mediated through the holiness of these things.*[57] Of significance for our study is that this observation may imply that

55. Milgrom is of the opinion that these chapters serve to encourage the priests and laity to maintain the cultic holiness of the priests and the offerings (*Leviticus 17–22*, p. 1793). Other scholars who seem to interpret the content of Leviticus 21–22 as having a strictly cultic function include Porter, *Leviticus*, pp. 166-79; Noordtzij, *Leviticus*, pp. 214-27; Gerstenberger, *Leviticus*, p. 315; Nihan, *From Priestly Torah to Pentateuch*, pp. 446-47. These commentators may accept that Israel's sanctification relied on the distinction between the holy and profane but they do not seem to consider that this is the primary purpose of Leviticus 21–22.

56. In explaining how a priest with a physical defect may 'profane' (חלל) the sanctuary (Lev. 21.23) Jan Joosten concludes that the 'root *ḥll* used in these verses probably implies the risk of impurity coming in contact with the holy abode of YHWH'. Within the same paragraph he qualifies this statement by saying that the verb 'means only that the holy is made, or treated as, profane; in other words, it describes only the first step towards impurity (since the profane may become impure)' (Joosten, *People and Land in the Holiness Code*, p. 126). But, since priests with defects can still consume the holy offerings (Lev. 21.22) Joosten's conclusion cannot be correct. By contrast, defiled priests may not eat these (Lev. 22.2-9).

57. One may also infer that the 'holiness' of the offerings is representative of divine 'holiness' from Lev. 22.9: ושמרו את־משמרתי ולא־ישאו עליו חטא ומתו בו כי יחללהו אני יהוה מקדשם ('They shall keep my charge, so that they do not bear sin for it and die thereby when they profane it. I am Yahweh who sanctifies them'). The

the תמים character of sacrificial animals represents an aspect of holiness. However, a consideration of this possibility shall be delayed until an examination is completed of the relationship between the appearance of the priests and animals, presented in Leviticus 21–22, and the holiness of God.

God's Holiness Is Displayed by the Priests's Officiation at the Altar
Not only does the text of Leviticus 21–22 indicate that the priests represent God's holiness, but it specifically identifies their work at the altar as that which expresses his holiness most clearly. For example, Lev. 21.8 reads:

וקדשתו כי־את־לחם אלהיך הוא מקריב קדש יהיה־לך כי קדוש
אני יהוה מקדשכם: ('You shall sanctify him, *for the food of your God he offers*, he shall be holy to you, for holy am I Yahweh who sanctifies you')[58]

One may interpret this verse as follows. First, the rationale for why the Israelites should pay attention to the holiness of the priests (i.e. וְקִדַּשְׁתּוֹ) is that they preside over the offerings at the altar (cf. v. 6). What is the connection between a priest's officiation at the altar and the requirement that the Israelites should observe their holiness? The following argument offered by Gorman, in relation to the prohibition against the high priest leaving the sanctuary while the anointing oil is on him (cf. v. 12), may apply here.

> The high priest is not to go outside the sanctuary because the anointing oil is upon him. It makes him holy and locates him within the realm of the holy; he shares the holy status of the tabernacle area (see Lev. 8). *His departure would disrupt the status of 'the holy'.*[59]

exegetical crux of this verse concerns the identity of the antecedent for the singular masculine suffixes of 'for *it*' (עליו); 'because of *it*' (בו); and 'when they profane *it*' (יחללהו). As most commentators observe, it is unlikely to be 'my charge' (משמרתי) because it is feminine. The most plausible remaining options are the 'bread' (לחם; cf. v. 7; Hoffmann, Noth, Elliger); the command not to eat forbidden carcasses (cf. v. 8; Milgrom); and God's 'holy name' (שם קדש). Among these it is arguable that Yahweh's 'holy name' is the antecedent of each pronominal singular third-person suffix in v. 9 (David Noel Freedman; cf. Milgrom, *Leviticus 17–22*, p. 1859). Most importantly, as Milgrom observes, the verb חלל forms an *inclusio* in vv. 2 and 9 and since its object in the former is 'my holy name' (masc. sing.) the same may be implied in v. 9 (Milgrom, *Leviticus 17–22*, p. 1860). Second, if Yahweh's 'holy name' is the referent of these suffixes it would indirectly include the profanation of the 'bread' and eating forbidden carcasses since both of these actions profane Yahweh's name. Thus, vv. 2-9 are ultimately concerned with preserving the sanctity of God's name by preventing the holy offerings from becoming profaned through defilement.

58. For my purposes it may not matter how one renders *piel* וְקִדַּשְׁתּוֹ 'You shall sanctify him' (e.g. Wenham, *Leviticus*, p. 288) or 'You shall treat him as holy' (e.g. Knohl, *The Sanctuary of Silence*, p. 191). Both have in mind the need for the laity to focus on the holiness of the priests which, as observed in the previous point, is representative of God's holiness.

59. Gorman, *Divine Presence*, p. 123.

In other words, the holiness of the high priest and the sanctuary share a degree of interdependence so that to remove one detracts from the holiness of the other.[60] In the same way one may speculate that a priest must maintain his holiness to avoid disrupting the status of the holy when making offerings. At this time he became most closely associated with the holiness of God through the offering of his 'food' (Lev. 21.6, 28, 17, 21; cf. Lev. 10.3).[61] One may argue that the command for Israel to observe the holiness of the priest (קדשתי) corresponds to his representation of God's holiness to the Israelites.

The second indication, within v. 8, that the priests were representative of God's holiness on these occasions is suggested by the clause which is subordinate to 'he shall be holy to you' (קדש יהיה־לך), namely *'for holy am I Yahweh* who sanctifies you' (כי קדש אני יהוה מקדשכם).[62]

Keeping in mind the parallel relationship between the priests and sacrificial animals within Leviticus 21–22, it seems possible that the 'without defect' (תמים) appearance of these animals fulfils a similar role in representing God's holiness.

The Physical Appearance of the Priests and Animals as a Means for Israel's Sanctification

Hartley's claim that the holiness of the priests and offerings were 'external expressions of the requirement to be holy as God is holy' may also be inferred from the rationale given for why the priests, and people (cf. Lev. 22.14-15), must avoid profaning Yahweh's name in Lev. 22.32.

---

60. Within the larger context of P the requirement for officiating priests to be 'without מום' and sacrificial animals to be תמים is complemented by the expectation that the altar be made with stones that are שלמה (Exod. 20.25). In his investigation of these parallels, it is noteworthy that Olyan seems to assume that one must conceive of the priests's bodies as תמים even though, as we have observed, this term is never applied to the priests (Saul M. Olyan, 'Why an Altar of Unfinished Stones? Some Thoughts on Ex 20,25 and Dtn 27,5-6', *ZAW* 108 [1996], pp. 161-71 [170]).

61. 'The holiness of the priests is related to their location in the sacred area and their enactment of sacred activity' (Gorman, *Divine Presence*, p. 122). Likewise, Gründwaldt suggests that 'Die Besonderheit des Hohenpriesters und der Priester ist in ihrer Funktion begründet. Der Hohepriester hat die Weihe des Salböls, weswegen er auch den heiligen Bezirk nicht verlassen darf (21,12), und die Priester gehen mit Dringen um, die im Opferkult in direkten Kontakt mit der Gottheit kommen (21,6.8.17; 22,15 u. ö.), ja sie kommen dem heiligen Gott selbst näher als irgend jemand sonst (21,23)' (Gründwaldt, *Das Heiligkeitsgesetz Leviticus 17–26*, p. 393).

62. Both Knohl and Joosten understand the subordination of the clause 'for I am Yahweh who sanctifies you' (כי אני יהוה מקדשכם) to 'he shall be holy to you' (קדש יהיה־לך) within Lev. 21.8 as an indication that the holy priest is at least one means by which Yahweh's holiness reaches the Israelites (Knohl, *The Sanctuary of Silence*, p. 191; Joosten, *People and Land in the Holiness Code*, p. 130).

ולא תחללו את־שם קדשי ונקדשתי בתוך בני ישראל אני יהוה
מקדשכם: ('You shall not profane my holy name so that I may be sanctified among the Israelites. I am Yahweh who sanctifies them')

The clause 'that I may be sanctified among the Israelites' (ונקדשתי בתוך בני ישראל) discloses *why* Yahweh's 'holy name' must not be profaned.[63] The relevant question seems to be, 'how is God sanctified among the Israelites'? Most commentators suggest that it is through their observance of *all* Yahweh's 'commandments'.[64] This suggestion assumes that the preceding verse (v. 31) indicates the means by which they will sanctify Him.

ושמרתם מצותי ועשיתם אתם אני יהוה ('You shall keep *my command-ments* and you shall do them. I am Yahweh')

At the very least, the reference to 'commandments' in this verse has in view Yahweh's commandments to maintain the appearance of the priests (Lev. 21.4, 9, 15), the sanctuary (Lev. 21.12), and the holy things (Lev. 22.15).[65]

---

63. Joosten regards the profanation of Yahweh's 'holy name' as profaning 'the bond between the people and their God, and leads to defilement of the sanctuary'. In a cor-responding footnote he suggests that this 'seems to be what is implied by the expression "to profane my holy name" (20.3; cf. 18.21; 19.12; 21.6; 22.2, 32): the "name of Yahweh" is probably to be connected with the frequent use of the formulas "I am Yahweh (your God)"' (Joosten, *People and Land in the Holiness Code*, p. 133). There are several problems with this view. First, the root חלל does not necessarily point to a danger of defilement. Priest's with defects would 'profane' the sanctuary but not defile it, as is implied by the fact that whereas they could eat the holy offerings, defiled priests could not (Lev. 21.22; 22.1-9). Second, it is not certain that the holiness of the 'name of Yahweh' represents the 'bond between the people and their God'. That Yahweh urges Israel not to profane his 'holy name' *so that* I [Yahweh] may be sanctified among the Israelites' (ונקדשתי בתוך בני ישראל) would seem to discount this view.

64. Milgrom, *Leviticus 17–22*, p. 1888; Hartley, *Leviticus*, p. 362. Nihan proposes that '[t]here is no rigid, definite division between Israel's holiness and Yhwh's holiness, but on the contrary a close interconnection: Israel's sanctification by means of *imitatio dei* (Lev. 19.2; 20.26!) enables in turn Yhwh to manifest his holiness within his commu-nity' (Nihan, *From Priestly Torah to Pentateuch*, p. 457; cf. Kornfeld, *Levitikus*, p. 89).

65. Scholars do not agree on what literary unit Lev. 22.31-33 serves as a conclusion. For those who see it as Leviticus 21–22 see B. Baentsch, *Exodus, Leviticus, Numbers* (HKAT, 1.2; Göttingen: Vandenhoeck & Ruprecht, 1903), p. 411; Elliger, *Leviticus*, p. 301. This understanding of these verses may be supported by the second person masculine plural suffix on מקדשכם ('who sanctifies you') in v. 32. Of the six occurrences of the participle מקדש in Leviticus 21–22, the central four have a third person masculine singular suffix whereas the outer two have the second person masculine suffix (Lev. 21.8; 22.32). This observation could support the view that Lev. 22.31-33 serves as a concluding exhortation for specifically Leviticus 21–22. For a scholar who see it as Leviticus 17–22 consult H.G. Reventlow, *Das Heiligkeitsgesetz: Formgeschichtlichuntersucht* (WMANT, 6; Neukirchen: Neukirchener, 1961), p. 100.

The appearance of these things, in addition to Israel's own growth in holiness, seems intended to represent God's holiness to Israel. This interpretation is in line with Kiuchi's interpretation of Lev. 22.32.

> Here the Lord alludes to his initial statement of the purpose concerning sanctuary worship in Exod. 29:45-46, the major protagonists of which are the priests. The *qdš* ni. appears just three times in Exodus–Leviticus (Exod. 29.43; Lev. 10.3; 22.32). The purpose of the Lord's self-identification and sanctification in Exod. 29.43 is mentioned; i.e. the priests are to become like the God of the Israelites (vv. 45-46).[66]

In keeping with this understanding, the final clause within v. 32 (i.e. 'I am Yahweh who sanctifies you', אני יהוה מקדשכם), and his recollection of his liberation of Israel from Egypt (Lev. 22.33), possibly disclose the intention of expressing God's holiness to the Israelites through the appearance of the priests and animals.[67] When observing the holiness of these things the Israelites were to learn about the holiness required of them in their service of Yahweh. The appearance of the priests *and* the sacrificial animals were possibly one element of God's sanctifying presence among the people of Israel.

A similar argument is made by Knohl who, like Kiuchi, acknowledges an allusion to Exodus 29 within Lev. 22.32. Knohl proposes that H

> connects the holiness of the priesthood to the special status of the entire nation. This is implied by the structure and content of the concluding verses of the daily offering pericope (Exod 29:42-46). The passage begins with an emphasis on God's meeting with the children of Israel and ends by declaring the purpose of the exodus as the indwelling of God among the community of Israel. In the middle of the passage we find the proclamation 'I will sanctify the Tent of Meeting and the altar, and I will consecrate Aaron and his sons to serve me as Priests' (v. 44). The sanctification of the Tent of Meeting and the priesthood is viewed as an expression of God's dwelling among the community of Israel.[68]

---

66. Kiuchi, *Leviticus*, p. 411.

67. Some scholars view the inclusion of a reference to the exodus as a clear indication that v. 33 is a later addition because they cannot comprehend a relationship between Israel's cult and salvation history. Most recently, in this regard, Gründwaldt comments on the inclusion of this verse as follows: 'Erstaunlich ist es, daß auch die Vorschriften für die Priester und den Gottesdienst in Lev 21–22 durch den Rekurs auf die Herausführung aus Ägypten (22, 31-33) beschlossen werden, den Kult und Geschichte gelten als zwei Theologoumena des Alten Testaments, die wenig miteinander zu tun haben' (Gründwaldt, *Das Heiligkeitsgesetz Leviticus 17–26*, p. 387). However, if my exegesis of the cultic prescriptions of Leviticus 21–22 is accepted the connection between cult and history may be stronger than Gründwaldt assumes. Both the cultic and historical texts are possibly intended to foster personal holiness among the Israelites. See also Bruno Baentsch, *Das Heiligkeits-Gesetz Lev. XVII–XXVI. Eine historisch-kritische Untersuchung* (Erfurt: Hugo Güther, 1893), p. 44.

68. Knohl, *The Sanctuary of Silence*, p. 190.

Moreover,

> God sanctifies Israel through dwelling among the people, and the Presence is concretized through the establishment of the Priestly institutions in the midst.[69]

As anecdotal evidence for this claim Knohl mentions the command for the laity to wear priest-like fringes on their garments (Num. 15.38-39) and proposes that[70]

> this pericope emphasizes the sanctity of all Israelites, as symbolized through the blue thread of the fringes, fashioned like the high priest's garments.[71]

Wenham likewise ventures, in relation to the command for the laity to wear blue tassels in Num. 15.38-39, that

> [t]he ark, God's throne, was wrapped in a blue cloth (Nu. 4:6) and blue curtains adorned the tabernacle indicating that this tent was the palace of the King of kings (e.g. Exod. 26.31, 36). Blue was also used in the high priest's uniform (Exod. 28.31, 37, etc.). No doubt it had a similar significance in the layman's tassel. The blue thread reminded him that he belonged to 'a kingdom of priests and a holy nation' (Exod. 19.6). Like the high priest he was called to exhibit holiness not only in his outer garb, but in his whole way of life.[72]

It seems reasonable to think that the symbolic connection between the priests and the laity echoes Exod. 19.6 in the way Wenham suggests. However, in view of my interpretation of Lev. 22.31-32, the tassels were possibly also intended to recall the sanctuary and priests which expressed God's holiness within Israel. Perhaps the resultant mindfulness of their association with this holy realm functioned to foster personal holiness (cf. Leviticus 18–20). If this possibility is accepted it would corroborate what I have argued concerning

---

69. Nevertheless, Knohl still recognizes that God is also sanctified through Israel's enactment of the commands given in Leviticus 21–22 (*The Sanctuary of Silence*, pp. 189, 191).

70. One does not need to look outside of Israel for an antecedent to the practice of attaching blue tassels to clothes (*pace* Noth, Bertman). Whatever background this practice had there seems to be a clear connection being drawn between the clothes of the laity and those of the priesthood. Since the colour blue was typically reserved for royal and cultic use, wearing these tassels 'would convert their dress into uniforms of the royal priests of God' (Milgrom, *Numbers*, p. 127; cf. S. Bertman, 'Tasselled Garments in the Ancient East Mediterranean', *BA* 24 [1961], pp. 119-128; Baruch A. Levine, *Numbers* [New York: Doubleday, 1993], pp. 400-401).

71. Knohl, *The Sanctuary of Silence*, pp. 191-92. Though Milgrom regards Knohl's proposal as 'patently forced' he does not demonstrate why this is so (*Leviticus 17–22*, p. 1809). Nihan similarly attempts to qualify Knohl's argument without critically engaging it (*From Priestly Torah to Pentateuch*, p. 454).

72. Wenham, *Numbers*, pp. 132-33.

the relationship between the holiness of priests, offerings, and sanctuary, and the sanctification of the laity in Leviticus 21–22: These were intended to express God's holiness to Israel as a model for what they were meant to be (i.e. Lev. 19.2).[73] However, as Knohl points out, the holiness to which they were to aspire could not be the cultic holiness of priests which is unattainable to the laity.[74] According to Num. 15.39 it is obedience to '*all* the commandments of Yahweh' *(את־כל־מצות יהוה)*.

Conclusion

The previous three points argue that the physical appearance of the sanctuary, the priests's officiation at the altar and the offerings are intended to express Israel's requirement to be holy as God is holy. *The appearance of the priests and sacrificial animals were one means of Israel's sanctification.* Below I shall argue that, when the term תמים is used to describe the 'holy' appearance of the sacrificial animals it, as a consequence, takes on a symbolic meaning that corresponds to one aspect of 'holiness' (קדש). Underlying the observations I shall make will be the two main arguments I have made in this Chapter. First, the lists of blemishes concerning priests and animals in Leviticus 21–22 closely parallel one another. Where a case can be made for viewing a particular word or cultic requirement as symbolic in one list, this parallel relationship will permit me to inquire if the same is true of the corresponding element in the other list. Second, the physical appearance of the priests and animals, which I have argued was of central importance in the legislator's composition of these lists, is intended to represent God's holiness to the Israelites for the latter's sanctification. When attempting to establish that תמים is intended to evoke human 'integrity' as a secondary domain of meaning within this context I shall make use of both of these insights.

Observations Which Suggest a Symbolic Meaning of תמים *in Leviticus 21–22*

The previous section argued that the term תמים was not applied to the priests without 'defect' (מום) in Leviticus 21 because the legislator wished to draw attention to the role of their physical appearance as representative of God's

---

73. Nihan, when taking into account the literary context of Leviticus 21–22 (i.e. Leviticus 18–20) and the interest the legislator shows in the relationship between the priests-sanctuary and the laity, similarly concludes that '[o]n the whole, the legislation [i.e. Leviticus 21–22] provides a fine complement to the previous section on the community's holiness in ch. 18-20. As programmatically announced in 19.30, it illustrates how the sanctification of the community itself depends first of all on the preservation of Yhwh's sanctuary as the very symbol of God's holiness, but also the unique role of the priests in this respect' (Nihan, *From Priestly Torah to Pentateuch*, p. 454).

74. Knohl, *The Sanctuary of Silence*, pp. 191-92.

holiness. This argument assumed that the primary domain of meaning of תמים is 'moral perfection' or human 'integrity' when applied to humans.[75] Nevertheless, from a cognitive linguistic perspective, it remains possible that תמים has a secondary symbolic meaning of human 'integrity' when applied to the animals in Leviticus 22. Several contextual factors seem to encourage this symbolic interpretation of תמים.

First, the parallel role that the priests and animals share in representing God's 'holiness' to the Israelites seems to imply that 'without מום' (i.e. priests) and תמים appearance symbolize an idea that extends beyond a 'cultic' meaning. Since the 'holiness' that they represent is also expected of the Israelites, it seems to have a partially 'ethical', in addition to a 'cultic', meaning.

Second, since we are dealing with literature, and not enacted ritual, the actual appearance of these things falls from view and we are left to consider the terms קדש, in the case of the priests, and תמים, in the case of the animals, as symbolic of God's holiness. The term תמים itself becomes an aspect of the animal's appearance. If so, then, from what was argued concerning the function of the appearance of priests and animals in Leviticus 21–22, one may reason that תמים becomes symbolic of God's holiness and of the life expected of the Israelites. From such a perspective a competent reader of Leviticus 22 may access a secondary symbolic domain of the term תמים, albeit during the post-crystallization period of interpretation. Moreover, that both קדש and תמים fulfil a parallel role in symbolizing God's 'holiness' within Leviticus 21–22 implies that they are closely related in meaning.[76]

Third, the interpretative process of resolving why the legislator omitted the term תמים from Leviticus 21, when it is used within the parallel list of Leviticus 22, may have heightened a reader's awareness of this term's potential ethical meaning. From a cognitive linguistic point of view, when one asks how the term תמים, as an animal's *literary* appearance, represents the holiness of God, the probability that one would access the secondary domain of human 'integrity' increases. Against the possibility that a reader would access this secondary domain of meaning in Leviticus 22 some scholars may point out that it is used of animals.[77] But a cognitive linguistic approach assumes that, though the primary domain accessed within this context is 'physical completeness', this does not exclude the possibility that an ethical

---

75. Milgrom, *Leviticus 17–22*, p. 1874.

76. This does not mean that these terms are synonymous. They are clearly not. However, it seems that they can both be used to refer to a particular aspect of God's holiness (cf. Deut. 18.13).

77. All commentators, with the exception of Kiuchi, assume that the term has only a cultic meaning in Leviticus 22. So Milgrom, Wenham, Noordtzij, Harrison, Porter, Budd, Kleinig.

meaning (i.e. as a secondary domain) is accessed in the post-crystallization period of interpretation (cf. Chapter 2).[78]

Fourth, a symbolic interpretation of תמים is possibly suggested by the parallel relationship between the priests and animals in Leviticus 21–22. It seems conceivable that the correspondence drawn between the priests and animals would encourage one to access what תמים means when applied to humans. I have already argued that the sacrificial animals perform, among other things, a symbolic function in relation to humans in Leviticus 1–16 (Chapter 5). If a reader were to presuppose that the same is true of the animals in Leviticus 22, the probability that their description as תמים would evoke the idea of human 'integrity' would seem to increase. That the corresponding priests are קדש may reflect that it shares some semantic overlap with תמים.

Fifth, related to the previous point, the 'acceptance' (רצון) of תמים animals on behalf of their offerers in Leviticus 22 may encourage one to access the symbolic meaning of תמים, as a secondary domain of meaning, in this context. Verses 19 and 20 are cited by several scholars as evidence that the 'burnt offering' is 'accepted' on an *offerer's behalf* in Lev. 1.3-4.[79]

> לרצנכם תמים זכר בבקר בכשבים ובעזים: (*'For acceptance on your behalf*, it shall be a without-defect male of the bulls or the sheep or the goats' Lev. 22.19)

> כל אשר־בו מום לא תקריבו כי־לא לרצון יהיה לכם: ('Anything that has a blemish in it you shall not offer, *for it will not be accepted for you'* Lev. 22.20)

Verse 21c implies that an animal's תמים character is critical for its, and consequently the offerer's (cf. vv. 19-20), acceptance.

> תמים יהיה לרצון כל־מום לא יהיה־בו: ('For acceptance it will be without-defect, it will not have any defect in it' Lev. 22.21c)

Nevertheless, though most scholars agree with this interpretation, it is often thought that the תמים character of the animal achieves acceptance by making the animal costly.[80] But this conclusion seems unlikely for three reasons. First, it does not take into account that these animals represent God's holiness. How a costly animal would symbolize holiness any more than a cheap one is not clear, unless the difference relates to their physical-appearance. Second, it overlooks that the three different species of animals offered differ significantly in costliness. For example, since a blind bull, disqualified from

---

78. For the use of תמים in relation to humans elsewhere in the Pentateuch see pages 202-206.

79. Kiuchi, *The Purification Offering*, p. 116; Milgrom, *Leviticus 1–16*, p. 149; Sklar, *Sin, Impurity, Sacrifice and Atonement* [PhD dissertation], pp. 187-88.

80. E.g. Hartley, *Leviticus*, p. 19.

the altar (Lev. 22.22), would presumably be worth far more than a תמים goat, the preference for a תמים goat over a blind bull would seem related to the former's appearance rather than its costliness. Third, if the value of the animal is of primary importance, it is unusual that the legislator has not set monetary guidelines for what constituted an acceptable animal (cf. Leviticus 27). With these things in mind the idea that it was the symbolic value of these animals (i.e. human 'integrity') that 'ransomed' their offerers remains plausible.

There seem sufficient grounds to speculate that, during the period of post-crystallization interpretation, a reader of Leviticus 21–22 would access an ethical *secondary domain* of תמים (Lev. 22.19, 21) despite that it is used of animals. The תמים character of these animals represents God's 'holiness', and parallels the 'holiness' of the priests. It seems possible that there is some semantic-overlap between the meanings of תמים and קדש within this context. Moreover, considering that the lists of defects in Leviticus 21–22 appear to have the purpose of encouraging holiness among the Israelites, this overlap possibly extends into the realm of ethics. The firmer exegetical basis of this interpretation supports the assumption that a lack of physical defects (i.e. wholeness) in animals symbolized 'moral integrity'.[81]

Conclusion

This Chapter sought to strengthen the argument made in Chapter 5 that, within ritual texts, the term תמים can be used of animals to symbolize an ethical aspect of holiness. It examined the parallel relationship between priests and sacrificial animals in Leviticus 21–22 and it argued that the legislator composed the regulations of these chapters to encourage his audience to view the physical completeness of priests and animals as representative of God's holiness. Furthermore, he presented the (literary?) appearance of these as a means by which Israel would be sanctified. In support of the argument made in Chapter 5, these findings suggest that the symbolic meaning of תמים (i.e. human 'integrity') within Leviticus 21–22 possibly constitutes an aspect of קדש.[82] Though this passage is part of H, it has significance for my contention that there is an ethical aspect to P's view of holiness because scholars agree that P and H use the relevant terminology in the same way within cultic contexts. Indeed, that both P (cf. Chapter 5) and H seem to use the term תמים to denote an aspect of holiness, within ritual texts, suggests that their respective views of holiness are more similar than what is commonly assumed.

81. E.g. Douglas, Wenham, Milgrom, Hartley.

82. Admittedly, the results of the present chapter concerning the symbolic meaning of תמים within Leviticus 21 are far from conclusive. Nevertheless, it is hoped that when viewed as a part of the overall argument presented in this book they may provide further encouragement for scholars to consider whether the concepts of holiness within P and H are as different as is often assumed.

Chapter 7

CONCLUSION

This study has proposed that an ethical dimension of holiness is implicit within P's ritual texts. In line with this proposal it suggested that there is possibly more coherence in the concepts of holiness found in P and H than is commonly assumed.

The justification for this study was based on two observations concerning the traditional assumption that P's concept of holiness is cultic and devoid of ethical concerns (Chapter 1). First, the historical contexts that scholars, such as Wellhausen, Milgrom and Knohl claim account for the Priestly writings do not explain why one should expect P's view of holiness to be unrelated to ethics. Second, though I acknowledged that an ethical view of holiness is not *explicit* in P, with the exception of Kiuchi, scholars have not investigated the possibility that such a view remains *implicit* within the ritual texts. This oversight seems to have resulted from the misguided assumption that such a concept *should* be explicit, as it is in H. Therefore, first, in the absence of a satisfactory historical theory for why one should expect an amoral view of holiness in P and second, by putting aside the assumption that such a view should be explicit, an examination of whether certain ritual texts assume an ethical idea of holiness did not seem inappropriate. In relation to this conclusion I hypothesized that a symbolic dimension to these texts was used by P to persuade the Israelites to be holy.

Chapter 2 outlined a method for interpreting the symbolic meaning of ritual texts. First, I indicated my intention to supplement the grammatical approach to semantics, advocated by James Barr, with cognitive linguistic analysis. Though attention to a term's paradigmatic and syntagmatic relations is essential for the interpretation of its 'primary domain' of meaning, a cognitive linguistic analysis provides a relatively objective means for identifying 'secondary domains' of meaning that a reader may access within a specific context. This method was judged to be of benefit to the present study which presupposed that symbolic meaning would be most likely found within the matrix of a term's secondary domains of meaning.

Second, my methodology regards the text as the proper object of interpretation when reading ritual texts. While this statement may sound like commonsense, it departs from a trend to locate ritual meaning by reconstructing 'what happened' when the prescribed rite was performed (e.g. Frank Gorman). By contrast, the present study hypothesized, based on Robert Alter's approach to Hebrew narrative, that there is an 'interfusion' between the meaning of P's ritual texts and their literary art. This method of interpretation was encouraged by, first, the observation that P's ritual texts do not seem to answer some important questions of a strictly practical nature and, second, that these texts are positioned immediately after the symbolic texts concerning the sanctuary (Exodus 25–40). In other words, considering that Leviticus presupposes Exodus 25–40 as important for its interpretation, it seemed reasonable to assume that the symbolic dimension of the latter text may extend into Leviticus. To my knowledge, the implications of this symbolic context for the interpretation of Leviticus have not been previously investigated.

Chapter 3 presented an argument, by way of an exegetical study of Leviticus 11, for considering that the command to 'be holy' (vv. 43-45) explicates a concern that is already present in P's 'dietary regulations' (vv. 1-42). This argument did not rely on an assumption that vv. 43-45 are the work of P, but on the presupposition that the author of these verses (i.e. H) was aware that P's 'dietary regulations' were composed to persuade the Israelites to 'be holy'. More specifically, it suggested that the legislator used literary art, in particular 'rhetorical progression', to convey the symbolic meaning of what it means to become 'unclean' to an audience familiar with Genesis 1–3. The food prohibitions recall Yahweh's command that the first humans should not eat the forbidden fruit and the human status of 'uncleanness' (טמא) represents the consequence of 'death' (מות) experienced by Adam and Eve after they rebelled against this command. According to Leviticus 11, to be 'unclean' was symbolic of a punitive 'exclusion from Yahweh's immediate presence' on account of the rebellion represented by eating or touching what was forbidden. In this way the 'dietary regulations' discouraged the Israelites from rebelling against Yahweh. Moreover, it seemed that they would encourage obedience to Yahweh's cultic and ethical commandments so that they could remain in his presence.

The insight that Leviticus 11 possibly fosters obedience to Yahweh's cultic and ethical commandments was significant for my hypothesis that the ethical thrust of Leviticus 11 is related to P's view of holiness. Some scholars (e.g. Milgrom; Douglas) argue that P has an ethical purpose without concluding that the latter is subsumed under P's idea of holiness. This argument rests on the distinction these scholars make between the ethical concerns of P and those which characterize the idea of holiness in H. That is, whereas in H the ethical life (i.e. holiness) consists in the observance of cultic and ethical commandments, they contend that P's ethical concern is limited to a general notion of 'respect for life'. By contrast, since I argue that the ethical concern of Leviticus 11 is similar to that which characterizes H's view of holiness, it seems that H's command to 'be holy' (Lev. 11.43-45) is in keeping with the program of the preceding legislation. Moreover, Chapter 3 concludes that P expected the Israelites to avoid the reality symbolized by 'uncleanness' (i.e. exile) by being holy.

Chapter 4 undertook an analysis of some of P's remaining 'purity regulations' (Leviticus 12–15). This analysis provided additional support for the conclusion reached in Chapter 3, that a person's status as 'unclean' symbolizes one's punitive 'exclusion from Yahweh's immediate presence'. It assisted my argument that P's 'dietary regulations' persuaded the Israelites to 'be holy' through their observance of certain cultic and ethical commandments.

Beginning with the legislation concerning the disease called צרעת (Leviticus 13) Chapter 4 argued that the legislator employed the technique of 'rhetorical progression', as he did in Levitiucs 11, to draw attention to the symbolic meaning of certain key terms, namely 'flesh' (בשר), the disease called צרעת and 'uncleanness' (טמא). First, with regard to 'flesh' (בשר), though its primary semantic domain in Leviticus 13 is 'human flesh', it seemed likely that someone familiar with the narrative of Genesis would access the secondary domain of 'human sinfulness' which is associated with this term in Genesis 6–9.

Second, Chapter 4 made a case for viewing the disease called צרעת as representative of divine judgment on 'flesh'. Since 'flesh' carries the *symbolic* meaning of 'human sinfulness' this view does not imply that P viewed people with צרעת as guilty of specific sin. Rather, the association between 'flesh' and צרעת served an educational function—*God's wrath falls on human sinfulness*. This idea is most graphically portrayed in the burning of the garment, which represents a person, that is infected with צרעת (Lev. 13.47-58).

Third, the symbolic meanings identified for 'flesh' and צרעת helped to confirm that the consequence of 'uncleanness' (טמא) represents a person's punitive 'exclusion from Yahweh's immediate presence' (cf. Chapter 3). Within Leviticus 13, 'uncleanness' is pronounced *after* the priest sees 'flesh' exposed or threatened by the disease צרעת. Moreover, the 'unclean' person is removed from the community and experiences a 'living-death' (Lev. 13.45-46). Thus, within this legislation, 'uncleanness' is a consequence of 'flesh' becoming afflicted with צרעת. *The person who had צרעת served as a 'walking advertisement' symbolizing the consequence of divine judgment upon human sinfulness.* This interpretation makes sense of the requirement that when such a person is healed he should undergo certain rites, including the offering of sacrifices which make כפר for him before his re-entry into the camp: *sinful humanity re-enters God's presence on the basis of* כפר (Lev. 14.1-32). These rites would have completed the educational purpose of the purity regulations.

The symbolic interpretation of Leviticus 13 offered in Chapter 4 gained in persuasiveness when the source of 'uncleanness' associated with childbirth

(Leviticus 12) and sexual discharges (Leviticus 15) was investigated. As was argued in relation to Leviticus 13, the source of uncleanness in these framing chapters is closely associated with the term 'flesh'.

The results of Chapter 4 supported the argument made concerning the meaning of 'uncleanness' in Leviticus 11. It seems that P's purity regulations (Leviticus 11–15) were aimed at persuading the Israelites to avoid the reality which stands behind the state of 'uncleanness' (presumably exile) by conforming themselves to Yahweh's will, presumably by keeping his cultic and ethical commandments (cf. Chapter 3). This, at least partial, ethical concern may reflect P's own view of holiness which is made explicit by H's command to 'be holy' in Lev. 11.43-45 (cf. Chapter 3). Nevertheless, since the holiness terminology in Leviticus 11 is confined to a section scholars regard as H, it remained necessary to investigate if P associates a concern for ethics with holiness elsewhere in its ritual texts. This was the aim of Chapter 5 which examined the prescription for the 'burnt offering' (Leviticus 1). This text was selected because, though holiness terminology does not occur, scholars commonly assume that the 'burnt offering' was P's 'most holy' (קדש קדשים) offering *par excellence* (see Appendix 2). Yet despite this assumption, to my knowledge, an investigation into whether the offering of this sacrifice might reflect that P required the offerer to 'be holy' had not been undertaken.

Chapter 5 presented an argument for viewing the 'burnt offering' as 'making ransom' (כפר) for its offerer by symbolizing human 'integrity' (תמים). This argument was based on the observation that the entire animal, which had to be 'without defect' (תמים), was the agent of כפר (Lev. 1.4). Taking into consideration the symbolic context of Leviticus 1, in which a 'human from among you' (אדם...מכם, Lev. 1.2) approaches Yahweh's presence at his Edenic-like sanctuary (cf. Exodus 25–40), the chapter contends that a reader would access a secondary domain of the term תמים, namely human 'integrity'. A case for this interpretation was argued, in part, because the 'burnt offering' appears in two narratives prior to Leviticus and on both of these occasions the one who offers the sacrifice is either called תמים (i.e. Noah, Gen. 6.9) or commanded to be תמים (i.e. Abram, Gen. 17.1). Chapter 5 proposes that within Leviticus 1 P presents the 'burnt offering' as a symbol of the life Yahweh finds acceptable (i.e. one characterized by 'integrity'). Moreover, considering that the 'burnt offering' is P's 'most holy' offering *par excellence* (see Appendix 2), I speculate that this symbolic meaning of תמים represents one aspect of what it means to be holy in P. Nevertheless, the chapter acknowledges that this argument is weakened by the lack of holiness terminology in Leviticus 1 and, for this reason, it was necessary to examine a ritual text in which both the terms תמים and קדש are present to see if there is a semantic overlap between them which extends into the realm of ethics.

Chapter 6 attempts to strengthen the proposal that the term תמים may be used of sacrificial animals to symbolize an aspect of קדש (cf. Chapter 5). For this purpose, the parallel lists of blemishes for priests and animals in Leviticus 21–22 were examined. Within these lists the priests are called 'holy' (קדש, Leviticus 21) whereas the corresponding sacrificial animals are described as 'without defect' (תמים, Leviticus 22). These lists presented an opportunity to see if their parallelism extends to the meaning of these terms. It did not seem to matter that Leviticus 21–22 is part of H because most scholars assume that P and H use the relevant terminology in the same way within ritual contexts.

First, from the list concerning priests (Lev. 21.16-24) Chapter 6 argued that their 'holy' (קדש) appearance was intended to represent divine holiness to the Israelites as a means for the latter's sanctification. Since the holiness the priests's appearance symbolized was to be emulated by the Israelites Chapter 6 concludes that it must extend beyond a cultic notion to an ethical one. In other words, though the legislator emphasizes the physical appearance of the priests in Leviticus 21, their holy appearance seems intended to bring to mind a view of holiness that is more than cultic.

Second, from the list concerning sacrificial animals (Lev. 22.17-25) Chapter 6 makes a case for viewing the term תמים as symbolic of the divine holiness which the Israelites were to emulate. That is, on the presupposition that the parallel drawn between priests and sacrificial animals in Leviticus 21–22 is important for their interpretation, I argued that the appearance of תמים animals performed the same function which I assigned to the appearance of the קדש priests: not only did the appearance of these animals symbolize divine holiness, but it also served as a means for Israel's sanctification. Several further observations, made from a cognitive linguistic perspective, strengthen this argument concerning the symbolic meaning of תמים in Leviticus 22. First, since their appearance comes to us within texts, Chapter 6 contends that one must interpret how the *terms* describing the physical appearance of the priests (i.e. קדש) and animals (i.e. תמים) relate to the idea of divine holiness symbolized in Leviticus 21–22. This observation has two implications for the meaning of תמים within Leviticus 22. On the one hand, the parallel relationship between the lists suggests that the terms קדש and תמים are closely related in meaning within this context. On the other hand, since I argue that the term קדש would possibly evoke an idea of holiness that surpasses a cultic meaning, when applied to the 'defect' (מום) free priests in Leviticus 21, the chapter suggests that the term תמים would do the same when used of the 'defect' (מום) free animals in Leviticus 22. Thus, it seems that the term תמים may evoke an ethical idea of holiness that the Israelites were expected to emulate. Second, Chapter 6 contends that the close correspondence the legislator has forged between priests and sacrificial animals within Leviticus 21–22 may also encourage one to access the domain of meaning תמים has when applied to humans (i.e. human 'integrity'). Third, Leviticus 22 presents the תמים character of the sacrificial animals as that which achieves a human's 'acceptance' (רצון) by Yahweh and this observation may further encourage one to view תמים as symbolic of a human quality.

For these reasons Chapter 6 concludes that, in the post-crystallization period of interpretation, a reader of Leviticus 21–22 may access an ethical domain of תמים (i.e. human 'integrity') when used of the sacrificial animals and associate this domain of meaning with the idea of 'holiness' (קדש) expected of the Israelites. If this conclusion is correct, it strengthens my argument that P views human 'integrity' as part of what it means to 'be holy' (cf. Chapter 5). Moreover, this conclusion supports my larger hypothesis that there is an ethical aspect to P's idea of holiness which has gone unnoticed by scholars, probably because they have not paid sufficient attention to the symbolic meaning of P's ritual texts.

Areas for Future Research Arising from This Study

There are several areas for future research arising from the present study. The first concerns the relationship between ritual and ethics in Leviticus. Previous attempts to resolve this issue are largely nuanced versions of one of either two approaches to the problem. The first is to argue that actions which lead to ritual impurity symbolize immoral behaviour which leads to impurity and expulsion from the land. For example, one may think of Hoffmann's suggestion that impurity arising from the disease צרעת represents those immoral practices that degrade the fabric of society.[1] Accordingly, by avoiding certain actions, which transgress ritual regulations, an Israelite was dissuaded from engaging in the corresponding immoral actions. The second, more recent, approach is to view the two systems as independent of one another. The main proponent of this view is Klawans who rejects the idea that there is a completely integrated symbolic system of impurity that embraces both ritual and

---

1. „Da nun der Leprosy als Sinnbild der Verbrechen gegen die Nebenmenschen gilt, so muss der davon Behaftete die ganze Gesellschaft meiden und einsam ausserhalb des Lagers wohnen.—Die Gesellschaft hat aber nur dann das Recht und die Pflicht, die ihr Schaden bringenden Elemente von sich auszuscheiden, wenn sie sich als eine Vereinigung Gleichgesinnter im Dienste Gottes Stehender betrachten darf. Eine Vereinigung zu egoistischen Zwecken darf ebensowenig den ihr Schadenden verbannen, wie etwa eine Societät von Kaufleuten ihren Concurrenten oder eine Räuberbande die ehrlichen Leute, deren Verrath sie fürchtet. Daher wird der Aussätzige nicht eher unrein, bis der als Vermittler des Gottesdienstes dastehende Priester ihn für unrein erklärt. Erst dann erscheint der Aussatz als Symbol eines Uebels, welche die Dienste Gottes stehende Gesellschaft gefährdet und benachtheiligt, und das aus der Gesellschaft zu verbannen, man berechtigt und verpflichtet ist" (Hoffmann, *Das Buch Leviticus*, pp. 317-18).

moral impurity.[2] According to him the impurity arising from both ritual and moral transgressions is real and a threat to Israel. The purity system does not encourage moral behaviour but the need to contain ritual impurity.

The present study may point to a third way of conceiving the relationship between ritual and ethics. I have argued that one of the functions of the ritual texts was to persuade the Israelites to be holy. Against Hoffmann, these texts do not present cultic misdemeanours as symbolic of immoral practices but serve to dissuade the reader from experiencing the reality represented by a period of uncleanness, namely exile from the land. Against Klawans, my argument that P's ritual texts persuaded the Israelites to be holy by associating uncleanness with a punitive 'exclusion from Yahweh's immediate presence' makes it seem likely that ritual and moral impurity comprise a single symbolic system in Leviticus. Both seek to dissuade the Israelites from rebelling against Yahweh by ignoring his cultic and ethical commandments. However, it still remains necessary to establish how this 'system' can be articulated more clearly.

The second area for further research arising from the present work relates to what it means to make כפר in 'cultic impurity' contexts. Does it mean to 'propitiate', 'expiate', 'purge', or 'ransom'? Though much has been written on this subject, recent scholars have commonly assumed that sin is not presupposed when כפר is made for ritually 'unclean' people. While the present study does not argue that such people are guilty of specific sin, it was proposed that, in their particular life circumstances, P has made them symbolize the relationship between sinful humanity and God. Their 'uncleanness' educates the Israelites that sinful humanity (בשר, Leviticus 12–15) must dwell apart from God's presence for it stands under his judgment (i.e. צרעת, Leviticus 13). However, God accepts sinful humanity back into his presence by the making of כפר. Interpreted in this way it may not be necessary to restrict the meaning of כפר to that of 'purification' but to view it as encompassing the idea of 'propitiation'. This area of research requires further attention.

Third, related to the previous point, the present study suggests that P viewed humanity as generally sinful. Since this idea is rejected by Jewish interpreters my proposal, in this regard, requires further assessment.

Finally the proposal that there is an ethical aspect to P's view of holiness requires a reassessment of the various historical contexts scholars have proposed as the setting for H. The results of both the Wellhausen and Knohl/ Milgrom schools of thought are largely dependent on what they consider is H's divergent view of holiness. In other words, the periods of history which these scholars suggest account for H are determined according to when they think a priestly school might have critiqued the cult in such a way that it led

2. Klawans, *Impurity and Sin in Ancient Judaism*, pp. 36-38.

to the extension of 'holiness' from the sanctuary to the laity.[3] In view of my contention that an ethical concern underlies P's view of holiness, this approach to the dating of H seems questionable.

3. Klawans has recently argued that scholars should allow for 'more critical reflection on the precise nature of the prophetic ethical advance. But turning to history, it is also important to think critically on when—or if—such an advance *ever* took place. Considering the fact that Third Isaiah (58.1-5) was complaining about some of the same issues as Amos (2.6-8), how can we be so sure that some substantive ethical advance was made in the eighth or seventh century B.C.E.' (Klawans, 'Methodology and Ideology in the Study of Priestly Ritual', pp. 12-13)?

THE RATIONALE FOR THE SELECTION OF CLEAN AND UNCLEAN ANIMALS IN LEVITICUS 11[1]

My exegesis of Leviticus 11 (Chapter 3) suggests that the selection of the various animals, and their identification as either clean or unclean, may have fulfilled a theological purpose. This suggestion does not imply that Israel had no dietary restrictions before the composition of Leviticus 11.[2] To the contrary, it seems likely that the pre-existing dietary significance of some animals would account for why they are included within the dietary regulations. Houston argues that, with the exception of the prohibition against eating all the creatures that 'swarm upon the ground', Israel's cultic customs reflect those of other cultures in the ANE.[3] If my interpretation of Leviticus 11 is correct, it seems possible that the legislator commandeers largely pre-existing dietary customs and fashions them into a text that is intended to facilitate Israel's commitment to Yahweh (cf. Lev. 11.43-45).[4] This idea allows for the possibility, Houston points out, that '[e]ven if the priests took over old customs, they could have reinterpreted them and given them new meaning'.[5]

1. For a comprehensive review and assessment of previous explanations for the rationale by which animals are identified as clean or unclean in Leviticus 11 see Houston, *Purity and Monotheism*, pp. 68-123; Jiří Moskala, 'Categorization and Evaluation of Different Kinds of Interpretation of the Laws of Clean and Unclean Animals in Leviticus 11', *BR* 66 (2001), pp. 5-41.

2. The 'dietary regulations' in Deuteronomy 14 are commonly assumed to post-date those found in Leviticus 11 (see W.L. Moran, 'The Literary Connection between Lev. 11:13-19 and Deut. 14:12-18', *CBQ* 28 [1966], pp. 271-77).

3. Houston, *Purity and Monotheism*, pp. 124-217.

4. Heinisch similarly suggests that the legislator of the food laws has taken over or assumed old existing rites. However, he does not suggest that they are re-fashioned to achieve the theological purpose I have suggested here. Heinisch, *Das Buch Leviticus*, p. 56.

5. Houston comments further that 'it grossly overestimates the power and intellectual independence of the priesthood to suppose that they could "impose" laws in food, of all things, without any reference to current custom. What they could do would be to support one tradition in their society against others.' And after reviewing archaeological data he concludes that '[t]he position is, then, that the biblical system of rules arose in a setting that was eminently compatible with it: it required no sharp changes in habitual

For example, the legislator may have given animals that the Israelites *unconsciously* avoided as food, *conscious* rationales for their uncleanness. Perhaps this process occurred with the creatures that 'swarm on the ground', since there is no evidence that other ANE cultures legislated against the eating of these.[6] If my suggestion that Genesis 1–3 is presupposed as important for the interpretation of Leviticus 11 (see Chapter 3), then it seems possible that the legislator identifies either the close relationship these animals have with the cursed 'ground' or their sharing of a serpent-like mode of locomotion (cf. Lev. 11.42) as a conscious reason for avoiding them. And within the progression of the regulations as a whole, this identification serves to emphasize the relationship between 'uncleanness' and the 'death' of Adam and Eve in Genesis 3.

However, from what has just been said, it is apparent that the present study reaches a different conclusion from that advocated by Houston in his analysis of the rationale underlying the selection of animals, and their identification as clean or unclean, in Leviticus 11. It will be helpful to review and evaluate Houston's explanation, in this regard, before contributing my own suggestion for such a rationale.

Walter Houston, Purity and Monotheism (1993)

Houston's initial examination of Leviticus 11 is diachronic, after which he offers a synchronic interpretation, taking into account H's final redaction of this chapter.[7] Since his synchronic conclusions are dependent on his diachronic arguments, our assessment can be limited to his explanation of the latter.

Beginning with vv. 2b-40, which he assigns to P, he develops an historical explanation for the cultic status acquired by the animals in this text.[8] Founda-

---

dietary and cultic practices general in the land and its environs at least since the beginning of the Middle Bronze Age. This is especially true of the accepted dietary and sacrificial customs in Israel' (Houston, *Purity and Monotheism*, pp. 20, 122, 177).

6. This is not to say that creatures which 'swarmed upon the ground' were eaten in such cultures, just that there is no evidence of legislation against such a practice in the ANE.

7. Houston maintains that the H redactor is responsible for vv. 41-45 and identifies vv. 1-2a and 46-47 as the work of a later editor (*Purity and Monotheism*, pp. 230, 248-53).

8. Apart from discussing what may account for the cultic status of the various animals mentioned in Leviticus 1, Houston also includes an examination of P's legislation on 'contact impurity' within Leviticus 11 (e.g. vv. 8, 11, 24-40). He argues that the prohibitions against touching unclean foods served as a warning to avoid customs that are dangerous to the Israelite society. '[U]ncleanness is thought of here as a contagious force, which may be transmitted from objects to people, and from the source of unclean-

tional for his study is the presupposition that 'the text [of Leviticus 11] is not concerned to impose a system on the populace in defiance of current custom, but rather to integrate custom into its system'.[9] Thus, Houston aims to iden-

ness to vessels. In dealing with unclean animals in this way, the text puts them in the same category with sexual sources of pollution, with "leprosy", and with human corpses. There is of course no surprise in this; the "implicit meanings" of unclean animals in the cultural background embrace those dangers perceived as most serious within the explicit social structure' (p. 245). But Houston sees the more immediate use of the prescriptions concerning 'contact impurity' as the 'defence of the sanctuary' for preserving Yahweh's presence (p. 245). One difficulty with this proposal, as Houston acknowledges, is that the sanctuary is not mentioned in Leviticus 11. To overcome this difficulty he appeals to the 'the symbolism of vermin as breaching the boundaries set within human society' (p. 246). He has in mind the eight 'swarming' (שרץ) animals mentioned in vv. 24-28 and in his opinion the boundaries threatened by these possibly symbolize not only those of the sanctuary but also its sacred personnel. Houston postulates that this concern, that any breach of purity within the camp would threaten the sanctity of the sanctuary, must reflect a vision of Israel 'as an armed camp surrounding the tabernacle of the God of Israel in close array and living so closely within the influence of its holiness that any pollution pollutes the sanctuary' (p. 247). He speculates that the historical context of such a vision was possibly 'the programme of a priestly elite of the *gôlâ* who in exile laid plans for the restoration of the community after a new Exodus' (p. 247).

However, the rationale by which Houston explains the laws on 'contact impurity' (Lev. 11.24-40) is only as certain as the historical context he thinks is presupposed by this text. The most likely time of its composition, he suggests, is the 'situation' one can 'envisage in which this vision could have arisen of the people of Israel in close array and living so closely within the influence of its holiness that any pollution pollutes the sanctuary itself' (p. 247). Suggesting that this time must have been the exilic or postexilic period he asserts that '[w]hile there can be no certainty that this is indeed the context in which we should understand the priestly work, it has the advantage of giving more practical significance to the historicizing form in which it is set than any other view' (p. 247). But, as Houston acknowledges, it is difficult to find certainty when attempting to identify a text's historical context. It would seem that the main weakness in his proposal relates to his presupposition that legislation on 'contact impurity' has in mind the threat impurity poses to the sanctuary. In the absence of any reference to the sanctuary he proposes that this concern may be inferred from the reference to eight 'swarming' animals (vv. 24-28) symbolized 'as breaching the boundaries set within human society' (p. 246). While I admit that the difficulty with these animals has, in part, to do with their ability to enter houses, it is not clear to me why they should bring to mind a possible threat to a sanctuary which is not mentioned. Therefore, though possible, for the time being we may put aside Houston's suggestion for why these animals are mentioned. Douglas, who understands Houston's explanation as treating 'the Levitical scheme as a relic of a pastoral way of life', suggests that for 'this to be serious there would need to be a theory of why some relics remain strong when their supporting context has passed away, while others are forgotten' (Douglas, *Leviticus as Literature*, p. 143). By anchoring the rationale for the selection of certain animals as clean or unclean in the context of the Pentateuch the present study avoids this weakness.

9. Houston, *Purity and Monotheism*, p. 236.

tify pre-existing customs, from both biblical and non-biblical sources, and explain how the redactor(s) have employed these to reinforce adherence to a (monotheistic) system of worship. A summary of his interpretation follows.

First, in attempting to account for the prescriptions concerning 'beasts' (בהמה); sea creatures; flying creatures (vv. 2b-23), Houston begins by observing that the clean 'beasts' (בהמה, vv. 2b-8) correspond to what was sacrificed by Semitic peoples. He argues that the criteria used to identify clean 'beasts'

> are derived…by comparison between the characteristics of the known sacrificial beasts, cattle, sheep and goats (and fallow deer?), and the known non-sacrificial beasts, particularly, it would be natural to expect, the domestic ones: dog, ass and pig.[10]

He suggests that the alignment of the clean beasts with those used within the cult was a means by which the Israelites could partake in the wider cultic practices (e.g. the animal sacrifices) which ensured God's blessing of them.[11] This view of the purpose fulfilled by the prescriptions for clean beasts informs Houston's wider reading of P's dietary prescriptions (i.e. vv. 2b-40). Presupposing a concentric organization of animals, people, and space within P's worldview, and based on his view that the prescriptions concerning beasts are formulated upon what was customarily sacrificed by Semitic peoples, he concludes that

> it is not the outer boundary—among the animals, that between clean and unclean—that is the key to their meaning, but the inner one, that marking off the sacrificial animals and the sacred realm. It is not so much that the sacrificial animals are a subset taken out of the edible animals (though this may be true in a historical sense), but that the edible animals are an extension of the set of the sacrificial animals at a lower level of significance. Since we find wild animals accepted for sacrifice at several other sites, it is likely that the whole set of clean animals are those accepted for sacrifice somewhere, though Jerusalem restricted victims to domestic animals.[12]

Therefore the significance of the clean animals within the legislator's system is that they represent what is acceptable within the cultic setting which was the source of blessing for P.[13] Nevertheless one is entitled to ask how Houston's explanation accounts for the criteria governing cleanness in sea creatures, which are not sacrificed in Israel, and birds. The possible answer is, according to Houston, that the legislator desired to give comprehensive prescriptions for

---

10. He cautions against the conclusion that the endorsement of these customs reflects ethnocentricity, on the part of the priests, or an expression of monotheistic Yahwism (Houston, *Purity and Monotheism*, p. 233).

11. Houston, *Purity and Monotheism*, p. 238.

12. Houston, *Purity and Monotheism*, p. 238.

13. Houston, *Purity and Monotheism*, p. 238.

the cleanness of all animal categories.[14] And as he claims is the case for the selection of clean beasts, he contends that the legislator likewise defined the cleanness of fish and birds on the basis of pre-existing dietary customs.

With regard to the sea creatures (vv. 9-12), Houston provides a persuasive account for why only animals with 'fins' and 'scales' were considered clean.[15]

> We have to assume...that the otherwise learned authors knew little about marine zoology. What they did know was that most of the fish normally eaten by Jews came from creatures that had scales and fins, and also perhaps that many others would be likely to be unacceptable because of their feeding habits... Hence, simply in order not to say nothing about a great section of the animal kingdom, the criterion of scales and fins was laid down.[16]

With regard to winged-creatures (vv. 13-23), citing parallels from certain ANE cultures, Houston suggests that they are possibly drawn from an 'international cultic tradition'.[17]

However, though Houston argues that the key to the meaning of P's dietary rules is to be found on the 'inner boundary' of Israel's threefold concentric view of her world (i.e. holy, clean, unclean), he still allows for the binary organization of Israelite life (clean vs. unclean; holy vs. common; cf. Lev. 10.10) to play a possible role in the shape of these rules. This move presupposes that various animals within the ANE had come to symbolize good and evil.[18] Thus, Houston proposes that the binary opposition of clean and unclean animals could still draw on such symbolism to

> symbolize the order of society or the disorder that surrounds and threatens it. The respect for God represented by abstinence from unclean flesh is at the same time respect for the explicit structure of society and acceptance that God's blessing is reserved for what is righteous and ordered according to traditional norms.[19]

Accordingly, Houston finds that two principles may account for how animals were assigned to clean and unclean categories within P's cultic dietary laws. On the one hand, the clean animals represented the inner circle of Israel's concentric view of the world. When it restricted its diet to clean animals it partook in what was acceptable for the cult and this was its source of bless-

14. Houston, *Purity and Monotheism*, p. 235.
15. I shall use this part of Houston's explanation below.
16. Houston, *Purity and Monotheism*, pp. 234-35.
17. He goes on to say that '[t]his is likely to be true at least of the original eight... No doubt they would be taken as representative of all birds with associations with bloodshed and the eating of blood and waste matter..., which made them unacceptable within the sacred sphere, and thus dangerous to the purity of the congregation' (Houston, *Purity and Monotheism*, p. 236).
18. Houston, *Purity and Monotheism*, pp. 21-25.
19. Houston, *Purity and Monotheism*, p. 239.

ing. On the other hand, it was possible that by excluding certain animals from its diet, the prescriptions of Leviticus 11 motivated the Israelites to abandon foreign cultic practices that would detract from their blessing.

Houston concludes his examination of the selection of animals in Leviticus 11 with an investigation of the prohibition against eating 'swarmers' (שרץ) in vv. 41-45, which he attributes to the H redactor.[20] Considering that this text comes immediately before H's characteristic exhortation to 'be holy' (vv. 44-45), he argues that this prohibition against eating 'swarming' creatures is representative of all those things Israel must avoid if it is to 'be holy'.[21] Nevertheless, observing that this is a strange location for what would be 'the apparently least likely of all of the possible breaches of the law', he proceeds to investigate what historical context might have made this prohibition such a poignant representation for practices that would be destructive for Israel's holiness.[22] He concludes that by prohibiting these animals H was responding to a 'cult of the dead'. Thus

> the priestly author may be seen as reacting against a particular extreme of an unofficial cult of the dead that did indeed involve the eating of such things as mice. The prohibition of their eating would then be required not just by system but by the real necessities of the day.[23]

If this conclusion is correct, then the position of this prohibition immediately before the call to 'be holy' would make sense.

> The prohibition [i.e. against eating swarming things]–implicitly all the prohibitions—can then be seen as a strong assertion that the powers of death and disorder must be excluded from the realm where the people of Israel dwell with their God. In confrontation with those who were employing the same symbolism in the opposite sense [ie. Cult of the dead—disorder] it functions as a call for the restoration of the traditional order of society with the proper relations of power and the traditional sexual restrictions.[24]

Houston's consideration of the H redaction of Leviticus 11 leads him to conclude that 'the function of the law [i.e. Leviticus 11] in Leviticus is to preserve the people's holiness in the sense of their dedication to their one God'.[25] The symbolism of the chapter is suggested as facilitating this function on two levels. On the one hand it functions as a 'bare sign' by recalling 'the separation demanded from all strange gods and all immoral behaviour, and the

---

20. Houston, *Purity and Monotheism*, pp. 248-53.
21. Houston, *Purity and Monotheism*, p. 250.
22. Houston, *Purity and Monotheism*, p. 250.
23. Houston, *Purity and Monotheism*, p. 251.
24. This is another example of the legislator using binary opposition to promote order within Israel (cf. Houston, *Purity and Monotheism*, p. 252).
25. Houston, 'Towards an Integrated Reading', p. 157.

cleaving to Yahweh alone'. On the other hand it is 'a true symbol, that is, a *motivated* sign, which carries its meaning within itself'. Thus, the first symbolizes the separation and the second enforces 'the separation of Israelites from all such cults'.[26]

Evaluation. Though I shall make use of Houston's explanation for why the clean sea creatures are limited to those having fins and scales, I find the following problems with his interpretation of what accounts for the distinction between clean and unclean animal classes in Leviticus 11. First, he is not consistent in the application of his presupposition that the key to the meaning of the clean animals is found within the inner boundary of Israel's concentric view of the world. For example, though it is helpfully applied to understanding the distinction between clean and unclean 'beasts' (vv. 1-8) Houston does not use it when accounting for the same distinction among other categories of animals. He attempts to overcome this problem by arguing that the legislator extends his prescriptions on clean 'beasts' (vv. 1-8) into the realms of water and flying creatures for the sake of being comprehensive. But the difficulty with this suggestion is that it excludes valid data from consideration before it is even examined. In other words, when identifying a possible source of the clean/unclean distinction within Lev. 11.1-23 he first omits vv. 9-23 and establishes a principle from vv. 1-8. He then overcomes the difficulty that his principle does not fit vv. 9-23 by speculating that the legislator desired to be comprehensive.

Making this approach even more difficult to accept is that one of these categories, namely that of flying creatures, contains animals that were sacrificed (i.e. birds). Yet instead of identifying the distinction between clean and unclean birds as corresponding to the 'inner boundary' of P's concentric view of the world, as he does for the 'beasts' (vv. 1-8), he proposes that unclean birds are only identified on the basis that they were (universally?) held as unclean. The question that needs to be answered is why would the legislator, who Houston argues desired to extend his treatment of the 'beasts' to other animal categories, feel it necessary to change the principle according to which the clean were distinguished from the unclean? It is accepted that fish were not sacrificed so that clean fish cannot correspond to fish sacrificed by Semitic peoples, but it seems odd that the legislator should not apply this principle to birds.

Second, Houston's proposal for why all 'swarming' creatures are identified as unclean in Lev. 11.41-42 seems overly speculative. He argues that the prohibition against eating one of these creatures may relate to their use within a 'cult of the dead' that appears to be operative at the time of Third Isaiah (cf. Isa. 65.3-5; 66.17). He suggests that these verses

26. Houston, *Purity and Monotheism*, p. 253.

offer some consistent evidence of a cult of the dead carried on in cemeteries and marked by the deliberate sacrifice and consumption of unclean food. In the case of 66.17 this would appear to have gone to the extreme of eating not just food generally recognized as unclean, like swine (65.4), but food not generally recognized as food. Of course, an interpretation is possible...that takes Lev. 11.41-42 as prior...and Isa. 66.17 as a satirical and ironic inversion of priestly standards. But assuming my interpretation can be sustained, the priestly author may be seen as reacting against a particular extreme of an unofficial cult of the dead that did indeed involve the eating of such things as mice.[27]

But how certain is Houston's reconstruction of the historical setting of this material? The lack of certainty in dating biblical texts is reflected by the conflicting results in the literature. Houston does not engage the proposals of Milgrom and Knohl that Leviticus undergoes its final stage of editorial work (by H) in the late eighth century BCE.[28] If these scholars are correct it introduces uncertainty into Houston's conclusions because, even if the cults he has in mind existed in pre-exilic times, the idea that a priestly group felt compelled to compose Leviticus 11 in order to prohibit the adoption of such pagan practices becomes less plausible.

Even if it could be demonstrated that Leviticus 11 were composed as late as postexilic times, this would not prove that this text presupposes knowledge of these particular cults as important for its interpretation. In this regard, Houston is liable to the same criticisms made of Gorman in Chapter 2.[29] By contrast, as argued in Chapter 3, Leviticus 11 presupposes knowledge of Genesis 1–3 as essential for its interpretation. As we shall see, this insight provides a more direct explanation for the inclusion of the animals that 'swarm upon the ground', than the suggestion that this prohibition reflects a *possible* practice that Isaiah *may* have referred to, at a time that is *not necessarily* contemporaneous with the composition of Leviticus 11.

Third, related to the previous criticism, Houston attributes too much significance to the symbolic meaning that the animals may have had in their original socio-historical context. In this sense, his work is analogous to the over-reliance on etymological studies in biblical semantics, at the expense of analyzing how words are *used* within a particular context.[30] Though I agree

27. Houston, *Purity and Monotheism*, p. 251.

28. Houston does not explain why he cannot deal with Milgrom's proposal (*Purity and Monotheism*, p. 249; cf. Milgrom, *Leviticus 1–16*, pp. 13-25; Knohl, *Sanctuary of Silence*, passim).

29. See pages 30-34.

30. Houston is aware that he is not interpreting the significance of animals as they occur within the text of Leviticus 11. On the one hand, this awareness is reflected in his stated interest that it is 'not so much the literary units' but 'the themes they encapsulate or point to, and these are not necessarily strictly confined to the units I have indicated'

that pre-existing cultic categories of animals might be partially determinative for the legislator's inclusion of them within the dietary regulations of Leviticus 11, it is argued here that the final symbolic meaning of these animals relies on how they are *used* within the text (see critique of Gorman in Chapter 2). Indeed, the latter approach yields more certain results considering the uncertain and hypothetical nature of reconstructed historical settings.

Despite the fact that I do not completely accept Houston's diachronic conclusions, his demonstration that the dietary customs of Israel are, with the exception of the prohibition against eating creatures that 'swarm upon the ground', at home among other cultures of the ANE is useful. It may shed light on why the legislator selects particular animals to achieve his theological purpose. For example, when the legislator desires to bring the idea of life to the reader's mind he mentions the sacrificial animals as clean; when he aims to imply the idea of death he refers to carnivores as unclean. In this sense, Leviticus 11 draws on Israel's pre-understanding of the animal world but uses it to perform a different function.

There are two implications this last insight has for identifying the rationale(s) underlying the selection of clean and unclean animals of Leviticus 11. First, the rationale(s) for why some animals are unclean no doubt remains in some way continuous with that responsible for the pre-existing custom. For this reason, archaeological studies and ancient interpreters may facilitate the identification of these rationales.[31] Second, it remains possible that the legislator alters the rationale of an existing custom, or introduces a new class of unclean animal, in order to achieve his goal. This possibility seems even more plausible considering that Leviticus 11 comes, first of all, within the narrative of the Pentateuch: by associating words, that have gained symbolic meaning through narrative development, with particular animals, the legislator may introduce a novel interpretation for why a particular animal is unclean. With these two possibilities in mind we may now begin the task of identifying the rationale underlying the selection of the animals, and why they are identified as either clean or unclean. *My interpretation proceeds on the assumption that, as literature, the dietary regulations are intended to encourage Israel to avoid exclusion from God's immediate presence (i.e. death) and embrace life in his presence through obedience to his will (cf. Chapter 3).*

(Houston, *Purity and Monotheism*, p. 230). Thus, for Houston, the dietary regulations are not literature so much as prescribed ritual practices. On the other hand, his exegesis at times relies on his hypothetical redactional reconstruction of this material. As Chapter 3 argued, many of these 'redactional seams' may be accounted for by the legislator's use of rhetorical progression.

31. The work of Houston is particularly helpful in this respect (*Purity and Monotheism*, Chapters 4–5).

A Literary Proposal

Lev. 11.1-8. The 'Beasts'

The section most obviously concerned with national diet (see Chapter 3) categorizes Israel's sacrificial quadrupeds as 'clean' food. But why are four unclean animals included within this section? If we may assume that the sacrificial animals represent 'life' as opposed to 'death' (i.e. uncleanness), then it would seem that these unclean animals emphasize this fact by almost conforming to the category of sacrificial animals. The camel and pig were possibly viewed as similar to the sacrificial animals on account of their domestic status.[32] Moreover, Houston has demonstrated that within the ANE the pig was regarded as both a carnivore and a scavenger.[33] If my understanding of Leviticus 11 is correct (cf. Chapter 3) this perspective on the pig may indicate that the use of the sacrificial animals to symbolize life in these verses is enhanced by excluding a domestic animal that is associated with the death of other animals. The rock badger and hare are similar to the sacrificial animals in that they are herbivorous and they appear to 'chew the cud'.[34] The legislator may have selected these four animals to draw attention to the type of animal that is permitted, namely the sacrificial 'life-giving' quadrupeds.[35] In terms of my progressive rhetorical reading of Leviticus 11 (cf. Chapter 3),

32. Domesticated pigs and camels were present in pre-exilic times according to Houston, *Purity and Monotheism*, pp. 135-42.

33. Houston, *Purity and Monotheism*, pp. 31, 190-93.

34. Houston finds virtually no evidence that either of these animals were eaten in Palestine at the relevant time period. To my knowledge, there is no evidence of any symbolic meaning attached to these animals within the ANE. This observation does not mean that the Israelites did not have a pre-existing reason for not eating them. It may have been enough for the legislator that they did not contribute to the culinary life of Israel to include them in order to highlight those that did. See Houston, *Purity and Monotheism*, pp. 142-43.

35. Douglas has recently suggested that the 'blood prohibition' accounts for the animals mentioned in Lev. 11.1-8. She thinks that the clean animals are chosen because they are herbivores. This is plausible, but it does not explain why the herbivorous camel, hare, and rock badger are included as unclean (following Houston [see below] it would seem that the pig was considered a carnivore). Douglas contends that it is because the law concerning the sacrificial quadrupeds, 'once formulated in terms of hoofs and cud-chewing generates its own exceptions which are legislated against specifically' (Douglas, 'The Forbidden Animals in Leviticus', pp. 17-18). But if the rationale to begin with is to confine Israel's diet to herbivores why not simply permit all the domesticated animals (בהמה) and prohibit carnivores? The argument that the clean quadrupeds are chosen because they symbolize something as sacrificial animals is able to more directly account why four other (non-sacrificial) animals, that overlap with the sacrificial ones in how they are perceived by the Israelites (i.e. either because they are domesticated [e.g. pig; camel] or appear to chew the cud etc [e.g. hare; rock badger]), are excluded as unclean.

this interpretation means that the chapter as a whole moves from the topic of life (vv. 1-3) to death (vv. 28-42) followed by an exhortation to remain in the realm of life (i.e. holiness, vv. 43-45).

Lev. 11.9-12. The 'Sea Creatures'

An implicit rationale for why the legislator restricts clean sea creatures to those which have 'fins' and 'scales' is difficult to identify. Houston's contention that this restriction may reflect the kind of fish that the Israelites were accustomed with seems most plausible.[36] Because of his desire to recall the animal categories of Genesis 1 the legislator might have included 'sea creatures' and, as Houston suggests, he used two prominent characteristics of fish the Israelites ate to define a category of clean 'sea creature'.

Lev. 11.13-19. 'Winged Creatures of the Air'

A literary rationale may explain the exclusion of carnivorous birds as 'unclean' for food in vv. 13-19.[37] The relationship between 'death' and uncleanness does not become explicit until vv. 39-40, so the mention of these carnivorous birds possibly brings to mind the idea of death and this may anticipate the more direct treatment of this subject in what follows. It seems plausible to speculate that the legislator selects birds that his intended audience already views as unclean on account of their carnivorous behaviour.[38] This possibility would increase the likelihood that the reference to these birds brought to mind the idea of death.[39]

Lev. 11.20-23. Winged Creatures that Leap 'Upon the Ground'

A literary rationale for the prohibited insects of vv. 20-22 is not easily identified. However, that the winged insects that are permitted are those with legs

---

36. Though, this conclusion may depend on what kind of sea animal is referred to as a תחשים in Exod. 25.5; 26.14; 35.23; 36.19; 39.34; Num. 4.6. Many scholars have assumed that this refers to non-scaly sea animals such as dolphins, porpoises and dugong, however this is not certain and some commentators prefer to translate it as 'goat', assuming that it is an archaic form of תיש. See Childs, *Exodus*, p. 523; John I. Durham, *Exodus* (WBC, 2. Waco, TX: Word Books, 1987), p. 350. Alternatively, Frank Cross suggests that the term refers to 'an imported specially finished leather' (cited in Houston, *Purity and Monotheism*, pp. 234-35).

37. Though not all of the twenty birds mentioned are identifiable to modern scholars, most commentators follow the Talmudic tradition that each of them is carnivorous (cf. *Mishnah Ḥullin* 3.6). Snaith suggests that the mentioned birds are unclean on account of their association with fresh blood (*Leviticus and Numbers*, p. 63).

38. Carnivorous birds were prohibited as food in some other ANE cultures (Houston, *Purity and Monotheism*, p. 156).

39. Houston points out that the bird section is the first to simply name kinds that may not be eaten rather than list morphological characteristics for excluding them. This

which allow these animals 'to leap by them upon the ground' (לנתר בהן
על־הארץ, v. 21b) is interesting. Is it possible that it is the relationship an
insect bears to the 'ground' that is determinative of their purity status?[40] This
understanding would require that 'ground' has a symbolic meaning in this
verse. In fact, the phrase 'upon/over the ground' (על־הארץ) occurs 32 times
before Leviticus 11 within the Pentateuch. With the exception of four of
these (Gen. 19.23; 41.34; 42.6; Exod. 16.14) they occur within the first
creation account (Gen. 1.1-2.4; × 8) and the Noahic narrative (Genesis 6–9; ×
20). The first of these passages presents everything 'upon/over the ground' as
'good'. However, the 20 occurrences of this phrase within the second passage
are associated with the corruption of the ways of 'all flesh' (כל־בשר) 'upon
the earth' (Gen. 6.12; 7.21[× 2]); God's watery judgment on 'all flesh' 'upon
the earth' (Gen. 6.17; 7.4, 6, 10, 12, 17, 18, 19); the animals 'upon the earth'
(cf. Genesis 1) that Noah encloses on the Ark (Gen. 7.14); God's removal of
water 'upon the earth' (Gen. 8.1); the re-creation of Genesis 1 animal life
'upon the earth' (Gen. 8.17[× 2], 19); God's announcement of his covenant
of preservation of all animals that live 'upon the earth' (Gen. 9.14, 16, 17).
From these references it seems that the phrase is associated with notions of
creation and divine judgment.[41] In this connection, the reference to 'upon the
ground' in Lev. 11.21 may allude to the creation account of Genesis 1. Given
what I have argued is a relatively explicit reference to the serpent through the
singular use of the term 'belly' (גחון) outside of Genesis 3 in Lev. 11.42 (cf.
Gen. 3.14; Chapter 3), it seems possible that the identification of insects
which are not able to remove themselves from 'upon the ground' by hopping
as 'unclean' is meant to bring the cursed serpent to mind once again.[42]

observation may serve to emphasize that it is the relationship these birds have with death
that makes them unclean (*Purity and Monotheism*, p. 43).

40. One may object to this possibility by observing that the 'winged swarmers' (שרץ
העוף, vv. 20-23) are a subset of the 'flying creatures' (העוף) mentioned in vv. 13-19.
Thus, it could be asked, 'Would not those clean winged creatures that hop on the
"ground" spend relatively more time on the ground than the unclean winged creatures in
vv. 13-19?' But such a comparison is not invited. Milgrom cites Ramban as defining
שרץ העוף in relation to the העוף mentioned in vv. 13-19 according to their number of
legs. '[T]wo-legged winged creatures mostly fly, hence they are called birds (vv 13-19),
but four-legged creatures mostly walk and for this reasons constitute a discrete group'
(Milgrom, *Leviticus 1–16*, p. 664). If this definition is correct then we are intended to
view the שרץ העוף as a class of winged creature that is associated with the 'earth'. In
this regard, the legislator uses the observation that some of these use a form of locomotion which removes them from the 'earth' more than others to make an association
between 'uncleanness' and the symbolic meaning of 'earth'.

41. It is noteworthy that this relationship does not apply to the term 'earth' (ארץ) on
its own.

42. That is, not through their anatomical features but by their association with the
ground.

Lev. 11.29-38. The Eight Animals that 'Swarm upon the Ground'
Chapter 3 argued that the eight animals that 'swarm upon the ground' (השרץ
על־הארץ) recall the serpent of Genesis 3. Not only do they live close to the
'earth' (cf. previous point) but they make one unclean by defiling clean food
(the latter may be analogous to the serpent's temptation of Eve to eat the
prohibited fruit). In addition to these observations, these animals are used to
bring together the ideas of 'death' and 'serpent': these serpent-like creatures
defile clean food when they die (Lev. 11.29-38). Houston's suggestion that
these eight animals are merely representatives of all animals that 'swarm' on
the ground overlooks the delimitation of them as a group '*among the* swarming things' (בשרץ, v. 29) and '*among all* that swarm' (בכל־השרץ, v. 31).[43]
Within the narrative of the Pentateuch it is possible that additional significance is given to these eight by establishing them as serpent-like.

Lev. 11.39-40. The Clean 'Beasts' which Die
As argued in Chapter 3, the clean quadrupeds are re-introduced in vv. 39-40
to establish the symbolic source of uncleanness. Though they are clean for
food (cf. Lev. 11.1-4) they render one unclean after they 'die' (מות) of natural
causes. Once again, it is acknowledged that the first-readers may have already
considered the flesh of these animals as unclean when they died of natural
causes. If so, the innovation of the legislator is to infuse a new rationale for
avoiding this flesh by associating it with what is meant by the term מָוֶת in the
Pentateuch (cf. Genesis 2–3).

Lev. 11.44-46. Creatures which 'Swarm upon the Ground'
Finally, the chapter finishes (vv. 41-46) with numerous references to the need
to avoid eating those animals which 'swarm upon the ground'. The phrase
'upon the ground' recurs four times in these verses, possibly adding further
support to my claim that this provides the rationale for why the legislator
nominates particular insects as unclean in vv. 20-23. Similarly, Milgrom
suggests that 'it is the association with the earth, the sphere of death, that led
to the exclusion of all land swarmers from Israel's diet'.[44] However, though
he arrives at this conclusion on the assumption that there is an intentional
association between the term 'earth' (ארץ) and 'Sheol' (שאל), it seems less
speculative to propose that the idea of the 'earth' being cursed is responsible
for their identification as unclean.[45]

---

43. More specifically, Houston suggests that these eight animals 'stand for any creatures that may invade the home of storeroom though they belong, ideally, elsewhere'
(Houston, *Purity and Monotheism*, p. 246).

44. Milgrom, *Leviticus 1–16*, p. 686.

45. Milgrom overlooks the possibility that a similar connection with the 'earth' may
account for why those insects that cannot hop are identified as unclean in Lev. 11.20-23
(*Leviticus 1–16*, p. 686).

Appendix 2

THE 'BURNT OFFERING' AS ISRAEL'S
'MOST HOLY' OFFERING *PAR EXCELLENCE*

The validity of the argument made in Chapter 5 requires that P's idea of holiness is latent within the prescription for the 'burnt offering' in Leviticus 1. Though P explicitly identifies the 'cereal offering' (מנחה), 'sin offering' (חטאת), and 'guilt offering' (אשם) as 'most holy',[1] it never uses the root קדש in connection with the 'burnt offering'.[2] However, that P knew of other offerings that were considered 'most holy' is implied by Num. 18.9a. Having informed Aaron that he had given him 'all the holy [offerings] of the Israelites' (לכל־קדשי בני־ישראל; Num. 18.8), Yahweh qualifies those that the priests may eat as

'*from* the most holy sacrifices, from the fire' (מקדש הקדשים מן־האש)

Those taken 'from the most holy' (מקדש הקדשים) are identified as the 'cereal offering', 'sin offering' and the 'guilt offering' (Num. 18.9b). In contrast to Snaith's conclusion to the contrary, Milgrom correctly observes that the partitive *mem* in מקדש הקדשים 'implies that there are other offerings of this type that are not the reserve of priests'.[3] In terms of the offerings prescribed in Leviticus 1–5, this observation leaves open the possibility that either, or both, the 'burnt offering' and 'peace offering' (שלמים) were considered 'most holy' despite never being identified as such.[4] There may have been contextual reasons governing the legislator's decision to identify the 'most holy' nature of some offerings but not others.[5] An attempt is made to unravel these contextual reasons in what follows.

---

1. Lev. 2.3, 10; 6.10, 18, 22, 7.1, 6; 10.12; 14.13.

2. Though see the discussion below concerning the legislator's command for 'most holy' sacrifices to be slaughtered at the place where the burnt offering is slaughtered.

3. Milgrom, *Leviticus 1–16*, p. 321. See also David P. Wright, 'Holiness (OT)', in *ABD*. III, pp. 237-49 (239).

4. A 'devoted thing' (חרם) is called 'most holy' to Yahweh (Lev. 27.28). However, the 'devoted things' refer to that which is devoted to Yahweh 'of man or beast and of the field' (מאדם ובהמה ומשדה). Since the term encompasses more than edible offerings it is not likely that they are among the 'most holy' offerings that the priests are warned not to eat in Num. 18.9.

5. A suggestion made by Kiuchi, *Leviticus*, p. 63. This possibility is overlooked by

It is possible to deduce that the 'burnt offering', and not the 'peace offering', was 'most holy' from an examination of how this phrase is used in relation to the מנחה, חטאת, and אשם offerings.[6] The phrase 'most holy' occurs within two contexts. First, when reference is made to the remaining edible parts of the מנחה, חטאת, and אשם offerings (Lev. 2.3, 10; 6.10, 22, 7.6; 10.12). Second, when it is stipulated that a particular offering should be slaughtered in the same place as the 'burnt offering' (Lev. 6.18; 7.2; 14.13)

Below I argue that both of these contexts make the use of the phrase 'most holy' unnecessary in connection with the 'burnt offering' and at the same time imply that the 'peace offering' did not have this status. After this argument is made I ask why the priests's מנחה and חטאת are not referred to as 'most holy' even though these offerings are referred to as such when offered by the laity. It is hoped that this study will provide further insight into the principle which governs the use of this phrase by P.

The Use of the Phrase 'Most Holy' to Protect the Remaining Edible Parts of Certain Offerings

Six times the legislator explicates his stipulation that the remaining edible parts of some offerings belong to Aaron and his sons with the phrase '[It is] most holy' ([הוא] קדש קדשים).[7] There are two sub-contexts in this regard, namely those addressed to the laity (Leviticus 1–5) and priests (Leviticus 6–7) respectively. Each of these is examined in turn below.

Passages Addressed to the Laity
When used in passages *addressed to the laity* the phrase 'most holy' seems to explain *why* the remaining edible parts of a particular offering *belong to the priests*.[8] Of the five sacrificial prescriptions addressed to the laity in Leviticus 1–5 (cf. Lev. 1.2; 4.2), the phrase occurs only in connection with the legislator's stipulation that the 'remainder' (הנתרת) of the 'cereal offering' *belongs to Aaron and his sons*' (לאהרן ולבניו, Lev. 2.3, 10). Significantly, the edible parts of the חטאת and אשם offerings are not mentioned in the prescriptions addressed to the laity, even though these offerings are elsewhere referred to as 'most holy'. This observation leads some scholars to regard Lev. 2.3, 10 as a later gloss,[9] but this overlooks two important contextual

---

Watts when he concludes that 'the observation that the *ōlāh* is especially sacred and important cannot be found in the biblical texts' (Watts, *Ritual as Rhetoric in the Book of Leviticus*, pp. 70-71).

6. Lev. 2.3, 10; 6.10, 18, 22; 7.2, 6; 10.12; 14.13.
7. Lev. 2.3, 10; 6.10, 22, 7.6; 10.12.
8. Kornfeld, *Levitikus*, p. 16; Hartley, *Leviticus*, p. 30; Kiuchi, *Leviticus*, p. 70.
9. Milgrom is somewhat inconsistent in his argument for why these verses are a

factors that seem to account for the presence of the phrase 'most holy' only within the prescription for the 'cereal offering' (Leviticus 2).

First, the prescription for the 'cereal offering', like all the prescriptions of Leviticus 1–5, is addressed 'to the Israelites' (אֶל־בְּנֵי יִשְׂרָאֵל, Lev. 1.2a; cf. 4.2a). In this regard it seems noteworthy that Lev. 2.3, 10 are the only occasions within Leviticus where it is specifically *the laity* who are informed of a sacrificial offering's 'most holy' nature.[10] Since it is used in relation to the rightful recipients of the offering's remaining edible portion, it is possible that its occurrence reflects the legislator's awareness that the 'cereal offering' was the only offering that the Israelites were liable to offer with the *intention* of eating. Two further observations may support this conclusion. First, the additional rite stipulated for the baked 'cereal offering', namely 'he shall deliver it' (הִגִּישָׁהּ, Lev. 2.8; 6.7), would appear to be aimed at ensuring that the 'cereal offering' was offered without any intention of benefiting from it materially. Observing that the term occurs in connection with the baked, but not the raw, 'cereal offering' Milgrom concludes that this additional rite was

> performed by the priest to show that the cereal offering was baked initially for the altar and not brought to the altar as an afterthought.[11]

But how could this rite prevent an offerer from bringing a baked 'cereal offering' as an afterthought? Would not the prohibition against adding yeast (Lev. 2.4) have served this purpose sufficiently?[12] Indeed, it is difficult to

latter addition. He begins by acknowledging that a surface reading of the stipulation that the remaining part of the baked 'cereal offering' will be 'for Aaron and his sons' (v. 10) contradicts Lev. 7.9 which indicates that the baked 'cereal offering' belongs to the officiating priest and not to his sons. However, he then observes that these verses are not necessarily contradictory because 'vv. 3-10 are addressed to the laity and not to the priests, and the fine distinction made by 7.9-10 would hardly be expected here... Moreover there may be no contradiction between the two passages, for in 7.9 the officiating priest, if he so desires, may share his perquisite with his fellow priests. That such a possibility is in fact presupposed by the text is shown by the distribution of the meat of the purification offering, which, though given to the officiant, may be eaten by any priest (6.19, 22). Thus, vv. 3 and 10 of this chapter refer not to the priestly owner of the cereal offering but to those who have the right to consume it, namely, the entire priestly cadre'. Milgrom appears to forget this conclusion at a latter point in his commentary when he states that vv. 3 and 10 'flatly contradict' Lev. 7.9 (*Leviticus 1–16*, pp. 187-88, 202; cf. Elliger, *Leviticus*, pp. 40, 44).

10. See observations concerning the 'most holy' חרם (Lev. 27.28) above.

11. Milgrom, *Leviticus 1–16*, p. 186.

12. Note that the absence of a prohibition against adding yeast to the raw 'cereal offering' probably supports this conclusion (Lev. 2.1-3). By simply prescribing the ingredients the legislator assumes that it is brought as an offering for the altar. He could safely assume that the raw 'cereal offering' had been brought without the offerer having entertained the prospect of eating it at home. By contrast, the prohibition against yeast in

explain the yeast-prohibition in any other way than that it served to remind the offerer that the 'cereal offering' was for the altar from the outset (Lev. 2.4).[13] As for the term הגישה, it seems more likely that it reminded the offerers that their baked 'cereal offering' was fully relinquished to Yahweh even though it would not be completely burnt.

Second, Leviticus 2 falls within a different literary context from that of the 'sin offering' (Lev. 4.1-5.13) and 'guilt offering' (Lev. 5.14-26). Whereas Leviticus 4–5 presupposes a situation in which a 'person' (נפש) has 'sinned' (חטא; cf. Lev. 4.2; 5.14), the prescription for the 'cereal offering' presumes a case in which a 'human' (אדם) brings an offering (Lev. 1.2). That is, the ritual for the 'cereal offering' comes as one of three prescriptions in Leviticus 1–3 that are subsumed under the general heading 'When a human from among you brings an offering' (אדם כי־יקריב מכם, Lev. 1.2).[14]

This context may help explain why the legislator chose to use 'most holy' in connection with only the remaining edible parts of the 'cereal offering' within the five prescriptions of Leviticus 1–5. The existence of another offering within Leviticus 1–3 that the offerer was entitled to eat (i.e. the שלמים, Leviticus 3; 7.11-21) presumably compelled the legislator to ensure that this did not happen with the other edible offering within this context. Moreover, this interpretation may also make sense of why the entire 'cereal offering' was presented to the altar, when this happened with only the burnt parts of other 'most holy' offerings, which the offerer may not have considered eating for other reasons (i.e. sin).[15] It was to remind the offerer that he had to relinquish the complete offering regardless of the fact that it would not all be burnt.

My examination of how 'most holy' is used in Leviticus 2 suggests that it was employed to ensure that the 'cereal offering' was offered without any intention of eating it. A corollary of this observation is that the 'peace offer-

---

Lev. 2.4 displays the legislator's concern that the offering be totally relinquished to Yahweh from the very moment a person determined to offer a 'cereal offering'.

13. After all, since yeast could be used in the offerings of the first fruits (Lev. 23.17, 20) it seems that it was only a problem in relation to the altar (Exod. 23.18; 34.25). Thus, to prohibit the addition of yeast was presumably a sign that this offering was destined for the altar.

14. As noted by Averbeck, 'Lev 1–3 form a unified whole. The repetition of the introductory formula and address to "the Israelites" in Lev. 4.1-2 (cf. 1:1-2) separates the rules for sin and guilt offerings in Lev. 4.1–6.7 from those in chs. 1–3' (Richard E. Averbeck, 'עלָה', in *NIDOTTE*, III, pp. 405-15 [408]). However, his conclusion that this is a literary reflection 'of the historical reality that before and even after the construction of the tabernacle, the burnt offerings and peace offerings, and the grain and drink offerings that normally came with them, constituted a system of offerings used by the faithful at solitary Yahwistic altars outside the tabernacle' seems unnecessary.

15. Milgrom, *Leviticus 1–16*, p. 186.

ing' was not regarded as 'most holy' because it was offered by the laity with an intention of eating some of it (cf. Lev. 7.11-21). This observation makes sense of the absence of the phrase in connection with the 'burnt offering'. Since it was completely burnt, to offer this offering with the intention of eating it was impossible. This is also the view of Rendtorff.

> Es ist aber auffallend, daß der Ausdruck *kodesch kodaschim* bei der *'ola* selbst nicht vorkommt, was seinen Grund darin hat, daß keine Opferteile zur weiteren Verwendung übrigbleiben.[16]

Passages Addressed to the Priests

That the phrase 'most holy' was used to avoid a potential mishandling of an offering is also suggested by its occurrence in passages addressed to priests (Lev. 6.10, 22; 10.12). In what follows I shall argue that, in contrast to the practical concerns underlying its use in Leviticus 2, the phrase is implemented in these passages to prevent priests from treating offerings in a way that contradicts their offerer's intention. A possible implication of this argument is that the holiness associated with offerings reflects the attitude of their offerers's hearts.

For example, to ensure that the priests did not bake the 'remainder' (הנתרת) of the 'cereal offering' with 'yeast' (חמץ, Lev. 6.10), something that was prohibited for the offerer (cf. Lev. 2.11), the legislator explains

> 'I have given it from the gifts. It is most holy like the sin and guilt offerings'
> נתתי אתה מאשי קדש קדשים הוא כחטאת וכאשם), Lev. 6.10b)

Two observations suggest that, on this occasion, the phrase is aimed at preventing the priests from handling the remaining edible part of the 'cereal offering' in a way that contradicts its offerer's intention. First, only the raw 'cereal offering' is dealt with in the prescription addressed to priests (i.e. Lev. 6.7-16). Various explanations are given for this observation,[17] but it seems possible that an awareness that the priests were liable to mishandle only the *raw* 'cereal offering' governed the legislator's decision not to refer to the baked version.[18] When addressing the priests concerning the 'cereal

---

16. Rendtorff, *Leviticus*, p. 102. One may also argue that the requirement to offer the 'most holy' 'grain offering' with a 'burnt offering' increases the likelihood that the latter was also 'most holy'.

17. For example, Milgrom suggests that only the raw 'cereal offering' is dealt with because, first, it was the most common, and, second, it has already been previously informed that the baked 'cereal offering' was to be unleavened (cf. Lev. 2.4-5). However, Milgrom's suggestion does not take into account the difference in addressee between Leviticus 2 and 6 respectively (*Leviticus 1–16*, pp. 390-91).

18. By contrast, the legislator dealt with both the raw (Lev. 2.4-15) *and* the baked (Lev. 2.1-3) מנחה when addressing the laity to ensure that they brought, and offered, it with the right intention. For example, with regard to the raw מנחה, it is warned that it is

offering', the legislator would have found it unnecessary to deal with the baked version because it had already been baked without yeast and presented with an additional rite (i.e. הגישה; cf. Lev. 2.8), thereby safeguarding it from being handled in a way that contradicted its 'most holy' status. Yet it still remained necessary for the legislator to ensure that the raw 'cereal offering' was treated in keeping with its intended destiny, namely the altar. Milgrom explains that

> [t]he presentation by the priest to the altar is an indispensable rite in the sacrificial procedure (see at 1.5); but whereas only the burnt parts of the other offerings are presented to the altar, the entire cereal offering undergoes presentation to the altar even though only its 'token' is burned. This is done to indicate that the entire offering in reality belongs to God that he, by his grace, has bestowed most of it as a perquisite to the priesthood. This point is stated explicitly in the priestly instructions 'I have assigned it (the cereal offering) as their portion from my food gifts' (6.10; see 10.12-13; 24.9). Perhaps for this reason...the priestly portion may not be eaten leavened (6.9-10) because, theoretically, all of it should be consumed on the altar on which leaven is prohibited (v. 11).[19]

Second, following on from the last sentence of Milgrom's statement above, that the phrase 'most holy' was used to ensure that the priests would treat the offerings in keeping with the spirit in which they were offered is likewise suggested by the equation of their eating of the 'cereal offering' with its consumption by fire on the altar. This is done by using the same terminology to describe the altar fire's consumption (תאכל, Lev. 6.3) of the 'burnt offering', in the immediately preceding passage (Lev. 6.1-6), and the priestly consumption (יאכלוה) of the 'remainder' (הנתרת) of the 'cereal offering' in Lev. 6.7-16.[20] What entered their mouths should be treated as though it was offered on the altar as 'most holy'.

קדש קדשים immediately after the stipulation that only the אזכרתה ('memorial portion') is burnt (Lev. 2.3). It would seem that on this occasion, reference to its 'most holy' nature was aimed at circumventing any desire the offerer had for partaking in what remained.

19. Milgrom, *Leviticus 1–16*, p. 186.

20. This parallel may warrant the literal translation of יאכלוה as 'he will eat it' (e.g. ESV, NRS, NJB). Since it would seem practically impossible for a single priest to eat all of the offering Milgrom prefers to translate 'he will enjoy it'. However, this translation misses that the legislator is simply going out of his way to draw a parallel between the priestly eating and the altar's burning of the 'most holy' offering (Milgrom, *Leviticus 1–16*, p. 402). A parallel between the altar and the priest is already adumbrated in Lev. 1.5-9 where the four occurrences of 'upon the altar' (על־המזבח) are paralleled by either 'the sons of Aaron, the priests' (בני אהרן הכהנים) or 'the sons of Aaron, the priest' (בני אהרן הכהן).

Thus, the phrase 'most holy' may have been used to ensure that the priests handled this offering in keeping with its intended destiny, symbolized by its presentation to the altar (cf. Lev. 2.8). The same rationale is evident for its use in relation to the remaining edible parts of the חטאת and אשם offerings (Lev. 6.22; 7.6; 10.12-13, 17). Since on each of these occasions it explicates why the priest should eat the remaining edible parts, it may be concluded that the legislator used it to protect the offering from being handled in a way that is inconsistent with the spirit in which it was offered. Of course, there was no such need to use the phrase in this way concerning the 'burnt offering'. Its complete consumption by fire (cf. Leviticus 1; 6.1-6) ensured that the offerer, nor even the priests, could have entertained the prospect of eating it.[21] As commented by Keil,

> [a]ll the holy sacrificial gifts, in which there was any fear lest a portion should be perverted to other objects,—were called most holy; whereas the burnt-offerings, the priestly meat-offerings (chap vi. 12-16) and other sacrifices, which were quite as holy, were not called most holy, because the command to burn them entirely precluded the possibility of their being devoted to any of the ordinary purposes of life.[22]

Thus, both sub-contexts in which 'most holy' occurs in relation to the remaining edible portions of offerings suggest that the contextual reason governing whether or not the legislator identified an offering as such was the perceived threat to the offering's intended destiny. With regard to the laity, it served to qualify what such an offering was, namely one offered with the full intention of relinquishing it to Yahweh.[23] With regard to the priests, it reminded them to treat such an offering in keeping with the will of the person who offered it. No such threat existed in relation to the 'peace offering' because the layperson was permitted to offer it with the intention of partaking in its eating. No threat was posed to the intended destiny of the 'burnt offering' because its ritual naturally prevented both the laity from offering it with the intention of eating it, and the priests from mishandling it.

---

21. Actually, the prescription for the 'burnt offering' addressed to the priests (Lev. 6.1-6) reflects the legislator's concern that the entire offering was burnt to ashes. It stipulates that the 'burnt offering' is to remain on the altar כל־הלילה עד־הבקר ('all the night until morning', Lev. 6.2); that אש המזבח תוקד בו ('the fire of the altar must be kept burning on it', Lev. 6.2) and, again, that האש על־המזבח תוקד־בו לא תכבה ('the fire on the altar must be kept burning. It shall not go out', Lev. 6.5) and finally, אש תמיד תוקד על־המזבח לא תכבה ('A continuing fire must be kept burning upon the altar. It shall not go out', Lev. 6.6).

22. Keil, *The Pentateuch*, p. 293. See similarly Rendtorff, *Leviticus*, p. 102.

23. For the dependence that the 'most holy' status of objects have on the will and intention of their offerers see N. Kiuchi, 'The Concept of Holiness in the Sacrificial Context' *Christ and Theology* 4 (1987), pp. 1-27 [Japanese].

Place of Slaughter

The designated place of slaughter is the other context in which the phrase 'most holy' occurs. When addressing the priests the legislator felt compelled to explain that the חטאת and אשם offerings were 'most holy' when stipulating that they were to be slaughtered (שחט) in the same place as the 'burnt offering' (Lev. 6.18; 7.2; 14.13).[24] On each occasion the place of slaughter is identified as either 'In the place where the burnt offering is slaughtered' (במקום אשר ישחטו את־העלה, Lev. 6.18; 7.2[25]) or 'In the place where one slaughters the sin offering and burnt offering' (במקום אשר ישחט את־החטאת ואת־העלה, Lev. 14.13). It would seem that these offerings were slaughtered in the same place as the 'burnt offering' *because* they were 'most holy'.[26] In this regard, Milgrom comments that

> [i]t is impossible to tell from the Bible when the status of 'most sacred' begins, but there is no doubt that it has happened before the offering is brought to the sanctuary. The wording of the text shows this, for example, 'this is the ritual for the purification offering. The purification offering shall be slaughtered before the Lord, at the spot where the burnt offering is slaughtered; it is most sacred' (6.18). That is to say, it is the prior status of the offering as most sacred that determines where it is to be slaughtered (cf. also 7.1-2 on the reparation offering)…in ancient Israel, sanctification took place as a result of a person's intention, expressed by word and deed, by declaration and setting aside.[27]

Once again, since unlike the other offerings the 'burnt offering' could only be offered with the intention of relinquishing it completely to Yahweh, this understanding favours the conclusion that the 'burnt offering' was a 'most holy' offering.[28] Alternatively, this interpretation disqualifies the 'peace

---

24. For some reason the place of slaughter is not stipulated for the laity in Leviticus 4. Milgrom seems right in saying that '[a]lthough sacrificial slaughter is performed by the lay offerer…, it falls on the priests to supervise the slaughter, that it be done in the proper manner and place' (Milgrom, *Leviticus 1–16*, p. 401). Nevertheless, why is this place not stipulated within the prescription for the burnt offering?

25. Whereas the phrase קדש קדשים הוא immediately follows the stipulation of the place of slaughter in Lev. 6.18, it is placed immediately prior to this in Lev. 7.1. Milgrom's explanation that the different word order of Lev. 7.1 derives from 'the author's desire to juxtapose the slaughter of the reparation animal and the dashing of its blood as was done in the prescription of the עלה (1:5)' seems correct (*Leviticus 1–16*, p. 408).

26. Milgrom, *Leviticus 1–16*, pp. 401-402.

27. Though, as demonstrated above, it would seem that it took place as soon as a person decided to offer such an offering. Milgrom, *Leviticus 1–16*, pp. 485-86.

28. Cf. a 'devoted thing' (חרם, Lev. 27.28). Because it was an irrevocable offering it was 'most holy'.

offering' from having a 'most holy' status. Of the four animal offerings, the 'peace offering' was the only one not slaughtered on the north side of the altar (cf. Lev. 1.11).[29] This observation is significant considering that the place of slaughter appears to signify ownership in P which can be inferred from Lev. 7.29:

> 'Whoever offers the sacrifice of his Peace Offering to Yahweh shall bring his offering to Yahweh from his Peace Offering' (המקריב את־זבח שלמיו
> (ליהוה יביא את־קרבנו ליהוה מזבח שלמיו

The partitive *mem* in מזבח שלמיו indicates that only part of the offerer's 'peace offering' is a אשי יהוה (v. 30a) that 'his [i.e. the offerer's] hands will deliver' (ידיו תביאינה, v. 30a) to Yahweh. As noted by Milgrom

> the second half of v 29b is not a pointless repetition of the first half. It stresses the difference between the well-being offering and the most sacred offerings. Whereas the latter become the property of the deity as soon as they are dedicated, the well-being offering continues to remain the property of the owner even after it is brought to the sanctuary—indeed, even after its blood and suet are offered up on the altar.[30]

Thus, it would seem that by not slaughtering the 'peace offering' in the same place as the 'burnt offering' (i.e. on the north side of the altar), the former offering was not offered with the intention of completely relinquishing it to Yahweh. As for the stipulation that the other offerings were to be slaughtered in the same place as the 'burnt offering', it would appear that this direction ensured that the priests officiated over these sacrifices in a way that was in keeping with the offerer's intention (cf. Leviticus 1–5). In relation to the place of slaughter Kiuchi comments that

> [t]he designation of the place for slaughtering indicates the animal ought to be slaughtered in *the same spirit* as the burnt offering.[31]

The conclusion that the 'burnt offering' was not just involved in, but foundational to P's concept of 'most holy' seems plausible.

The Non-Mention of 'Most Holy' in Relation to the Priestly מנחה *and* חטאת *Offerings*

The absence of the term קדש in passages that prescribe the priestly 'cereal offering' (Lev. 6.12-16) and 'sin offering' (Lev. 6.23) provides further evi-

---

29. As commented by Milgrom, its place of slaughter 'is termed "before the Lord" (Lev. 3.7) in its limited sense of "at the entrance to the Tent of Meeting" (Lev. 3:2, 13)' (Milgrom, *Leviticus 1–16*, p. 165).

30. Milgrom, *Leviticus 1–16*, p. 429.

31. Kiuchi, *Leviticus*, p. 127 (emphasis mine).

dence for why the 'burnt offering' was never referred to as 'most holy' despite having had such a status. Though the remaining edible portions of the מנחה and חטאת offerings made by the laity are elsewhere referred to as 'most holy' (Lev. 6.22; 7.6; 10.12-13, 17), the command to completely burn these offerings when they are offered by priests (Lev. 6.15, 23) made it unnecessary for the legislator to refer to these offerings as 'most holy'.[32] Moreover, it should not be missed that the legislator's prohibition against priests eating their own 'most holy' offerings adds support to the idea that this phrase referred to things that were completely relinquished by their offerers.

Conclusion

An examination of P's use of the phrase 'most holy' in relation to the offerings of Leviticus 1–7 reveals that the phrase not only encapsulates what has become the deity's personal property, but also the offerer's intention to completely relinquish this possession as his own. In this sense, it is possible to view P's 'most holy' offerings as symbolic evidence of an offerer's willingness to dedicate a possession in its entirety to Yahweh.[33] This finding makes the absence of holiness terminology in connection with the 'burnt offering' understandable because the practical nature of this offering (i.e. its complete consumption by fire) precludes any possibility of offering it with the intention of eating it. On the one hand, I contend that the complete burning of the 'burnt offering' accomplished what the legislator sought to achieve by using the phrase 'most holy' elsewhere, namely the offering of a sacrifice in keeping with the intention of how it was offered. On the other hand, I argue that the place in which the 'burnt offering' was slaughtered is symbolic of the attitude underlying the 'most holy' offerings. It may be inferred from these observations that the 'burnt offering' was P's 'most holy' offering *par excellence*. That is, there is a sense in which the phrase was not applicable to the offering because it had indeed been completely offered to Yahweh. To offer the 'burnt offering' was to accept without question that one was relinquishing something from one's possessions to Yahweh. Thus, Kiuchi seems correct when he concludes that

> it is the burnt offering that represents the essence of 'the most holy thing': it is entirely burnt to ashes. But why is only the burnt offering not described as most holy? Because as an offering destroyed completely by fire, there was no

32. As is the case for the 'burnt offering'.

33. This view of what is meant by 'most holy' receives support from the concept of חרם ('things devoted'). To devote something to Yahweh 'was a more solemn and irreversible vow than ordinary dedication' (Wenham, *Leviticus*, p. 341). The things that the Israelites devoted to Yahweh could not be sold or redeemed because 'every devoted thing is most holy to Yahweh' (כל־חרם קדש־קדשים הוא ליהוה, Lev. 27.28b).

reason to warn the Israelites against touching remaining parts. Since part of the *minhâ*, *hattā't* and *'āšām* remained, it was essential to alert the offerer to its holy nature because it represents what was to be wholly offered to the Lord: it must disappear. This remaining part was consumed by the priest or lay individual. Thus it seems that the mention of 'the most holy' in reference to the *minhâ*, *hattā't* and *'āšām* functions simply to warn the Israelites that the remaining parts of the offerings ought to be handled with utmost care. It by no means indicates that those offerings were *holier* than the burnt offering. Thus the essence of holiness is expressed by the burnt offering, which is never explicitly called 'holy'.[34]

The ruling of the Mishnah,[35] and the assumption made by most modern commentators,[36] that the 'burnt offering' was 'most holy' seems justified.

34. Kiuchi, *Leviticus*, p. 63.
35. *m.* Zebah. 5.1; 6.1.
36. Keil, *The Pentateuch*, p. 293; Rendtorff, *Leviticus*, p. 102; Levine, *In the Presence of the Lord*, p. 73; Milgrom, *Leviticus 1–16*, p. 183; Wright, 'Holiness', p. 239; Kiuchi, *Leviticus*, pp. 63-64.

BIBLIOGRAPHY

Allwood, J., 'Meaning Potential and Context: Some Consequences for the Analysis of Variation in Meaning', in Cuyckens, Dirven and Taylor (eds.), *Cognitive Approaches to Lexical Semantics*, pp. 29-65.

Alter, Robert, *The Art of Biblical Narrative* (London: George Allen & Unwin, 1981).

Amit, Yairah, 'Progression as a Rhetorical Device in Biblical Literature', *JSOT* 78 (2003), pp. 3-32.

André, G., and Helmer Ringgren, 'טמא', in Botterweck and Ringgren (eds.), *Theological Dictionary of the Old Testament*, pp. 330-342.

Aquinas, Thomas, *Summa theologica*, II (Chicago: William Benton, 1952).

Astruc, Jean, *Conjectures sur la Genèse: Introduction et notes de Pierre Gibert* (orig. 1773; Classiques de l'histoire des religions. Paris: Noêsis, 1999).

Averbeck, Richard E., 'טמא', in VanGemeren (ed.), *NIDOTTE*, II, pp. 365-76.

—'עלה', in VanGemeren (ed.), *NIDOTTE*, III, pp. 405-15.

—'Clean and Unclean', in VanGemeren (ed.), *NIDOTTE*, IV, pp. 477-86.

Baentsch, Bruno, *Exodus, Leviticus, Numbers* (HKAT, I/2. Göttingen: Vandenhoeck & Ruprecht, 1903).

—*Das Heiligkeits-Gesetz Lev. XVII–XXVI. Eine historisch-kritische Untersuchung* (Erfurt: Hugo Güther, 1893).

Bähr, K.C.W.F., *Symbolik des mosaischen Cultus* (2 vols.; Heidelberg: Mohr, 1837–39).

Baillet, M., *Qumran Grotte 4 III (4Q482–4Q520)* (DJD, 7; Oxford: Clarendon Press, 1982).

Baker, D.W., 'Leviticus 1–7 and the Punic Tariffs: A Form Critical Comparison', *ZAW* (1987), pp. 188-97.

Balentine, Samuel E., *Leviticus* (Louisville, KY: John Knox Press, 2002).

—*The Torah's Vision of Worship* (Minneapolis: Fortress Press, 1999).

Ball, Edward. (ed.), *In Search of True Wisdom: Essays in Old Testament Interpretation in Honour of Ronald E. Clements* (JSOTSup, 300. Sheffield: Sheffield Academic Press, 1999).

Bamberger, Bernard J., *The Torah: A Modern Commentary. Leviticus* (New York: Union of American Hebrew Congregations, 1979).

Barr, James, 'Hebrew Lexicography: Informal Thoughts', in Bodine (ed.), *Linguistics and Biblical Hebrew*, pp. 137-51.

—'Is God a Liar? (Genesis 2–3) – and Related Matters', *JTS* 57 (2006), pp. 1-22.

—*The Garden of Eden and the Hope of Immortality* (London: SCM Press, 1992).

—*The Semantics of Biblical Language* (Oxford: Oxford University Press, 1961).

Barton, John, *The Nature of Biblical Criticism* (Louisville, KY: John Knox Press, 2007).

—*Understanding Old Testament Ethics: Approaches and Explorations* (Louisville, KY: Westminster/John Knox Press, 2003).

—(ed.), *The Biblical World*, II (London: Routledge, 2002).

Baumgarten, J.M., 'The 4Q Zadokite Fragments on Skin Disease', *JJS* 41 (1990), pp. 153-65.

Baumgartner, W. (ed.), *Festschrift für A. Bertholet* (Tübingen: Mohr, 1950).

Beardsley, M., 'Metaphorical Senses', *Nous* 12 (1978), pp. 3-16.

Becker, J., *Das Heil Gottes: Heils- und Sündenbegriffe in den Qumrantexten und im Neuen Testament* (SUNT, 3. Göttingen: Vandenhoeck & Ruprecht, 1964).

Begrich, J., 'Die priesterliche Torah', in Volz, Stummer and Hempel (eds.), *Werden und Wesen des Alten Testament*, pp. 63-88.

Bergen, Wesley J., *Reading Ritual: Leviticus in Postmodern Culture* (JSOTSup, 417; London: T. & T. Clark, 2005).

Bernoulli, M., *Vocabulaire biblique* (Neuchâtel: Delachaux & Niestlé, 1954).

Bertholet, A., *Leviticus* (Tübingen: J.C.B. Mohr, 1901).

Bertman, S., 'Tasselled Garments in the Ancient East Mediterranean', *BA* 24 (1961), pp. 119-28.

Bibb, Bryan D., *This is the Thing That the Lord Commanded You to Do: Ritual Words and Narrative Worlds in the Book of Leviticus* (PhD dissertation, Princeton Theological Seminary, 2005).

Blenkinsopp, Joseph, *Prophecy and Canon* (Notre Dame: University of Notre Dame Press, 1977).

Blum, Erhard, *Studien zur Komposition des Pentateuch* (Berlin: W. de Gruyter, 1990).

Bodine, Walter R. (ed.), *Linguistics and Biblical Hebrew* (Winona Lake, IN: Eisenbrauns, 1992).

Botterweck, G.J., and H. Ringgren (eds.), *Theological Dictionary of the Old Testament* (Grand Rapids: Eerdmans, 1986).

Bratsiotis, N. P, 'בָּשָׂר', *TDOT*, II, pp. 317-32.

Brovarski, E., 'The Doors of Heaven', *Orientalia* 46 (1977), pp. 107-15.

Brown, F., S.R. Driver and C.A. Briggs (eds.), *Hebrew and English Lexicon of the Old Testament* (Oxford: Clarendon Press, 1929).

Buber, M., and F. Rosenzweig (eds.), *Die Schrift und ihre Verdeutschung* (Berlin: Schocken, 1936).

Budd, J.P., *Leviticus* (NCB; Grand Rapids: Eerdmans, 1996).

Caird, G.B., *The Language and Imagery of the Bible* (Philadelphia: Westminster Press, 1980).

Caquot, A., and M. Delcor (eds.), *Mélanges bibliques et orientaux en l'honneur de M. Henri Cazelles* (AOAT, 212; Kevelaer: Butzon & Bercker; Neukirchen–Vluyn: Neukirchener Verlag, 1981).

Calvin, John, *Genesis* (trans. John King; Grand Rapids: Eerdmans, 1948).

Carmichael, Calum A., *The Origins of Biblical Law: The Decalogues and the Book of the Covenant* (Ithaca, NY: Cornell University Press, 1992).

Carson, D.A., and John D. Woodbridge (eds.), *Hermeneutics, Authority, and Canon* (Carlisle: Paternoster Press, 1986).

Cassuto, U., *A Commentary on the Book of Exodus* (Jerusalem: Magnes Press, 1983).

—*A Commentary on the Book of Genesis I* (Jerusalem: Magnes Press, 1964).

Childs, Brevard S., *Exodus* (London: SCM Press, 1974).

Cholewinski, A., *Heiligkeitsgesetz und Deuteronomium* (AnBib, 66. Rome: Biblical Institute Press, 1976).

Cohen, Aryeh, and Shaul Magid (eds.), *Beginning/Again: Towards a Hermeneutics of Jewish Texts* (New York: Seven Bridges Press, 2002).

Cole, P., and J. Morgan (eds.), *Syntax and Semantics: Speech Acts*, III (New York: Academic Press, 1975).

Croft, William, and D. Allen Cruse, *Cognitive Linguistics* (Cambridge: Cambridge University Press, 2004).

Cuyckens, H., R. Dirven and J.R. Taylor (eds.), *Cognitive Approaches to Lexical Semantics* (Berlin: Mouton–de Gruyter, 2003).

Davies, Phillip R., 'Ethics and the Old Testament', in Rogerson, Davies and Carroll (eds.), *The Bible in Ethics. The Second Sheffield Colloquium*, pp. 164-73.

Delitzsch, Franz, *Commentar zum Hebräerbrief* (Leipzig: S. Hirzel, 1857).

Dillmann, August, *Die Bücher Exodus and Leviticus* (2nd edn; Leipzig: S. Hirzel, 1880).

Dillmann, August, and V. Ryssel, *Exodus and Leviticus* (Leipzig: S. Hirzel, 1897).

Douglas, Mary, 'Deciphering a Meal', *Daedalus* 101 (1972), pp. 61-81.

—*Jacob's Tears: The Priestly Work of Reconciliation* (Oxford: Oxford University Press, 2004).

—*Leviticus as Literature* (Oxford: Oxford University Press, 1999).

—*Natural Symbols: Explorations in Cosmology* (London: Barrie & Rockliffe, 1970).

—*Purity and Danger* (London: Routledge & Kegan Paul, 1966).

—'The Forbidden Animals in Leviticus', *JSOT* 59 (1993), pp. 3-23.

Driver, G.R., 'Leprosy', in J. Hastings, F.C. Grant and H.H. Rowley (eds.), *Dictionary of the Bible*, pp. 575-78.

Driver, S.R., *An Introduction to the Literature of the Old Testament* (Edinburgh: T. & T. Clark, 1897).

Durham, John I., *Exodus* (WBC, 2. Waco, TX: Word Books, 1987).

Eerdmans, B.D., *Das Buch Leviticus* (Giessen: Alfred Töpelmann, 1912).

Eichrodt, Walther, *Theology of the Old Testament*, II (London: SCM Press, 1967).

Eilberg-Schwartz, Howard, 'Creation and Classification in Judaism: From Priestly to Rabbinic Conceptions', *HR* 26 (1987), pp. 357-81.

Eissfeldt, Otto, *The Old Testament: An Introduction* (trans. Peter R. Ackroyd; Oxford: Blackwell, 1965).

Elliger, Karl, *Leviticus* (Tübingen: J.C.B. Mohr, 1966).

Emerton, J.A. (ed.), *Congress Volume: Jerusalem 1986* (Leiden: E.J. Brill, 1988).

—*Studies in the Pentateuch* (Leiden: E.J. Brill, 1990).

Enns, Peter, *Exodus* (Grand Rapids: Zondervan, 2000).

Fabry, H.J., and H.W. Jüngling (eds.), *Levitikus als Buch* (BBB, 119. Berlin: Philo, 1999).

Falk, Daniel K., Florentino García Martínez and Eileen M. Schuller (eds.), *Sapiential, Liturgical and Poetical Texts From Qumran. Proceedings of the Third Meeting of the International Organization for Qumran Studies, Oslo 1998* (STDJ, 35. Leiden: E.J. Brill, 2000).

Feldman, E., *Biblical and Post-Biblical Defilement and Mourning* (New York: Ktav, 1977).

Feucht, Christian, *Untersuchungen zum Heiligkeitsgesetz* (Berlin: Evangelische Verlagsanstalt, 1964).

Firmage, Edwin, 'The Biblical Dietary Laws and the Concept of Holiness', in Emerton (ed.), *Studies in the Pentateuch*, pp. 177-208.

Firmage, Edwin, Bernard G. Weiss and John W. Welch (eds.), *Religion and Law: Biblical-Judaic and Islamic Perspectives* (Winona Lake, IN: Eisenbrauns, 1999).

Fishbane, M., 'Biblical Colophons, Textual Criticism and Legal Analogies', *CBQ* 42 (1980), pp. 438-49.

Fitzpatrick-McKinley, Anne, *The Transformation of Torah from Scribal Advice to Law* (JSOTSup, 287; Sheffield: Sheffield Academic Press, 1999).

Fox, Michael V., *A Time to Tear Down and a Time to Build Up: A Rereading of Ecclesiastes* (Grand Rapids: Eerdmans, 1999).

Fredericks, D.C., 'נֶפֶשׁ', in VanGemeren (ed.), *NIDOTTE*, III, pp. 133-34.

Freedman, D.N. (ed.), *Anchor Bible Dictionary* (6 vols.; New York: Doubleday, 1992).

Friedman, Richard. E., *Commentary on the Torah* (San Francisco: Harper, 2001).

Fretheim, Terence E., *Exodus* (Louisville, KY: John Knox Press, 1991).

Frey, Jörg, 'The Notion of "Flesh" in 4QInstruction and the Background of Pauline Usage', in Falk, Martínez and Schuller (eds.), in *Sapiential, Liturgical and Poetical Texts from Qumran. Proceedings of the Third Meeting of the International Organization for Qumran Studies*, pp. 197-226.

Fritz, V., *Tempel und Zelt. Studien zum Tempelbau in Israel und zu dem Zeltheiligtum der Priesterschrift* (WMANT, 47; Neukirchen–Vluyn: Neukirchen Verlag, 1977).

Frymer-Kensky, Tikva, 'Pollution, Purification, and Purgation in Biblical Israel', in Myers and O'Connor (eds.), *The Word of the Lord Shall Go Forth. Essays in Honor of David Noel Freedman in Celebration of his Sixtieth Birthday*, pp. 399-410.

Gane, Roy, *Cult and Character: Purification Offerings, Day of Atonement, and Theodicy* (Winona Lake, IN: Eisenbrauns, 2005).

Gerstenberger, E.S., *Leviticus* (OTL; Louisville, KY: Westminster/John Knox Press, 1996).

Gese, H., *Essays in Biblical Theology* (trans. K. Crim; Minneapolis: Augsburg, 1981).

Gilders, William K., *Blood Ritual in the Hebrew Bible: Meaning and Power* (Baltimore: Johns Hopkins University Press, 2004).

Ginzberg, Louis, *The Legends of the Jews*, III (Philadelphia: Jewish Publication Society of America, 1909–38).

Gorman, Frank. H., 'Ritualizing, Rite and Pentateuchal Theology', in Reid (ed.), *Prophets and Paradigms: Essays in Honor of Gene M. Tucker*, pp. 173-86.

—*Divine Presence and Community: A Commentary on the Book of Leviticus* (International Theological Commentary; Grand Rapids: Eerdmans, 1997).

—*The Ideology of Ritual: Space, Time and Status in the Priestly Literature* (JSOT Press; Sheffield: Sheffield Academic Press, 1990).

Grabbe, Lester L., *Leviticus* (Sheffield: Sheffield Academic Press, 1993).

Graf, Karl Heinrich, *Die geschichtlichen Bücher des Alten Testaments: Zwei historische-kritische Untersuchungen* (Leipzig: T.O. Weigel, 1866).

Green, Garrett, '"The Bible as...": Fctional Narrative and Scriptural Truth', in Green (ed.), *Scriptural Authority and Narrative Interpretation*, pp. 79-96.

—(ed.), *Scriptural Authority and Narrative Interpretation* (ed. Garrett Green. Philadelphia: Fortress Press, 1987).

Grelot, Pierre, *The Language of Symbolism: Biblical Theology, Semantics, and Exegesis* (trans. Christopher R. Smith; Peabody, MA: Hendrickson Publishers, 2006).

Grice, H.P., 'Logic and Conversation', in Cole and Morgan (eds.), *Syntax and Semantics*: *Speech Acts*, III, pp. 41-58.

Grisanti, Michael A., 'שֶׁקֶץ', in VanGemeren (ed.), *NIDOTTE* IV, pp. 243-46.

Gründwaldt, Klaus, *Das Heiligkeitsgesetz: Leviticus 17–26* (Berlin: W. de Gruyter, 1999).

Gunkel, Hermann, *Genesis* (orig. 1901; Macon, GA: Mercer University Press, 1997).

Harrington, Hannah, *The Purity Texts* (London: T. & T. Clark International, 2004).

Harrison, R.K., *Leviticus* (Leicester: IVP, 1980).

Hartley, John E., *Leviticus* (WBC; Dallas: Word Books, 1992).

Hastings, J. (ed.), *Encyclopedia of Religion and Ethics* (New York: Charles Scribner's Sons, 1951).

Hastings, J., F.C. Grant and H.H. Rowley (eds.), *Dictionary of the Bible* (2nd rev. edn; New York: Scribner's, 1963).

Hayes, Christine E., *Gentile Impurities and Jewish Identities* (Oxford: Oxford University Press, 2002).

Heinisch, Paul, *Das Buch Leviticus* (Bonn: Hanstein, 1935).

Hoffmann, David Z., *Das Buch Leviticus* (2 vols.; Berlin: Poppelauer, 1905–1906).

Houston, Walter, *Purity and Monotheism: Clean and Unclean Animals in Biblical Law* (JSOTSup, 140; Sheffield: Sheffield Academic Press, 1993).

—'Towards an Integrated Reading of the Dietary Laws of Leviticus', in Rendtorff and Kugler (eds.), *The Book of Leviticus: Composition and Reception*, pp. 142-61.

Houtman, Cornelis, *Exodus* (Leuven: Peeters, 2000).

Hulse, E.V., 'The Nature of Biblical Leprosy', *PEQ* 107 (1975), pp. 87-105.

Janowski, Bernd, *Sühne als Heiligeschehen* (Neukirchen–Vluyn: Neukirchener Verlag, 1982).

Jastrow, Morris, 'The So-called Leprosy Laws: An Analysis of Leviticus, Chapters 13 and 14', *JQR* (1913–14), pp. 357-418.

Jenni, E., and C. Westermann (eds.), *Theologisches Handwörterbuch zum Alten Testament* (2 vols.; Munich: Kaiser, 1971–76).

Jenson, Phillip, *Graded Holiness: A Key to the Priestly Conception of the World* (JSOTSup, 106; Sheffield: JSOT Press, 1992).

Jones, Larry Paul, *The Symbol of Water in the Gospel of John* (JSNTSup, 145. Sheffield: Sheffield Academic Press, 1997).

Joosten, Jan, *People and Land in the Holiness Code: An Exegetical Study of the Ideational Framework of the Law in Leviticus 17–26* (Leiden: E.J. Brill, 1996).

Jouon, Paul, and T. Muraoka, *A Grammar of Biblical Hebrew* (Rome: Editrice Pontificio Istituto Biblico, 1996).

Kaiser, W.C., 'The Book of Leviticus', in Keck (ed.), *The New Interpreter's Bible*, I, pp. 985-1119.

Kalisch, Marcus M., *Leviticus*, II (London: Longmans, 1867–72).

Kaufmann, Y., *The History of Israelite Religion* (4 vols.; Tel Aviv: Dvir, 1937–56 [Hebrew]).

Kearny, P.J., 'Creation and Liturgy: The P Redaction of Exodus 25:40', *ZAW* 89 (1977), pp. 375-87.

Keck, L. (ed.), *The New Interpreter's Bible*, I (Nashville: Abingdon Press, 1994).

Kedar, Benjamin, *Biblische Semantik* (Stuttgart: W. Kohlhammer, 1981).

Kedar-Kopfstein, B., 'תמם', in Botterweck and Ringgren (eds.), *TDOT*, XV, pp. 699-711.

Keil, C.F., *Commentary on the Old Testament*. I. *The Pentateuch* (orig. 1866–91; Peabody, MA: Hendrickson, 1996).

Keil, K., 'Die Opfer des Alten Bundes nach ihrer symbolischen und typischen Bedeutung', *Lutherische Zeitschrift*, 1856.

Kellogg, S.H., *The Book of Leviticus* (The Expositor's Bible; New York: Funk & Wagnalls, 1900).

Kiuchi, Nobuyoshi, 'A Paradox of the Skin Disease', *ZAW* 113 (2001), pp. 505-14.

—*A Study of Ḥāṭā' and Ḥaṭṭāʾt in Leviticus 4–5* (Tübingen: J.C.B. Mohr [Paul Siebeck], 2003).

—*Leviticus* (Apollos. Leicester: IVP, 2007).

—'The Concept of Holiness in the Sacrificial Context', *Christ and Theology* 4 (1987), pp. 1-27 [Japanese].

—*The Purification Offering in the Priestly Literature: Its Meaning and Function* (Sheffield: JSOT Press, 1987).

—'Propitiation in the Sacrificial Ritual', in *Christ and the World*, XV (Inzai, Chiba: Tokyo Christian University, 2005), pp. 35-50.

Klawans, Jonathan, *Impurity and Sin in Ancient Judaism* (Oxford: Oxford University Press, 2000).

—'Methodology and Ideology in the Study of Priestly Ritual', in Schwartz, Wright, Stackert and Meshel (eds.), *Perspectives on Purity and Purification in the Bible*, pp. 84-95.

—'Pure Violence: Sacrifice and Defilement in Ancient Israel', *HTR* 94 (2001), pp. 135-57.

—*Purity, Sacrifice, and the Temple: Symbolism and Supersessionism in the Study of Ancient Judaism* (Oxford: Oxford University Press, 2006).

Kleinig, John W., *Leviticus* (Saint Louis, MO: Concordia Publishing House, 2003).

Klostermann, August, 'Beiträge zur Entstehungsgeschichte des Pentateuchs', *ZLThK* 38 (1877), pp. 401-45.

—*Der Pentateuch* (Leipzig: Deichert, 1893).

Knierim, Rolf P., 'שׁגג', in Jenni and Westermann (eds.), *THAT*, pp. 869-72.

—*Die Hauptbegriffe für Sünde im Alten Testament* (2nd edn; Gütersloh: Mohn, 1967).

—*Text and Concept in Leviticus 1:1-9* (Tübingen: J.C.B. Mohr, 1992).

Knohl, Israel, *The Sanctuary of Silence: The Priestly Torah and the Holiness School* (Minneapolis: Fortress Press, 1995).

Koch, K., *Die Priesterschrift von Exodus 25 bis Leviticus 16. Eine überlieferungsgeschichtliche und Literarkritische Untersuchung* (FRLANT, 53; Göttingen: Vandenhoeck & Ruprecht, 1959).

Koehler, L., and W. Baumgartner (eds.), *HALOT* (trans. M.E.J. Richardson; Leiden: E.J. Brill, 1994–2000).

Kornfeld, W., *Das Buch Levitikus* (Die Welt der Bibel. Kleinkommentare zur Heiligen Schrift, 15; Dusseldorf: Patmos, 1972).

Kornfeld, W., and H. Ringgren, 'קדשׁ', in Botterweck and Ringgren (eds.), *Theological Dictionary of the Old Testament*, XII, pp. 521-45.

Kugler, R.A., 'Holiness, Purity, the Blood and Society: The Evidence for Theological Conflict in Leviticus', *JSOT* 76 (1997), pp. 3-27.

Kurtz, J.H., *Sacrificial Worship of the Old Testament* (orig. 1863; trans. James Martin; Grand Rapids: Baker Book House, 1980).

Lakoff, George, *Philosophy in the Flesh* (New York: Basic Books, 1999).

—'The Contemporary Theory of Metaphor', in Ortony (ed.), *Metaphor and Thought*, pp. 202-51.

—*Women, Fire, and Dangerous Things: What Categories Reveal about the Mind* (Chicago: University of Chicago Press, 1987).

Lakoff, George, and Mark Johnson, *Metaphors We Live By* (Chicago: University of Chicago Press, 1980).

Langacker, Ronald W, *Concept, Image, and Symbol: The Cognitive Basis of Grammar* (2nd edn; Cognitive Linguistics Research, 1. Berlin: Mouton–de Gruyter, 2002).

Leupold, H.C., *Exposition of Genesis* (London: Wartburg Press, 1942).

Levin, S., *The Semantics of Metaphor* (Baltimore: Johns Hopkins University Press, 1977).

Levine, Baruch A., *In the Presence of the Lord* (Leiden: E.J. Brill, 1974).
—*Leviticus* (Philadelphia: Jewish Publication Society of America, 1989).
—*Numbers* (New York: Doubleday, 1993).
—'The Descriptive Tabernacle Texts of the Pentateuch', *JAOS* 85 (1965), pp. 307-18.
Lewis, Gilbert, 'A Lesson from Leviticus: Leprosy', *Man* 22 (1987), pp. 593-612.
Liss, Hanna, 'Kanon und Fiktion: Zur literarischen Funktion biblischer Rechtstexte', *BN* 121 (2004), pp. 7-34.
—'Ritual Purity and the Construction of Identity – The Literary Function of the Laws of Purity in the Book of Leviticus', in Römer (ed.), *The Books of Leviticus and Numbers*, pp. 329-54.
Lockshin, Martin I., *Rashbam's Commentary on Leviticus and Numbers: An Annotated Translation* (BJS, 330. Providence, RI: Brown Judaic Studies, 2001).
Louth, Andrew, *Discerning the Mystery: An Essay on the Nature of Theology* (Oxford: Clarendon Press, 1983).
Maccoby, Hyam, *Ritual and Morality: The Ritual Purity System and its Place in Judaism* (Cambridge: Cambridge University Press, 1999).
Maass, Fritz, 'אָדָם', in Botterweck and Ringgren (eds), *TDOT*, I, pp. 75-87.
MacCulloch, J.A., 'Hand', in Hastings (ed.), *Encyclopedia of Religion and Ethics*, pp. 492-99.
Macht, David I., 'A Scientific Appreciation of Leviticus 12:1-5', *JBL* (1933), pp. 253-60.
Magonet, Jonathan, ' "But if it is a girl she is unclean for twice seven days..." The Riddle of Leviticus 12.5', in Sawyer (ed.), *Reading Leviticus: A Conversation with Mary Douglas*, pp. 144-52.
Matthews, R., 'Concerning a "Linguistic Theory" of Metaphor', *Foundations of Language* 7 (1971), pp. 413-25.
McConville, J. Gordon, ' "Fellow-Citizens": Israel and Humanity in Leviticus', in McConville and Möller (eds.), *Reading the Law. Essays in Honour of Gordon J. Wenham* (London: T. & T. Clark International, 2007), pp. 10-32.
McEvenue, S.E., *The Narrative Style of the Priestly Writer* (AnBib, 50; Rome: Biblical Institute Press, 1971).
Meyers, Carol L., 'Lampstand', *ABD*, IV, pp. 141-43.
—*The Tabernacle Menorah* (Missoula, MT: Scholars Press, 1976).
Meyers, Carol L., and M. O'Connor (eds.), *The Word of the Lord Shall Go Forth. Essays in Honor of David Noel Freedman in Celebration of his Sixtieth Birthday* (Winona Lake, IN: Eisenbrauns, 1983).
Milgrom, Jacob, 'H$_R$ in Leviticus and Elsewhere in the Torah', in Rendtorff and Kugler (eds.), *The Book of Leviticus: Composition and Reception*, pp. 24-40.
—*Leviticus 1–16: A New Translation with Introduction and Commentary* (AB, 3; New York: Doubleday, 1991).
—*Leviticus 17–22: A New Translation with Introduction and Commentary* (AB, 3A; New York: Doubleday, 2000).
—*Leviticus 23–27: A New Translation with Introduction and Commentary* (AB, 3B; New York: Doubleday, 2001).
—*Numbers* (Philadelphia: Jewish Publication Society of America, 1990).
—'The Changing Concepts of Holiness in the Pentateuchal Codes with Emphasis on Leviticus 19', in Sawyer (ed.), *Reading Leviticus. A Conversation with Mary Douglas*, pp. 65-75.
Miller, Cynthia L. (ed.), *The Verbless Clause in Biblical Hebrew: Linguistic Approaches*, (Linguistic Studies in Ancient West Semitic; Winona Lake, IN: Eisenbrauns, 1999).

Miller, Douglas B., *Symbol and Rhetoric in Ecclesiastes: The Place of Hebel in Qohelet's Work* (Atlanta: Society of Biblical Literature, 2002).

Moberly, R.W.L., 'Did the Serpent Get It Right?', *JTS* 39 (1988), pp. 1-27.

Moran, W.L., 'The Literary Connection between Lev. 11:13-19 and Deut. 14:12-18', *CBQ* 28 (1966), pp. 271-77.

Moskala, Jiří, 'Categorization and Evaluation of Different Kinds of Interpretation of the Laws of Clean and Unclean Animals in Leviticus 11', *BR* 66 (2001), pp. 5-41.

Muraoka, Takamitsu, *Emphatic Words and Structures in Biblical Hebrew* (Leiden: E.J. Brill, 1985).

—'The Tripartite Nominal Clause Revisited', in Miller (ed.), *The Verbless Clause in Biblical Hebrew: Linguistic Approaches*, pp. 187-213.

Nihan, Christophe, *From Priestly Torah to Pentateuch: A Study in the Composition of the Book of Leviticus* (PhD dissertation, University of Lausanne, 2005).

Noordtzij, A., *Leviticus* (trans. T. Togtman; Bible Student's Commentary; Grand Rapids: Zondervan, 1982).

—*Numbers* (trans. Ed. van der Maas; Grand Rapids: Zondervan, 1983).

Noth, Martin, *Leviticus* (trans. J.E. Anderson; OTL; Philadelphia: Westminster Press, 1965).

Ogden, C.K., and I.A. Richards, *The Meaning of Meaning* (New York: Harcourt, Brace & Co, 1945).

Olyan, Saul M., 'Mary Douglas's Holiness/Wholeness Paradigm: Its Potential for Insight and its Limitations', *Journal of Hebrew Scriptures* 8 (2008), pp. 2-9.

—*Rites and Rank: Hierarchy in Biblical Representations of Cult* (Princeton: Princeton University Press, 2000).

—'Why an Altar of Unfinished Stones? Some Thoughts on Ex 20,25 and Dtn 27,5-6', *ZAW* 108 (1996), pp. 161-71.

Ortony, A. (ed.), *Metaphor and Thought* (2nd edn; Cambridge: Cambridge University Press, 1993).

Ostrer, Boris S., 'Birds of Leper: Statistical Assessment of Two Commentaries', *ZAW* 115 (2003), pp. 348-61.

Otto, Eckart, *Theologische Ethik des Alten Testaments* (Theologische Wissenschaft, 3/2; Stüttgart: W. Kohlhammer, 1994).

Otto, Rudolf, *The Idea of the Holy* (London: Oxford University Press, 1923).

Ottosson, Magnus, 'Eden and the Land of Promise', in Emerton (ed.), *Congress Volume: Jerusalem 1986*, pp. 177-88.

Parry, D.W., 'Garden of Eden: Prototype of Sanctuary', in Parry and Ricks (eds.), *Temples of the Ancient World*, pp. 126-52.

Parry, D.W., and S.D. Ricks (eds.), *Temples of the Ancient World* (Salt Lake City: Deseret, 1994).

Peet, T. Eric, 'A Historical Document of Ramesside Age', *JEA* 10 (1924), pp. 120-24.

Péter-Contesse, R., *Lévitique 1–16* (CAT, 3a; Geneva: Labor & Fides, 1993).

—[Péter, René] 'L'imposition des mains dans l'Ancien Testament', *VT* 27 (1977), pp. 48-55.

Philip, Tarja S, *Menstruation and Childbirth in the Bible: Fertility and Impurity* (SBL, 88; New York: Peter Lang, 2006).

Poorthuis, M.J.H.M., and Baruch J. Schwartz (eds.), *Purity and Holiness: The Heritage of Leviticus* (Jewish and Christian Perspectives Series, 2; Leiden: E.J. Brill, 2000).

Provan, Iain, V. Philips Long, and Tremper Longman, III, *A Biblical History of Israel* (Louisville, KY: Westminster/John Knox Press, 2003).

Rad, Gerhard von, *Old Testament Theology: The Theology of Israel's Historical Traditions* (orig. 1957; 2 vols.; trans. D.M.G. Stalker; Edinburgh: Oliver & Boyd, 1973).

Rainey, A., 'The Order of Sacrifices in Old Testament Ritual Texts', *Biblica* 51 (1970), pp. 485-98.

Rashbam, *Rashbam's Commentary on Leviticus and Numbers: An Annotated Translation* (ed. and trans. Martin I. Lockshin; Providence, RI: Brown Judaic Studies, 2001).

Reid, Stephen Breck (ed.), *Prophets and Paradigms: Essays in Honor of Gene M. Tucker* (Sheffield: Sheffield Academic Press, 1996).

Reiner, E., 'Lipšur Litanies', *JNES* 15 (1956), pp. 129-49.

Rendsburg, Gary A., 'The *Inclusio* in Lev. xi', *VT* 43 (1993), pp. 418-21.

Rendtorff, Rolf, *Die Gesetze in der Priesterschrift* (FRLANT, 62; Göttingen: Vandenhoeck & Ruprecht, 1963).

—*Leviticus* (BKAT, 3/1; Neukirchen–Vluyn: Neukirchener Verlag, 1985).

—'What Happened to the "Yahwist"? Reflections after Thirty Years' (paper at the International SBL Meeting, Edinburgh, 2006).

Rendtorff, Rolf, and Robert A. Kugler (eds.), *The Book of Leviticus: Composition and Reception* (VTSup, 93; Leiden: E.J. Brill, 2003).

Reventlow, H.G., *Das Heiligkeitsgesetz formgeschichtlich untersucht* (WMANT, 6; Neukirchen: Neukirchener Verlag, 1961).

Rodriguez, A.M., *Substitution in the Hebrew Cultus and in Cultic-Related Texts* (PhD dissertation, Andrews University, 1980).

Rogerson, John W., Margaret Davies and M. Daniel Carroll R. (eds.), *The Bible in Ethics: The Second Sheffield Colloquium* (JSOTSup, 207. Sheffield: Sheffield Academic Press, 1995).

Römer, T. (ed.), *The Books of Leviticus and Numbers* (Colloquium biblicum lovaniense, 55; Leuven: Peeters, 2008).

Rosenzweig, F., 'Das Formgeheimnis der biblischen Erzählungen', in Buber and Rosenzweig (eds.), *Die Schrift und ihre Verdeutschung*, pp. 239-61.

Ross, Allen P., *Holiness to the Lord: A Guide to the Exposition of the Book of Leviticus* (Grand Rapids: Baker Academic, 2002).

Rost, Leonhard, 'Erwägungen zum israelitischen Brandopfer', in *Vom Ugarit nach Qumran: Festschrift O. Eissfeldt* (BZAW, 77; Berlin: W. de Gruyter, 1958), pp. 177-83.

Ruwe, Andreas, *'Heiligkeitsgesetz' und 'Priesterschrift:' literaturgeschichtliche und rechtssystematische Untersuchungen zu Leviticus 17:1–26:2* (Tübingen: J.C.B. Mohr [Paul Siebeck], 1999).

Sailhamer, John H., *The Pentateuch as Narrative* (Grand Rapids: Zondervan, 1992).

Sarna, Nahum M., *Exploring Exodus: The Origins of Biblical Israel* (New York: Shocken Books, 1986).

—*Genesis* (Philadelphia: Jewish Publication Society of America, 1989).

Sawyer, J.F.A. (ed.), *Reading Leviticus: A Conversation with Mary Douglas* (JSOTSup, 227; Sheffield: Sheffield Academic Press, 1996).

Schäfer, Peter, *Studien zur Geschichte und Theologie des rabbinischen Judentums* (Leiden: E.J. Brill, 1978).

Scharbert, Josef, *Fleisch, Geist und Seele im Pentateuch* (Stüttgart: Verlag Katholisches Bibelwerk, 1966).

Schenker, A., 'Welche Verfehlungen und welche Opfer in Lev. 5, 1-6?', in Fabry and Jüngling (eds.), *Levitikus als Buch*, pp. 249-61.

Schwartz, Baruch J., 'Israel's Holiness: The Torah Traditions', in Poorthuis and Schwartz (eds.), *Purity and Holiness: The Heritage of Leviticus* (Jewish and Christian Perspectives Series, 2; Leiden: E.J. Brill, 2000), pp. 47-59.

Schwartz, Baruch J., David P. Wright, Jeffrey Stackert and Naphtali S. Meshel (eds.), *Perspectives on Purity and Purification in the Bible* (London: T. & T. Clark International, 2008).

Searle, John R., 'Metaphor', in Ortony (ed.), *Metaphor and Thought*, pp. 92-123.

Seebass, H., 'נֶפֶשׁ', in Botterweck and Ringgren (eds.), *TDOT*, IX, pp. 497-519.

Seidl, Theodor, 'שׂגנ/שׂגה', in Botterweck and Ringgren (eds.), *TDOT*, XIV, pp. 397-405.

—*Tora für den 'Aussatz'-Fall: Literarische Schichten und syntaktische Strukturen in Levitikus 13 und 14* (St Ottilien: EOS Verlag, 1982).

Sherwood, Stephen K., *Leviticus, Numbers, Deuteronomy* (Berit Olam. Studies in Hebrew Narrative and Poetry; Collegeville, MN: Liturgical Press, 2002).

Shimasaki, Katsuomi, *Focus Structure in Biblical Hebrew: A Study of Word Order and Information Structure* (Bethesda, MD: CDL Press, 2002).

Silbermann. A.M. (ed.), *Pentateuch with Targum Onkelos, Haphtaroth and Rashi's Commentary: Leviticus* (trans. A. Blashki and L. Joseph; Jerusalem: Silbermann Family, 1932).

Silva, Moisés, *Biblical Words and their Meaning: An Introduction to Lexical Semantics* (Grand Rapids: Academie Books, 1983).

Sklar, Jay A., *Sin, Impurity, Sacrifice and Atonement* (PhD dissertation, Cheltenham and Gloucester College of Higher Education, 2001).

—*Sin, Impurity, Sacrifice, Atonement: The Priestly Conceptions* (Sheffield: Sheffield Phoenix Press, 2005).

Snaith, Norman H., 'A Note on Numbers xviii 9', *VT* 23 (1973), pp. 373-75.

—*Leviticus and Numbers* (London: Thomas Nelson, 1967).

Soden, W. von, 'Religiöse Unsicherheit, Säkularisierungstendenzen und Aberglaube zur Zeit der Sargoniden', in *Studie biblica et orientalia* (AnBib, 12; Rome: Pontifical Biblical Institute Press, 1959), pp. 356-67.

Sommer, Benjamin D., 'Conflicting Constructions of Divine Presence in the Priestly Tabernacle', *Int* 9 (2001), pp. 41-63.

—'Expulsion as Initiation: Displacement, Divine Presence, and Divine Exile in the Torah', in Cohen and Magid (eds.), *Beginning/Again: Towards a Hermeneutics of Jewish Texts*, pp. 23-48.

Sparks, Kenton L., *Ancient Texts for the Study of the Hebrew Bible: A Guide to the Background Literature* (Peabody, MA: Hendrickson Publishers, 2005).

Speiser, E.A., *Genesis* (New York: Doubleday, 1964).

Staubli, Thomas, 'Die Symbolik des Vogelrituals bei der Reinigung von Aussätzigen (Lev. 14,4-7)', *Biblica* 83 (2002), pp. 230-37.

Stern, Josef, *Metaphor in Context* (Cambridge, MA: MIT Press, 2000).

Stern, Josef, 'Metaphor, Literal, Literalism', *Mind and Language* 21 (2006), pp. 243-79.

Stevenson, William Barron, 'Hebrew *'Olah* and *Zebach* Sacrifices', in Baumgartner (ed.), *Festschrift für A. Bertholet*, pp. 488-97.

Stiver, Dan R., *The Philosophy of Religious Language: Sign, Symbol and Story* (Oxford: Blackwell, 1996).

Stordalen, T., *Echoes of Eden: Genesis 2–3 and Symbolism of the Eden Garden in Biblical Hebrew Literature* (Leuven: Peeters, 2000).

Trevaskis, Leigh M., 'On a Recent "Existential" Translation of *ḥāṭā*', *VT* 59 (2009), pp. 313-19.

—review of *Blood Ritual in the Hebrew Bible: Meaning and Power* (Baltimore: Johns Hopkinss University Press, 2004), by William K. Gilders, in *EJT* 17 (2008), p. 184-85.

—'The Purpose of Leviticus 24 within its Literary Context', *VT* 59 (2009), pp. 295-312.

Turner, Victor W., *The Forest of Symbols* (Ithaca, NY: Cornell University Press, 1967).

VanGemeren, W.A. (ed.), *New International Dictionary of Old Testament Theology and Exegesis* (5 vols.; Grand Rapids: Zondervan, 1997).

Vanhoozer, Kevin J., *Is There a Meaning in This Text?* (Grand Rapids: Zondervan, 1998).

—'The Semantics of Biblical Literature: Truth and Scripture's Diverse Literary Forms' in Carson and Woodbridge (eds.), *Hermeneutics, Authority, and Canon*, pp. 51-104.

Vaux, Roland de, *Studies in Old Testament Sacrifice* (Cardiff: University of Wales Press, 1964).

Volz, Paul, Friedrich Stummer, and Johannes Hempel (eds.), *Werden und Wesen des Alten Testament* (BZAW, 66; Berlin: Alfred Töpelmann, 1936).

Waltke, Bruce K., and Michael P. O'Connor, *An Introduction to Biblical Hebrew Syntax* (Winona Lake, IN: Eisenbrauns, 1990).

Wardlaw, T.R., *Conceptualizing Words for 'God' within the Pentateuch: A Cognitive-Semantic Investigation in Literary Context* (LHS, 495; New York: T. & T. Clark, 2008).

Warning, Wilfried, *Literary Artistry in Leviticus* (Leiden: E.J. Brill, 1999).

Watts, James W., ''Ōlāh: The Rhetoric of Burnt Offerings', *VT* 56 (2006), pp. 125-37.

—*Ritual and Rhetoric in Leviticus: From Sacrifice to Scripture* (Cambridge: Cambridge University Press, 2007).

Weinfeld, Moshe, *Deuteronomy and the Deuteronomic School* (Winona Lake, IN: Eisenbrauns, 1992).

—'Sabbath, Temple and the Enthronement of the Lord: The Problem of the Sitz im Leben of Gen. 1:1–2:3', in Calquot and Delcor (eds.), *Mélanges bibliques et orientaux en l'honneur de M. Henri Cazelles*, pp. 501-12.

—'Social and Cultic Institutions in the Priestly Source against their Near Eastern Background', in *Proceedings of the Eighth World Congress of Jewish Studies, Bible Studies, and Hebrew Language. 1981* (Jerusalem: World Union of Jewish Studies, 1983), pp. 95-129.

Wellek, René, and Austin Warren, *Theory of Literature* (London: Jonathan Cape, London, 1949).

Wellhausen, Julius, *Die Composition des Hexateuchs und der historichen Bücher des Alten Testaments* (orig. 1899; Berlin: W. de Gruyter, 1963).

—*Prolegomena to the History of Israel* (orig. 1883; trans. J. Sutherland Black and A. Menzies; Atlanta: Scholars Press, 1994).

Wenham, Gordon J., *Genesis 1–15* (WBC, 1; Dallas: Word Books, 1987).

—*Genesis 16–50* (WBC, 1; Nashville: Thomas Nelson Publishers, 1994).

—*Numbers* (Leicester: IVP, 1981).

—'Original Sin in Genesis 1–11', *Churchman* 104 (1990), pp. 309-28.

—'Purity', in Barton (ed.), *The Biblical World*, II, pp. 378-94.

—'Sanctuary Symbolism in the Garden of Eden Story', in *Proceedings of the Ninth World Congress of Jewish Studies, Division A: The Period of the Bible* (Jerusalem: World Union of Jewish Studies, 1986), pp. 19-25.

—*Story as Torah: Reading the Old Testament Ethically* (Edinburgh: T. & T. Clark, 2000).

—*The Book of Leviticus* (Grand Rapids: Eerdmans, 1979).

—'Why Does Sexual Intercourse Defile (Lev. 15:18)?', *ZAW* 95 (1983), pp. 432-44.

Wessely, N.H., 'Leviticus', in Mendelssohn (ed.), *Netivot Ha-shalom*, III (Vienna: von Schmid und Busch, 1846).
Westermann, Claus, *Genesis 1–11* (London: SPCK, 1984).
—*Genesis 12–36* (Minneapolis: Augsburg, 1985).
Whitekettle, Richard, 'Leviticus 12 and the Israelite Woman: Ritual Process, Liminality and the Womb', *ZAW* 107 (1995), pp. 393-408.
—'Leviticus 15.18 Reconsidered: Chiasm, Spatial Structure and the Body', *JSOT* 49 (1991), pp. 31-45.
Wilkinson, John, 'Leprosy and Leviticus: A Problem of Semantics and Translation'. *SJT* 31 (1978), pp. 153-66.
Wright, David P., 'Holiness (OT)', in Freedman (ed.), *ABD*, III, pp. 237-49.
—'Holiness, Sex, and Death in the Garden of Eden', *Biblica* 77 (1996), pp. 305-29.
—'Observations on the Ethical Foundations of the Biblical Dietary Laws: A Response to Jacob Milgrom', in Firmage, Weiss and Welch (eds.), *Religion and Law: Biblical-Judaic and Islamic Perspectives*, pp. 193-98.
—'The Gesture of Hand Placement in the Hebrew Bible and in Hittite Literature', *JAOS* 106 (1986), pp. 433-46.
Wright, David P., and R.N. Jones, 'Leprosy', in Freedman (ed.), *ABD*, IV, pp. 277-82.

INDEX OF REFERENCES

HEBREW BIBLE

Genesis		2.4–2.34	199	5.1-2	100
1–Leviticus 12	139, 143-45	2.4	100	5.2	200
		2.7	85	6–9	142, 144, 170, 232, 249
1–11	65, 207	2.9	95		
1–3	93, 96-97, 106, 144, 162, 165, 231, 239, 245	2.15-17	100		
		2.15	93-94	6.1–9.29	140
		2.16-17	97	6	206
		2.17	92, 94, 99-100	6.3	140
				6.9	202, 204, 233
1.1–2.4	198, 249	2.19	93		
1.1–2.3	198-99	2.21	93, 143	6.12-13	216
1	26, 82, 86, 94, 96-97, 101, 165, 199, 201, 248-49	2.23	143	6.12	140-41, 249
		2.24	140, 143, 163, 167, 199	6.13	140
				6.17	140, 249
		3	89, 92, 95-100, 109, 156, 162, 207, 239, 249-50	6.19	140
1.5	85			7.4	249
1.6-10	26			7.6	249
1.10	85			7.10	249
1.20	84-86, 97-98			7.12	249
		3.1-6	98	7.14	249
1.24	97-98	3.3	79	7.15	140
1.26-27	200	3.4	95, 99	7.16	140
1.26	200	3.6	95	7.17	249
1.27-28	201	3.7	95, 142	7.18	249
1.28	161	3.8	93	7.19	249
1.29-30	65	3.10	142	7.21	140, 249
1.31	198	3.11	142	8	205
2–3	93-94, 96-101, 140, 161, 201, 250	3.14	37, 98, 249	8.1	249
		3.16	96	8.9	205
		3.21	65, 94, 96	8.17	140, 249
		3.23-24	99	8.19	249
2	93-94, 161, 168, 199	3.23	94	8.20-21	205
		3.24	94-95	8.20	205
2.1	198	4.4	65	9	97
2.2	198	4.5	65	9.1-7	65
2.3	198	5	201	9.3-6	58, 62

9.3-4	97	4.7	139, 142	26.36	225
9.4	59, 140	7.18	91	27.31	63
9.9-18	66	8.9	91	28.9-14	94
9.11	140	9.9-11	149	28.20	94
9.13	140	9.9	148	28.30	204
9.14	249	9.10	148	28.31	225
9.16	140, 249	12.5	204	28.37	225
9.17	140, 249	12.22	79	28.38	53, 182-83
9.22	142	12.44	141	28.41	94
9.23	142, 149	12.48	141	28.42-43	143
9.24	149	13.2	74	28.42	142
15	205	13.12	74	28.43	53, 142
15.9	205	13.13	177	29	224
15.10	205	13.21	149	29.1-37	51
15.17	149	14	26	29.1	204
17	141-44,	14.24	149	29.8	94
	164, 207	16.14	249	29.36	15-16
17.1	204, 233	19	50	29.37	79
17.11	141	19.2	223	29.42-46	224
17.13	141	19.6	225	29.43	224
17.14	141	19.12	79	29.44	224
17.23	141	20.10	73, 216	29.45-46	224
17.24	141	20.22–23.3	34	30.11-16	65
17.25	141	20.25	222	30.11	197
19.23-24	149	20.26	95, 142	30.17	197
19.23	249	21.28	216	30.22	197
21.4	141	22.22	74	30.26-30	51
22	177	22.29	74	30.29	79
22.2-13	204	22.30	91	30.32	143
22.16	129	23.12	73	30.34	197
25.27	204	23.18	254	31.1	197
28.2	79	23.19	58, 62	31.12-18	198
29.14	141	24.15	197	31.12-17	198
33.13	91	25–40	26-27, 32,	31.12	197
34.15	141		34, 197-98,	32.34	100
34.17	141		201, 207,	34.19	74
34.22	141		231, 233	34.25	254
34.24	141	25–31	197	34.26	58, 62
34.27	91	25.1	197	34.29	129
37–50	26	25.5	129, 248	34.30	129
37.34	155	25.7	94	34.35	129
40.19	139, 141	25.16	95	35–40	197, 198
41.34	249	25.18-22	94, 199	35.7	129
42.6	249	25.31-35	94	35.23	129, 248
42.9	142	25.32	199	36.8	94
42.12	142	26.1	94	36.19	129, 248
		26.14	129, 248	36.29	204
Exodus		26.24	204	36.35	94
3.2	149	26.31	94, 225	37.7-9	94, 199
3.15	50				

Exodus (cont.)

37.18	199		208, 209,	2	174, 192,	
39–40	198		210, 233,		254, 255	
39.32	198		239, 251,	2.1-3	253, 255	
39.34	129, 248	1.1-9	257	2.1	103, 127,	
39.43	198	1.1-2	176		200, 201,	
40	190	1.1	254		253	
40.14	94	1.2-4	197, 199	2.3-10	253	
40.33	198	1.2	181	2.3	251, 252,	
40.34-35	197		22, 127,		253, 256	
40.35	190, 197,		192, 199,	2.4-15	255	
	199		200, 201,	2.4-5	255	
			202, 205,	2.4	253, 254	
			207, 233,	2.8	253, 256,	
Leviticus			252, 253,		257	
1–16	1, 2, 3, 9,		254	2.10	251, 252,	
	21, 26, 29,	1.3-4	178, 179,		253	
	30, 31, 48,		181, 184,	2.11	255	
	49, 51, 52,		187, 228	3	21, 24, 25,	
	56, 62,	1.3	23, 173,		174, 254	
	68, 72, 73,		179, 180,	3.1	203	
	100, 101,		181, 182,	3.2	259	
	103, 203,		183, 184,	3.3-5	64	
	228		191, 193,	3.6	203	
1–12	143		194, 195,	3.7	259	
1–10	172, 173		197, 202,	3.9-11	64	
1–7	22, 23, 27,		204, 205,	3.13	259	
	56, 76,		210	3.14-16	64	
	127, 174,	1.4	23, 29,	4.1–6.7	254	
	177, 195,		173, 175,	4–5	175, 202,	
	196, 199,		176, 179,		206, 254	
	200, 211,		180, 181,	4.1–5.13	175, 254	
	260		182, 183,	4	29, 36, 39,	
1–5	22, 32, 39,		185, 186,		114, 258	
	251, 252,		188, 189,	4.1-2	254	
	253, 254,		190, 191,	4.2	52, 53,	
	259		192, 193,		103, 127,	
1–3	30, 174,		194, 195,		201, 252,	
	175, 202,		197, 233		253, 254	
	254	1.5-9	256	4.3	36, 203	
1	10, 29, 31,	1.5	186, 195,	4.6	195	
	171, 172,		197, 256,	4.7	195	
	173, 174,		258	4.8	39	
	175, 177,	1.9	176, 177	4.11	140	
	178, 181,	1.10	184, 205	4.13	52, 140	
	188, 189,	1.11	259	4.17	195	
	192, 195,	1.13	177	4.18	195	
	197, 199,	1.14-17	204, 205	4.20	15	
	203, 205,	1.14	184, 205	4.22-26	202	
	206, 207,	1.17	177, 205	4.22	52	

4.23	203	6.19	253
4.25	195	6.20	79
4.26	15	6.22	251-53,
4.27-35	202		255, 257,
4.27	127, 201		260
4.30	195	6.23	259-60
4.31	15, 37	7.1-9	177
4.34	195	7.1-2	258
4.35	15	7.1	251, 258
5	202	7.2	252, 258
5.1	52, 103,	7.6	251-52,
	127, 201		257, 260
5.2-4	88	7.8	129
5.2	79	7.9-10	253
5.3	79, 200	7.9	253
5.4	103, 127,	7.11-35	24
	201	7.11-21	186, 254-
5.6	15		55
5.7	79	7.18	53, 181,
5.10	15		186-87,
5.14-26 [Eng. 5.14-6.7]			193-94
	53, 175,	7.19	79
	254	7.20-21	67, 103
5.14	254	7.21	79, 127,
5.15	127, 201-		200-201
	203	7.24	91
5.17-19	52, 53	7.25	127
5.17	53, 127,	7.26-27	73, 76
	201	7.27	103
5.18	202-203	7.28	200
5.21	127	7.29	259
5.25 [Eng. 6.6]	202-203	7.30	36, 259
6–7	252	8	68, 221
6	203, 255	8.10-30	51
6.1-6	256-57	8.10-12	51
6.2	257	8.10-11	1
6.3 [Eng. 5.22]	201, 256	8.12	172
6.5	257	8.13	94
6.6	257	8.15	1
6.7-16	255-56	8.30	1, 143, 172
6.7	253	9.7	175
6.9-10	256	10.1-3	95, 159
6.10	251-52,	10.2	149
	255-56	10.3	1, 172,
6.11	79, 256		222-24
6.12-16	257, 259	10.6	155
6.15	260	10.10	56, 57, 67-
6.18-20	13		69, 121,
6.18	251-52,		242
	258		

10.12-13	256-57,
	260
10.12	251-52,
	255
10.17	257, 260
11–15	27, 29, 37-
	38, 48-49,
	53-54, 56,
	60-61, 63,
	66-67, 69,
	96-97, 144,
	160-62,
	164, 168,
	196, 206,
	233
11–14	162
11	1, 10, 21,
	37, 46, 49-
	50, 52-56,
	58, 62, 70,
	71, 73-82,
	87-91, 93,
	95-98, 100-
	101, 103,
	105-106,
	108-110,
	114, 125-
	26, 130,
	139, 144,
	159-62,
	170-72,
	206, 231,
	233, 238-
	40, 243,
	244-47,
	249
11.1-42	106, 160,
	170, 231
11.1-23	81-82, 86,
	244
11.1-8	82-84, 86,
	130, 244,
	247
11.1-4	250
11.1-3	248
11.1-2	239
11.2-40	239, 241
11.2-23	241
11.2-8	81, 241

Leviticus (cont.)
11.2-3	92
11.2	97
11.3	104
11.4	82, 97, 104
11.5	82, 104
11.6	82 104
11.7	82
11.8-40	82
11.8-12	84
11.8	82-84, 86, 97, 103, 239
11.9-23	69, 82, 86-89, 244
11.9-12	82, 242, 248
11.9	76
11.10-12	74
11.10	82, 84, 97
11.11	83-84, 103, 239
11.12	82, 84
11.13-23	242
11.13-19	73, 82, 248-49
11.13	82, 97
11.20-23	82, 248-50
11.20-22	248
11.20	82, 97
11.21	249
11.24-45	81
11.24-40	81, 82, 87, 92, 239-40
11.24-28	27, 62, 81, 86-87, 90, 92, 240
11.24	69, 80, 87, 90, 165
11.25	69, 80, 87-88
11.26	80, 87
11.27	80, 87
11.28-42	248
11.28	69, 80, 87-88
11.29-42	81, 87, 89
11.29-40	89-90
11.29-38	78, 87, 90, 114, 250
11.29-30	77, 92, 98-99
11.29	90, 98, 250
11.31-32	80, 91, 32
11.31	80, 90, 91-92, 98, 100, 250
11.32-38	90
11.32	80, 88, 90-92, 100
11.33	80, 90
11.34	80, 84, 90
11.35-38	90
11.35	80, 90
11.36	80, 84, 90, 98
11.38	80, 84, 90
11.39-42	87
11.39-40	90, 92, 248, 250
11.39	69, 80, 90-92, 100
11.40	69, 80, 88
11.41-46	250
11.41-45	239, 243
11.41-42	69, 81, 87, 90, 244-45
11.41	99
11.42	82, 96, 98, 239, 249
11.43-45	1, 8, 10, 46-47, 49, 53, 54, 61, 70, 78-81, 83, 100-102, 105-106, 108, 110, 127, 160, 170-71, 173, 206, 231, 233, 238, 248
11.43-44	83, 102-103
11.43	87, 103
11 44-46	250
11.44-45	61, 70, 75, 78, 100, 102-103, 160, 172, 178
11.44	47, 97, 103 104
11.45	81-82, 239
11.46-47	
12-15	10, 105, 107-109, 114, 166, 169-70, 232, 236
12-13	166, 168-69
12	56-57, 96, 109, 143-44, 160-66, 168, 170, 233
12.2	127, 161, 164-65
12.3	141, 162, 164, 166
12.4	88, 165
12.5	161, 165
12.6	165-66
13-14	56, 96-97, 109, 114, 151-52, 157, 162, 166
13	27, 45, 108-10, 112-13, 115-27, 129-30, 132, 134-40, 143-45, 148, 149, 152, 159-60, 162-63, 165-66, 168-70, 232-33, 236
13.1-46	125, 157-59
13.1-8	148
13.1	126
13.2-46	115

13.2-44	117	13.14-15	134-36,	13.31	137
13.2-17	126, 129,		148	13.32	134, 137,
	148	13.14	45, 116,		151
13.2-8	126-27,		118, 124,	13.33	116
	129, 130-		136	13.34	137, 151
	34, 139,	13.15	130-31,	13.35	116, 118,
	148, 151-		134, 136-		151
	52		40, 144,	13.36	134, 151
13.2-4	129		148	13.38-39	126, 150-
13.2	110, 126-	13.16-17	134		53
	32, 139,	13.16	138, 158	13.38	126-27,
	148, 153,	13.17	137, 158		148, 153
	200	13.18-28	130, 139,	13.39	151-53
13.3-17	110		145, 147-	13.40-46	126, 149,
13.3-8	127, 133		49		152, 154-
13.3	116, 130,	13.18-27	126		55, 158
	133, 137-	13.18-23	110, 139,	13.40-44	150-51,
	39		148, 152		154
13.4-8	131	13.18	126, 129-	13.40	126-27,
13.4	131, 139,		30, 144,		153
	158		148, 150,	13.41	153
13.5-8	131, 151		153	13.42-44	150
13.5	128	13.19	148	13. 42-43	158
13.6	128, 137,	13.20	151-52,	13.42	151, 153
	151		158	13.43	137, 149
13.7	116, 118,	13.22	148, 151-	13.44	154-55
	128, 151		52	13.45-46	112, 123,
13.8	128, 151	13.23	148, 151-		152, 154-
13.9-17	126, 128,		52		55, 158-59,
	130-34,	13.24-28	110, 126,		232
	138, 139,		139, 144,	13.45	155
	145, 148		148	13.46	123, 155-
13.9	126, 128,	13.24	126, 129-		56
	132-34,		30, 148-50,	13.47-59	108, 124-
	138, 139,		153		26, 156,
	148, 153,	13.25	137, 151-		159
	157		52, 158	13.47-58	157, 232
13.10-12	134, 136	13.27	137, 148,	13.47-49	157
13.10	132-33,		151-52	13.47	126, 153,
	158	13.28	148, 151-		157
13.11	133, 139		52	13.48	162
13.12-17	135	13.29-37	126, 129-	13.50	137
13.12-15	157		30, 149-52	13.51	137
13.12-13	133-34	13.29-30	151	13.52	158
13.12	138, 150-	13.29	126-27,	13.53	151
	51		129, 151,	13.55	137, 151,
13.13	116-19,		153		158
	124, 135,	13.30	134, 137,	13.56	124
	150, 158		150	13.57	151, 158

Leviticus (cont.)		15.19-30	96	19	40, 75, 77,
13.58	159	15.19-24	161, 167		160
13.59	124, 156	15.19	127, 167,	19.2-3	40
14	27, 109,		168-69	19.2	2-3, 78,
	114, 156,	15.23	141		208, 223,
	159, 170	15.24	141		226
14.1-32	109, 125,	15.25-30	167	19.5	182
	157, 159,	15.25	127, 141,	19.7	181
	162, 170,		167, 169	19.8	127
	232	15.31	167	19.9-18	40
14.1-8	169	15.32-33	167	19.12	223
14.2	117	15.32	164	19.20	127
14.4-7	114, 123	16	2, 89, 113	19.30	226
14.13	251-52,	16.6	37	20.2	62, 127
	258	16.16	52	20.3	223
14.20	175	16.17	200	20.3-5	177
14.33-53	108-109,	16.21	52, 187-89,	20.7	2-3
	124, 160		192	20.9	127
14.34	115, 122,	16.24	189	20.13-15	68
	149	17–26	1-3, 8-10	20.24-26	104-105
14.39	151	17–24	72	20.26	2-3, 223
14.43	151	17–22	223	20.27	127
14.44	151	17	4, 64-65,	21–23	2
14.45	27		92	21–22	10, 75, 77,
14.48	151	17.1-11	58-59		79, 174,
15	27, 56-57,	17.3-4	59, 64		207, 209,
	96, 109,	17.7	62		214-29,
	160-62,	17.8	127		234-35
	166-70,	17.10-13	76	21	7, 207,
	233	17.10-14	58, 62		210-11,
15.1-33	167	17.10	59, 63, 127		214, 216-
15.1-18	96	17.11	17, 59,		17, 219,
15.2	127, 137,		63-65, 78,		226-27,
	167-69		103, 127,		229, 234
15.2-15	169		190, 192,	21.1-4	56
15.3	168-69		195	21.2-3	68
15.5	88	17.12	59	21.4	220, 223
15.6	88	17.13	127	21.6	8, 214,
15.7	88, 169	17.14	73, 127		220-23
15.10	88	17.15	80, 88, 91,	21.7	8, 214, 219
15.11	88, 141		127	21.8	2, 3, 8,
15.13	88, 169	17.21	177		221-23
15.14	141	18–20	105, 216,	21.9	127, 223
15.16-18	68		219, 225-	21.10	155
15.16-17	167		26	21.12	221-23
15.16	127, 164,	18.5	201	21.13-14	219
	167, 169	18.21	62, 223	21.15	223
15.17	103, 164	18.29	127	21.16-24	208, 210,
15.18	164, 167-	19–20	219		212, 216,
	68				234

21.17	208, 213, 222	22.25	179, 181	12.9	112	
		22.29	182	12.12	123-24	
21.18	127, 212	22.31-33	223-24	14.6	155	
21.20	211, 212	22.31-32	225	15.38-39	225	
21.21	208, 213, 222	22.31	223	15.39	226	
		22.32-33	2-3	16.35	159	
21.22	208, 220, 223	22.32	2, 8, 213, 222-24	18.5-6	94	
				18.8	251	
21.23	208, 213, 220, 222	22.33	224	18.9	251	
		23.11	182	19.1-13	123	
21.28	222	23.15	209	23.1-6	176	
22	202-203, 207, 209, 210, 215, 217-18, 227-28, 234-35	23.17	254	27.18-23	187	
		23.20	254	30.16	52	
		23.29	127	31.48	65	
		24.9	256			
		24.15	127	*Deuteronomy*		
		24.16-22	78	5.14	73	
22.1-16	215	24.17	127, 200	10.16	141	
22.1-9	214, 223	24.19-20	75	11.31–28.68	4	
22.2-9	220-21	24.19	127	12.21	60	
22.2	220-23	24.21	200	14	238	
22.3	67	25–27	72	14.3-21	91	
22.4	68	25	2	14.21	58, 62, 91	
22.6	80, 88	25.26	127	15.21	215	
22.7	221	25.29	127	17.1	215	
22.8	91, 221	25.30	209	18.10	177	
22.9	220-21	26	4, 89, 106	18.13	173, 202, 204, 206, 215, 227	
22.10-13	8	26.12	93			
22.11	103	26.14-46	101			
22.14-15	222	27	1, 3, 229	22.21	91	
22.14	127	27.2	127	23.2 [Eng. 23.1]	211	
22.15	222	27.14	127	23.12-15	168	
22.17-25	203, 208, 210, 234	27.28	251, 253, 258, 260	23.15	93, 168	
				25.11-12	212	
22.19-20	228	27.29	201	28.15-69	101	
22.19	182, 210, 215, 228-29			28.27	149	
		Numbers		28.35	149	
22.20	179, 182, 213, 228	3.1	100	30.6	141	
		3.7-8	94	30.15	91, 100	
22.21	127, 182-83, 210, 215, 228-29	4.6	225, 248	30.19	91, 100	
		4.14	63	31.26	95	
		5.2-4	56	32	208	
		5.15-16	52	32.4	208	
22.22	212-13, 229	6.9-12	56	32.5	208	
		7.89	94	34.9	187	
22.23	181, 212-13	8.7	140			
		8.26	94	*Joshua*		
22.24	211, 212-13	11.1-3	159	2.19	154	
		12.1-15	110	7.15	91	

Judges
6   176
11.31   177
13   176

1 Samuel
3.13   216
4.12-18   38
17.38   158
18.4   158
24.1-7   158
24.15   91

2 Samuel
1.11   155
3.29   112
7.6-7   93
7.14   112
15.21   91
22.1   100
22.31   208

1 Kings
2.32   154
7.29   94
8.6-7   94
8.63   66
18   176

2 Kings
3   176
3.27   177
5   112
5.27   112
11.4-20   6
11.14   155
11.18   6
15.5   110
19.1   155
20.7   149
22.11   155
22.19   155

Isaiah
1.17   75
1.18   116
11.16   100
38.21   149
40.2   181

43.2   149
56.7   182
58.1-5   237
65.3-5   244
65.4   245
66.17   82, 244-45
66.24   91

Jeremiah
6.20   182

Ezekiel
1.26   41
8.10   82
10.19   94
11.1   94
24.17   155
24.22   155
33.4   154
43.1-4   94
43.22–23   15
44.26-27   56
44.31   91
47.1-12   94

Amos
2.6-8   237
7.17   102

Hosea
4.6-8   216
9.3   102

Ezra
9.5   155

Malachi
2.4-7   216

Psalms
15.2   204, 208
51.9   116
105.29   91

Proverbs
6.28   149

Job
1.5   175

2.7   149
18.13   123
42.8   91, 175

Ecclesiastes
9.4   91
10.1   91

Daniel
12.10   116

2 Chronicles
3.7   94
3.10-14   94
5.7-8   94
26.18-21   112
26.19   110

New Testament
Mark
2   110

Romans
7.5-6   145
7.8   145

1 Corinthians
5.5   145

Galatians
3.3   145
4.29   145
5–6   145

Philippians
3.3 145

INDEX OF AUTHORS

Allwood, J. 17
Alter, R. 34, 35, 37, 46, 80, 231
Amit, Y. 38, 81
Aquinas, T. 48
Astruc, J. 3
Averbeck, R.E. 48, 68, 191, 254

Baentsch, B. 223-24
Bähr, K.C.W.F. 17, 35
Baker, D.W. 111
Balentine, S.E. 71, 80, 82, 97, 120, 200-201, 210, 216-17, 219
Bamberger, B.J. 112, 131, 163
Barr, J. 12-16, 18, 20-21, 25, 78, 99, 100-101, 230
Barton, J. 113
Baumgarten, J.M. 111
Beardsley, M. 44
Becker, J. 147
Begrich, J. 10
Bergen, W.J. 27, 31
Bernoulli, M. 187
Bertholet, A. 187
Bertman, S. 225
Bibb, B.D. 32
Blenkinsopp, J. 198
Blum, E. 97-98, 176
Bratsiotis, N.P. 140-41
Brovarski, E. 95
Budd, J.P. 25, 120, 227

Caird, G.B. 42, 43
Calvin, J. 85
Carmichael, C.A. 95
Cassuto, U. 65, 142-43, 198
Childs, B.S. 198, 248
Cholewinski, A. 10
Croft, W. 17, 19, 20
Cruse, D.A. 17, 19, 20

Delitzsch, F. 35
Dillmann, A. 118
Douglas, M. 9, 37, 53-54, 69, 70-80, 82, 89, 96, 98, 106, 120-22, 124, 156, 173, 203, 206, 209, 213, 217-19, 229, 231, 240, 247
Driver, G.R. 135
Driver, S.R. 2, 91
Durham, J.I. 248

Eerdmans, B.D. 1
Eichrodt, W. 7
Eilberg-Schwartz, H. 37
Eissfeldt, O. 3, 22
Elliger, K. 81, 135-37, 161, 164, 187, 221, 223, 253
Enns, P. 199

Feldman, E. 57
Feucht, C. 10
Firmage, E. 37, 66, 84
Fishbane, M. 110, 148
Fitzpatrick-McKinley, A. 35
Fox, M.V. 91
Fredericks, D.C. 103
Friedman, R.E. 200
Fretheim, T.E. 26
Frey, J. 145-47
Fritz, V. 23, 127
Frymer-Kensky, T. 113, 156, 160, 164

Gerstenberger, E.S. 25, 27, 80-81, 120, 127, 132, 148, 187, 189, 210, 215, 220
Gese, H. 192
Gilders, W.K. 22, 33-34, 174, 191, 195
Ginzberg, L. 111
Gorman, F.H. 22, 30-34, 79, 213, 217-18, 221-22, 231, 245-46
Grabbe, L.L. 104
Graf, K.H. 3

Green, G. 35
Grelot, P. 34, 41
Grice, H.P. 44
Grisanti, M.A. 82
Gründwaldt, K. 10, 211, 222-24
Gunkel, H. 93

Harrington, H. 91, 109, 111
Harrison, R.K. 80-81, 118, 217, 227
Hartley, J.E. 22, 25-26, 30, 31, 34, 37, 47, 52, 71, 109, 113, 118, 120, 122, 126-28, 134-37, 156, 157, 162, 164, 172, 176-77, 182-83, 188-89, 192, 197, 200-201, 210, 212, 217-19, 222-23, 228-29, 252
Hayes, C.E. 102
Heinisch, P. 61, 108, 128, 163, 166, 177, 211, 238
Hoffmann, D.Z 82-83, 109, 113-15, 119, 129, 134, 148, 163-66, 173, 184, 189, 192-93, 201, 203-204, 221, 235-36
Houston, W. 2, 7, 54, 28, 66, 71, 77, 81-82, 84, 87, 92, 97, 99, 102, 238-48, 250
Houtman, C. 143
Hulse, E.V. 118

Janowski, B. 185, 187, 189, 191-93
Jastrow, M. 136
Jenson, P. 71, 161
Johnson, M. 16
Jones, L.P. 41, 42-43, 109
Jones, R.N. 118
Joosten, J. 7, 220, 222-23
Jouon, P. 128

Kaiser, W.C. 176
Kalisch, M.M. 163
Kaufmann, Y. 5, 50
Kearny, P.J. 198
Kedar, B. 14-15
Kedar-Kopfstein, B. 173
Keil, C.F. 2, 56, 80, 85, 88, 98-99, 172, 257, 261
Keil, K. 35
Kellogg, S.H. 2, 3
Kiuchi, N. 14, 15, 35-37, 39, 47, 59, 63-65, 88, 93, 96-98, 115-19, 124, 128, 138, 159, 161-62, 172-74, 178-79, 181-82, 188, 191-97, 199, 201-202, 204, 224, 227-28, 230, 251-52, 257, 259-61

Klawans, J. 9, 27, 30, 66-67, 71, 85, 89, 111, 196, 235-37
Kleinig, J.W. 128, 154-55, 164, 227
Klostermann, A. 3
Knierim, R.P. 22-23, 27-29, 31-32, 36, 39, 52, 173, 179-87, 189-90, 193-94, 197, 203, 210-11
Knohl, I. 2-3, 5-10, 48, 50-53, 56-57, 70, 217, 219, 221-22, 224-26, 230, 236, 245
Koch, K. 26
Kornfeld, W. 7, 125, 137, 161, 223, 252
Kugler, R.A. 68
Kurtz, J.H. 17, 35

Lakoff, G. 17, 45
Langacker, R.W. 16, 18-19
Leupold, H.C. 86
Levin, S. 44
Levine, B.A. 22-25, 30-31, 34, 71, 80, 109, 118, 127, 137, 172, 176-77, 182, 185, 189-91, 196-97, 225, 261
Lewis, G. 109, 119
Liss, H. 35, 63, 90
Lockshin, M.I. 129, 131
Long, P.V. 27, 34
Longman III, T. 27, 34

Maccoby, H. 56, 77, 110, 112, 135, 157
Maass, F. 127
MacCulloch, J.A. 187
Macht, D.I. 161
Magonet, J. 163
Matthews, R. 44
McConville, J.G. 127
McEvenue, S.E. 212
Meyers, C.L. 94, 199
Milgrom, J. 1-10, 21, 29-30, 36-37, 47-48, 51-76, 78-86, 88-92, 96-98, 102-104, 106, 108-109, 111-12, 115, 117-18, 120-27, 129-35, 137, 148-51, 154-59, 162, 164-69, 172-77, 179-80, 182-83, 187-88, 194, 199-200, 202-203, 205-206, 209-17, 220-21, 223, 225, 227-31, 236, 245, 249-56, 258-61
Miller, C.L. 136
Miller, D.B. 44
Moberly, R.W.L. 99-101
Moran, W.L. 238

Moskala, J. 238
Muraoka, T. 128, 136

Nihan, C. 5, 23, 26, 77, 166, 214, 219-20,
    223, 225-26
Noordtzij, A. 22, 25, 37, 48, 82, 86, 125,
    128, 131, 135, 156, 164, 172, 179, 182,
    189, 192, 214, 220, 227
Noth, M. 3, 21-22, 37, 49, 83-84, 87-88,
    125, 127, 137, 161, 173, 175, 179, 182,
    187, 189, 192, 197, 199, 221, 225

O'Connor, M.P. 197
Ogden, C.K. 11, 43
Olyan, S.M. 8, 217, 222
Ostrer, B.S. 113
Otto, R. 7, 50
Ottosson, M. 106

Parry, D.W. 93
Péter-Contesse, R. 118, 161, 182
Philip, T.S. 161
Provan, I. 27, 34

Rad, G. von 7
Rainey, A. 22
Rashbam 129, 131, 197
Reiner, E. 52
Rendsburg, G.A. 104
Rendtorff, R. 22, 23, 31, 37, 53, 54, 172,
    175, 177, 180-82, 185, 187-89, 194,
    197, 202, 255, 257, 261
Reventlow, H.G. 223
Richards, I.A. 11, 43
Ringgren, H. 7
Rodriguez, A.M. 179, 185, 187-88, 194,
    197
Rosenzweig, F. 198
Ross, A.P. 81, 102
Rost, L. 174
Ruwe, A. 94

Sailhamer, J.H. 81, 96, 161-62
Sarna, N.M. 26, 66, 85, 140, 173, 198-99,
    202
Schäfer, P. 198
Scharbert, J. 139, 142, 170
Schwartz, B.J. 2, 172

Searle, J.R. 44
Seebass, H. 103
Seidl, T. 124, 125, 132, 134-36, 139, 148
Sherwood, S.K. 110, 158
Shimasaki, K. 136
Silva, M. 13-16
Sklar, J.A. 47, 63-64, 159, 179, 181-82,
    184, 187-88, 194-95, 228
Snaith, N.H. 48, 52, 82, 88, 102, 172, 180,
    183, 194, 211, 248, 251
Soden, W. von 5
Sommer, B.D. 198
Sparks, K.L. 62
Speiser, E.A. 85, 93
Staubli, T. 113
Stern, J. 41-45
Stevenson, W.B. 25
Stiver, D.R. 41
Stordalen, T. 94, 95

Trevaskis, L.M. 9, 77, 118-19, 138, 174
Turner, V.W. 29

Vanhoozer, K.J. 25, 42
Vaux, R. de 194

Waltke, B.K. 197
Wardlaw, T.R. 17-21, 144
Warning, W. 87
Warren, A. 41-42
Watts, J.W. 21, 77, 177-78, 252
Weinfeld, M. 5, 198
Wellek, R. 41, 42
Wellhausen, J. 3-5, 7, 161, 230, 236
Wenham, G.J. 25, 27, 30, 56, 66, 71, 81,
    85, 90, 93-95, 97, 102, 104, 113, 118,
    120-21, 125-28, 132, 134, 137, 140-41,
    148, 155-56, 158, 160, 164, 166, 173,
    177, 179, 182, 188-90, 202, 207, 210,
    213, 216-17, 219, 221, 225, 227, 229,
    260
Wessely, N.H. 129, 166
Westermann, C. 86, 95
Whitekettle, R. 160, 167-68
Wilkinson, J. 109
Wright, D.P. 9, 66, 93-95, 112-13, 118,
    172, 180, 185-88, 194, 251, 261

Abraham 204-206, 233
Adam and Eve 190, 199-201, 206, 231
Altar 64-65, 72-76, 95, 121, 142, 195, 203-204, 208, 210-11, 213-14, 216, 221-22, 224, 226, 229, 253-54, 256-57, 259
Ancient Near East
  Impurity 6, 55, 57, 62, 164
  literature 23-25, 66, 93
  priests 211, 216
  religious ideas 62, 113, 174, 238, 239, 242, 246, 247, 248

biblical narrative 22-26, 33-35, 37-38, 42, 46, 65-66, 112-113, 115, 124-25, 139, 142, 177, 190, 204, 231, 232, 233, 246, 250
'blood prohibition' 58-59, 62-63, 65, 76, 247
burnt offering
  'atonement gift' 176, 191
  birds 184, 204-205, 241-242
  diachronic interpretation 175, 181, 195
  'divine acceptance' 179
  expiatory 29, 174-75
  'gift of entreaty' 176-77
  'item of worth' 179, 195-96, 205-206
  religious ideal 177-78
  sin 188-89, 192, 206
  symbolism 178, 196, 206, 233
  theological interpretation 176, 233

cherubim 94, 199
chiasmus 85, 167-68, 212
childbirth 96, 120, 160-62, 164, 232
clean animals (see unclean animals)
clothes 80, 88, 155, 157, 225
cognitive linguistic theory 11, 16-21, 45, 204, 227, 230, 234
  centrality 18
  crystallization 20, 143-44, 163, 227-29, 235
  dynamic construal 19

encyclopaedic knowledge 18-19
  prescriptive context 19
  primary domain 18, 46, 143-44, 204, 215, 227, 230
  semantic domain 18
  semantic frame 17-18
  symbolism 11
creation theology 26
cultic
  definition 40
  sins 53
cultic terminology
  appropriateness 48-50

Day of Atonement 52, 89, 113, 156, 189, 200
defilement (see impurity)
dietary legislation ('dietary regulations'; 'food laws') 1
  ethical basis/purpose 21, 54, 231
  rationale 60-61, 70, 76, 79, 104, 246
  'respect for life' 54, 60, 62, 79, 231
  read as literature 80, 98, 105, 108, 246
'dietary system' 58, 60, 62-63, 67
divine judgment 109, 111-12, 115, 122, 124-25, 140-41, 144-45, 148-49, 154, 159-60, 170, 232
divine presence 2, 72, 89, 93, 104-105, 117, 172
Documentary Hypothesis 3-5

ethics
  definition 40
  and ritual 235-36
ethical commands 51-52, 56, 216
exclusion from divine presence 57, 88-89, 92-93, 99, 101-102, 105, 107, 109, 122, 125, 155-56, 159, 170, 214, 231-32, 236, 246
exile 26, 31, 72-73, 89, 101, 106, 170, 199, 232-33, 236, 240

flesh (בשר) 45, 232
and human rebellion 144-45, 147-48,
152, 160, 163, 170, 232
forbidden fruit 98-100, 104, 106, 231
food prohibition 58, 60-61, 66-67, 97-98,
104, 106, 114, 161, 231

Garden of Canaan 101
Garden of Eden 101, 106, 140, 142-43, 156,
167, 190, 197, 199, 200, 201, 207, 233
sanctuary symbolism 26, 93-95, 99,
105-106, 190, 197, 226, 231, 233
genital discharges 56, 67, 96, 160, 166
Grain Offering (מנחה) 29, 175, 215, 254-
55
ground as cursed 239, 250
guilt-offering 174-75, 189, 202, 206, 251,
254-55

hand-leaning 178-96
birds 205
consecration 185, 187
identification 185, 192
item of worth 179, 194, 195, 195, 205,
206
legal relinquishment 180
ownership 185, 186, 194
substitution 179, 185, 187, 188, 192,
193, 194, 195, 196, 206
transference 185, 187, 188
holiness
cultic 1-2, 6, 51, 102, 217, 219-20, 226
distinction between cultic and
ethical 1-10, 47-49, 219, 236
cultic and ethical commandments 2,
51, 53, 89, 101, 106, 160, 170,
231-33
ethical 1-2, 10, 21, 49, 219, 230
'forces of life' 57-60, 68
numinous 50
personal 48-50, 224-25
profaned 59, 186, 213, 220-23
semantic overlap with תמים 174, 196,
206-210, 216-18, 221-22, 226-29,
233-35
unrelated to ethics 6-7, 61, 229
'wholeness' 120-22, 218-19
Holiness Code
historical context 3-6, 9-10, 236-37

human (אדם) 126,-28, 130, 132-33, 139-
40, 146, 150, 191-92, 196, 199, 200-
201, 233, 254
human mortality 66, 127, 140, 166

illegitimate totality transfer 15, 21, 25
impurity (טמא)
anthropology 71, 120, 160
cleansing 14, 15, 68, 114, 117, 120,
124-25, 160, 163, 165, 191
conceptualization 54, 57, 61
death 51, 56-60, 67-68, 70, 89, 92, 95,
105-106, 109, 114, 117, 122-24,
155, 160, 214, 220, 231-32, 239,
246-49
'forces of death' 56-58, 60, 68, 89
metaphysical substance 47, 51, 54-55,
57-58, 61-62, 67, 69, 72
symbolism 80-81, 84, 86-87, 89-90,
92, 95-96, 101-102, 105-109, 114,
117, 120, 122, 125, 138, 144, 157,
159-60, 165, 170, 214, 231-33
interpretation
extra-linguistic factors 17, 21, 38, 45-
46, 65, 113
object of interpretation 22, 30-39, 46,
231
symbolic 9, 17, 21, 30, 35, 43, 45-46,
78, 115, 118, 145, 147, 196, 200,
202, 210, 220, 227-28, 232
כפר 14-15, 23, 37, 39, 59, 64-65, 109,
159, 170, 173, 175-76, 178-84, 186,
188-93, 195-96, 203, 206, 232, 233,
236
language
distinction between metaphor and
symbol 40-45
leprosy 108, 110-11, 119-20, 135, 235, 240
Leviticus, The Book of
'ring structure' 75, 77

Mesopotamian ritual documents 52, 55,
112
metaphor
definition 40-45
deviance account 44-45
tenor and vehicle 42-43
menorah 72, 94, 199
moral impurity 236

nakedness 95-96, 142
narrative analogy 34, 37
narrative art 34-35
Noachide narrative 66, 204

offerer
    intention 255, 259-60
offering
    relationship with offerer 178-96

פשעים 52

Peace Offering (שלמים) 23-24, 29, 59, 63-
    64, 174-77, 186, 203, 213, 250-52, 254,
    257, 259
Pentateuch 3, 19, 32, 45, 62, 89, 93, 97,
    102, 104, 126, 139, 141-42, 145, 149,
    159, 190, 203-204, 228, 240, 246,
    249-50
priest 37, 207
    ethical standards 215
    garments 225
    symbolic of God's presence 227
    physical appearance 209-26
    relationship with altar 221-22
    uncleanness of 214
priestly tradition (desire for the offer to be
    holy) 173, 178, 186, 196
purification offering (חטאת) 15, 29, 26,
    47, 88, 113, 186, 189, 191, 203, 251-
    53, 255, 258-60
purity
    'forces of life' 57, 60, 68
purity laws
    educational function 105, 116, 119-20,
        170, 232
    symbolic system 30, 120, 196, 235-36

Qumran 110-11, 132, 139, 145, 147, 216

reader
    extra-linguistic situation 16, 45-46,
        65, 113
rhetorical progression 36-38, 42, 81, 98,
    106, 110, 131, 151, 231-32, 246
ritual impurity (see impurity)
ritual text
    conceptualities 31-32
    drama 27, 30-31
    enactment 25, 27-34, 72-73

ethical purpose 21, 40, 49, 53-54, 72,
    74, 231
genre 22-24, 26, 32-33
fictive mode 35
implicit theology 1, 8-10, 26-27, 29-
    30, 35, 47, 49, 53, 79, 106, 110,
    160, 171, 173, 230
literary approach 31, 35, 115, 119,
    213-14
literary art 22, 33-39, 47, 80, 83, 209,
    213-14, 231
meaning 21-39
object of interpretation 22, 30-40
paucity of information 26-32
practical purpose 23, 26
procedure 21, 23, 36
repetition 36-37, 39, 84, 169
symbolism 9, 10, 11, 17, 178, 196,
    202, 230, 231
theology 22-26, 29-31, 34-37, 46, 80

sacrificial animals
    literary appearance 216, 227
    symbolism 218, 219, 221, 224, 226-
        29, 234
    tripartite systematization 209, 213, 217
sacrificial blood 59-60, 63-65, 76, 95, 123,
    156, 190-92, 195-96, 203
sanctuary
    Symbolism 26, 93-95, 99, 104-106,
        142, 198, 200-201, 231, 233
צרעת
    previous explanations 96, 97, 108-25
    symbolic of divine judgment 145, 149,
        152, 154, 156, 159-60, 170, 232,
        236
serpent 37, 96, 98-99, 239, 249-50
sexual discharges 56, 67, 96, 109, 112,
    137, 160, 162-63, 166-69 233
sexual intercourse 52, 68, 167-68
sin offering (see Purification Offering)
symbol
    definition 40-45
symbolic interpretation 9, 17, 78, 115,
    118, 145, 147, 196, 200, 202, 210, 220,
    227-28, 232

tabernacle (see Sanctuary) 26, 198
תמים 10, 28, 195, 196, 202-22, 226-28
    Abraham 204-206, 233

human integrity 10, 173, 196, 202-
   10, 215, 217, 219-20, 226-29, 233,
   234-35
  Noah 204-206, 233
  relationship with קדש 10, 172, 174,
   207-22, 226-29, 233
  symbolism 10, 202, 205, 206, 226-29
term (see word)
tree
  knowledge of good and evil 89, 100
  of life 94-95, 199

unclean animals
  detestable 76, 78, 82, 86, 99, 102-103
  rationale for selection 238-50
  theological interpretation 37
uncleanness (see impurity)
yeast prohibition 253-56

words
  concept 11-12
  hyponym 14
  paradigmatic relations 13-15, 19, 230
  semantic analysis 14
  sense 11-12
  supernym 14
  symbolic meaning 11, 46, 230
  synonyms 14
  syntagmatic relations 13, 15-16, 19,
   46, 229
  tenor 42
  vehicle 42

Printed in the USA
CPSIA information can be obtained
at www.ICGtesting.com
LVHW011644120124
768841LV00005B/458

9 781906 055981